LIBRARY OF NEW TESTAMENT STUDIES

436

formerly the Journal for the Study of the New Testament Supplement series

THE DANIELIC ESCHATOLOGICAL HOUR
IN THE JOHANNINE LITERATURE

STEFANOS MIHALIOS

t & t clark

Published by T&T Clark International
A Continuum imprint
The Tower Building, 11 York Road, London SE1 7NX
80 Maiden Lane, Suite 704, New York, NY 10038

www.continuumbooks.com

British Library Cataloguing-in-Publication Data
A catalogue record for this book is available from the British Library

ISBN: HB: 978-0-567-36720-4

Typeset by Pindar NZ, Auckland, New Zealand
Printed and bound in Great Britain

To my parents,
Yannis and Chrysoula,
and
to my mentor,
Gregory K. Beale.
εἰδὼς παρὰ τίνων ἔμαθον καὶ ἐπιστώθην

CONTENTS

Acknowledgments

The present study is a lightly revised version of my doctoral dissertation presented to Wheaton College in 2009. When the task of this research project first appeared before me, I felt both the inviting excitement of biblical research and the lingering anguish of completing the project. The realization of a work like this requires more than personal diligence and rigorous attention. It calls for the support of people who can equip, guide, encourage and teach, whether it be faculty, friends, or family. For this reason, I would like to express my gratitude to those who have contributed to the completion of this research project.

First, I would like to express my gratitude for my professor and mentor, Dr. Greg Beale. Along with my parents, I dedicate this dissertation to him, due to the tremendous impact he had on my scholarly formation. His exegetical mastery resembles that of a skilled surgeon, who carefully approaches the task with utmost precision. I thank him for his initial suggestion to undertake the topic of this work, as well as for his invaluable mentorship, his constant exhortation to excel, his wise counsel and constructive comments.

I am also indebted to my second reader, Dr. Hassell Bullock, for reading the dissertation and for providing helpful comments. He has guided me in several areas, especially since I also served as his teaching assistant. Dr. Daniel I. Block and Dr. Craig Keener served as additional readers, and I thank them for their useful notes and suggestions. Finally, I have also benefited from Dr. Hans-Josef Klauck, who read and commented on one of my chapters when it was still in its preliminary stages.

For the shaping of this work, I would like to thank D. Susan Dillon for her contribution and advice regarding English expression and prepositions. I am grateful for her willingness to patiently read with me the entire work and also indicate areas for improvement in the flow of argument. Also, my close friend Aris Angelakopoulos has given from his time to help me with the final formatting.

My parents, Yannis and Chrysoula Mihalios, have been a great support over these past years; I would not have managed to be here without their care and support. For their many sacrifices and loving care, not only in recent years, but throughout my life, I dedicate this work to them. Finally, my wife, Manon, deserves my utmost gratitude and thanks, for she has been a constant supporter, an excellent encourager, a loving spouse, and a permanent source of joy.

June, 2010

LIST OF ABBREVIATIONS

AB	Anchor Bible
ABR	*Australian Biblical Review*
ACEBT SS	*Amsterdamse Cahiers voor Exegese en bijbelse Theologie, Supplement Series*
ACNT	Augsburg Commentaries on the New Testament
AJSL	*American Journal of Semitic Languages and Literatures*
AnBib	Analecta Biblica
ANRW	*Aufstieg und Niedergang der römischen Welt*
AOTC	Apollos Old Testament Commentary
APB	*Acta Patristica et Byzantina*
ASTI	*Annual of the Swedish Theological Institute*
ATD	Das Alte Testament Deutsch
BASOR	*Bulletin of the American Schools of Oriental Research*
BBR	*Bulletin for Biblical Research*
BECNT	Baker Exegetical Commentary on the New Testament
BETL	Bibliotheca ephemeridum theologicarum lovaniensium
BI	*Biblical Illustrator*
Bib	*Biblica*
BibS(F)	*Biblische Studien (Frieburg)*
BIS	Biblical Interpretation Series
BN	*Biblische Notizen*
BNTC	Black's New Testament Commentaries
BSac	*Bibliotheca Sacra*
BT	Biblical Theology
BTB	*Biblical Theology Bulletin*
BU	Biblische Untersuchungen
BZ	*Biblische Zeitschrift*
CBC	Cambridge Bible Commentary
CBET	Contributions to Biblical Exegesis and Theology
CBNTS	Coniectanea Biblica New Testament Series
CBQ	*Catholic Biblical Quarterly*
CBQMS	*Catholic Biblical Quarterly*, Monograph Series
CJT	*Canadian Journal of Theology*
CTJ	*Calvin Theological Journal*
DBSJ	*Detroit Baptist Seminary Journal*
EKKNT	Evangelisch-Katholischer Kommentar zum Neuen Testament
ETL	*Ephimerides theologicae lovanienses*

ETS	Erfurter theologische Studien
EvJ	*Evangelical Journal*
EvQ	*Evangelical Quarterly*
ExpTim	*Expository Times*
FOTL	The Forms of the Old Testament Literature
FRLANT	Forschungen zur Religion und Literatur des Alten und Neuen Testaments
Greg	*Gregorianum*
HBT	*Horizons in Biblical Theology*
HCOT	Historical Commentary on the Old Testament
Hor	*Horizons*
HSM	Harvard Semitic Monographs
HSS	Harvard Semitic Studies
HTR	*Harvard Theological Review*
HTS	Harvard Theological Studies
IBS	*Irish Biblical Studies*
ICC	International Critical Commentary
Int	*Interpretation*
IVPNT	IVP New Testament Commentary Series
JBL	*Journal of Biblical Literature*
JETS	*Journal of the Evangelical Theological Society*
JNES	*Journal of Near Eastern Studies*
JOTT	*Journal of Translation and Textlinguistics*
JSNT	*Journal for the Study of the New Testament*
JSNTSup	*Journal for the Study of the New Testament*, Supplement Series
JSOTSup	*Journal for the Study of the Old Testament*, Supplement Series
JSP	*Journal for the Study of the Pseudepigrapha*
JSPSup	*Journal for the Study of the Pseudepigrapha*, Supplement Series
JSS	*Journal of Semitic Studies*
JTS	*Journal of Theological Studies*
LDSS	The Literature of the Dead Sea Scrolls
MNTC	Moffatt New Testament Commentary
NAC	New American Commentary
NCB	New Century Bible
NCBC	New Cambridge Bible Commentary
Neot	*Neotestamentica*
NICNT	New International Commentary on the New Testament
NICOT	New International Commentary on the Old Testament
NIGTC	The New International Greek Testament Commentary
NovT	*Novum Testamentum*
NovTSup	*Novum Testamentum*, Supplements
NSBT	New Studies in Biblical Theology
NTS	*New Testament Studies*
OG	The Old Greek translation of the OT books

OTL	Old Testament Library
OTS	*Oudtestamentische Studiën*
PNTC	Pillar New Testament Commentary
PTL	*Poetics and the Theory of Literature* (Currently as *Poetics Today: A Journal for Theory and Analysis of Literature and Communication*)
ResQ	*Restoration Quarterly*
RevExp	*Review and Expositor*
SBAB	Stuttgarter biblische Aufsalzbände
SBL	Society of Biblical Literature
SBLDS	SBL Dissertation Series
SBLSCS	SBL Septuagint and Cognate Studies
SBT	Studies in Biblical Theology
SBTS	Sources for Biblical and Theological Study
Scr	*Scripture*
SJT	*Scottish Journal of Theology*
SNTSMS	Society for New Testament Studies Monograph Series
SP	Sacra pagina
ST	*Studia Theologica*
StudBL	Studies in Biblical Literature
SVTP	Studia in Veteris Testamenti pseudepigrapha
SwJT	*Southwestern Journal of Theology*
TBC	Torch Bible Commentaries
TH	The Theodotion Version of the Greek translation of the OT
TJ	*Trinity Journal*
TOTC	Tyndale Old Testament Commentaries
TynBul	*Tyndale Bulletin*
VT	*Vetus Testamentum*
WBC	Word Biblical Commentary
WMANT	Wissenschaftliche Monographien zum Alten und Neuen Testament
WTJ	*Westminster Theological Journal*
WUNT	Wissenschaftliche Untersuchungen zum Neuen Testament
ZAW	*Zeitschrift für die alttestamentliche Wissenschaft*
ZBKNT	Zürcher Bibelkommentare NT
ZNW	*Zeitschrift für die neutestamentliche Wissenschaft*
ZTK	*Zeitschrift für wissenschaftliche Theologie*

1

INTRODUCTION

The topic of the use of the Old Testament in the New Testament has gained considerable attention in the past century,[1] broadly affecting the area of biblical studies. The text of the NT takes on a new significance with the proper appreciation of the OT context. A significant number of those in the scholarly guild have realized more and more that the books of the NT were written with the OT and the Jewish milieu as a background. This use of the OT by the NT authors has often been described with terms borrowed from literary studies, such as "quotation," "allusion," and "echo," and it has recently been identified with the notion of "intertextuality."[2]

While the notion of "intertextuality" has begun its history of development within the parameters of linguistic and literary studies,[3] the use of terms such as

---

1.   The following is only a representative sample of the significant studies in the area. For more studies in this area, consult the bibliography. C. H. Dodd, *According to the Scriptures* (London: Nisset, 1953); E. Earle Ellis, *Paul's Use of the Old Testament* (Edinburgh: Oliver and Boyd, 1957); Joseph A. Fitzmyer, 'The Use of Explicit Old Testament Quotations in Qumran Literature and the New Testament', *NTS* 7 (1960–1961), pp. 297–333; Barnabas Lindars, *New Testament Apologetic: The Doctrinal Significance of the Old Testament Quotations* (London: SCM, 1961); M. Black, 'Christological Use of the Old Testament in the New Testament', *NTS* 18 (1971), pp. 1–14; D. A. Carson and H. G. M. Williamson (eds), *It is Written: Scripture Citing Scripture: Essays in Honor of Barnabas Lindars* (Cambridge: Cambridge University Press, 1988); R. B. Hays, *Echoes of Scripture in the Letters of Paul* (New Haven: Yale University Press, 1989); Craig A. Evans and James A. Sanders (eds), *Early Christian Interpretation of the Scriptures of Israel: Investigations and Proposals* (JSNTSup, 148; Sheffield: Sheffield Academic Press, 1997); M. J. Mulder (ed.), *Mikra: Text, Translation, Reading, and Interpretation of the Hebrew Bible in Ancient Judaism and Early Christianity* (Minneapolis: Fortress, 1990); G. K. Beale and D. A. Carson (eds), *Commentary on the New Testament Use of the Old Testament* (Grand Rapids: Baker, 2007).

2.   In this study I will primarily deal with the notion of allusion. See pp. 8–10 for criteria on recognizing an allusion.

3.   Approximately in the late '70s. The term "intertextuality" (*intertextualité*) appears to have originated with Julia Kristeva, *Desire in Language: A Semiotic Approach to Literature and Art* (New York: Columbia University Press, 1980), translated from French, 1969. Also, idem, *Revolution in Poetic Language* (New York: Columbia University Press, 1984). Kristeva's "intertextuality" "has nothing to do with matters of influence by one writer upon another, or with the sources of a literary work"; rather, it involves "the transposition of one or

"quotation," "allusion," and "echo" have acquired a different sense within the field of biblical studies.[4] On the one hand, linguists have used the term "intertextuality" with a concern for the system of codes that surrounds a specific text, which could include any literary work or other conventional means of communication within the culture. On the other hand, biblical scholars have generally used the term "intertextuality" with a concern for the text's "relation to a prior text," which also displays a "genetic or causal" explanation.[5] In other words, within the area of biblical studies, the recognition of a quotation, allusion, or echo in a specific biblical text (e.g. Jn 5.28-29) exposes the influence of a prior text (e.g. Dan. 12.2) on the author of the subsequent work (e.g. John). This influence of the prior text is expressed in the writing of the subsequent work either consciously or subconsciously (see pp. 8–10 for criteria on determining an allusion).

The above emphasis on the use of the OT in the NT has attracted the attention of several scholars who have examined the use of the OT in the Fourth Gospel and the rest of the Johannine literature.[6] Although John does not cite OT scripture as often

more *systems* of signs into another, accompanied by a new articulation of the enunciative and denotative position" (Kristeva, *Semiotic*, p. 15; idem, *Revolution*, pp. 59–60). For example, a word or phrase that has acquired a certain meaning within the system of codes of the conventional culture is now used within a different literary context to interact with this context for the production of a new meaning.

4.   See also Stanley E. Porter, 'The Use of the Old Testament in the New Testament: A Brief Comment on Method and Terminology', in Craig A. Evans and James A. Sanders (eds), *Early Christian Interpretation of the Scriptures of Israel: Investigations and Proposals* (SNTSup, 148; Sheffield: Sheffield Academic Press, 1997), pp. 79–96 (84).

5.   Hays, *Echoes*, p. 15. The examination of the NT use of OT texts has also been influenced by the study of Jewish literature, where one finds specific methods of interpretation of the OT, such as the midrashic method.

6.   C. K. Barrett, 'The Old Testament in the Fourth Gospel', *JTS* 48 (1947), pp. 155–60; F. W. Young, 'A Study of the Relation of Isaiah to the Fourth Gospel', *ZNW* 46 (1955), pp. 215–33; Aileen Guilding, *The Fourth Gospel and Jewish Worship* (Oxford: Clarendon, 1960); E. D. Freed, *Old Testament Quotations in the Gospel of John* (NovTSup, 11; Leiden: Brill, 1965); Günter Reim, *Studien zum Alttestamentlichen Hintergrund des Johannesevangeliums* (SNTSMS, 22; Cambridge: Cambridge University Press, 1974); J. V. Dahms, 'Isaiah 55.11 and the Gospel of John', *EvQ* 53 (1981), pp. 78–88; Severino Pancaro, *The Law in the Fourth Gospel: The Torah in the Gospel, Moses and Jesus, Judaism and Christianity According to John* (NovTSup, 42; Leiden: E. J. Brill, 1975); Craig A. Evans, 'On the Quotation Formulas in the Fourth Gospel', *BZ* 26 (1982), pp. 79–83; R. T. Fortna and B. R. Gaventa (eds), *The Conversation Continues: Studies in Paul and John: In Honor of J. Louis Martyn* (Nashville: Abingdon, 1990); M. Hengel, 'The Old Testament in the Fourth Gospel', *HBT* 12 (1990), pp. 19–41; A. T. Hanson, *The Prophetic Gospel: A Study of John and the Old Testament* (Edinburgh: T&T Clark, 1991); B. G. Schuchard, *Scripture Within Scripture: The Interrelationship of Form and Function in the Explicit Old Testament Citations in the Gospel of John* (SBLDS, 133; Atlanta: Scholars, 1992); M. J. J. Menken, *Old Testament Quotations in the Fourth Gospel: Studies in Textual Form* (CBET, 18; Kampen, Netherlands: Kok, 1996); Andreas Obermann, *Die christologische Erfüllung der Schrift im Johannesevangelium:*

as some other NT authors do, his writings are, nevertheless, full of allusions and indirect references to OT ideas.[7] With this research, I hope to contribute in this area by establishing an OT background of the use of *hour* (ὥρα) in the writings of John.

Many scholars have recognized the presence of eschatological language in John. John's use of eschatological language expresses a duality in eschatology, namely that which is *already, but not yet realized.*[8] One of John's ways of expressing this eschatological dualism is through the concept of the hour. On the one hand, John (through Jesus' *ipsissima verba* or *ipsissima vox*) indicates that the hour *has* come or that it *is* here; on the other hand it seems that this hour is still to come in the future.[9] No one, however, has fully explored the possibility that the hour in John has an OT background, although a small number of scholars have made the suggestion in a few passages.

The eschatological significance of the hour in John is apparent throughout his writings (Jn 2.4; 4.21, 23; 5.25, 28; 7.30; 8.20; 12.23, 27; 13.1; 16.2, 4, 21, 25, 32; 17.1; 1 Jn 2.18; Rev. 3.3, 10; 14.7, 15), since it is directly associated with such latter-day notions as the glory of God (e.g. Jn 17.1), the coming of the Spirit (e.g. Jn 4.23), the resurrection (e.g. Jn 5.25), Christ as the Son of Man (e.g. Jn 12.23), the

Eine Untersuchung zur johanneischen Hermeneutik anhand der Schriftzitate (WUNT, 83; Tübingen: Mohr [Siebeck], 1996). Consult the bibliography for more studies on this area.

7. Scholars have struggled with John's use of the OT. In many instances there exists ambiguity about whether John quotes or alludes to an OT text. See Johannes Beutler, 'The Use of Scripture in the Gospel of John', in R. Alan Culpepper and C. Clifton Black (eds), *Exploring the Gospel of John: in Honor of D. Moody Smith* (Louisville: Westminster John Knox, 1996), pp. 147–62. Nevertheless, OT imagery predominates in the Fourth Gospel (e.g. "tabernacle," "serpent," "manna," "water," "shepherd," "vine," etc.). See Jörg Frey, Jan G. van der Watt, and Ruben Zimmermann, *Imagery in the Gospel of John: Terms, Forms, Themes, and Theology of Johannine Figurative Language* (WUNT, 200; Tübingen: Mohr [Siebeck], 2006). Also, Saeed Hamid-Khani, *Revelation and Concealment of Christ: A Theological Inquiry into the Elusive Language of the Fourth Gospel* (WUNT, 120; Tübingen: Mohr [Siebeck], 2000); and Ruben Zimmermann, *Christologie der Bilder im Johannesevangelium: Die Christopoetik des vierten Evangeliums unter besonderer Berücksichtigung von Joh 10* (WUNT, 171; Tübingen: Mohr [Siebeck], 2004).

8. John's eschatology has become the locus for much discussion. See Jörg Frey, *Die johanneische Eschatologie I: Ihre Probleme im Spiegel der Forschung seit Reimarus* (WUNT, 96; Tübingen: Mohr [Siebeck], 1997); idem, *Die johanneische Eschatologie II: Das johanneische Zeitverständis* (WUNT, 110; Tübingen: Mohr [Siebeck], 1998); idem, *Die johanneische Eschatologie III: Die eschatologische Verkündigung in den johanneischen Texten* (WUNT, 117; Tübingen: Mohr [Siebeck], 2000). See also Hartwig Thyen, *Studien zum Corpus Iohanneum* (WUNT, 214; Tübingen: Mohr [Siebeck], 2007), pp. 512–27.

9. Brown has distinguished between those passages that say that the hour has not come (2.4; 4.21, 23; 5.25, 28-29; 7.30; 8.20; 16.2, 25, 32), and those that say that the hour has come (12.23, 27; 13.1; 17.1). See Raymond E. Brown, *The Gospel According to John* (AB, 29; New York: Doubleday, 1966), p. 517.

final judgement (e.g. Jn 5.28-29), and the cross as an end-time event of judgment and glorification (e.g. Jn 12.27-33).[10]

This book especially attempts to demonstrate the contribution of Danielic eschatology to John's concept of the hour. The book of Daniel (Old Greek [not TH]) also mentions the term *hour* (ὥρα), which denotes an eschatological hour (see the LXX of Dan. 4.26; 8.17, 19; 9.21; 11.35, 40, 45; 12.1, 13), and is the only use of hour in the OT canon that does so.[11] In this examination of the Johannine hour, we will determine the possibility of a Danielic influence and thus hopefully also gain a better understanding of the hour in John.[12] This endeavor should not surprise us, since along with the books of Isaiah and Psalms, scholars have recognized that Daniel is one of the books "most frequently quoted and alluded to in the New Testament."[13] Danielic influence has been discerned in several themes that prevail in the NT, such as God's kingdom, eternal life, resurrection, and the Son of Man (three of which themes occur in John).[14] Moreover, the Danielic prophecies have influenced the eschatological discourses in Mark and Matthew, and they have also

10. See especially, D. G. van der Merwe, ' "Ὥρα, A Possible Theological Setting for Understanding Johannine Eschatology', *Acta Patristica et Byzantina* 13 (2002), pp. 255–87. Also, Thomas Knöppler, *Die theologia cruces des Johannesevangeliums: Das Verastandnis des Todes Jesu im Rahmen der johanneischen Inkarnations – und Erhöhungschristologie* (Düsseldorf: Neukirchener Verlag, 1994), especially his third chapter, 'Die Rede von der ὥρα Jesu' (pp. 102–15).

11. The term ὥρα appears 53 times in the books of the OT (LXX). It appears 13 times in Daniel (LXX), 9 of which are clearly eschatological (more than any other book in the Hebrew Bible). The references in Job (7 times), 2 Kings (5 times) and Exodus (5 times) are not eschatological uses of the term. The rest of the 23 uses are scattered throughout the OT books, and most of them are not eschatological (1 time in Numbers, Leviticus, Esther, Nehemiah, Ruth, Joshua, 1 Samuel, 2 Samuel, Isaiah, Hosea, Zechariah, Psalms; 2 times in Ezra, 1 Kings; 3 times in Genesis; and 4 times in Deuteronomy). Apart from Daniel, the word ὥρα appears in the prophets only in Hos. 2.9; Zech. 10.1; and Isa. 52.7. The first two instances refer to the hour of corn and rain; the latter refers to the hour of the blooming of the mountains (in Spring) as an image that denotes the coming salvation of Yahweh. The Danielic use of hour seems to be the only one specifically related and relevant to the Johannine uses.

12. My focus will be on the Gospel of John and the Johannine epistles, while the book of Revelation will be given little attention. I will later provide the reasons for this restriction. Also, the fact that my interest lies with the Danielic influence in John's concept of the hour, this does not mean that other OT influences will not be considered; it only means that the focus of this book is to examine the contribution of Daniel to John's concept of the hour.

13. Craig A. Evans, 'Daniel in the New Testament: Visions of God's Kingdom', in John J. Collins and Peter W. Flint (eds), *The Book of Daniel: Composition and Reception* (Vol. 2; Leiden: Brill, 2001), pp. 490–527. See also Dodd, *Scriptures*.

14. On God's kingdom, see Evans, 'Daniel' (and the bibliography he cites in pp. 526–27). On the eternal life, see U. E. Simon, 'Eternal Life in the Fourth Gospel', in F. L. Cross (ed.), *Studies in the Fourth Gospel* (London: A. R. Mowbray, 1957), pp. 97–110. On the resurrection, see N. T. Wright, *The Resurrection of the Son of God* (Minneapolis: Fortress, 2003). On the Son of Man, see Delbert Burkett, *The Son of the Man in the Gospel of John* (JSNTSup,

affected the book of Revelation.[15] The effort to discern a Danielic background to yet another word or theme, specifically the theme of the hour, holds promise, since it seems to correspond well with the general NT emphasis and the thematic development in John.

I. *History of Investigation*

One of the most apparent Danielic allusions in the Gospel of John is that in Jn 5.28-29, which reads: "Do not be amazed at this; for the hour is coming, in which all who are in the tombs will hear his voice, and will come forth; those who did good to a resurrection of life, those who committed evil to a resurrection of judgement." As we will see in a subsequent chapter,[16] most commentators agree that this saying alludes to the Danielic resurrection in Dan. 12.2. However, as far as I know, no commentary on the Gospel of John mentions that both resurrection descriptions, the one in John and the one in Daniel, are set to occur within the same eschatological hour (Jn 5.28; Dan. 12.1). Indeed, it seems plausible that the above-recognized allusion to the Danielic resurrection may also involve the Danielic hour. The significance of this observation lies with the fact that Jesus uses the hour as a theme that points to his own passion, cross, and resurrection. In this case, the Danielic hour of judgment and resurrection has begun its fulfillment in the ministry of Jesus. While the commentaries on John may have missed this connection, a small number of scholars have discerned and suggested a parallel between the Johannine hour and the hour in Daniel.

In his monograph, *L' "ORA" Di Cristo Nel Quarto Vangelo*, Giuseppe Ferraro examines the notion of hour in the Gospel of John.[17] In doing this, he has discerned a Danielic background to the hour in John 5 and devotes a few pages to it. Within this chapter, Ferraro provides a chart in which he compares the various Danielic phrases (from Daniel 7, 11, 12) with the corresponding phrases in John 5. It is here, in this chart, that he makes explicit the connection between the hour in Jn 5.25, 28 and the Danielic hour. As important as this earlier suggestion may be, Ferraro does not flesh out the significance of this connection when he comments on the use of hour in the Johannine passages. Surprisingly, the only subsequent comment that he makes in reference to Daniel is at the end of his section on John 5, which reads as follows:

> The focus on the hour of salvation becomes Christological with [Jesus']
> access to the mystery of the Father. We reach . . . a similar result with the one

56; Sheffield: Sheffield Academic Press, 1991); and idem, *The Son of Man Debate: A History and Evaluation* (SNTMS, 107; Cambridge: Cambridge University Press, 1999).

15. G. K. Beale, *The Use of Daniel in Jewish Apocalyptic Literature and in the Revelation of St. John* (Lanham: UPA, 1984); idem, *John's Use of Old Testament in Revelation* (JSNTSup, 166; Sheffield: Sheffield Academic Press, 1998).

16. See Chapter 5 on John 5.

17. Giuseppe Ferraro, *L' 'ORA' Di Cristo Nel Quarto Vangelo* (Rome: Herder, 1974).

achieved in the text of 4.21-23, and together we have discerned a shift in the meaning of "hour" as being realized in the Fourth Gospel, in comparison to the text in Daniel, which may have been the inspiration behind the use of the term "hour" and the notion of resurrection, as we have argued in an earlier section.[18] (Author's translation.)

Nevertheless, Ferraro's contribution is meaningful, especially since he is one of the few that has traced the Johannine hour back to Daniel.

The first scholar to actually engage the Danielic hour and to integrate it into the exegesis of the Johannine text is G. K. Beale, in his commentary on the book of Revelation. Beale relates the eschatological use of hour in Rev. 3.10; 14.7, 15; 17.12; 18.10, 17, 19, with that in Dan. 4.17; 11.45; and 12.1.[19] He argues that John has used the Danielic hour to depict the eschatological time of judgment and tribulation. Following Beale, other scholars have made similar observations (e.g. Osborne and Smalley).[20] Moreover, Beale has extensively argued for a Danielic background of the Johannine hour as it appears in 1 Jn 2.18.[21] He attempts to show that the combination of the words "last" and "hour" is unique in Daniel and therefore John's *last hour* probably refers to the eschatological hour as it appears in Daniel. D. A. Carson has recently evaluated as plausible Beale's suggestion that the *last hour* of 1 Jn 2.18 goes back to Daniel.[22]

The next scholar in line (chronologically) to have acknowledged a Johannine allusion to the Danielic hour is Frey, who has argued convincingly for a general Danielic background of Jn 5.28-29. He specifically argues that the resurrection reference in Jn 5.28-29 relates to the final resurrection from the dead as it appears in Dan. 12.2. To establish this allusion, he has observed several common elements between the resurrection descriptions in Jn 5.28-29 and in Dan. 12.1-2, among which he also mentions the common use of hour in Dan. 11.40, 45; 12.1 (LXX);

18. Ibid., p. 150.

19. G. K. Beale, *The Book of Revelation: A Commentary on the Greek Text* (NIGTC; Grand Rapids: Eerdmans, 1999), pp. 292, 751–52, 879, 907–8.

20. Grant R. Osborne, *Revelation* (BECNT; Grand Rapids: Baker, 2002); Stephen S. Smalley, *The Revelation to John: A Commentary on the Greek Text of the Apocalypse* (Downers Grove: InterVarsity, 2005). See the concluding chapter for a brief summary of the use of hour in Revelation.

21. G. K. Beale, 'The Old Greek of Daniel as a Background to the "Last Hour" in 1 Jn 2.18', (Read at the 'Greek Bible' Section at the Annual Meeting of the SBL in Boston; November, 2008); see the discussion later in the chapter on 1 John. The initial idea for this book in the form of dissertation also came from G. K. Beale. On the general Danielic background of the "last days" in 1 Jn 2.18 cf. also Raymond E. Brown, *The Epistles of John* (AB, 30; New York: Doubleday, 1982), p. 331; and Hans-Josef Klauck, *Der erste Johannesbrief* (EKK, 23/1; Zurich: Benziger Verlag, 1991), p. 147.

22. Carson, '1–3 John', in G. K. Beale and D. A. Carson (eds), *Commentary on the New Testament Use of the Old Testament* (Grand Rapids: Baker, 2007), pp. 1063–67 (1064–65).

and Jn 5.25, 28.[23] For Frey, the eschatological hour in Jn 5.25, 28 is linked to the final resurrection and serves as part of the evidence for a Danielic background. While Frey has devoted only a single paragraph in reference to the Danielic hour, his contribution is significant, since the general attempt of the book is to build the notion of eschatology in the Gospel of John.

Johannes Beutler, in *Judaism and the Jews in the Gospel of John*,[24] following Ferraro and Frey, also makes reference to the Danielic use of hour and attempts to interpret the hour in John in the light of the eschatological hour in Daniel. Like Ferraro, Beutler has not elaborated much on the proposed connection.[25] He only mentions the Danielic background in passing, without commenting on the significance of the Danielic influence. His attempt to make a connection, nevertheless, is commendable and serves as another witness to the presence of a Danielic allusion in the use of hour in John.

Finally, two additional scholars have discerned a Danielic background to the use of hour in Mark 14. While the presence of hour in Mark 14 is not a Johannine usage, it refers to the theme of Jesus's hour in general, which is most probably attributable to Jesus himself. First, Evans has discerned a Danielic background to the hour in Mk 14.35. He writes:

> The hour theme derives from Jesus himself, who probably drew upon vocabulary and themes from Daniel (4.17, 26; 5.5; 8.17, 19; 11.35, 40, 45), where the idea of "hour" figures prominently, often with eschatological overtones. The Johannine hour motif represents an independent and greatly developed expression of this theme.[26]

Similarly, Pitre closely links the eschatological hour in Mk 14.35, 41 with that in Dan. 11.35, 40, 45.[27] The eschatological nature of the latter hour, especially since it includes tribulation, illuminates the use of hour in Mark 14, which speaks about Jesus's final hour of persecution and pain. Later, in speaking on the same passage, Pitre parallels Mark's references to the *Son of Man*, *hour*, and *cup* with those in Jn 12.27-28 and 18.10-11.[28]

---

23. Frey, *Eschatologie 3*, pp. 382–84.

24. Johannes Beutler, *Judaism and the Jews in the Gospel of John* (Rome: Editrice Pontificio Istituto Biblico, 2006).

25. Concerning the use of hour in John 5, Frey appears to be the only one to have used the Danielic hour in a way that significantly bears upon the interpretation of John 5 (see Frey, *Eschatologie 3*, pp. 382–84).

26. Craig A. Evans, *Mark 8.27–16.20* (WBC, 34B; Dallas: Word, 2002), p. 411. However, Evans also mentions that 'ἡ ὥρα, "the hour," is at most only loosely related to the Johannine hour motif (e.g. Jn 17.1); it offers no evidence of contact between the synoptic and Johannine traditions' (ibid., p. 411).

27. Brant Pitre, *Jesus, the Tribulation, and the End of the Exile* (Grand Rapids: Baker, 2005), p. 482.

28. Ibid., pp. 495–96. See also his mentioning of the Johannine hour as a reference to

The above brief sketch of the history of research on the Danielic background of the hour in John provides multiple attestations in favor of the proposed connection. In this book, I seek to examine the above proposal and, if possible, establish the presence of an allusion to the Danielic hour, not only more deeply and thoroughly in John 5, but throughout its various uses in John. In addition to validating the presence of such an allusion throughout John, there will also be elaboration of the interpretative significance of the allusion.

II. *Methodological Considerations*

a. *Setting the Criteria for Determining an Allusion*

As I have already mentioned, the study of identifying the presence of OT references in the NT has been largely influenced by literary approaches.[29] Apart from the literary terminology (e.g. modes of references such as quotations, allusions, and echoes), the method of studying the NT's dependence on the OT has often been to identify word and thematic parallels, repetition, similar or unique contextual meaning, etc. If there is an OT background for hour (ὥρα) in John, then out of the three literary modes of references mentioned above, it would probably be an allusion.[30] The initial purpose of this research, therefore, is to examine whether an allusion to Daniel behind the Johannine hour exists.[31] Before any proposal is made on the methodology that will serve as a means to identify an OT allusion, the mere attempt to ground an allusion on the basis of one word needs to be justified.

Can the presence of *one* NT word be justified as an allusion to the OT? Is the attempt of this monograph warranted? First, one can hardly deny the existence of one-word allusions elsewhere in the NT, since such allusions have already been verified.[32] Second, one must realize that an allusion (or echo) does not reproduce the

Jesus's death in Jn 2.4; 12.23, 27; 17.1 on p. 498.

29. See Hays, *Echoes*, who refers to John Hollander, *The Figure of Echo: A Mode of Allusion in Milton and After* (Berkeley: University of California Press, 1981). See also Porter, 'Use of the Old Testament', pp. 79–96.

30. Quotations may appear in the texts under examination and may contribute to our understanding of the use of the hour. However, the specific use of an OT word in the NT could never be regarded as a direct quotation, because a mere word cannot fulfill the criteria for a quotation.

31. The essential difference between an allusion and an echo is that an allusion is consciously made by an author and the allusion depends upon the alluded text for understanding, while an echo may not involve either of these two things. Therefore, in the case of allusion, the author would likely intend for the reader to recognize the allusion to the OT text, while in an echo the author may not have such an intention. For criteria on identifying connections between texts see, Richard D. Altick and John J. Fenstermaker, *The Art of Literary Research* (New York: Norton, 1993), pp. 106–19. For the intentional nature of the allusion, see Earl Miner, 'Allusion', in Alex Preminger and T. V. F. Brogan (eds), *The New Princeton Encyclopedia of Poetry and Poetics* (Princeton: Princeton University Press, 1993), pp. 38–39.

32. Some examples are the concept of "water" in John, especially Jn 4.10, 14 and 7.38;

exact phrasing of the alluded OT text; rather, it reproduces enough wording so that the idea behind the OT text is conveyed to the reader of the NT text. Depending on the idea that is conveyed, the NT author may have used one, two, or even four words to establish an allusion.[33] However, an allusion may exist in the presence of only one word. The question then becomes whether there are enough indications for the Johannine hour to be an allusion to the Danielic hour. This needs to be verified by establishing the appropriate criteria, and then testing the evidence by these criteria.

Several attempts have been made to establish appropriate criteria for determining an allusion.[34] These criteria have been generally based on the earlier work of Hays.[35] In this work, I use those criteria that have been generally applied and verified by these scholars, upon which I elaborate directly below. Also, when I refer to the notion of allusion, I do so as the "conscious, though subtle, yet specific" reference to an OT text or idea,[36] which as we will argue has exegetical implications.

In order to investigate whether the use of hour in John is an allusion to Daniel, I use the following specific criteria.[37] First, verbal parallelism is an initial indication that a connection exists between the NT text and the alleged OT source text. In this case, the word ὥρα must appear in both texts. Second, since the hour in John is an eschatological one, I investigate exegetically whether the concept of hour in the OT text is an eschatological hour. Third, the larger cluster of words or phrases

---

the name "Hagar" in Gal. 4.24-25; and the words "Gog" and "Magog" in Rev. 20.8. See for example, Larry Paul Jones, *The Symbol of Water in the Gospel of John* (Sheffield: Sheffield Academic Press, 1997). Other examples of one-word allusions in John may be the reference to "tabernacle" in Jn 1.14, the "shepherd" motif in John 10, and the use of "serpent" in Jn 3.14.

33. If the reference to the OT text has more than five words, then the reference is generally regarded as a quotation (see Ziva Ben-Porat, 'The Poetics of Literary Allusion,' *PTL* 1 [1976], pp. 105–28 [107]). In case of an echo, the words used by the NT author may simply betray the author's scriptural and theological background.

34. For example, see the following studies on allusions in the Gospel of John and the criteria they establish. Hamid-Khani, *Revelation*, pp. 91–120, 251–85; Andrew C. Brunson, *Psalm 118 in the Gospel of John: An Intertextual Study on the New Exodus Pattern in the Theology of John* (WUNT, 158; Tübingen: Mohr [Siebeck], 2003), pp. 7–16; and Gary T. Manning, Jr., *Echoes of a Prophet: The Use of Ezekiel in the Gospel of John and in Literature of the Second Temple Period* (London: T&T Clark, 2004), pp. 3–19. On the subject of issuing criteria for determining an allusion, see the useful treatments in Timothy W. Berkley, *From a Broken Covenant to Circumcision of the Heart: Pauline Intertextual Exegesis in Romans 2.17-29* (SBLDS, 175; Atlanta: Society of Biblical Literature, 2000), pp. 17–66; and Christopher A. Beetham, *Echoes of Scripture in the Letter of Paul to the Colossians* (BIS, 96; Leiden: Brill, 2009).

35. Hays, *Echoes*, pp. 29–32.

36. This definition is based partly on Hamid-Khani, *Revelation*, p. 94. This definition of "allusion," which involves the consciousness of the NT author, defers from the definition that reader-oriented literary critics give to the notion of "intertextuality."

37. Since the proposed allusion of this monograph concerns the book of Daniel, I consider that this allusion already meets the criterion of *availability*, that is, the book of Daniel was probably available to John or Jesus.

in the parallelism indicates a stronger possibility for the existence of an allusion.[38] Fourth, if the context of the NT verse that mentions the hour and the context of the possible alluded OT text (i.e. Daniel) have parallel themes or allude to the same OT texts,[39] then this is another indication for an allusion between the NT and the OT texts.[40] Fifth, the presence in the NT context of other verified OT quotations, allusions or echoes from the same OT book, strongly suggests the presence of an allusion.[41] Finally, I have searched the Jewish literature in order to assess the use of eschatological language and the use of eschatological OT texts in the Jewish tradition, especially those from the relevant Danielic passages where hour occurs. This reveals whether the Jewish authors understood the specific OT texts that are under investigation in a way similar to or different from John, and, as we will see, it reinforces the argument of an OT background for the hour in John.[42] The above criteria have been applied throughout the book, either through the research of the primary extra-biblical sources or exegesis of the biblical texts.

b. *Definition of Eschatology*

This book repeatedly refers to the concept of *eschatology*, since it attempts to qualify both the concept of hour and a number of OT passages as being eschatological. Moreover, at several points, I speak of a specific theme (e.g. resurrection) as having an eschatological import. For this reason, I find it necessary to provide a definition of the term *eschaton* or *eschatology*, so that it is clear as to what I mean when I use the term.

The term has come to signify many things, depending on which school of thought one adheres to, or under which field of theology one studies (ST or BT). In the

---

38. The vocabulary cluster does not necessarily require the use of exact words or phrases; the concept may also appear in a synonym or a synecdoche. This criterion corresponds to Hays' test of *volume* (Hays, *Echoes*, p. 30).

39. There are many instances where two different biblical passages allude to the same OT sources. Of course, the mere fact that the two passages have used the same OT source does not necessitate a connection between them. However, if there exist other indications that the two biblical passages might be linked to each other (one passage alludes to the other), then the common reference to the same OT sources reinforces the argument that sees the two passages in relation to each other. For example, in investigating the relationship between Dan. 11.36–12.4 and Jn 5.24-29 (both of which mention the hour) one finds that both texts, the LXX of Daniel and John, allude to the same OT passages (Isaiah 26, Ezekiel 37, and Daniel 7).

40. This criterion represents the idea of *thematic coherence* and *common intertextual sources*. Thematic coherence between any two texts is an indication for a link between the texts, especially when the theme involved is a rare concept in the OT.

41. This corresponds to Hays' criterion of *recurrence*.

42. This will satisfy the criterion of *historical plausibility*. If Second Temple Judaism and Late Judaism relate the concept of Danielic hour to similar eschatological themes with those in John, this will reinforce the argument for a connection between the Johannine hour and Daniel. In other words, if others have borrowed the Danielic hour to denote the coming eschatological era, then Jesus and John may have done so as well.

following, I will briefly mention some of the definitions already provided, and then give my own estimation of what eschatology means.[43] Some of the definitions proposed are as follows.[44]

- A form of expectation that is characterized by finality. The eschaton is the goal of the time process that after which nothing further can occur. It is the climax of theological History.[45]
- Eschatology is a doctrine or a complex of ideas about the last things, which is more or less organically coherent and developed. Every eschatology includes in some form or other a dualistic conception of the course of history and implies that the present state of things and the present world order will suddenly come to an end and be superseded by another of an essentially different kind.[46]
- The expectations for a final and eternal world order.[47]

---

43. For some helpful sources on the definition of "eschatology" see the following: I. Howard Marshall, 'Slippery Words: I. Eschatology', *The Expository Times* 89 (1978), pp. 264–69; Donald E. Gowan, *Eschatology in the Old Testament* (Edinburgh: T&T Clark, 2000); Dirk H. Odendaal, *The Eschatological Expectation of Isaiah 40–66 with Special Reference to Israel and the Nations* (Philadelphia: Presbyterian and Reformed, 1970), pp. 1–58; Sigmund Mowinckel, *He That Cometh: The Messiah Concept in the Old Testament and Later Judaism* (Grand Rapids: Eerdmans, 2005); Geerhardus Vos, *The Eschatology of the Old Testament* (Phillipsburg: P&R Publishing, 2001); Magne Saebø, 'Old Testament Apocalyptic in its Relation to Prophecy and Wisdom: The View of Gerhard von Rad Reconsidered', in Knud Jeppesen, Kristen Nielsen and Bent Rosendal (eds), *In the Last Days: On Jewish and Christian Apocalyptic and its Period* (Aarhus: Aarhus University Press, 1994), pp. 78–91; idem, 'Eschaton und Eschatologia im Alten Testament—in traditiongeschichlicher Sicht', in Jutta Hausmann and Hans-Jürgen Zobel (eds), *Alttestamentlicher Glaube und biblische Theologie: Festschrift für Hosrt Dietrich Peuss zum 65. Geburtstag* (Stuttgart: Kohlhammer, 1992), pp. 321–30; Yair Hoffman, 'Eschatology in the Book of Jeremiah', in Henning Graf Reventlow (ed.), *Eschatology in the Bible and in Jewish and Christian Tradition* (JSOTSup, 243; Sheffield: Sheffield Academic Press, 1997), pp. 75–97; Christian Link, 'Points of Departure for a Christian Eschatology', in Henning Graf Reventlow (ed.), *Eschatology in the Bible and in Jewish and Christian Tradition* (JSOTSup, 243; Sheffield: Sheffield Academic Press, 1997), pp. 98–110; Henning Graf Reventlow, 'The Eschatologization of the Prophetic Books: A Comparative Study', in Henning Graf Reventlow (ed.), *Eschatology in the Bible and in Jewish and Christian Tradition* (JSOTSup, 243; Sheffield: Sheffield Academic Press, 1997), pp. 169–88.

44. The definitions are selected from Hoffman, 'Eschatology', pp. 75–76. Hoffman has proposed three conditions that he finds necessary, although not sufficient, for defining the concept of eschatology: 1) future perspective; 2) universal overview; and 3) miraculous, supernatural elements (p. 77).

45. S. B. Frost, 'Eschatology and Myth', *VT* 2 (1952), pp. 70–80.

46. Mowinckel, *He That Cometh*, p. 125.

47. Y. Kaufman, *Toldot Haemunah Hyisraelil* (Jerusalem: Mosad-Bialik-Devir, 1960), p. 629.

- The certainty that history will be finally broken off and abolished in a new age.[48]
- The study of ideas and beliefs concerning the end of the present world order and the introduction of a new order.[49]
- The knowledge of the end of this period, this time, and of the rather short space of time that precedes the end.[50]

The common element in the above definitions is the notion of finality and the presence of two distinct ages: the one that ends and the one that begins.

G. B. Caird has beautifully mapped out the history of signification concerning the term *eschatology*.[51] He has identified different kinds of eschatologies (e.g. individual, historical, imminent, realized, existential, purpose), all of which, in one way or another, include the notions of finality and the existence of two distinct ages. However, the development of the definition of the term *eschatology* indicates that there must be more than one aspect to the meaning of the eschatological "end" and the shifting between the two ages. One should try to incorporate as many aspects as possible into the definition of the *eschaton*. In this case, while *eschatology* can be found to be affecting the inner existence of the individual, it also affects the body; while it is perceived in the present, it is also about the future; and while one may expect the eschaton to arrive imminently, it is also distant.

The term *eschatology* should not be defined in terms that merely reflect the very end of history. The eschaton as it is described in the Old and New Testaments has primarily to do with God's intervening act in history in order to transform it. Eschatology relates to the transformation of reality as we know it, and it involves the presence of two distinct eras. Whenever God has acted in a way to transform reality and to inaugurate the beginning of a new era, one that cannot be reversed, this should be perceived as an eschatological act. In order to discern whether a theme or a text is eschatological, one must also observe elements of a future final goal and a universal perspective; however, this future goal and universal perspective may have their beginning in history. Eschatology, therefore, is the transforming act of God in history, towards a progression that leads to the final consummation of all things.[52]

---

48. Walther Eichrodt, *Theology of the Old Testament* (Vol. 1; London: SCM Press, 1961), p. 385.

49. R. E. Clements, *Prophecy and Covenant* (London: SCM Press, 1965), p. 104.

50. J. P. M. van der Ploeg, 'Eschatology in the Old Testament', *OTS* 17 (1972), pp. 89–99.

51. G. B. Caird, *The Language and Imagery of the Bible* (Grand Rapids: Eerdmans, 1980), pp. 243–71.

52. In this case, an eschatological promise (or prophecy) can have both a temporal fulfillment and a final fulfillment. The temporal fulfillment need not be of a different nature (non-eschatological) from the final fulfillment (which is eschatological), since the temporal fulfillment carries out the same salvific plan of God and inaugurates the process by which the "eschaton" will be fulfilled.

c. *Setting the Structure*

In order to provide the OT background of the eschatological hour in John, I proceed as follows. In my Chapter 2, I investigate the use of the phrases "in that time" and "time of distress" in the Old Testament, especially as these relate to the same expressions in Dan. 12.1. In doing this, I attempt to make the possible intertextual connections between the various passages to which the evidence points. My focus is especially on the use of the above expressions in the book of Daniel, especially as they relate to the use of ὥρα in the Old Greek of Daniel. Research of such eschatological language in the OT and Daniel shows how the OT authors understood the eschaton and the eschatological hour. This should also reveal the words and themes that relate to the eschatological hour in the OT (e.g. final judgement and resurrection).

In Chapter 3, I examine the use of eschatological time or hour in the literature of Second Temple Judaism. The Jewish interpretative tradition may provide us with alternative or similar interpretations of the OT passages. How does Jewish tradition understand the eschaton, especially in relation to the Danielic concept of a coming hour? How does Judaism use the notion of an eschatological hour? How does Judaism refer to the Danielic passages that contain reference to hour?

In Chapters 4 through 8, I explore the use of eschatological hour in specific passages in the Gospel of John and his first epistle.[53] Special attention is given to the exegesis of the Johannine passages in relation to their immediate context. This investigation has led to certain connections between John and Daniel. Verbal and thematic parallels between the texts, common use of OT passages, and John's contextual reference to other already verified allusions from the book of Daniel, all provide the criteria for substantiating a relationship between the texts. I also provide a comparison of the different variants of the primary OT biblical texts and — if needed — the Jewish texts as well. This reveals the particular textual tradition that John may have in mind when alluding to the OT text.

Additional attention is given to John's textual and interpretative use of the Danielic eschatological references. How does John use the term hour in context? How does the existence of a Daniel allusion affect our interpretation of hour in John?

---

53. I will thoroughly examine the OT background of certain Johannine passages, rather than examining every occurrence of the eschatological hour in John. Therefore, although I will deal to some extent with all of the references of the eschatological hour in the Johannine corpus, the focus will be on Jn 4.19-26; 5.19-30; 12.20-36; 16.20–17.1; and 1 Jn 2.18-25 (there exists only one reference to the hour in the Johannine Epistles, in 1 Jn 2.18). The book of Revelation will not be considered for the following reasons: work has already been done on the use of the Old Testament in Revelation; a Danielic background to the hour in Revelation has been asserted by other scholars; and the Johannine authorship of the book has been debated (see Beale, *Use of Daniel*; Beale and Carson, *Use of Old Testament*; and Steve Moyise, *The Old Testament in the Book of Revelation* [JSNTSup, 115; Sheffield: Sheffield Academic Press, 1995]).

How does the OT allusion enhance the rhetorical force of the Johannine text for the original readers and hearers?

On the basis of these explorations, hermeneutical and theological inferences have been proposed for John's gospel and the Johannine epistles.[54] As I attempt to show, the use of the Danielic hour in the Fourth Gospel will enforce an *already and not yet* notion of fulfillment recognized by previous scholarship. The focusing on the uses of Daniel's hour in John fleshes out and refines this previously acknowledged notion, especially by showing what prophecies from Daniel are part of the fulfillment idea. The concept of the eschaton as it is used in the NT will hopefully be better understood in light of this OT background. Moreover, the present research holds potential that the reader will arrive at a greater appreciation of the mission of Christ in relation to the Son of Man (Dan. 7.13) and the Danielic eschatological hour.

Finally, the book is designed to contribute towards the clarification of the use of the OT in the NT. More specifically, the study shows that John has not used the word and concept of hour for merely rhetorical purposes, but in relation to the OT context.

---

54. The following are some of the further questions that this study may affect. What kind of eschatology do John's writings convey? How does John's use of the hour relate to our understanding of God's plan for the world and of our expectation for God's eschatological acting in history? How does John's use of the hour help one achieve a better understanding of the Johannine concept of fulfillment?

2

THE USE OF ESCHATOLOGICAL HOUR IN THE OT

I. *Introduction*

The present chapter is devoted to the survey of certain eschatological uses of hour as it appears in the Old Testament. In the first part of the survey, I examine the use of the eschatological word עֵת in the OT (MT), apart from Daniel. In this section, I specifically target the phrase בָּעֵת הַהִיא ("at that time"), as well as those occurrences of עת that express a time of distress (עֵת צָרָה). While the Old Testament uses other words or expressions to denote an eschatological time (e.g. מוֹעֵד, קֵץ, and בְּאַחֲרִית הַיָּמִים, for the MT, and ὥρα, καιρός, συντελεία, and πέρας, for the LXX),[1] I have limited the scope of this survey to the particular eschatological expressions that appear in Dan. 12.1, since this is the main text to which the Johannine hour potentially alludes. More specifically, in the book of Daniel, the word ὥρα in the Old Greek (OG) translates the Hebrew word עֵת in the instances most relevant to this study (Dan. 8.17; 11.40; 12.1),[2] and the word עת appears within the Hebrew phrase בָּעֵת הַהִיא (κατὰ τὴν ὥραν ἐκείνην) in Dan. 12.1 and is also associated with a time of distress in the same verse (עֵת צָרָה). The purpose of this first section is to understand how the OT utilizes the word עֵת, when the word is used in a similar manner to that in Dan. 12.1. This will potentially reveal the general OT background behind the Danielic use of "time" (עת). Therefore, the eschatological "time" in the OT is examined in relation to the

---

1. One may also add to the list the phrases "day of the Lord" and "in that day." For more information on such expressions, see John R. Wilch, *Time and Event: An Exegetical Study of the Use of 'ēth in the Old Testament in Comparison to Other Temporal Expressions in Classification of the Concept of Time* (Leiden: Brill, 1969); Simon J. DeVries, *Yesterday, Today and Tomorrow* (Grand Rapids: Eerdmans, 1975); Gerhard von Rad, 'The Origin of the Concept of the Day of Yahweh', *JSS* 4 (1959), pp. 97–108. See also the study of Peter Andreas Munch, *The Expression Bajjôm Hāhū': Is it an eschatological terminus technicus?* (Oslo: I Kommisjon Hos Jacob Dybwad, 1936).

2. The word עת appears in Dan. 8.17; 9.21, 25; 11.6, 13, 14, 24, 35, 40; 12.1, 4, 9, 11, and the word ὥρα in Dan. 4.17, 19, 26; 5.5; 8.17, 19; 9.21; 11.6, 35, 40, 45; 12.1, 13. In the whole of the OT (LXX), the word עת is translated as καιρός (162 times), ὥρα (26 times), and χρόνος (2 times). Almost half of the instances of ὥρα translate the word עת.

following twofold division: (1) the time of God's intervention (בְּעֵת הַהִיא); and (2) the time of distress (עֵת צָרָה).

The second part of this survey investigates the use of the Greek word ὥρα in the OG of Daniel. The use of other eschatological expressions are only considered as needed for understanding the word ὥρα. This section specifically deals with the hour theme as it develops from Dan. 8.17, 19, to Dan. 11.6, 30, 35, 40, 45, and Dan. 12.1, 13. The use of the phrase "latter days" in Dan. 10.14 (cf. Dan. 2.28-29, 45) is also given some attention, since it affects the Danielic concept of time. In conjunction with this, we will observe the use of other eschatological themes that affect the understanding of hour, since the primary purpose of this section is to understand Daniel's use of the eschatological ὥρα.

In this chapter, there is a discussion of the Hebrew text of Daniel and intertextual connections with other Hebrew OT books and intertextual links within the book itself. This discussion not only helps us understand the connections with other OT passages made by the writer of Daniel, but it also forms part of a background of which the OG translator, Judaism, and the NT writers may have been aware to varying degrees. In addition, there will be discussion of the OG translation of Daniel and the intratextual relationships that he draws between earlier parts of his translation and later parts. This will also form a background of which Judaism and the NT writers may also have been aware to different degrees.

The survey as a whole aims at a better understanding of the above eschatological words or phrases as they appear in different OT passages, and especially in Daniel. Hopefully, by the end of this chapter, the eschatological hour will be understood better in association with these Danielic expressions and themes.

II. *The Use of Eschatological* עֵת *in the OT*

a. *The Time of God's Intervention:* בְּעֵת הַהִיא
One of the phrases that Daniel uses to depict the eschatological moment of God's judgment, of the restoration of Israel, and of the final resurrection, is the phrase הַהִיא בְּעֵת ("in that time").[3] This is the precise phrase that the OG translator renders κατὰ τὴν ὥραν ἐκείνην in Dan. 12.1. A survey of the eschatological uses of the phrase "in that time" in the rest of the OT will reveal the eschatological tone of the phrase in the Prophets and will provide an interpretative framework for the eschatological hour in Dan. 12.1.[4]

---

3.   Daniel 12.1-2 depicts the final act of God, which is the climax in God's redemptive plan, as it appears in Daniel 7–12.

4.   The phrase בְּעֵת הַהִיא occurs twice in Dan. 12.1. In the Hebrew Bible, the phrase occurs a total of 68 times. Apart from the book of Jeremiah, most of the instances of this phrase deal with events that are historical in nature. In most of these cases, the phrase "in that time" connects an event of the past with an event of the present (Gen. 21.22; 38.1; Num. 22.4; Deut. 1.9, 16, 18; 2.34; 3.4, 8, 12, 18, 21, 23; 4.14; 5.5; 9.20; 10.1, 8; Josh. 5.2; 6.26; 11.10, 21; Judg. 3.29; 4.4; 11.26; 12.6; 14.4; 21.14, 24; 1 Kgs 8.65; 11.29; 14.1; 2 Kgs 8.22; 16.6; 18.16;

Most often, the depicted event that occurs "in that time" is connected with the preceding events in the narrative. The phrase "in that time" seems to function as a conventional linguistic means to connect events within the narrative flow.[5] While the phrase "in that time" does not have eschatological overtones outside the prophetic books, we will see below that, in the prophetic literature, "in that time" is primarily used with an eschatological sense. Apart from Dan. 12.1, "in that time" possibly depicts an eschatological era in Joel 4.1; Mic. 3.4; Zeph. 1.12; 3.19-20; and Jer. 3.17; 4.11; 8.1; 38.1 (LXX; 31.1 in MT); 33.15; 27.4, 20 (LXX; 50.4, 20 in MT).[6]

In most of the above cases, the LXX translates the phrase בָּעֵת הַהִיא with the Greek phrase ἐν τῷ καιρῷ ἐκείνῳ,[7] which is significant, since the Theodotionic version of Dan. 12.1 twice renders בָּעֵת הַהִיא with the same Greek phrase, ἐν τῷ καιρῷ ἐκείνῳ.[8] In all of the above instances, we will see that the expression "in that time" denotes the expectation of a future era at which God will deliver Israel from her enemies and will restore her to a state of permanent peace. In this sense, inasmuch as the foretelling of this future era represents God's ultimate goal for Israel's restoration, the phrase "in that time" reflects an eschatological expectation.

In the first instance, the context of Joel 4.1 is rich in eschatological themes. "In that time" most certainly refers to the preceding events described in Joel 3. The time in Joel 4.1 probably refers to the Day of the Lord (2.1; 3.4), which involves

20.12; 24.10; 1 Chron. 21.28, 29; 2 Chron. 7.8; 13.18; 16.7, 10; 21.10; 28.16; 30.3; 35.17; Ezra 8.34; Neh. 4.16; Est. 8.9; Isa. 18.7; 20.2; 39.1). Wilch dedicates much of his book to this specific use of "time." He distinguishes between different types of relationships of events, such as comparison, direct relationship, causal relationship, etc. For more information, see Wilch, *Time*, pp. 34–77. Also, for a further elaboration on the phrase, see John E. Goldingay, 'Kayyom Hazzeh "On This Very Day"; Kayyom "On The Very Day"; Ka'et "At The Very Time"', *VT* 43 (2001), pp. 112–15.

5. It is interesting to note that whatever the function of the phrase בָּעֵת הַהִיא is — whether it merely links together two separate historical events or whether it points to a future acting of God — in most instances, it relates different events that occur within the literary confines of the book. This linkage, therefore, need not always be a chronological linkage, since the intent of the biblical authors could have been to provide a thematic contextual relationship of these events (see Wilch, *Time*, p. 71).

6. I am only dealing with those occurrences of the phrase "in that time" in the prophets that have a possible eschatological reference. The rest of the occurrences of the Hebrew phrase "in that time" are Amos 5.13 and Isa. 18.7; 20.2. More broadly, the Hebrew word עֵת appears to have a future reference in the following prophetic passages: Joel 4.1; Amos 5.13; Mic. 2.3; 3.4; Zeph. 1.12; 3.19, 20; Jer. 3.17; 4.11; 8.1, 12; 10.15; 11.12, 14; 30.7; 31.1; 33.15; 50.4, 20; 51.33; Ezek. 21.25, 29; 22.3; 30.3; and Dan. 8.17; 11.24, 35, 40; 12.1, 4, 9.

7. The three exceptions are Zeph. 1.12 (ἐν ἐκείνῃ τῇ ἡμέρᾳ; cf. the same rendering in one of the occurrences in Dan. 12.1, LXX); Jer. 38.1 (ἐν τῷ χρόνῳ ἐκείνῳ); and Jer. 33.15, which does not have a Greek equivalent. The Greek phrase κατὰ τὴν ὥραν ἐκείνην appears only in the OG of Daniel, which adds to the fact that the concept of the eschatological hour has been uniquely developed as a Danielic theme.

8. The same Greek translation (ἐν τῷ καιρῷ ἐκείνῳ) of the Hebrew phrase "in that time" also appears in Amos 5.13 and Isa. 18.7.

the outpouring of the Spirit (3.1-2), the signs of blood, fire and smoke (3.3),[9] and the darkening of the sun (3.4).[10] This day of reckoning will result in the salvation of those who will call upon God's name (3.5).[11] Finally, Mount Zion becomes the place where the elect will live (3.5), an image that resembles the mountain in Isa. 2.2.[12] According to this description, God's intervention to establish his reign involves both judgment and restoration. Interestingly, the eschatological end in Joel 2 also involves the removal of the northern army, which threatens God's people (2.20). After the destruction ends, a new era begins, which is characterized by the outpouring of the Spirit, the presence of God, and the salvation of those who will call upon God's name (Joel 2.28-32).

While these themes may not directly relate to the resurrection reference in Dan. 12.1, they nevertheless relate to the general Danielic themes of judgment and restoration. The similar reference to the destruction of the northern army in Dan. 11.40-45 could possibly point to a literary connection between Joel 2 and the final battle in Daniel. Indeed, the divine army in Joel is one whose "like has never been from of old, nor will be again after them in ages to come" (2.2), an expression that resembles the nature of the "tribulation" in Dan. 12.1, "such as never occurred since there was a nation until that time." By employing the phrase "in that time" (twice in Dan. 12.1), Daniel may have drawn upon a prophetic tradition that combines Joel with other prophetic texts.[13] The above observations indicate the common use of the phrase "in that time" in Joel and in Daniel. By the time Daniel wrote his book, this phrase could have become a *terminus technicus* for referring to the eschaton.[14] To say the least, the thematic emphasis in the context of Joel 4.1 qualifies

9.   The association of blood with fire also occurs in Ezek. 38.22. See James L. Crenshaw, *Joel: A New Translation with Introduction and Commentary* (AB. 24C; New York: Doubleday, 1995), p. 168.

10.   The darkness of the sun resembles the description in the following passages: Isa. 13.10; 34.4; Jer. 4.23; Ezek. 32.7-8; Amos 8.9. Crenshaw relates the redness of the moon with Zeph. 1.17 (Crenshaw, *Joel*, p. 168). The phrase "in that time" in Amos 5.13 refers to a similar depiction of darkness (5.18); the time there refers to the day of the Lord that will bring God's judgment (5.18-20).

11.   Garrett identifies the salvation described here with the salvation of the Gentiles. See Duane A. Garrett, *Hosea, Joel* (NAC, 19A; Nashville: Broadman & Holman, 1997), p. 375, who also refers to Willem A. VanGemeren, 'The Spirit of Restoration', *WTJ* 50 (1988), pp. 81–102.

12.   The Isaianic theme of the gathering of the nations appears in the context of Joel, in Joel 3.1 and 4.2.

13.   An army that invades from the north is also depicted in the eschatological passages of Ezek. 38.5, 15.

14.   The phrases "in that time" and "in that day" may have been interpreted by early Judaism and Jesus as a *terminus technicus* referring to the eschatological day of the Lord. The close association of the two phrases throughout the prophetic literature denotes a common use (see the discussion on pp. 19–27), especially since the Hebrew phrase "in that time" (הַהִיא בָּעֵת) is translated as "in that day" (ἐν ἐκείνῃ τῇ ἡμέρᾳ) in the OG of Dan. 12.1. For certain,

the phrase "in that time" as having eschatological import, which is significant for our study of the same phrase in Daniel.[15]

The significance of the reference to "that time" in Joel 4.1 also lies in the fact that it occurs within a particular expression (בַּיָּמִים הָהֵמָּה וּבָעֵת הַהִיא), the exact equivalent of which appears only in Jer. 33.15 and Jer. 50.4, 20.[16] The close association of the two phrases, "in that day" and "in that time," strengthens the idea that "time" may function as a reference to the Day of the Lord. Interestingly, as we will see later, a similar association between "time" (ὥρα) and "day" (ἡμέρα) occurs in Dan. 12.1, 13, which indicates that the final ὥρα in Daniel may represent the eschatological day on which the Lord will intervene with judgment, but also with restoration.

The phrase "in that time" also occurs in Mic. 3.4, which speaks about a time of judgment because of the sins of Israel.[17] At first glance, the eschatological nature of "time" in this text may not be evident,[18] since it probably refers to the time of God's judgment through the Babylonian invasion.[19] However, inherent in these predictions is God's ultimate restoration through the Messiah, whose kingdom will extend to "the ends of the earth" (Mic. 5.3-4); God's redemption will come through the providence of an ideal king (cf. Mic. 2.13), whose kingdom will have universal effects. Also, the time of judgment in Micah 3 should not be disconnected from the eschatological blessings and restoration in Micah 4. This latter chapter begins with

the New Testament generally interprets the phrase ἐν ἐκείνῃ τῇ ἡμέρᾳ (equivalent of הַהוּא בַּיּוֹם) eschatologically (e.g. Mt. 7.22; Lk. 17.31; Jn 14.20; 16.23, 26; 2 Tim. 1.18; 4.8). Even Munch, who argues against a *terminus technicus* for the phrase "in that day," acknowledges that, in later periods, Judaism and Christianity may have developed an eschatological understanding of the phrase (Munch, *Bajjôm Hāhū'*, p. 57).

15. I take Joel 4.1 as a reference to the restoration of Israel's fortunes, rather than her return from the captivity (so David A. Hubbard, *Joel and Amos* [TOTC; Downers Grove: InterVarsity, 1989], p. 74). See the parallel phrase in Zeph. 3.20 in association with the phrase "in that time," as well as Ezek. 39.25 in context (so Hans Walter Wolff, *Joel and Amos* [Hermeneia; Philadelphia: Fortress, 1977], p. 76, who sees this restoration as "final").

16. I will explore the phrase in Jeremiah later. Crenshaw argues that the double expression is used here as a parallel that aims at greater precision. He thus sees the two temporal phrases as synonymous. See Crenshaw, *Joel*, p. 173.

17. Smith has noticed a connection between Mic. 3.2 and Amos 5.14-15, due to the common use of the phrase "in that time." Both texts speak about the defiance of good by the people and the admonition to hate evil. Smith also mentions Isa. 1.16-17 (Ralph L. Smith, *Micah-Malachi* [WBC, 32; Dallas: Word, 1984], p. 31).

18. I see the "time" here as a reference to the future, as most scholars do. Contra Andersen and Freedman (Francis I. Andersen and David Noel Freedman, *Amos: A New Translation with Introduction and Commentary* [AB, 24A; New York: Doubleday, 1989], p. 355). The eschatological connotation of the expression "in that time" in Mic. 3.4 may be subtle due to this being one of the earlier uses of the phrase. The same could be said about Amos 5.13 and Isa. 18.7; 20.2.

19. Mays sees this "time" as "a temporal reference to a distant future" (James Luther Mays, *Micah: A Commentary* [OTL; Philadelphia: Westminster, 1976], p. 80). Notice the reference to an "evil time" in Mic. 2.3.

a reference to the "latter days"[20] and ends with the promise of the eschatological king (Mic. 4.14–5.3). Surely, the judgment that comes upon Israel is due to the lack of appropriate leadership (Mic. 3.9-10). It is the absence of a proper king in Israel that has brought them pain, similar to that of a woman bearing a child:

> Now, why do you cry out loudly? Is there no king among you, or has your counselor perished, that agony has gripped you like a woman in childbirth? Writhe and labor to give birth, daughter of Zion, like a woman in childbirth; for now you will go out of the city, dwell in the field, and go to Babylon. There you will be rescued; there the Lord will redeem you from the hand of your enemies.[21]

(Mic. 4.9-10)

The fact that the emphasis on restoration in Micah 4 relates to the desolation described in Micah 3 is also evident from the contrast that exists in the state of the temple as it appears in Mic. 3.12 and 4.1. In the last days, the restored temple will replace the desolated one. Mount Zion, mentioned in Mic. 4.2 (cf. Isa. 2.2), will be the place out of which God will reign forever (Mic. 4.7). All of these are expected to be fulfilled as the solution to Israel's problems in Mic. 3.4, which take place "in that time." In context, this time leads up to and is thus linked to God's appointed time for intervention,[22] and together with its equivalent phrase "in that day" (Mic. 4.6), this reference to "time" can probably be located within the "latter days" of Mic. 4.1, or closely linked to it.

Israel's experience of the historical particularity of the Babylonian exile serves as the ground from which the realization of God's eschatological promises spring. Here, in Micah, one may perceive the beginnings of prophetic eschatology, "which painted a dark horizon of judgment and then fractured that darkness with bright hues of the breaking new day."[23] This new day is introduced within the confines of historical reality. While Mic. 3.4 is not quoted or alluded to in Daniel, the phrase "in

---

20. Micah 4.1-3 quotes Isa. 2.2-4 (though it is possible that the latter quotes the former). The whole section begins with the phrase וְהָיָה בְּאַחֲרִית הַיָּמִים ("And it will be in the later days"). Shaw argues for the literary connection of Mic. 3.1-12 and 4.1-8 on the basis of rhetorical and thematic parallels. See Charles S. Shaw, *The Speeches of Micah: A Rhetorical-Historical Analysis* (JSOTSup, 145; Sheffield: Sheffield Academic Press, 1993), pp. 101–5. Contra Bob Becking, 'The Exile Does Not Equal the Eschaton: An Interpretation of Mic. 4.1-5', in F. Postma, K. Spronk and E. Talstra (eds), *The New Things Eschatology in Old Testament Prophecy: Festschrift for Henk Leene* (Maastricht, Netherlands: Shaker, 2002), pp. 1–7.

21. Throughout the book I have used the NASB translation, except for a few instances, where I have used my own translation.

22. See Bruce Waltke, 'Micah', in Thomas Edward McComiskey (ed.), *The Minor Prophets: An Exegetical and Expository Commentary* (Vol. 2; Grand Rapids: Baker, 1993), pp. 591–764 (659).

23. C. Hassell Bullock, *An Introduction to the Old Testament Prophetic Books* (Chicago: Moody Publishers, 2007), pp. 133–34.

that time" is used in both texts to denote a coming judgment that will be replaced by an extended period of restoration. The expectations for renewal with which the phrase "in that time" relates in Mic. 3.4 (i.e. the coming of the end-time king, the permanent defeat of Israel's enemies, the restoration of Israel and the temple, and the establishment of a worldwide kingdom) are themes that also appear in the book of Daniel, in one way or another.

In the case of Zeph. 1.12 and 3.19-20, the eschatological language that surrounds the phrase "in that time" is immediately discernable.[24] In the former instance, the "time" concerns God's judgment: "It will come about at that time that I will search Jerusalem with lamps, and I will punish the men who are stagnant in spirit, who say in their hearts, 'the Lord will not do good or evil!'" (1.12). This time of judgment is equivalent to the great day of judgment (Zeph. 1.8, 10, 14), when God will judge not only Jerusalem, but also the rest of the world.[25] Zephaniah characteristically declares: "A day of wrath is that day, a day of trouble and distress, a day of destruction and desolation, a day of darkness and gloom, a day of clouds and thick darkness" (1.15). This is, further, a day of blood and fire (1.17-18), similar to that described in Joel 3.[26] The words "time" (עֵת in 1.12) and "day" (יוֹם in 1.15) are again used interchangeably to refer to the same moment or period of time. God's wrath culminates in a cataclysmic end that affects all nations on earth (3.8).[27]

Following God's judgment, the final part of the book (Zeph. 3.9-20) conveys the hope that will accompany this judgment, at "that time" (3.9); the people will be

---

24. The Greek phrase ἐν τῷ καιρῷ ἐκείνῳ also appears in Zeph. 3.16, translating the Hebrew phrase בָּעֵת הַהוּא.

25. The eschatological nature of the "day" references in Zephaniah is confirmed by (1) other eschatological descriptions of this day in the rest of the book of Zephaniah; (2) the final and universal nature of Israel's restoration (3.20); and (3) the radical transformation that these promises introduce, a transformation that differs from reality as it is known. As Sweeney notes, scholars have suggested that expressions such as "in that day" or "in that time" are redactional, partly because of their eschatological connotations. Sweeney rightly objects by saying that the formula "in that day" (or "in that time") does not inherently mark an eschatological era, but takes its eschatological meaning from its context (Marvin A. Sweeney, *Zephaniah* [Hermeneia; Philadelphia: Fortress, 2003], pp. 92–93). However, Sweeney does not recognize the eschatological context of Zephaniah.

26. In fact, the wording of Zeph. 1.15 can be found in Joel 2.2, which indicates a literary dependence between the two texts (Raymond Dillard, 'Joel', in Thomas Edward McComiskey (ed.), *The Minor Prophets: An Exegetical and Expository Commentary* [Vol. 1; Grand Rapids: Baker, 1992], pp. 239–314 [271]). The Day of the Lord, one of the main themes in Zephaniah, also appears in the book of Amos. Smith observes some of the similarities that exist between the references to the "day" in the two books: "Amos and Zephaniah both used the term הַ 'hush' in referring to the day. Amos uses the words חֹשֶׁךְ 'darkness' (5.18, 20), אָפֵל 'gloom' (5.20), and מַר 'bitter' (8.10) to describe the day" (Smith, *Micah-Malachi*, pp. 131–32).

27. David W. Baker, *Nahum, Habakkuk, Zephaniah* (TOTC; Downers Grove: InterVarsity, 1988), p. 114.

purified, and a remnant will be preserved. In Zeph. 3.19-20, the prophet portrays this hope in the following words:

> Behold, I am going to deal *at that time* with all your oppressors. I will save the lame and gather the outcast, and I will turn their shame into praise and renown in all the earth. *At that time* I will bring you in, even *at the time* when I gather you together; indeed, I will give you renown and praise among all the peoples of the earth, when I restore your fortunes before your eyes, says the Lord. (Emphasis is mine.)

The fulfillment of the promises will take place "in that time" (בָּעֵת הַהִיא) and will bring about the restoration of Israel in terms of the gathering of "those who have been scattered" (3.19).[28] The involvement of those who are lame occurs in other eschatological passages, such as Isa. 35.6; Jer. 31.8; and Mic. 4.6-7, the contexts of which also speak about the regathering of the dispersed Israel. We also notice in the above text (Zeph. 3.19-20) that God's restoration will have universal effects, that is, "among all the peoples of the earth" (3.20). Furthermore, this restoration will bring abundant joy to the people of Mount Zion (Zeph. 3.14),[29] a joy that is linked with the following promise: "The king of Israel, the Lord, is in your midst; you shall fear disaster no more" (Zeph. 3.15). Once again, the phrase "in that time" looks forward to the deliverance of Israel not merely as the restoration of the people of God, but also as the establishment of God's own kingship.[30]

The use of the phrase "in that time" in Zephaniah supports the suggestion that this phrase carries eschatological connotations linked with God's worldwide judgment and restoration. It is commonly used by the prophets in reference to the outworking of God's restorative plan, which will initiate the final era of peace.

Jeremiah's use of the phrase "in that time" (בָּעֵת הַהִיא) also appears within contexts that reiterate eschatological themes (Jer. 3.17; 4.11; 8.1; 31.1; 33.15; 50.4, 20). We have seen that Micah and Jeremiah's contemporary, Zephaniah, had already used this phrase in reference to God's final judgment and restoration.[31] In harmony with this use, Jeremiah employs the phrase in connection to similar eschatological promises.

Jeremiah 3.17 is the first instance in which the theme of the restoration of Israel appears.[32] The prophet begins with God's appeal to repentance, in Jer. 3.14-15, and

---

28. The restoration of Israel's fortunes appears in Zeph. 3.20 and in Joel 4.1, both of which place this restoration "at that time."

29. The prophet mentions the additional element that this day will be a time of purification for the remnant of Israel (Zeph. 3.9).

30. Scholars have maintained that the repetition of the phrase "in that time" in Zeph. 3.19-20 denotes the time of the eschaton (DeVries, *Yesterday*, pp. 64–74, 202–5).

31. In Mic. 3.4 and Zeph. 1.12; 3.19, 20. The phrase has also been used by Joel (4.1) and Daniel (12.1), only at a later time.

32. The verb שׁוּב, in Jer. 3.14, could mean either "to repent" or "to return." In the former case, God calls Israel to return to Him; in the latter case, God calls Israel to return to the land.

then enters into a description of God's vision of Israel's restoration in Jer. 3.16-18. The expression "in those days" (בַּיָּמִים הָהֵמָּה), in 3.16, already creates an expectation of the day in which God will act for deliverance.[33] Similarly, the phrase "in that time" (בָּעֵת הַהִיא), in 3.17, awaits God's salvific act. While this act refers primarily to God's intervention in Israel's near future, it also prefigures the final restoration of God's people. The time or the event spoken about is one characterized by God's reign over Jerusalem, the absence of a confined temple and expansion of the Holy of Holies over Jerusalem,[34] the presence of God in an unusual way, and the gathering of all the nations to Jerusalem (3.17-18).[35] God's reign in Jerusalem, the throne of the Lord, will also result in the regaining of the land (Jer. 3.19). This is Jeremiah's first glance at God's restorative plan, and the language is reminiscent of later prophetic passages that speak of a future eschatological era in which the temple will be transformed or expanded (e.g. Ezekiel 37, Zechariah 1–2, Daniel 2; cf. also John 4).[36] As Huey comments, "true faith does not depend on symbols or external forms in order to worship God."[37]

The next two occurrences of the phrase "in that time" are in Jer. 4.11 and Jer. 8.1. The former instance (Jer. 4.11) is preceded by an appeal for Israel to repent (Jer. 3.21–4.4). The admonition specifically involves the circumcision of their hearts. However, this plea for repentance is followed by judgment, which implies Israel's disobedience to the plea. The phrase "in that time" is coupled with the phrase "in that day" (בַּיּוֹם־הַהוּא in Jer. 4.9), and refers to God's act of judgment upon

I find the former rendering to be the most probable, since, according to Jeremiah, Israel was to return back to the land after 70 years. For further discussion on the topic, see Jeremiah Unterman, *From Repentance to Redemption: Jeremiah's Thought in Transition* (JSOTSup, 54; Sheffield: Sheffield Academic Press, 1987), pp. 131–32. Note also the return motif in Deut. 4.29-30.

33. The combination of the phrases "in these days" and "in that time" must have some significance, since they appear together consistently in Jeremiah. Lundlom acknowledges this connection and further states that "for Jeremiah, Ezekiel, and Second Isaiah, more than for the eighth century prophets, the future is to have important discontinuities with the past" (Jack R. Lundbom, *Jeremiah 1–20* [AB, 21A; New York: Doubleday, 1999], pp. 314–15).

34. G. K. Beale argues that the point of Jer. 3.17 is the expansion of the Holy of Holies (or God's throne room) over Jerusalem. This expansion will not merely encompass the whole of Jerusalem, but the entire earth (universal application). For Beale's argument see G. K. Beale, *The Temple and the Church's Mission: A Biblical Theology of the Dwelling Place of God* (NSBT; Downers Grove: InterVarsity, 2004), pp. 113, 140, 142–43.

35. Thompson has characterized this state of events as the description of the true religion (J. A. Thompson, *The Book of Jeremiah* [NICNT; Grand Rapids: Eerdmans, 1980], pp. 202–3). The transformation described here is similar to that of Isa. 2.2-4 and Mic. 4.1-4, which also involve an expanded eschatological temple (Peter C. Craigie, Page H. Kelley, and Joel F. Drinkard, Jr. *Jeremiah 1–25* [WBC, 26; Dallas: Word, 1991], p. 61).

36. Beale, *Temple*, pp. 126–33, 138–54.

37. Huey has a reference to Jn 4.23 (F. B. Huey, Jr., *Jeremiah, Lamentations* [NAC, 16; Nashville: Broadman & Holman, 1993], p. 76).

Israel, specifically upon their leaders, priests and prophets.[38] Jeremiah's use of the phrases "in that day" and "in that time" awaits a future era, the nature of which will be expounded later in the book of Jeremiah. In a similar manner, the phrase "in that time" in Jer. 8.1 relates to the coming of days (הִנֵּה יָמִים בָּאִים in Jer. 7.32) when all in Jerusalem will die. The "time" in Jer. 8.1, therefore, is one of judgment and punishment, since the people of God have decisively disobeyed him (7.21-28). While these references to a future "time" may not initially appear to denote an eschatological era, their association with the time references in Jeremiah 30–33 explains God's intervention as part of a greater plan that involves the eschaton.[39]

Indeed, while on one level the language of Jeremiah in chs 30–33 relates to the restoration from the exile (esp. Jer. 31.2-14), on another level, it involves the final and complete restoration of Israel. The expressions "in those days" and "in that day" used in these chapters (30.3, 8; 31.27, 29, 31, 33, 38; 33.14) are surrounded by several eschatological images that describe this era as both troublesome and salvific. Such images are the pains of the birth of a child (30.6);[40] distress as it has never been before (30.7);[41] and God's judgment (30.5, 11, 24); but also the utterance of the covenantal formula (30.22; 31.33);[42] joy through suffering (31.13; 33.10-11); the new covenant (31.31); a complete knowledge of God and the forgiveness of sins (31.34; 33.8); and the promise of the latter-day king (33.15-16). Also, the mention of both Mount Zion and the theme of joy in Jer. 31.6-7 and 12-14 resembles the description of joy in Zeph. 3.14, where the prophet speaks of a permanent, end-time, restoration. The period of time mentioned in Jer. 31.1 and 33.15 ("in that time") should be taken to include all of the above promises.[43]

---

38. In Jer. 4.11, the enemy of God becomes his people. The phrase to describe God's people is "my daughter, my people" or "my daughter people" (Huey, *Jeremiah*, p. 82; William L. Holladay, *Jeremiah 1: A Commentary on the Book of the Prophet Jeremiah, Chapters 1–25* [Hermeneia; Minneapolis: Fortress, 1986], p. 156). God's people are mentioned within the phraseology of covenantal language.

39. As Bullock observes, "Jeremiah's eschatology elsewhere . . . is in agreement with the plan of the future set forth in the Book of Consolation" (Jeremiah 30–31) (Bullock, *Introduction*, p. 243).

40. The LXX version of Jer. 30.6 has the phrases καὶ περὶ φόβου and καὶ σωτηρίαν, which do not appear in the MT. See William McKane, *Jeremiah Vol 2* (ICC; Edinburgh: T&T Clark, 1996), p. 758.

41. Such a terrible day is also portrayed in Isa. 13.6, 9; Joel 2.11; 3.4; Hos. 2.2; Zeph. 1.14; and Mal. 3.23. McKane mentions Kimchi, who parallels this distress with the war described in Ezekiel 38–39, as the final challenge to the sovereignty of God (McKane, *Jeremiah*, p. 759). Thompson parallels this distress with the Day of the Lord in Amos 5.18-20; Isa. 2.12-21; and Zeph. 1.14-18 (Thompson, *Jeremiah*, p. 555). Lundbom sees "the beginnings" of an eschatological, messianic, understanding in the transformation that takes place in 30.8-9 (Jack R. Lundbom, *Jeremiah 21–36* [AB, 21B; New York: Doubleday, 2004], p. 385).

42. The covenantal formula also appears in Jer. 7.23; 11.4; and 24.7. The LXX does not translate Jer. 30.22.

43. Huey relates the phrase "in that time" with the relevant language of Jer. 30.3, 8, 22,

The eschatological nature of this "time" is strengthened by Jeremiah's use of "latter days" in 30.24 (right before the use of "in that time" in 31.1). This phrase, along with the rest of Jer. 30.23-24, alludes to Jer. 23.19-20, where the expression "latter days" is employed (23.20) to portray the time of God's wrath upon the false prophets of Israel (23.19).[44] It is precisely in the "latter days" that God's intentions will be accomplished, and the people will gain an understanding of these purposes.[45] Almost exactly the same wording (see underlined text) is used in both Jer. 23.19-20 and Jer. 30.23-24.[46]

Jer. 23.19-20	*Jer. 30.23-24*
Behold, the storm of the Lord has gone forth in wrath, even a whirling tempest; It will burst on the head of the wicked. The anger of the Lord will not turn back until he has performed and carried out the purposes of his heart; In the last days you will understand this clearly.	Behold, the storm of the Lord has gone forth in wrath, even a sweeping tempest; It will burst on the head of the wicked. The fierce anger of the Lord will not turn back until he has performed and carried out the purposes of his heart; In the last days you will understand this.
הִנֵּה סַעֲרַת יְהוָה חֵמָה יָצְאָה וְסַעַר מִתְחוֹלֵל עַל רֹאשׁ רְשָׁעִים יָחוּל לֹא יָשׁוּב אַף־יְהוָה עַד־עֲשֹׂתוֹ וְעַד־הֲקִימוֹ מְזִמּוֹת לִבּוֹ בְּאַחֲרִית הַיָּמִים תִּתְבּוֹנְנוּ בָהּ בִּינָה	הִנֵּה סַעֲרַת יְהוָה חֵמָה יָצְאָה סַעַר מִתְגּוֹרֵר עַל רֹאשׁ רְשָׁעִים יָחוּל מְזִמּוֹת לִבּוֹ לֹא יָשׁוּב חֲרוֹן אַף־יְהוָה עַד־עֲשֹׂתוֹ וְעַד־הֲקִימוֹ בְּאַחֲרִית הַיָּמִים תִּתְבּוֹנְנוּ בָהּ

The repetition of nearly the exact phrasing indicates that Jeremiah intends to communicate the same event in both cases. The reference is to the same wrath, the same understanding, and also the same "latter days." The text in Jer. 30.24 adds the word "fierce anger" (חָרוֹן), possibly to stress the magnitude of God's wrath and relate it to the distress in Jer. 30.7.

The same association between "time" and "days" also exists in Jer. 33.14-16 (בָּאִים יָמִים in 33.14, and בַּיָּמִים הָהֵם in 33.16). The latter passage introduces the messianic

and 24. Huey, *Jeremiah*, p. 269.

44. Notice that God will reveal his intentions with the coming of his wrath (Walter Brueggemann, *A Commentary on Jeremiah: Exile and Homecoming* [Grand Rapids: Eerdmans, 1998], p. 280). Brueggemann correctly relates the wrath of God with the context of Jeremiah 30, rather than relating it to the context of Jer. 23.20. Therefore, the wrath of God does not come upon the prophets, but rather upon the imperial power that opposes God's restoration (Brueggemann, *Jeremiah*, p. 279).

45. Once again, the people do not understand what their destiny entails according to God's purposes (Cf. Deut. 32.28-29). This understanding will be gained in the "latter days" (Jer. 23.19-20; 30.23-24).

46. Jeremiah 30.23-24 relates to the eschatological time of distress in Jer. 30.7 (see pp. 28-30)

reference to the righteous branch of David, who will be Israel's king (33.15).[47] This reference is a clear allusion to Jer. 23.5:[48]

Jer. 23.5	Jer. 33.15
Behold, *the days are coming*, declares the Lord, when I will raise up for David a righteous Branch (לְדָוִד צֶמַח צַדִּיק); and he will reign as king and act wisely and execute justice and righteousness in the land (וְעָשָׂה מִשְׁפָּט וּצְדָקָה בָּאָרֶץ).	*In those days* and *at that time* I will cause a righteous Branch of David (צַדִּיק לְדָוִד צֶמַח) to spring forth; and he will execute justice and righteousness in the land (וּצְדָקָה בָּאָרֶץ וְעָשָׂה מִשְׁפָּט).

Therefore, Jeremiah twice in chs 30–33 alludes back to ch. 23 in a way that connects the references to "time" and "day" with the "latter days." The focal point of all these eschatological prophecies is not merely Israel's restoration, but a restoration unto God's kingdom and under God's appointed king.

The characteristic expression "in those days and in that time," which is used in Jer. 33.15 (בַּיָּמִים הָהֵם וּבָעֵת הַהִיא) can be found elsewhere only in Jer. 50.4, 20; and Joel 4.1, all of which contexts speak of God's deliverance. The occurrence of the phrase in Jer. 50.4 and 20 is a linguistic means for Jeremiah to refer to the promised eschatological acts of chs 30–33. More specifically, these verses reiterate the promises of the new covenant and the forgiveness of sins. In Jer. 50.4, the people of God repent and seek God in Zion, and this repentance leads to their unification with God in an eternal covenant (50.5). Similarly, in Jer. 50.20, Jeremiah links "that time" with the forgiveness of sins promised in 31.34 and 33.8.[49]

It is interesting to note that every single instance of the phrase "in that time" in Jeremiah is associated with a similar phrase of the "day" or the "days." The following chart illustrates this point.

The phrase "in that time"		The "day" or "days"	
Jer. 3.17	בָּעֵת הַהִיא	Jer. 3.16	בַּיָּמִים הָהֵמָּה
Jer. 4.11	בָּעֵת הַהִיא	Jer. 4.9	בַּיּוֹם־הַהוּא
Jer. 8.1	בָּעֵת הַהִיא	Jer. 7.32	הִנֵּה יָמִים בָּאִים

47. This messianic prophecy is reminiscent of the promises introduced by the phrase "in the latter days" in Gen. 49.1 and Num. 24.14.

48. Thompson identifies the parallel of Jer. 33.15-16 with Jer. 23.5-6 (Thompson, *Jeremiah*, p. 601).

49. Holladay acknowledges that the forgiveness of sins in Jer. 50.5 parallels the promise given in Jer. 31.34. He also connects Jer. 50.4 with Jer. 31.9, where the phrase "walking and weeping they shall go" is repeated. Further on, Holladay links Jer. 50.20 with Jer. 30.15-17 and 31.34b, on the basis that the words "guilt" and "sin" appear together in Jer. 30.15 and are dealt in Jer. 30.17 and 31.34b (Holladay, *Jeremiah 1*, pp. 415–16, 418).

The phrase "in that time"		The "day" or "days"	
Jer. 31.1	בָּעֵת הַהִיא	Jer. 30.24	בְּאַחֲרִית הַיָּמִים
Jer. 33.15	בָּעֵת הַהִיא	Jer. 33.14	יָמִים בָּאִים
		Jer. 33.15	בַּיָּמִים הָהֵם
Jer. 50.4	בָּעֵת הַהִיא	Jer. 50.4	בַּיָּמִים הָהֵם
Jer. 50.20	בָּעֵת הַהִיא	Jer. 50.20	בַּיָּמִים הָהֵם

The same association of the phrase "in that time" with the "days" is also evident in the contexts of Joel 4.1; Mic. 3.4; and Zeph. 1.12; 3.19-20, as we have already seen. This association reinforces the eschatological significance of the phrase "in that time," since the time of God's intervention is linked to the final day of the Lord. Although one would expect this end-time period to involve solely God's judgment and punishment, it also involves God's restorative plan and the establishment of his kingdom through a messianic agent. The phrase "in that time" has been used enough in OT eschatological contexts to establish a tradition of its own, possibly even becoming a *terminus technicus* for the end-time period of judgment and restoration.

In this survey of the phrase "in that time," we have observed that this expression has been employed by the prophets to denote the coming of an eschatological era. This "time" has been consistently associated and compared with the eschatological "day" in which God will execute his judgment upon the nations and Israel will be restored. This will be a time of purification for God's people, who will eventually receive the promise of the Spirit and enjoy the restoration of their covenantal relationship with God, through the erection of a new temple and the establishment of a new reign. When Daniel uses the phrase "in that time" twice in Dan. 12.1, he likely used it in association with its use in the prophetic tradition (a *terminus technicus*) and meant it as the culminating eschatological point already mentioned by his predecessors. We will see that the immediately preceding and following contexts of Dan. 12.1 bear out such a conclusion.

b. *The Time of Distress:* עֵת צָרָה

The exact phrase "time of distress" (עֵת צָרָה) occurs eight times in the Hebrew Bible (Judg. 10.14; Neh. 9.27; Ps. 37.39; Isa. 33.2; Jer. 14.8; 15.11; 30.7; and Dan. 12.1). Generally, the word עֵת is used many times in reference to a time of distress.[50] The notion of a distressful time appears extensively in the prophets.[51] The idea was

50. References of "time" to such a distress appear in Judg. 10.14; 2 Chron. 28.22; Neh. 9.27; Job 38.23; Ps. 10.1; 37.19; Eccl. 9.12; Isa. 33.2; Jer. 2.27-28; 6.15; 8.12; 10.15; 11.12, 14; 14.8, 19; 15.11; 30.7; 46.21; 49.8; 50.27, 31; 51.6, 18, 33; Ezek. 7.7, 12; 21.25, 29; 30.3; 35.5; and Dan. 9.25; 12.1. The fact that the word "time" is closely associated with the notion of "distress" or "trouble" is also attested by the fact that the plural noun "times" (עִתִּים) is sometimes used as a substitute for "trouble" (e.g. Ps. 31.16; Isa. 33.6; Dan. 11.6, 13-14).

51. The word that is mostly used to describe the period of "distress" is צָרָה (Judg. 10.14; Neh. 9.27; Ps. 10.1; 37.39; Isa. 33.2; Jer. 14.8; 15.11; 30.7; Dan. 12.1). Apart from this word,

known at least from the times of Isaiah (Isa. 33.2), if not earlier,[52] and later, Jeremiah and Ezekiel use the notion of a distressful time to refer to God's judgment or punishment, either upon his people or upon the nations (Jer. 2.27-28; 6.15; 8.12; 10.15; 11.12; 14.8; 15.11; 30.7; 46.21; 49.8; 50.27, 31; 51.18; Ezek. 21.30, 34; 35.5). In this section, I will specifically deal with the period of distress in Jer. 30.7,[53] which is similar to the final tribulation in Dan. 12.1. Since the "time" in Dan. 12.1 is one of great distress, the prophetic text in Jeremiah serves as the best background to the Danielic distress. The purpose of this investigation is to better understand the "time of distress" in Dan. 12.1 and ultimately its connection to the OG's use of hour in Dan. 12.1.

Commentators have acknowledged the "time of distress" in Jer. 30.7 as the appropriate background behind the very same phrase in Dan. 12.1.[54] In the immediate context of Jer. 30.7, God promises that he will restore Israel (30.3);[55] however, the way that God will bring about this restoration is through pain and terror. God's

the word רָעָה is also used (Ps. 37.19; Eccl. 9.12; Jer. 2.27-28; 11.12; 15.11; Amos 5.13; Mic. 2.3), as well as the words פֶּקֶד and פְּקֻדָּה (Jer. 6.15; 8.12; 10.15; 46.21; 49.8; 50.27, 31; 51.18). Finally, Ezekiel uses the unique phrase בְּעֵת עֲוֹן קֵץ (Ezek. 21.30, 34; 35.5).

52. In the earlier uses of the phrase "time of distress," the distress is not eschatological; it refers to the different political and sociological troubles that Israel experienced (2 Chron. 28.22; Neh. 9.27; Job 38.23; Ps. 37.19; Eccl. 9.12). The presence of this distress somehow implied the passive stance of God towards his disobedient people (Judg. 10.14; Ps. 10.1). At times, God is portrayed as the sole deliverer in such time of distress (Neh. 9.27; Isa. 33.2).

53. This is the passage most closely associated with Dan. 12.1. Although see also the reference in Isa. 33.2. Isaiah speaks of God protecting Israel in the time of distress (צָרָה; ἐν καιρῷ θλίψεως), which probably refers to Israel's exile. Without doubting the reference to a historical situation, the images and expressions that Isaiah uses in the immediate context of this distress, also involve God's actions in the eschaton. God promises to pour out the Spirit on his people (32.15), the outcome of which will be eternal peace and security in the land (32.17-18). This restoration will be done through the provision of a king (Isa. 32.1), who is later identified with God himself (Isa. 33.17, 21). The exilic time of distress in Isaiah will be replaced by an era of peace that will include the outpouring of the Spirit and the establishment of God's kingdom. It could be that Isaiah projects the eschatological image of the new Jerusalem in contrast to the imminent state of distress.

54. E.g. John J. Collins, *Daniel: A Commentary on the Book of Daniel* (Hermeneia; Minneapolis: Fortress, 1993), pp. 390–91; Ernest Lucas, *Daniel* (AOTC; Downers Grove: InterVarsity, 2002), p. 294.

55. The LXX translates with χρόνος στενός ("time of straitness"). Other references to a great judgment that has never occurred before are Ezek. 21.30, 34 and Dan. 12.1 (cf. Exod. 9.24). Regarding the time of distress in Jeremiah, it may also be found in Jer. 2.27-29; 6.15, where it refers to Israel's punishment for her misdeeds. Also, the time of judgment for Israel in Jer. 11.12 becomes the time of prayer (11.14), since the distress has caused the people to respond with a plea for deliverance. Similarly, there is a strong plea for God's mercy and deliverance from the time of distress (צָרָה) in Jer. 14.8, 19; and 15.11; however, God's decision for judgment is irrevocable. The rest of the passages in Jeremiah using צָרָה either are not

act of judgment will deliver Israel from her captivity. This is evident especially in Jer. 30.18–31.1, where the prophet talks about the restoration of the "latter days" (30.24) in a way that also involves God's wrath (30.23). This wrath is the focus of attention in Jer. 30.5-11.[56]

The day of distress is depicted as one of terror and fear,[57] a day with no peace (30.5), which resembles the day of the Lord as it is narrated in Isa. 2.10-17.[58] In Jer. 30.6, the image of the laboring woman is brought into the picture to describe the people on whom God's judgment will fall.[59] The inability to bear children could imply the desolate state into which God will bring Jerusalem. Furthermore, the magnitude of the distress will be incomparable to anything that has happened before.

The description of the "time," in Jer. 30.7 as a day of great distress[60] that has never occurred before resembles the language in Dan. 12.1, the latter of which probably alludes to the former:

Jer. 30.7	Dan. 12.1
Alas! for that day (הַיּוֹם הַהוּא) is great, there is none like it (כָּמֹהוּ מֵאַיִן); and it is Jacob's time of distress (וְעֵת־צָרָה), but he will be saved from it.	And there will be a time of distress (עֵת צָרָה), such as never has been (לֹא־נִהְיְתָה) since there was a nation till that time (הָעֵת הַהִיא). But at that time (וּבָעֵת הַהִיא) your people shall be delivered . . .

In both of the above passages, the outcome of the great distress is the deliverance of God's people.[61] Also, both passages seem to talk about a universal distress, since in Jer. 30.11 God promises to completely destroy all the nations. In addition, Jeremiah mentions that, while Israel will eventually be saved, she will not be left undisciplined

eschatological (Jer. 8.12; 10.15; 11.12, 14) or have already been discussed (Jer. 3.17; 4.11; 8.1; 31.1; 33.15; 50.4, 20).

56. The poetic genre of Jer. 30.1–31.40 attests to the unity of this large section (William L. Holladay, *Jeremiah 2: A Commentary on the Book of the Prophet Jeremiah, Chapters 26–52* [Hermeneia; Minneapolis: Fortress, 1989], pp. 155–56).

57. According to McKane, the great day of terror parallels God's judgment on Gog (Ezekiel 38–39). The great day of terror also appears in Hos. 2.2; Joel 2.11; 3.4; Isa. 13.6, 9; Zeph. 1.14; Mal. 3.23. See McKane, *Jeremiah*, p. 759.

58. Gerald L. Keown, Pamela J. Scalise, and Thomas G. Smothers, *Jeremiah 26–52* (WBC, 27; Dallas: Word, 1995), pp. 92–93.

59. The image of the pains of childbirth is also used in Jer. 4.31; 6.24; and 22.23 to describe a great distress. Thompson agrees with most scholars that since the image is used elsewhere to describe a curse upon the enemy soldiers, its similar use here serves to denote God's curse upon Israel (Thompson, *Jeremiah*, p. 556).

60. The word צָרָה is explicitly connected to the pains of a woman bearing a child in Jer. 4.31, in which context we have already seen the description of God's judgment occurring "in that time" (4.11) or "in that day" (4.9).

61. Brueggemann rightly observes the adversative preposition of Jer. 30.7b, which emphasizes the reassuring conclusion of the distress: terror will be turned into assurance. See Brueggemann, *Jeremiah*, p. 273.

(30.11), which also parallels the purifying nature of the Danielic distress.[62] Even as Israel experiences the distressful day of God's wrath, *in that same time*, they will also experience God's deliverance; Yahweh will be their God, and they will be his people (30.24–31.1).[63]

The exilic distress mentioned in Jer. 30.7 portrays Israel under the judgment of God. The "time of distress" points forward to the time of Israel's suffering due to her disobedience. Nevertheless, despite the magnitude of this distress, vindication will eventually take place. Its apparent use by Daniel shows that, not long after Jeremiah, this distress was viewed as foreshadowing the great end-time tribulation.

c. *Summary of Use of Eschatological Time Expressions in the OT*
The scope of the earlier section of this chapter was to survey those eschatological expressions that appear in the OT and relate to the Danielic eschatological hour ("in that time" and "time of distress"). The disadvantage of such a broad survey is the fact that it is impossible to maintain the in-depth study that some of the passages require. Nevertheless, this survey has brought to light those passages that likely provide the backdrop to similar expressions in the book of Daniel and the eschatological hour therein.

The survey in the OT has shown that these time references are directly associated with the eschaton, especially with respect to Israel's destiny, which involves both judgment and restoration. One may draw the following conclusions: the expressions "in that time" and "time of distress" are often directly linked with eschatological notions and are to be understood within an eschatological framework. By "eschatological" we mean God's appointed time in history that introduces a distinct era in which reality as we know it is transformed; this eschatological time points to God's final goal for history.

Moreover, we have seen that the eschatological concept of time in the phrases surveyed entails both the judgment of the disobedient and the vindication of the remnant/saints; thus, Israel is depicted as both suffering and being vindicated. The phrase בָּעֵת הַהִיא, in particular, appears in contexts with eschatological language, denoting the time of Israel's final restoration, the establishment of peace, the renewal of the covenant, and the forgiveness of sins. This phrase is especially linked to the "latter days" era and the rise of God's end-time king. The word "time" is further closely associated with the concept of eschatological distress (Jer. 30.7), which reflects God's act of judgment.

In the OG of Daniel, we will further see that the term "hour", which translates עֵת in the initial clause of Dan. 12.1, depicts the end-time period in which God will

---

62. See Dan. 11.35, "and some of the wise shall stumble, so that they may be refined, purified, and made white, until the time of the end, for it still awaits the appointed time"; and Dan. 12.10, "Many will be purged, purified and refined, but the wicked will act wickedly; and none of the wicked will understand, but those who have insight will understand."

63. Once again, notice how the notion of "time," in Jer. 30.7, is used interchangeably with the idea of "day" in Jer. 30.3, 7-8.

execute his judgment to the effect that any opposition against him no longer exists. The defeat of God's end-time opponent will result in the vindication of God's people and their resurrection to eternal life.

III. *The Use of the Eschatological* ὥρα *in Daniel*

In the past, there have been great difficulties with the interpretation of the book of Daniel. The difficulties concern several matters such as the literary form of the book and its structure, the preservation of the book in two languages,[64] the book's genre, its dating, etc. It is, indeed, a challenge for any scholar to introduce this book. Nevertheless, there has been some agreement pertaining to some of these issues. Generally, the book is perceived as an apocalyptic work of literature. Also, the book's twofold division has been acknowledged, the first being a narrative in which Daniel is mentioned in the third person (chs 1–6), and the second being an apocalyptic work of which Daniel is the first person narrator (chs 7–12).[65] The first section narrates stories of Daniel in Babylon, while the later focuses on Daniel's visions, which describe the rise and fall of different earthly nations.[66] Most modern scholars date the book in the second century, although there is a minority who support an earlier date.[67]

The focus of this section is the examination of the eschatological ὥρα in the LXX of Daniel generally, and in Dan. 12.1 specifically. I examine those Danielic verses that explicitly use the term ὥρα eschatologically (Dan. 8.17, 19; 11.6, 35, 40, 45; 12.1, 13). Although the focus is on the Septuagint's use of the word ὥρα, references are also made to the Hebrew text, wherever necessary.

The purpose of examining the concept of ὥρα in Daniel is to understand how this temporal notion has been developed in Daniel and to see how the author discusses this hour in relation to other eschatological themes. After I briefly summarize the broader context of the eschatological hour in Daniel, I examine the use of ὥρα and its eschatological background as it occurs in Dan. 8.17, 19; 11.6, 35, 40, 45; 12.1, 13,[68] with a brief digression on the use of the "latter days" in Dan. 10.14. A more

---

64. Hebrew (Dan. 1.1–2.4; 8.1–12.13) and Aramaic (Dan. 2.4–7.28).

65. The language of Daniel does not fit with this division. Dan. 2.4–7.28 is written in Aramaic, while the rest of Daniel (Dan. 1.1–2.3 and 8.1–12.13) is written in Hebrew. There have been several attempts to deal with this problem of language, most of which end up with some kind of multi-editing theory for the book.

66. Block provides a good overview of Daniel and argues for a unified reading of the book (Daniel I. Block, 'Preaching Old Testament Apocalptic to a New Testament Church', *CTJ* 41 [2006], pp. 17–52).

67. For the latter, e.g. see Joyce G. Baldwin, *Daniel: An Introduction and Commentary* (TOTC; Downers Grove: InterVarsity, 1978); Edward J. Young, *The Prophecy of Daniel: A Commentary* (Grand Rapids: Eerdmans, 1957).

68. The word ὥρα also occurs in the OG of Dan. 4.17, 19, 26; 5.5; and 9.21. In ch. 4, it refers to Nebuchadnezzar's hour of judgment (4.17), Daniels' perplexity (4.19), and the restoration of Nebuchadnezzar's kingdom (4.19); in Dan. 5.5, ὥρα represents the time at

extensive exegetical discussion of the literary unit of Dan. 12.1-4 will clarify the significance of hour in Dan. 12.1.

a. *The Broader Context of the Eschatological Hour in Daniel*

The book of Daniel is full of eschatological language and images; specific references to an eschatological end first appear in Dan. 2.28, 29, 45, where the phrase "latter days" (ἐπ' ἐσχάτων τῶν ἡμερῶν) occurs. Daniel interprets Nebuchadnezzar's dream pertaining to the future of his kingdom and the kingdoms that will follow.

The references to an eschatological end continue in Dan. 8.17, 19, 23; 10.14; 11.6, 13, 20, 27, 29, 35, 40, 45; 12.1, 4, 6, 9, 13. These references are part of three visions (Daniel 8–12) that expand the vision of Daniel 7. The four visions (Daniel 7, 8, 9, 10–12) are parallel in some respects, and so many of the themes are repeated.[69] Chapter 7 describes four beasts that represent four kingdoms. Out of the fourth beast a king will rise (small horn), who will boast against God and will attack the people of God. At that time, the Son of Man will execute judgment upon the nations, deliver God's people, and establish an everlasting kingdom. Daniel's second vision, in ch. 8, explicates the first vision in more detail, focusing on the rise of the insolent king and the persecution of the saints. In his third vision (ch. 9), an angel reveals to Daniel the time at which all this will happen, as well as the appearance and the cutting off of the Messiah. Finally, the last vision of chs 10–12 is a detailed description of the rise and fall of different nations, the battles between them, the suffering of the people of God, and the final victory of God over his enemies.[70] All four visions culminate in a final end, which is God's victory over his enemies and the deliverance of God's people in the eschaton.

b. *The Use of* ὥρα *in Dan. 8.17, 19*

In ch. 8, Gabriel informs Daniel that the vision involving the cessation of the regular sacrifice and the transgression that makes Israel desolate pertains to the time

---

which the human hand wrote on the wall; and in Dan. 9.21, it refers to the time of the evening sacrifice, at which Gabriel came to speak to Daniel. Likewise, ὥρα occurs in Theodotion of Dan. 3.5-6, 15; 4.19, 33; 5.5; 9.21. In ch. 3, it refers to the hour at which the people were instructed to worship Nebudchanezzar's image. These references do not affect directly the rest of the uses concerning the hour of the end. In Theodotion, ὥρα does not occur in Dan. 8.17, 19; 11.6, 35, 40, 45; 12.1, 13.

69. Lucas argues for a closer connection between visions 1 and 2 (chs 7 and 8), and 3 and 4 (chs 9 and 10–12) respectively (Lucas, *Daniel*). However, this does not exclude the interrelationship that exists between all visions. For example, one finds many parallels between visions 1 and 4 as well.

70. The commentators are virtually unanimous in their interpretation of ch. 11, except when they reach vv. 21, 36, or 40 of the chapter. Most scholars have described the despicable king of 11.21 as Antiochus IV Epiphanes. Others have proposed a change of subject at either 11.36 or 11.40. I contend that the king of 11.36, although it could be a reference to Antiochus, primarily represents God's adversary in the eschaton (see my discussion later on this issue). For different interpretations on the reference of these verses, see Lucas, *Daniel*, pp. 292–93.

of the end (8.17, 19). This end will be a period of wrath, the outpouring of God's judgment upon those who disobey. The tribulation of desolation is the climax of what the little horn or the insolent king will do to the Israelites (8.9, 23); both the sanctuary and God's people will be trampled by him (8.13, 24). According to the vision's interpretation, this king who will grow strong in power will persecute and deceive God's people (8.24-29). He will think himself to be so great (8.25) as to oppose even the Prince of princes. Finally, he will be destroyed, although not by human power (8.25). The "end" in 8.17, 19 appears to relate to a specific time in history in which these events will occur.[71]

In the OG of Dan. 8.17, we find the expression εἰς ὥραν καιροῦ, which refers to the appointed time of the vision's fulfillment. The eschatological nature of this phrase arises from its Hebrew equivalent, לְעֶת־קֵץ, which literally reads "at the time of the end." The phrase in Dan. 8.19, εἰς ὥρας καιροῦ συντελείας ("appropriate time of consumption"), is parallel to that in Dan. 8.17, and its Hebrew equivalent literally means "at the appointed time of the end" (לְמוֹעֵד קֵץ). The fact that the above phrases are parallel and synonymous is attested by Theodotion's translation of Daniel (TH), which renders both phrases the same: εἰς καιροῦ πέρας ("for the end of time").

The particular wording used in Dan. 8.17, 19 suggests the eschatological nature of the hour. First, the word ὥρα is connected with the phrase καιροῦ συντελείας in the Old Greek of Dan. 8.19 (literally "time of consummation"). The LXX translator (OG) has probably added the word συντελείας ("consummation" or "end") in 8.19 to elaborate on the eschatological nature of the hour in 8.17; this addition also better reflects the equivalent word in Hebrew, קֵץ. The addition is evident in the following parallel:

Dan. 8.17	Dan. 8.19
ἔτι γὰρ	ἔτι γὰρ
εἰς ὥραν	εἰς ὥρας
καιροῦ	καιροῦ συντελείας

Also, one may notice that both of the above phrases (8.17, 19) begin with the construction ἔτι γὰρ. The construction ἔτι γὰρ always introduces the time of the end in Daniel (8.17, 19, 26; 10.14; 11.27, 35; 12.13)[72] and connotes the idea that the eschaton (time of the end), although not yet here,[73] is expected to arrive.

---

71. In Daniel 8–12, the word "end" (קֵץ) occurs 15 times. In vv. 8.17, 19; 11.27, 35, 40; 12.4, 9 the word appears in a phrase that bears either the meaning "time of the end" or the "appointed time of the end." Therefore, Daniel sees the end-time as being determined.

72. Outside Daniel, it appears in Gen. 7.4; 45.11; 46.30; Deut. 31.27; Job 36.2; Isa. 10.25, always connoting a somewhat unexpected outcome. It may be that the prophetic utterances in Daniel await an unexpected fulfillment.

73. For a more extensive exegetical treatment of the Danielic hour, see my comments on Dan. 11.36–12.4.

Other pointers to an eschatological use of the hour may be the presence of the words מוֹעֵד (8.19) and קֵץ (Dan. 8.17, 19) in the Hebrew text. First, the word מוֹעֵד (Dan. 8.19) appears with the meaning of "appointed time" six times in Daniel (8.19; 11.27, 29, 35; 12.7), all of which refer to the end of times.[74] The fact that the word עֵת in 8.17 parallels the word מוֹעֵד in 8.19 shows that both terms refer to the same particular time appointed by God (the OG translates both with ὥρα).[75]

Second, the word קֵץ (Dan. 8.17, 19) appears 67 times in the Hebrew Bible and its main meaning is "end."[76] The significance of the word "end" here in Daniel (8.17, 19; 9.26; 11.6, 13, 27, 35, 40, 45; 12.4, 6, 9, 13) lies in the fact that it is specifically used to connote an eschatological reality within history (the end of reality as presently experienced), although it is also used to project Israel's final destiny according to the purposes of God. A similar use of קֵץ ("end") in Daniel appears in the book of Ezekiel (Ezek. 7.2, 3, 6; 21.30, 34; 35.5). The LXX translation of the above passages in Ezekiel reinforces the eschatological dimension of the word in the specific texts, since every instance of קֵץ is rendered with the Greek word πέρας,[77] except for Ezek. 35.5 which has ἐπ' ἐσχάτῳ.

It is likely that the translator of Daniel (TH) has in mind the "end" in Ezekiel, especially since the combination of the words καιρός and πέρας, apart from Hab. 2.3,[78] occurs only in Ezek. 21.30, 34, and Dan. (TH) 8.17, 19; 11.27, 35, 40;

---

74. The word מוֹעֵד occurs 224 times in the Hebrew Bible, out of which most of the references have the meaning of a "meeting place" (e.g. Exod. 29.4, 10, 30; 33.7; 35.21; Lev. 3.2, 8, 13; 6.16, 26; Num. 3.7, 8, 25, etc.). Another meaning of the word is "festival" (e.g. Lam. 1.4; Zech. 8.9), and yet another is "appointed time" (e.g. Num. 9.2, 13; 15.3; 28.2; Deut. 31.10; 1 Sam. 9.24; 31.8; 1 Chron. 23.31; Neh. 10.33; Isa. 1.14; 33.20; Jer. 8.7; Ezek. 36.38; 44.24; 46.9; Hos. 2.9, 11; Zeph. 3.18; etc.). Elsewhere in the Hebrew Bible, the word מוֹעֵד occurs twice in relation to the word עֵת (2 Sam. 24.15; Ps. 102.14).

75. The word עֵת may take on the meaning of "appointed time," especially when it is directly associated with such words as מוֹעֵד (2 Sam. 24.15; Ps. 102.14), זְמָן (Ezra 10.14; Neh. 10.35; 13.31; Eccl. 3.1), or קֵץ (Dan. 8.17; 11.13; 11.35; 11.40; 12.4, 9). Also, עֵת takes on the notion of "appointed time" when it becomes the subject of the verb בּוֹא (Isa. 13.22; Jer. 27.7; 51.33; Ezek. 7.7, 12; 22.3; Hag. 1.2). There are instances where the word עֵת is closely associated with "a day" that is coming (בּוֹא) (e.g. Jer. 33.14; 46.21; 50.27; 50.31; Ezek. 21.30, 34).

76. Most of the occurrences refer to the end of a period of time, whether this is days, months or years (e.g. Gen. 8.6; 41.1; Deut. 9.11; Judg. 11.39; 1 Kgs 2.39; etc.). Some instances refer to the end of a person's life (e.g. Job 6.11; Jer. 51.13; Lam. 4.18), while others have the meaning of "limit" or "border" (e.g. Job 16.3; Ps. 39.4; 119.96). When the word קֵץ is negated, it also conveys the notion of endlessness or eternity (e.g. Job 22.5; Eccl. 12.12; Isa. 9.7).

77. The word πέρας is used only in the Theodotionic version of Daniel: Dan. (TH) 7.29; 8.17, 19; 11.27, 35; 12.6, 9.

78. Habakkuk 2.3 describes a vision that will take place at the appointed time (מוֹעֵד), which is described as the end (קֵץ). The LXX translates: ἔτι ὅρασις εἰς καιρὸν καὶ ἀνατελεῖ εἰς πέρας. Habakkuk 2.4 speaks of the desolation of the boastful one, and the rest of ch. 2 describes this boastful figure, whose end is destruction. Then, Habakkuk 3 goes on to speak

12.9.[79] This may explain why the Theodotion version renders both Hebrew phrases, לְעֶת־קֵץ ("time of the end") and לְמוֹעֵד קֵץ ("appointed time of the end") in 8.17 and 8.19, respectively, with the Greek phrase ἔτι γὰρ εἰς καιροῦ πέρας. The Ezekiel passages speak of the coming judgment upon Israel.[80] In all of the above instances, an emphasis is placed on the fact that the time of God's judgment is near and is certain.[81] This is most evident in Ezek. 7.2, 3, and 6, where the word "end" is repeated three times in verses 7.2-3 and another three times in 7.6, the repetition of which probably indicates the certainty of the judgment, as well as the magnitude of the destruction.[82] A similar emphasis exists in Ezek. 21.30, 34, and 35.5.[83]

When Daniel speaks of the time of an eschatological end, he does not introduce a novel story about the eschaton; rather, he draws from what has already been said and gives it new significance. The background of Ezekiel 7, 21, 35 indicates that the time of the end in Dan. 8.17, 19 is God's foretold judgment upon those who disobey God's ordinances.[84] Daniel's eschatological ὥρα contains the fulfillment of God's promises regarding justice and vindication.

---

of God's deliverance, a deliverance, however, that is accomplished through a time of distress (ἐν ἡμέρᾳ θλίψεως).

79. The Hebrew text also combines עת with קץ in Ezek. 21.30, 34; 35.5 and Dan. 8.17; 11.35, 40; 12.4, 9.

80. Ezekiel 7 refers to the Day of the Lord (see the translation of the LXX in 7.10). The verb בוא in Ezek. 7.7 is not a dittograph; this is supported by the fact that in 7.10 we also have the presence of two verbs with the same subject. The form of Ezekiel 7 is interesting in that it provides room for paralleling verses 7.7 and 7.12, where "time" occurs. Both instances are preceded by the idea that the "end" or the "day" has already come (7.6 and 7.10). See Leslie C. Allen, *Ezekiel 1–19* (WBC, 28; Dallas: Word, 1994), pp. 107–8.

81. The nearness of the Day of the Lord also appears in Ezek. 30.3; Joel 1.15; 2.1; and Zeph. 1.7, 14. The nearness in Ezekiel is evident by the presence of the verb בוא, which not only indicates the proximity of God's judgment, but also seems to guarantee its certainty. The expression used in 7.2 is בָּא קֵץ, and in 7.6 this "coming end" is intensified through the following chiasm: קֵץ בָּא בָּא הַקֵּץ. Block lists a number of parallel phrases that relate to the notion of the "coming day" and then links Ezek 7.7 with Isa. 22.2, 5 (Daniel I. Block, *The Book of Ezekiel: Chapters 1–24* [NICOT; Grand Rapids: Eerdmans, 1997], p. 253). Another argument for the eschatological use of the word "to come" can be found in Arie van der Kooij, '"Coming" things and "Last" Things: Isaianic Terminology as Understood in the Wisdom of Ben Sira and in the Septuagint of Isaiah', in F. Postma, K. Spronk and E. Talstra (eds), *The New Things Eschatology in Old Testament Prophecy: Festschrift for Henk Leene* (Maastricht, Netherlands: Shaker, 2002), pp. 135–40.

82. Ezekiel emphasizes the *coming* of the end.

83. The phrase that is used in Ezek. 21.30 and 34 is בְּעֵת עֲוֹן קֵץ. This phrase is twice connected to the "coming of the days" (אֲשֶׁר־בָּא יוֹמָם) and refers to the wicked, godless leader of Israel. Ezekiel 35.5 also speaks of a time of distress that will happen in the end; this is the same "end" mentioned in Ezek. 21.30, 34, and is linked by the use of the exact phrase, בְּעֵת עֲוֹן קֵץ.

84. The expression "the end has come" is a prophetic formula that should have brought fear to those hearing it. Block attempts to find the significance of the phrase in Amos 8.2, thus

The Danielic hour of the end (Dan. 8.17, 19) pertains to an eschatological moment in history, since, at this hour, the end-time opponent brings about the destruction of the sanctuary and the cessation of the sacrifices (Dan. 8.11-13; cf. Dan. 9.26-27; 12.11), the messianic agent appears (8.25; 9.26), and a new epoch is inaugurated. The transition from one era to another is implied with the defeat of God's final adversary in Dan. 8.25.

Daniel does not disclose everything about the eschatological ὥρα in Daniel 8; rather, the development of the hour theme later in the book reveals to us more about the new era. This end-time period involves more than mere judgment, persecution, and the defeat of God's final opponent. The reader will have to wait until the description of the final vision in Daniel 11–12, where the hour appears again in connection to additional end-time events.

c. *The "Latter Days" in Dan. 10.14*

Before I comment on the use of ὥρα in Daniel 11–12, a short exegetical comment on the "latter days" in Dan. 10.14 advances the notion of a coming eschatological era in Daniel and further links the hour to the establishment of God's kingdom.[85] Daniel 10.14 reads, "Now I have come to give you an understanding of what will happen to your people in the latter days (בְּאַחֲרִית הַיָּמִים in MT, ἐπ᾽ ἐσχάτου τῶν ἡμερῶν in OG), for the vision pertains to the days yet future." The meaning (or referent) of the phrase "latter days" as it is generally used in the OT is disputed.[86] Being consistent with the definition of eschatology in my introduction and because of the wider context of Daniel 7–12, I view the phrase "latter days" in Dan. 10.14 as signifying a specific time (or event) that occurs in history and also contributes towards the transformation of all things at the end of time.[87] The eschatological import of this phrase

---

connecting Ezekiel 7 with Amos 8.2 (Block, *Ezekiel*, p. 248). Amos 8.2 introduces a vision, which also speaks of the coming end of Israel (ἥκει τὸ πέρας), and is qualified eschatologically by the repetition of the phrase ἐν ἐκείνῃ τῇ ἡμέρᾳ (בַּיּוֹם הַהוּא) in 8.9 and 13 and the use of the phrase ἡμέραι ἔρχονται (יָמִים בָּאִים) in 8.11. The vision is introduced with a parallel between the "ripe fruits" and the "time of the end." Andersen and Freedman acknowledge the eschatological connotation of the word "end," especially as it relates to the phrase "in that day" (Andersen and Freedman, *Amos*, p. 797).

85. In this section I will focus on the MT and at points refer to the OG.

86. Hoffman sees the phrase "in the latter days" functioning "sometimes, but not always . . . as an eschatological term." He denies the eschatological nature of the term in such passages as Gen. 49.1; Deut. 4.30; 31.29; Jer. 23.20, while he affirms it in Isa. 2.2; Mic. 4.1; Ezek. 38.16; Hos. 3.5; and Jer. 30.24 (Hoffman, 'Eschatology', pp. 75–97). Oswalt also, who agrees with Buchanan that the phrase "latter days" is not used in a technical way, acknowledges the fact that in some instances the phrase can be used in a more technical way (cf. Jer. 48.47; 49.39; Ezek. 38.16; Dan. 10.14; Hos. 3.5), to indicate the consummation of history (John N. Oswalt, *The Book of Isaiah: Chapters 1–39* [NICNT; Grand Rapids: Eerdmans, 1986], p. 116).

87. Contra G. W. Buchanan, 'Eschatology and the "End of Days"', *JNES* 20 (1961), pp. 188–93; and Hans Kosmala, 'At the End of the Days', *ASTI* 2 (1963), pp. 27–37. Hans

is strengthened when both קֵץ and אַחֲרִית appear in the same context. Although the two words are distinct, their combined use affects the meaning and referent of both.[88]

In Dan. 10.14, the phrase appears within the context of Daniel's revelatory experience. There, an angelic figure reveals to Daniel what will happen in the "latter days." On the one hand, the phrase "latter days" depicts the era of the prophetic descriptions in Dan. 11.2–12.4; the events narrated there will certainly occur in the "latter days." However, the phrase also functions so as to allude to the "latter days" in Dan. 2.28-29, 45. The author of the book of Daniel intends to communicate that the events of the vision that are about to be revealed concern the kingdom succes-sions of Daniel 2. Indeed, in ch. 2, Daniel's interpretation of Nebuchadnezzar's dream is sandwiched with the *inclusio* of the phrase אַחֲרֵי דְנָה ($\dot{\epsilon}\pi'$ $\dot{\epsilon}\sigma\chi\dot{\alpha}\tau\omega\nu$ $\tau\hat{\omega}\nu$ $\dot{\eta}\mu\epsilon\rho\hat{\omega}\nu$, Dan. 2.28-29 and 2.45).[89] The focus of the narrative there, having depicted the rising of one kingdom after the other, is on God's establishment of a kingdom that will last forever.

The history of the phrase "latter days" (בְּאַחֲרִית הַיָּמִים) betrays a concern for Israel's destiny as a reigning institution and emphasizes the future coming of a messianic figure that will establish God's kingdom for Israel and the nations (see Gen. 49.1;

Kosmala, in dealing with the phrase "in the latter days" as it generally appears in the OT, argues that the phrase is distinct from the idea of a "final end." His argument, though, seems to be in contrast with his findings in the Qumran, the NT, and the Targumim (he sees a development of the meaning throughout the centuries). Kosmala limits his opponents to two schools of thought on OT eschatology, which both translate the phrase "in the last days" or "at the end of the days" and represent the two extremes (Kosmala seems to be following J. Lindblom, 'Gibt es eine Eschatologie bei den alttestamentlichen Propheten?' *ST* 6 [1953], pp. 79–114). However, one can hardly limit the definition of "latter days" in such a way, for the following reasons: 1) it disregards the rest of the views concerning the relation of OT eschatology to the prophets; 2) it limits the eschatological scope of the phrase "latter days" — or the definition of the term eschatology — to be either at the end of history or not at the end of history.

On the use of the phrase "latter days" in the OT, see also Cees Houtman, 'An der Swelle zum Eschaton: Prophctische Eschatologie im Deuteronomium', in F. Postma, K. Spronk and E. Talstra (eds), *The New Things Eschatology in Old Testament Prophecy: Festschrift for Henk Leene* (ACEBT, SS3; Maastricht, Netherlands: Shaker, 2002), pp. 119–28; Becking, 'The Exile', pp. 1–7; and E. Lipinski, 'b'hryt hymym dans les texts preexiliques', *VT* 20 (1970), pp. 445–50 (445–48).

88. Contextual factors such as eschatological themes, radical historical changes, the word "end," etc. signify that the phrase "latter days," in Dan. 10.14, pertains to an eschatological reality.

89. Notice also the phrase בְּאַחֲרִית יוֹמַיָּא in Dan. 2.28.

Num. 24.14;[90] Deut. 4.30; 31.29;[91] Isa. 2.2 and Mic. 4.1;[92] Hos. 3.5;[93] Jer. 23.20; 30.24; 48.47; 49.39;[94] and Ezek. 38.16[95]). It is significant that, throughout the OT, the "latter days" are concerned with the formation of God's kingdom. This emphasis

90. In Gen. 49.9, Judah is portrayed as the lion, which everybody dreads, to whom the royal scepter (שבט) will ultimately belong, and whom all the people will obey (Gen. 49.10) in the "latter days" (ἐπ' ἐσχάτων τῶν ἡμερῶν in Gen. 49.1). The characteristic picture of Judah as the lion that lies down and whom nobody dares to rise up is picked up in Num. 23.24 and 24.9. This individual will come out of Israel and will exterminate Israel's enemies (Num. 24.17) again in the "latter days" (ἐπ' ἐσχάτου τῶν ἡμερῶν in Num. 24.14). The "latter days" point to a radical change in history, which will introduce the following two distinct eras: the era *before* Israel's reign and the era *of* Israel's reign. In this sense, the expression "latter days" involves the time of Israel's kingdom.

91. In Deut. 31.29, Moses predicts that Israel will live in disobedience to God and, therefore, will experience God's punishment in the "latter days" (ἔσχατον τῶν ἡμερῶν). Israel seems to have failed to live up to her destiny. In Deuteronomy, the "latter days" (ἐπ' ἐσχάτῳ τῶν ἡμερῶν in Deut. 4.30) are primarily identified with Israel's distress (Deut. 4.25-28). (Hamilton parallels Deut. 31.29 with Gen. 49.1 based on contextual similarities; Victor P. Hamilton, *The Book of Genesis: Chapters 18–50* [NICOT; Grand Rapids: Eerdmans, 1995], p. 646; so also does Claus Westermann, *Genesis 37–50: A Continental Commentary* [Minneapolis: Augsburg, 1986], p. 223.)

92. Beginning with Isaiah and Micah, the phrase "latter days" (ἐν ταῖς ἐσχάταις ἡμέραις in Isa. 2.2 and ἐπ' ἐσχάτων τῶν ἡμερῶν in Mic. 4.1) takes on a new significance: it has more explicit universal implications; and also, in the "latter days" there will be a radical transformation in history. The imagery of the mountain is reminiscent of the mountain Sinai, where God's law was first given. In this case, the "latter days" may refer to a renewal of the covenant and a renewal of the giving of the law; however, this renewal will be one that will encompass all people.

93. Hosea 3.5, similarly, relates the "latter days" (ἐπ' ἐσχάτων τῶν ἡμερῶν) with an era in which Israel will regain her king and kingdom (Hos. 3.4 describes Israel without a king, and Hos. 3.5 describes Israel with a king).

94. The "latter days" (ἐπ' ἐσχάτου τῶν ἡμερῶν) in Jer. 23.20 portrays God's wrath upon the false prophets of Israel (Jer. 23.19) and the repetition of the same phrase in the context of Jer. 30.24 (MT; 37.24 in LXX) includes God's restorative plan. Although the phrase "latter days" in the contexts of Jer. 48.47 (MT) and 49.39 (MT; 25.19 in LXX) does not have an immediate eschatological association, it nevertheless carries over some of the eschatological implications of the earlier occurrences of the phrase. Jeremiah's favorite theme of God's deliverance through distress and suffering is brought up in these passages in connection with the use of the "latter days" in order to indicate the universal nature of God's deliverance.

95. The phrase in Ezek. 38.16 (ἐπ' ἐσχάτων τῶν ἡμερῶν) can hardly be denied any eschatological associations, due to its immediate eschatological context. Gog's attack against Israel in the "latter days" will be done in fulfillment of past prophecies (Ezek. 38.17). Yet, the attack will only function as an excuse for the destruction of God's enemies (Ezek. 38.18–39.20) and the vindication of God's people (Ezek. 39.21-29). The prophecies speak of a final battle, where all of God's enemies will be destroyed and Israel's restoration will be final.

has probably attracted Daniel to use it in his depiction of the time when God will act to destroy all human power and establish his reign forever.

Indeed, the visions in Daniel 7–12, with their interpretations, depict this time, namely the succession of the various earthly kingdoms and the establishment of the one kingdom that will last forever (Dan. 7.18, 27). This is also true of the fourth vision in Dan. 11.2–12.4, which describes Israel's final restoration in terms of a final resurrection from the dead (12.1-2). Thus the phrase "latter days" in Dan. 10.14 refers to the rise and fall of ungodly kingdoms and the persecutions of God's people that culminate in a definitive defeat and victory only for the saints.

The "latter days" (Dan. 10.14) should not be disconnected from the eschatological "time of the end" or "hour" in Daniel 8, 11, 12, especially since the phrase "latter days" refers to the period that involves the events in Daniel 11–12. Moreover, some OG manuscripts (967 and 88-Syh) have directly connected the phrase "latter days" with the eschatological hour by ending Dan. 10.14 with the phrase "the hour is yet for days," instead of the usual "the vision is yet for days."[96] This textual variant indicates that at least some scribes perceived the "last days" in connection to the hour.

The above understanding of the "latter days" in Daniel qualifies the eschatological hour of Dan. 12.1 with yet another theme: the establishment of God's kingdom for Israel. One may even argue that the culminating point of "eternal life" in Dan. 12.2 represents the means by which God's people will reign.

d. *The Use of* ὥρα *in Daniel 11*

Before we enter into the exegesis of Dan. 12.1-4, a preliminary look at the hour in Daniel 11 will demonstrate the significance of the hour theme in Daniel and will illustrate the literary development of this hour in the narrative. In Daniel 11, the author consistently mentions the word ὥρα, especially in relation to the end. The OG intends to connect the time references in Daniel 11 with the hour of Dan. 8.17, 19, indicating that the events in the narrative explicate and unfold the events described in the vision of ch. 8. More specifically, the first reference to the hour, in Dan. 11.6, alludes to Dan. 8.19 to make the above point. The following chart illustrates the allusion:

Dan. 8.19	*Dan. 11.6*
He said, "Behold, I am going to let you know what will occur at the final period of the indignation, for it pertains to the appointed hour of consummation (εἰς ὥρας καιροῦ συντελείας μενεῖ)."	At the consummation of the years (εἰς συντέλειαν ἐνιαυτῶν) they will form an alliance, and the daughter of the king of the South will come to the king of the North to carry out a peaceful arrangement. But she will not retain her position of power, nor will he remain with his power, but she will be given up, along with those who brought her in and the one who sired her as well as he who supported her in that hour (μενεῖ εἰς ὥρας).

96. Beale, "'Last Hour' in 1 Jn 2.18'.

Daniel expounds on the notion of the eschatological hour as it was first introduced in the vision of Daniel 8. The construction εἰς ὥρας occurs again in Dan. 11.35 and also probably alludes to Dan. 8.19. This time the allusion is slightly stronger:

Dan. 8.19	*Dan. 11.35*
He said, "Behold, I am going to let you know what will occur at the final period of the indignation, for it pertains to the appointed hour of consummation (ἔτι γὰρ εἰς ὥρας καιροῦ συντελείας μενεῖ)."	Some of those who have insight will fall, in order to refine, purge and make them pure until the time of consummation (καιροῦ συντελείας); because it is still to come at the appointed hour (ἔτι γὰρ καιρὸς εἰς ὥρας).

Throughout the development of the battle in Daniel 11, the reader is repeatedly reminded that these events occur within God's appointed time:

Dan. 11.6   καὶ εἰς συντέλειαν . . . καὶ μενεῖ εἰς ὥρας
Dan. 11.13   κατὰ συντέλειαν καιροῦ
Dan. 11.20   καὶ ἐν ἡμέραις ἐσχάταις
Dan. 11.27   ἔτι γὰρ συντέλεια εἰς καιρόν
Dan. 11.29   εἰς καιρόν
Dan. 11.35   ἕως καιροῦ συντελείας ἔτι γὰρ καιρὸς εἰς ὥρας

The inclusion of the events of the battle in the final hour indicates that the Danielic hour does not represent a particular moment, but a period within which these events will take place. This period need not be placed at the very end of historical time to have an eschatological import. Rather, the use of the word ἔσχατος in Dan. 10.14 (ἐπ' ἐσχάτου τῶν ἡμερῶν) and in Dan. 11.20 (ἐν ἡμέραις ἐσχάταις) indicates that the OG translator viewed this period as part of the eschaton, even though the events take place within the parameters of history. This eschatological perception of the hour is probably due to the overall emphasis of the book, which has these events and this hour culminating in the radical transformation of eternal resurrection (Dan. 12.1-2).

The eschatological nature of the Danielic hour is enhanced with the rise of the insolent king in 11.36, the description of which alludes to the end-time opponent in Daniel 7 and 8. Indeed, the reference to the hour in Dan. 11.35 is connected with the appearance of the arrogant king in 11.36, whose actions and death certainly occur within the parameters of the Danielic hour:

Dan. 11.40   καθ' ὥραν συντελείας
Dan. 11.45   ἥξει ὥρα τῆς συντελείας αὐτοῦ

In the OG, both the hour of the end in Dan. 11.40, 45 and the eschatological hour in 11.35 use the word ὥρα in connection to the "end" (συντέλεια). As we will see later, within this same hour (κατὰ τὴν ὥραν ἐκείνην), the great tribulation and the final resurrection occur (12.1-2).

The suggestion that Dan. 11.36-45 describes God's end-time opponent, is evident from a shift that occurs between 11.35 and 11.36. The literary unit of Dan. 11.36-39 differs from its preceding context in that it presents to us the character of God's opponent, rather than his deeds.[97] Indeed, the chronological order of the narration is paused in order for the king to be portrayed. Verbs such as "to exalt himself" and "to make himself great" are generally used in the Hebrew Bible of either God or those who oppose God (e.g. Isa. 10.15). While the king in 11.36 could be taken to be the "despicable" person of 11.21, thus retaining the subject of the preceding passage, a change of subject in 11.36 suggests that the specific description of a historical figure (i.e. Antiochus Epiphanes) has been replaced with the general depiction of God's end-time opponent.

The king's portrait in 11.36-39 resembles the description of God's end-time opponent in Daniel 7–8. His boasting (11.36) provokes God's wrath and makes his own end certain (see Dan. 8.25; 11.45). This boasting parallels the boasting of God's end-time opponent in Dan. 7.25, especially since the idea of "a time, times and half a time" is applied to both figures (Dan. 7.25; 12.7).[98] Ironically, the king claims for himself the power and the glory that belongs to God's Messiah.[99]

Also, the king's attitude to "do as he wishes" resembles the attitude in Dan. 8.4; 11.3; and 11.16. His desire to magnify himself against every god reminds us of the similar campaign against God of the little horn in Dan. 8.10-11.[100] This horn caused "some of the hosts and some of the stars" to fall down to the earth. The notion of "stars" as a reference to angels is not foreign to the Hebrew Bible.[101] In this case, the actions of God's adversary in 8.10-11 have consequences in the heavenly realm. It would not be contrary to Daniel's custom to portray a heavenly battle in Daniel 8.[102]

---

97. From here to the end of this section, the discussion will be generally based on the MT, though the MT's ideas are also maintained in the OG.

98. The reference in Dan. 12.7 probably signifies a limitation to the duration of the persecutions in 11.36-45 and the time of trouble in 12.1.

99. Numbers 24.7-8 mentions how God's king is to be exalted and he will devour the nations, in a passage that later prophesies about the last days: "a scepter shall rise from Israel." Later, in his oracle (Num. 24.24), Balaam refers to the "ships of Kittim," to which Dan. 11.30 alludes. In Ps. 2.6, God's king has been installed upon the Holy Mountain, despite the opposition of the earthly kings in 2.2. In Psalms 24 the king of Glory shall stand in God's Holy Place. In Psalms 68, God is the deliverer (v. 20), the King himself (v. 24), who defeats the kings of this earth (vv. 12, 14) and subdues them to His reign (v. 29).

100. Clifford argues for an Egyptian legend being the background for this magnifying (Richard J. Clifford, 'History and Myth in Daniel 10–12', *BASOR* 220 [1975], pp. 23–26 [25]; see also Collins, *Daniel*, p. 386). For those who see Antiochus Epiphanes as the background for this verse, the following title has been found on his coins: BASILEOS ANTIOCHOU THEOU EPIPHANOUS (M. Hengel, *Judaism and Hellenism: Studies in Their Encounter in Palestine During the Early Hellenistic Period* [Vol. 1; London: SCM, 1974], p. 285; in Collins, *Daniel*, p. 386).

101. In Judges 5.20, the stars fight for Israel from heaven. See also Dan. 12.3, where the resurrected people of God are to become like the stars.

102. Isaiah 14.13-14 and Ezek. 28.2, 6, 9, also portray the ongoing character of God's

Moreover, the phrase "until the indignation (ὀργή; זַעַם) is finished" in 11.36 prob-ably refers to God's wrath against Israel, as it was also the case with the indignation (ὀργή; זַעַם) in Dan. 8.19.[103] This wrath, although initiated in God himself, is usually carried out by different nations, which in this case could be the nation represented by the king of our passage.[104]

Furthermore, the phrase "he will show no regard for the gods of his father" (11.37) is problematic to those that see Antiochus Epiphanes as the king of 11.36, because Antiochus is not elsewhere portrayed to have abandoned the gods of his people.[105] In addition, the phrase "a god whom his fathers did not know" in 11.38 creates similar difficulties of interpretation for those who identify the king of this passage with Antiochus.[106]

adversaries and could have served as a source for Daniel. The king there will also "speak wondrous things against the god of gods." Compare with Dan. 7.8, 20; 8.11 and 8.23.

103. The phrase "until the indignation is finished" (11.36) may refer either to God's wrath against Israel (Baldwin lists the following verses in support of this view: Isa. 10.23; 13.5; 26.20, 21; 30.27; 66.14; Jer. 10.10; Dan. 8.19; Baldwin, *Daniel*, p. 197) or to the king's wrath against the people of God (Collins, *Daniel*, p. 386). Although the verbal form of the word "indignation" (זַעַם) has been used earlier in reference to the king of the north (Dan. 11.30), there are enough reasons to link the indignation in 11.36 with God. The noun in the Hebrew Bible always refers to God's wrath, except for once. Out of the 22 times that the noun זַעַם occurs in the Hebrew Bible, only in Hos. 7.16 does it refer to God's adversaries and even there it does not have the meaning of wrath (translated as "insolence"). The rest 21 uses relate to God's wrath (Ps. 38.3; 69.24; 78.49; 102.10; Isa. 10.5, 25; 13.5; 26.20; 30.27; Jer. 10.10; 15.17; 50.25; Lam. 2.6; Ezek. 21.31; 22.24, 31; Dan. 8.19; Nah. 1.6; Hab. 3.12; Zeph. 3.8.). Also, Daniel uses the noun זַעַם once more, in 8.19, and he does so in reference to God. Finally, the phrase "he will prosper until the indignation is finished" makes more sense if it were God's wrath, since God will do the ending according to the next phrase.

104. This is displayed in Zech. 1.12, thus also the petition to God to remove the wrath (Lucas, *Daniel*, p. 220).

105. The main god of the northern kingdom would be Apollo, whom Antiochus wor-shiped, at least early in his life. Collins believes that Daniel construed this portrait of Antiochus in order to promote the king's impiety. He asserts that the reference is to all the other gods apart from Zeus, since there is a historical connection between Antiochus and Zeus (Collins, *Daniel*, p. 387). Lucas also believes that this phrase is a "polemical exaggeration," concluding with Collins that the reference here is to Antiochus' preference for Zeus (Lucas, *Daniel*, p. 290). The "beloved of women" has been described to be either Tammuz-Adonis (see H. Ewald's proposal in connection with Ezek. 8.14 in James A. Montgomery, *A Critical and Exegetical Commentary on the Book of Daniel* [ICC; Edinburgh: T&T Clark, 1950], p. 462) or Dionysus (Lucas, *Daniel*, p. 290). Both deities were worshiped in Egypt, which would make Daniel's argument as follows: the king worshiped neither the god of the northern kingdom (Apollo), nor the god of the southern kingdom (Adonis or Dionysus).

106. Collins once again attributes this to a "polemical exaggeration" employed by Daniel (Collins, *Daniel*, p. 388). The phrase "he will honor a god of fortresses" in 11.38 has also posed difficulties in its interpretation. Theodotion and Jerome translate מָעֻזִּים as a proper name. Others have identified this god with Jupiter Capitolinus (Montgomery, *Daniel*, p. 461; Robert

The proposal that the insolent king in 11.36-39 has been idealized as an eschato-logical figure becomes even more evident in 11.40-45. Modern scholarship sees 11.40 as the transition from "*ex eventu* prophecy to real (and erroneous) prediction at this point,"[107] mainly because they see the text only through the lens of Antiochus's life. Daniel 11.40-45 cannot be applied to Antiochus, because the events described in these verses do not correspond to Antiochus's life or death,[108] so the only poss-ible solution according to this view would be to say that this portion of Daniel is an erroneous prediction.

For example, the boastful king is said to meet his end "between the seas and the beautiful Holy Mountain" (11.45), that is, within the area of Palestine (somewhere between the Mediterranean Sea and Jerusalem). However, none of the different accounts that we have for Antiochus's death match the description in 11.45. All four accounts relate Antiochus's death with the robbery of the temple in Persia and situate his death in the east.[109]

A different approach is that of Jerome, who attributed this passage, starting from 11.21, as a reference to the Antichrist. D. W. Gooding also relates the prophecy to the Antichrist.[110] Since Gurney has argued that the phrase "at the time of the end" signals a change of subject in 11.40,[111] this change may also be argued for 11:36 in light of its preceding verse. Goldingay agrees that "the phrase 'at the time of the end' (contrast v. 35) seems to preclude our taking the verses as a résumé of Antiochus's career as a

Charles, *A Critical and Exegetical Commentary on the Book of Daniel* [Oxford: Clarendon, 1929], p. 316). Hengel identifies this god with Zeus Akraios (Hengel, *Judaism and Hellenism*, p. 284), which is very improbable, since 2 Macc. 6.2 mentions Antiochus imposing Zeus Olympius on the Jews (Collins, *Daniel*, p. 387). In Dan. 11.7, 10, and 19, the Hebrew word for "fortress" (מָעֻזִּים) refers to the defenses of the northern kingdom, and in Dan. 11.31, the same word refers to the defense of the holy place in Jerusalem. The word מָעֻזִּים is repeatedly used in the Hebrew Bible in connection to Yahweh; however, in this context, the word (whether it is used as a proper name or not) must have some other referent, which remains unknown to the reader.

107. Collins, *Daniel*, p. 388.

108. Morkholm argues that Antiochus went east, where he remained until his death after one-and-a-half years (O. Morkholm, *Antiochus IV of Syria* [Copenhagen: Gyldendalske Boghandel, 1966], pp. 166–80).

109. The four accounts that we have are as follows: 1) Antiochus was struck down by madness after having robbed a temple in Elymais (Plybius, *Hist.* 31.9); 2) Antiochus died out of melancholy after his robbing the temple in Elymais and after realizing that his melancholy was due to his robbing the temple in Jerusalem (1 Macc. 6.1-17); 3) Antiochus was murdered while robbing a temple in Persia (2 Macc. 1.11-17); 4) He was struck with a disease by God after his attempt to rob a temple in Persia. For more information on the accounts see Collins, *Daniel*, pp. 389–90; and Lucas, *Daniel*, p. 291.

110. D. W. Gooding, 'The Literary Structure of Daniel and Its Implications', *TynBul* 32 (1981), pp. 43–79.

111. R. J. M. Gurney, *God in Control* (Worthing, England: H. E. Walter, 1980), pp. 146–52.

whole."[112] Assuming that part of Daniel 11 includes the life and doings of Antiochus Epiphanes (11.21-35), I argue that the figure of Antiochus has become the pattern for God's final adversary, who appears in the end-time hour. The king of 11.36-45 represents the actual eschatological enemy of God.[113]

The hour of the end in 11.40 (καθ᾽ ὥραν συντελείας; קֵץ וּבְעֵת) situates the actions of God's adversary within the Danielic eschatological era. Collins argues that the word קֵץ in itself does not necessarily connote a final ending.[114] This meaning is probably correct here, since the events described do not end the historical process of time. Nevertheless, the phrase "hour of the end" signifies that the events do take place within a period of time, the complexion of which embodies the eschaton.[115]

Indeed, Dan. 11.36-45 leads up to Dan. 12.1-4, which also involves the Danielic eschatological hour (12.1). It is within this hour that God executes his final acts of judgment, resurrection, and eternal life (Dan. 12.1-3), thus leading his people in a victorious, transformed state of being.

e. *The Use of* ὥρα *in Dan. 12.1-4*
Beginning with Dan. 12.1, the battle scene shifts to the image of Michael rising up to protect God's people. Michael's rising has been defined as a judicial act.[116] The construction עָמַד עַל in the Hebrew text has the following meanings in the book of Daniel: "stand upright" (Dan. 8.18; 10.11); "rise against" (11.14); "rise in his place" (11.20, 21); and "stand over," "protect" (12.1).[117] Both the OG and TH translate ὁ ἑστηκὼς

---

112. See Goldingay's comments on Dan. 11.40 (John E. Goldingay, *Daniel* [WBC, 30; Dallas: Word, 1998], p. 305).

113. Other considerations point to an OT background of Dan. 11.36-45, which links Daniel to different Old Testament prophecies that talk about the eschaton. For example, the king in Daniel 11 may stand as the representative of God's adversaries in general, similar to Gog in Ezekiel 38–39. Ezekiel 38.5 and 15 depict Gog and his forces coming from the north, invading Israel in the last days (38.16). Moreover, Gog's death takes place in a valley east of the sea (Ezek. 39.11), which could be the same geographical reference for the place of the king's death in Dan. 11.45. Similarly, the eschatological end in Joel 2 involves the removal of the northern army that threatens God's people (Joel 2.20). After the destruction ends, a new era begins, which is characterized by the outpouring of the Spirit, the presence of God, and the salvation of those who will call upon God's name (Joel 2.28-32).

114. Collins, *Daniel*, p. 337.

115. We have already seen the eschatological use of the word "end" (#qe) in Dan. 8.17, 19 (cf. also 12.4, 6). In Daniel 8–12, the word "end" occurs 15 times. Daniel sees the end-time as being determined.

116. Nickelsburg has argued for a judicial understanding of עָמַד (especially argues from Zech. 3.1). He states, "The disputants in a lawsuit stand. Yahweh will stand to judge. In Zechariah 3, the accusing angel stands, as does in *Jub.* 48.9. In *Jub.* 18.9, the defending angel stands before God and before the accuser" (G. W. E. Nickelsburg, *Resurrection, Immortality, and Eternal Life in Intertestamental Judaism* [HTS, 26; Cambridge, MA: Harvard University Press, 1972], p. 12; see also Collins, *Daniel*, p. 390).

117. The verb עָמַד occurs in the book of Daniel in the following verses: Dan. 1.4, 5, 19;

ἐπί ("who stands over"). The scenery of Dan. 12.1 is parallel to that of Daniel 7, where the context uses judicial language: standing before God, sitting before the court, and opening the books. The figure and role of Michael resembles the figure and role of the Son of Man in Daniel 7, who is given the authority to judge and to vindicate. Nickelsburg also notes that Michael stands up in court in *T. Dan.* 6.2 and Jude 9.[118] Therefore, when Michael executes judgment and vindicates God's people, he does so as the representative of God and his Messiah (Son of Man). Yet, while Michael's role seems to be primarily judicial, a military function is not necessarily excluded. In light of Michael's role in Daniel 10, one might say that Michael's responsibilities here, as the executor of judgment, are both judicial and military.[119]

The deliverance of the people appears to be from the attack of the insolent king (in the immediate context), but it also involves a deliverance from all evil.[120] Not all the people will be delivered, but only those written in the book of life (see Dan. 7.10; 10.21).[121] Deliverance in this context can refer either to preservation through the persecution or to deliverance from death; as we shall see, the language of Dan. 12.2 prefers the latter understanding of deliverance.

The phrase κατὰ τὴν ὥραν ἐκείνην in the OG of Dan. 12.1 sets the time frame of this deliverance. The hour refers to the eschatological ὥρα in Dan. 8.17, 19, and Dan. 11.35, 40, 45. The interrelationship that exists among Dan. 8.17, 19, Dan. 11.35-40, and Dan. 12.1-2 is important for one's understanding of the hour in Daniel, since it shows that Daniel has consistently upheld the theme of an eschatological ὥρα. The manner by which the book of Daniel emphasizes this eschatological ὥρα has set a precedent for later NT interpreters of the Danielic eschaton.[122]

A development of the hour theme, at least in the LXX, is apparent, especially if one notices the following connection between Dan. 8.19 and Dan. 12.1. The OG of Dan. 12.1 relates to Dan. 8.19 through the use of the phrase τοὺς υἱοὺς τοῦ λαοῦ σου, which in Dan. 8.19 appears almost in identical form: τοῖς υἱοῖς τοῦ λαοῦ σου.[123] The

8.4, 6, 7, 15, 18, 22, 23, 25; 10.11, 13, 16, 17; 11.1, 2, 3, 4, 6, 7, 8, 11, 13, 14, 15, 16, 17, 20, 21, 25, 31; 12.1, 5, 13.

118. Nickelsburg, *Resurrection*, pp. 11–27.

119. Young, *Daniel*, p. 255.

120. Such as the one described in Isa. 25.8.

121. In Dan. 7.10, the books are opened as the court sits to judge, and in Dan. 10.21, the angel is about to narrate what is written in the book of truth. For the mention of the "book" compare also with Isa. 4.3; Exod. 32.32-33; Ps. 69.28 (book of life); Also, compare with Mal. 3.16-18 and its immediate context.

122. Not only is this "time" characterized by the term "end," but it is also associated with various eschatological themes, such as the execution of judgment (Daniel 7), the coming of the Son of Man (Daniel 7), the reference to Messiah (Daniel 9), the destruction of God's adversary (Daniel 11), and the resurrection of the dead (Daniel 12).

123. The OG of Dan. 8.19 adds the phrase τοῖς υἱοῖς τοῦ λαοῦ σου, which does not appear in the MT. Jeansonne rightly concludes that this is an exegetical addition provided by the translator. The added phrase is taken from Dan. 12.1, which has ἐπὶ τοὺς υἱοὺς τοῦ λαοῦ σου, in order to make the connection between the times of distress in Dan. 8.19 and 12.1. See

interesting thing, however, is that the above phrase appears neither in the Hebrew nor in the Theodotion of Dan. 8.19. Did the OG translator have a different *Vorlage* in front of him, or did he add the phrase on his own? In the former instance, we have a *Vorlage* in which even the Hebrew of Dan. 12.1 alludes to Dan. 8.19. In the latter instance, we have a translator who has most probably taken the phrase from Dan. 12.1 and inserted it into Dan. 8.19; apparently, he thought that the two verses were describing the same event. In either case, the OG testifies to the connection.

In addition, it is evident that the hour of Dan. 12.1 refers to the hour of Dan. 11.35, 40, and 45 (and especially to the events described in Dan. 11.40-45).[124] Not only does the word ὥρα appear in all of the above, but also the use of "the wise" (οἱ συνιέντες; הַמַּשְׂכִּלִים) in Dan. 12.3 is a reiteration of "the wise" in Dan. 11.33, 35.[125] Moreover, the phrase "until the time of the end" (ἕως καιροῦ συντελείας; עַד־עֵת קֵץ) in Dan. 12.4 repeats the same phrase from Dan. 11.35.[126]

Therefore, the eschatological hour of Dan. 12.1 functions, first, as the development and culmination of the hour as it appears in Dan. 8.17, 19 and Dan. 11.35-45; and second, it functions as the summation of the eschatological end-time events as they appear in the above contexts. Indeed, the hour of Dan. 12.1 is an hour of persecution and distress, as well as the time of God's judgment; nevertheless, it is also an hour of vindication for God's people, and one that includes the eschatological resurrection from the dead.

However, if the hour in Dan. 12.1 has the special function of summarizing the eschatological end — at least in the OG of Daniel — why is it that the OG does not translate the phrase "in that time" (וּבָעֵת הַהִיא) consistently, since it appears three times in Dan. 12.1?[127] The OG translates the first phrase as κατὰ τὴν ὥραν ἐκείνην, while the others are translated as τῆς ἡμέρας ἐκείνης and ἐν ἐκείνῃ τῇ ἡμέρᾳ. The OG translator uses the word ὥρα in the first instance, and then uses the word ἡμέρα for the other two. Does this difference in translation indicate that the OG does not place any special emphasis on the word "hour"? While one may think that the difference in translation represents different eschatological moments, there are strong indications to think otherwise (this could very well be a stylistic variation).

First, it is important to note that the Hebrew phrase וּבָעֵת הַהִיא appears in Daniel

---

Sharon P. Jeansonne, *The Old Greek Translation of Daniel 7–12* (CBQMS, 19; Washington: The Catholic Biblical Association of America, 1988).

124.   The link between these texts is acknowledged by most scholars (e.g. Lucas, *Daniel*, p. 293; Stephen R. Miller, *Daniel* [NAC, 18; Broadman & Holman, 1994], p. 313; Collins, *Daniel*, p. 390).

125.   Similarly, the use of "the many" (רַבִּים) alludes to Dan. 11.33, 34, 39, 44. Goldingay is correct to note about Dan. 12.1 that, "the threefold 'that time' in v. 1 reinforces the impression that the whole verse is resumptive, as do the allusions to 'the discerning' and 'the multitude' in v. 3. The 'time of trouble' is thus a resumptive summary reference to the troubles of 11.40-45, not a new event" (Goldingay, *Daniel*, p. 306).

126.   Daniel 11.40 also has בְּעֵת קֵץ, so the links are even more extensive in the Hebrew text.

127.   The phrase appears twice as וּבָעֵת הַהִיא and once as הָעֵת הַהִיא.

only in 12.1, and it does so three times. Second, the three-time repetition of the Hebrew phrase in Dan. 12.1 should point to the significance of the phrase in relation to the events described. Third, the TH translation renders all three occurrences of the phrase in virtually the same way, twice as ἐν τῷ καιρῷ ἐκείνῳ and once as τοῦ καιροῦ ἐκείνου, which indicates that the translator viewed the phrases as referring to the same event.

Moreover, as we have already seen, the phrase בָּעֵת הַהִיא has been used before to indicate the eschatological time of God's final act (Joel 4.1; Mic. 3.4; Zeph. 1.12; 3.19-20; and Jer. 3.17; 4.11; 8.1; 31.1; 33.15; 50.4, 20).[128] One can hardly deny that Daniel was at least aware of the phrase and its eschatological significance in the above contexts. Although Daniel may not explicitly intend to allude to the above OT texts, the similar contexts of judgment and restoration in which the phrase occurs, would have given Daniel at least an eschatological framework.[129] This would imply that Daniel does not disclose a new eschatological plan, but rather generally projects what has already been said into a future fulfillment.

The variation in the OG translation of the phrase "in that time" — once as "in that hour" and twice as "in that day" — may indicate that Daniel, or at least the OG translator, has the above OT texts in mind, since, as I have previously shown, all of the above passages relate the phrase "in that time" to the theme of "the day" (whether this is the day of the Lord, the "latter days," or a variation of the phrase "in that day"). Therefore, it seems that the OG translation betrays an interpretative attempt to relate the eschatological hour with the eschatological "day," qualifying the Danielic hour as the ultimate fulfillment of the preceding eschatological prophecies.

The above argument is further intensified by Dan. 12.13, where the Hebrew construction לְקֵץ ("at the end") is rendered in the OG as ἔτι γὰρ εἰσιν ἡμέραι καὶ ὧραι εἰς ἀναπλήρωσιν συντελείας ("for there are yet *days* and *hours* to the fulfillment of the end").[130] Why has the OG translator combined the notions of "days" and "hours" in this verse? On the one hand, the addition of ὧραι indicates that the fulfillment of the end is linked to the prophetic utterances in Dan. 8.17, 19; 11.40, 45; and 12.1. We have already encountered the construction ἔτι γάρ in Dan. 8.17 and 19, which may function in a way to indicate the unexpected nature of the fulfillment at hand. On the other hand, the coupling of the hour with the word "day" in the OG of Daniel, occurs only in Dan. 4.17 and 12.1.[131] Therefore, the addition of ἡμέραι indicates that

---

128.   Collins also mentions some of these passages (Collins, *Daniel*, p. 390). See my comments in the earlier section of this chapter.

129.   Perhaps, by Daniel's time, the phrase בָּעֵת הַהִיא had become a *terminus technicus* to refer to the end-time restoration.

130.   The Theodotion version of 12.13 translates, ἔτι γὰρ ἡμέραι εἰς ἀναπλήρωσιν συντελείας ("for there are yet *days* to the fulfillment of the end") thus retaining only the "days" of the OG.

131.   The former speaks about the time of God's judgment upon Nebuchadnezzar, while the latter speaks about God's judgment upon God's final adversary. A judgment, however, that is coupled with deliverance and vindication.

the eschatological hour should be interpreted in conjunction with the eschatological "day," just as it was done in the former prophecies.

Daniel further indicates a connection to Jeremiah specifically, with his reference to a "time of distress, one as never occurred since there was a nation until that time" (Dan. 12.1).[132] As we have already seen, a probable background for this time of distress is Jer. 30.7, which depicts Israel's eschatological hardships, and which results in a time of eschatological blessings, namely the salvation of Israel and the reign of David's descendant (30.9). The exact phrase עֵת צָרָה ("time of distress") occurs seven times in the Hebrew Bible.[133] The occurrence in Jer. 30.7 specifically refers to the time of the second exodus and uses the image of a woman in labor, an image that is also used in Isa. 26.16-17 and 66.7-9. All of these passages portray the time of distress as the pains of a woman who is about to bear a child. This image conveys the notion that suffering is integral to deliverance. Distress is God's way of bringing about new life. Daniel 12.1-2 similarly shows that the resurrection to new life follows distress and persecution.[134]

The resurrection reference in Dan. 12.2 indicates that the hour in Dan. 12.1 is also the hour in which the eschatological resurrection will take place: "Many of those who sleep in the dust of the ground will awake." Daniel 12.2 is not necessarily the only place in the Hebrew Bible where the notion of a bodily resurrection is present.[135] The reference resembles that of Isa. 26.19: "Your dead will live; their corpses will rise. You who lie in the dust, awake and shout for joy."[136] The allusion to Isa. 26.19 reinforces Daniel's concern to reiterate past restoration passages and

132.   While both the Hebrew texts of Dan. 12.1 and Jer. 30.7 use the phrase עֵת צָרָה, the OG of Daniel translates with ἡμέρα θλίψεως ("day of distress"), and the LXX of Jeremiah has χρόνος στενός ("time of straitness"). The OG translator of Daniel may have used ἡμέρα θλίψεως in order to connect this distress with the one found in Isa. 26.16 (notice that this distress occurs "in that day," 26.1).

133.   Judg. 10.14; Ps. 37.39; Isa. 33.2; Jer. 14.8; 15.11; 30.7; Dan. 12.1.

134.   Daniel 12.2 speaks of the resurrection from the dead and alludes to Isa. 26.19: "Your dead will live; Their corpses will rise. You who lie in the dust, awake and shout for joy."

135.   On the theme of the resurrection in the OT see Collins, *Daniel*, pp. 394–98; Gerhard von Rad, 'Life and Death in the OT', *TDNT* 2:847; Robert Martin-Achard, *From Death to Life: A Study of the Development of the Doctrine of the Resurrection in the Old Testament* (Edinburgh: Oliver & Boyd, 1960); and Daniel I. Block, 'Beyond the Grave: Ezekiel's Vision of Death and Afterlife', *BBR* 2 (1992), pp. 113–41. See also the introduction in N. T. Wright, *Resurrection*, pp. 3–31"

136.   For the use of the term "sleep" to designate death, Goldingay notes: "The OT's standard way of envisaging dying and coming back to life is by speaking of lying down and sleeping, then of waking and getting up. The former is an extreme form of the latter, which thus provides the metaphor for it (2 Kgs 4.31; 13.21; Isa. 26.19; Jer. 51.39, 57; Job 14.12)" (Goldingay, *Daniel*, p. 307). For other associations between sleep and death in the OT see Thomas H. McAlpine, *Sleep, Divine and Human in the Old Testament* (JSOTSup, 38; Sheffield: JSOT, 1987), pp. 135–49.

to foresee yet another exodus from the exilic distress.[137] Although some believe that Isa. 26.19 refers to national restoration,[138] Childs has observed that a sharp distinction between national restoration and individual resurrection is a modern suggestion that should not be made.[139] N. T. Wright reaffirms Childs' suggestion by holding national restoration and individual resurrection together. More particularly, he states that the bodily resurrection of Dan. 12.2 is "the form that national restoration takes."[140] Therefore, it is not improbable that Daniel saw both Israel's national restoration and a bodily resurrection in the Isaianic passage. Collins believes that Daniel understood Isa. 26.19 in terms of an actual resurrection, especially because of the use of the word "corpse."[141] Also, F. Garcia Martinez has argued for an individual resurrection in Dan. 12.2 based on the Aramaic text of 4QpsDaniel.[142] There exists, therefore, a conceptual connection between Isa. 26.19 and Dan. 12.2,[143] which depicts God's renewing work, both nationally and individually.

However, for the first time Daniel introduces the idea of a double resurrection, that of the righteous and that of the wicked.[144] Daniel 12.2 specifically reads, "Many of those who sleep in the dust of the ground will awake, some to eternal life, and some to disgrace and eternal contempt." The repetition of "*some . . . and some*" refers to a subdivision of the *many* (both righteous and wicked are resurrected) and

---

137.   See the related articles by Daniel P. Bailey, 'The Intertextual Relationship of Daniel 12.2 and Isa. 26.19: Evidence from Qumran and the Greek Versions', *TynBul* 51 (2000), pp. 305–308; and Gerhard F. Hasel, 'Resurrection in the Theology of Old Testament Apocalyptic', *ZAW* 92 (1980), pp. 267–84.

138.   E.g. Lucas, *Daniel,* p. 294. For the two views see Hasel, 'Resurrection', pp. 267–84. See also Nickelsburg, *Resurrection,* p. 18.

139.   Brevard S. Childs, *Isaiah* (OTL; Louisville: Westminster John Knox Press, 2001), p. 192.

140.   Wright, *Resurrection,* p. 116.

141.   Most modern scholars agree with this. See Collins, *Daniel,* pp. 391–92; Nickelsburg, *Resurrection,* p. 23.

142.   F. Garcia Martinez, *Qumran and Apocalyptic: Studies on the Aramaic Texts from Qumran* (Leiden: Brill, 1992), p. 146. Fragment 2 of 4Q245 (4QpsDan^c ar) reads:

  1. . . .
  2. in order to eradicate wickedness
  3. those in blindness, and they have gone astray
  4. they then shall arise
  5. the holy, and they will return
  6. wickedness

See Florentino Garcia Martinez and Eibert J. C. Tigchelaar, *The Dead Sea Scrolls: Study Edition* (Vol. 1; Grand Rapids: Eerdmans, 1997), p. 493.

143.   Bailey has offered further observations that strengthen the connection between Isa. 26.19 and Dan. 12.2 (Bailey, 'Daniel 12.2 and Isaiah 26.19', pp. 305–8).

144.   Although Collins believes that Judaism had already introduced the idea of resurrection in the Enoch corpus (*1 En.* 22; 27; 91.10; 93.2; 104.1-6), it could very well be that *1 Enoch* borrowed from Daniel rather than the other way around (Collins, *Daniel,* p. 396).

does not contrast the *some* with others that are not resurrected (as has been argued). It is the most natural reading to see both groups being resurrected.[145]

The phrase עוֹלָם לְחַיֵּי ("to eternal life"; OG and TH, εἰς ζωὴν αἰώνιον) occurs only here (Dan. 12.2) in the Hebrew Bible. The duration of this eternal life is not indicated, although it seems to be unlimited. The life is contrasted with the notions of "reproach" and "disgrace." Interestingly, the word דְּרָאוֹן ("disgrace") occurs elsewhere only in Isa. 66.24, the context of which speaks about God's deliverance through birth pains (Isa. 66.7-9).[146]

Finally, the hour in Dan. 12.1 may also have messianic connotations, since in Dan. 12.1-3 one finds language reminiscent of the suffering servant in Isaiah. More specifically, the OG of Dan. 12.2 describes the saints as being "lifted up" (ὑψωθήσεται) in the same manner as the servant in Isaiah is "lifted up" (ὑψωθήσεται in Isa. 52.13). In addition, the use of the participial form οἱ συνιέντες (or מַשְׂכִּלִים; "those who are wise") in Dan. 12.3 may reflect the status of the servant in Isa. 52.13 (συνήσει; שׂכל; "will understand").[147] The following chart illustrates the proposed connection:

Isa. 52.13	*Dan. 12.1-3*
Behold, my servant will understand (συνήσει), and be lifted up (ὑψωθήσεται), and glorified exceedingly.	And at that hour . . . on that day the whole people will be lifted up (ὑψωθήσεται), every one that is written in the book. . . . And those who understand (οἱ συνιέντες) will shine like the brightness of the sky.

In support of the above suggestion, in Isa. 53.11, the suffering servant is said to justify the many, which parallels the description of those who justify many in Dan. 12.3.[148] It is possible that the Danielic use of these terms may have a messianic reference, and the redemption-through-suffering motif of Dan. 11.36–12.4 have messianic connotations. Although the use of "the wise" may not explicitly refer to the Messiah, it is possible that the Messiah was understood to be one of the "wise" in Dan. 12.3. The presence of God's Messiah in Daniel 12 is reinforced by the fact that the Son of Man has been introduced to us in Daniel 7 as "the eschatological agent of God,"[149] who will execute God's judgment on earth; Michael may represent this figure in Daniel 12.[150] Whatever the influence may be, the fact remains that in

145.   Collins, *Daniel*, p. 393; contra Louis F. Hartman and Alexander A. Di Lella, *The Book of Daniel*, (AB, 23; Garden City: Doubleday, 1978), p. 308.

146.   The Greek phrase αἰσχύνην αἰώνιον (Dan. 12.2) appears in Isa. 54.4, again in association with the barren woman who will eventually be fruitful. The context in Isaiah 54 is one of deliverance.

147.   See also Ps. 2.10; 14.2; 53.2 and Dan. 11.33, 35; 12.10; Amos 5.13.

148.   Montgomery, *Daniel*, p. 472.

149.   Barnabas Lindars, *Jesus Son of Man: A Fresh Examination of the Son of Man Sayings in the Gospels* (London: SPCK, 1983), p. 160.

150.   Michael is also portrayed to be the representative of God and his Messiah in

Dan. 12.1-3, the saints — along with the Son of Man — are depicted along the line of the servant in Isaiah.

Our passage in Daniel ends in 12.4 with the sealing of the book, a book that most probably refers to the vision given in Dan. 10.11–12.3. The idea behind the sealing is that no one will be able to know more about the time of the end until the book is reopened. The quest for further revelation will be futile, as the phrase "many will run to and fro" implies.[151]

The word ὥρα in the OG of Dan. 12.1 summarizes the Danielic visions and bring to a culmination the eschatological prophecies of the end. Moreover, the word ὥρα is used specifically with the intention to emphasize the eschatological hour as it has been developed in Daniel, namely that moment or era in history that will end all opposition and establish God's kingdom. Finally, the hour, as part of the phrase "in that time," connects the eschatological visions of Daniel with former OT eschatological prophecies, depicting the restoration of Israel through the refining process of hardship.

f. *Summary of Use of Eschatological Hour in Daniel 8–12*

The eschatological hour in Daniel 8–12 is a time of persecution for the people of God, caused by God's final adversary. This hour depicts an eschatological era, since it involves the end-time battle that will take place between God's adversary and the people of God (11.40-45); thus, it initiates the eschaton as it is revealed in Dan. 8.17, 19; 10.14; 11.35, 40, 45; 12.1. The hour of 12.1 also refers to the judicial representation of God's people, which resembles the court imagery in Dan. 7.13-14 with the Son of Man possibly representing the people of God. It is within this final period, the hour, that the kingdom of God will also be given to the saints. As a final outcome, this hour involves the eschatological resurrection of the dead unto eternal life (for some) and eternal disgrace (for others). Within this eschatological age, suffering will give birth to life (a motif associated with God's servant in Isaiah 53). In conclusion, the hour of Dan. 12.1 can be summarized as such: *in God's final hour, suffering is integral for deliverance to take place, a deliverance through judgment and resurrection.*

Rev. 12.7-10. In Rev. 12.7-9, Michael with his angels battle against the evil forces and subdue them. In Rev. 12.10, this victory represents God's kingdom and the Messiah's authority. G. K. Beale has traced these verses back to Daniel, arguing that Michael's victory over Satan does not happen apart from Christ's victory on the cross. He says: "Christ's redemptive work on earth unleashes the effect in heaven of Michael's victory" (Beale, *Book of Revelation*, p. 652). Beale has indicated the rich associations that exist between Rev. 12.7-10 and the book of Daniel (especially Daniel 2, 7, 10, and 12).

151.   This is a probable allusion to Amos 8.12 (see especially the context). Baldwin also mentions Isa. 29.9-11, where the people are blind because God has sealed the book that contains his plans (Baldwin, *Daniel*, p. 206.).

3

THE USE OF ESCHATOLOGICAL HOUR IN JEWISH LITERATURE

I. *Introduction*

The primary aim of this book is to investigate whether John's use of the term "hour" has a Danielic background. A survey of the Jewish exegetical tradition of the relevant Danielic passages will indicate whether these traditions anticipate an eschatological hour similar to that found in Daniel. Indeed, if John has borrowed the term "hour" from the book of Daniel, this means that he must likely have approached the Danielic text with some kind of hermeneutic. However, before establishing the existence of such an interpretative approach by John, the question must be asked: How do the earlier and later Jewish writings interpret the relevant Danielic passages? In what way does the Jewish tradition treat the Danielic "time" or hour?

In this chapter, I examine those passages from the Jewish tradition that bear the following characteristics: 1) they quote from, allude to, or expand on those Hebrew or OG Danielic passages that explicitly refer to the final time or hour (Dan. 8.17, 19; 10.14; 11.6, 35, 40, 45; and 12.1-3, 13); 2) they also specifically mention the expectation of a future time or hour in allusion to either the Hebrew or Greek text of Daniel; 3) they are dated early enough to be prior or contemporary to John's writings (up to the first century AD);[1] 4) they may be interpreted in an eschatological sense.[2] First, I comment on the relevant Apocryphal/Pseudepigraphical passages, and then I examine the references in the Dead Sea Scrolls.

---

1. The Apocryphal books of *4 Ezra* (2 Esdras 3–14) and *2 Baruch* are the only ones examined here with a date near the end of the first or the beginning of the second century. These works, although they are contemporary to John, are still Jewish, reflecting the theological crisis of the Jews after the destruction of the second temple in AD 70. Their perspective is useful to us, since they reflect the Jewish hermeneutic of the OT around John's time. See Larry R. Helyer, *Exploring Jewish Literature of the Second Temple Judaism* (Downers Grove: InterVarsity, 2002), pp. 392–93, 423; Craig A. Evans, *Ancient Texts for New Testament Studies: A Guide to the Background Literature* (Peabody: Hendrickson, 2005), pp. 34, 36.

2. While this later criterion can become subjective, several of the Jewish passages have been characterized as potentially eschatological. By "potentially eschatological," I mean that at least some scholars view these passages speaking about the end-time.

The purpose of this survey is to demonstrate that the conceptual connection between the eschatological hour and the Danielic eschatological themes (judgment, resurrection, the restoration of God's people, and the defeat of God's final adversary) is not unique to John. There is precedence of such a connection in the Jewish exegetical tradition, which, if established, demonstrates the following: (1) already in the Jewish tradition there is anticipation of the fulfillment of the Danielic eschatological "time"; (2) this end-time expectation is linked to the Danielic eschatological events of judgment and resurrection; (3) the connection between the hour in Daniel and the Danielic eschatological themes was familiar to the Jews, and therefore, its use by Jesus or John would not have been received as unique or extraordinary.

II. *The Use of the Danielic Hour in the Apocryphal/ Pseudepigraphal Literature*[3]

a. *The Book of Similitudes: 1 Enoch 37–71*

One of the books in which reference to a future hour or "time" occurs in the midst of Danielic allusions is *1 Enoch*.[4] Most scholars would acknowledge the interdependence that exists between Daniel 7–12 and *1 En.* 46–48.[5] The beginning of this section (*1 En.* 46.1-3) strongly alludes to Dan. 7.9, 13-14, as is evident from the following:

---

3. I have grouped the Apocrypha and the Pseudepigrapha together, because the only Apocryphal books I will refer to are *4 Ezra* (2 Esdras 3–14) and *2 Baruch*, both of which are usually listed in the Pseudepigrapha. Also, while *3 Enoch* was written at a later time (probably between the fifth and the sixth century AD), and thus reflects later Rabbinic thought, I will nevertheless include it in this group, since 1) it expands on the Enochic themes (*1 and 2 Enoch*), and 2) it claims to represent the theology of the early second century AD (on the dating of *3 Enoch*, see note 15 below).

4. The book of *1 Enoch* is divided into five parts, each of which may have been written at a different date. A very plausible date would be somewhere between 200 BC and AD 50 (Evans, *Ancient Texts*, p. 29; E. Isaac, '1 (Ethiopic Apocalypse of) Enoch', in James H. Charlesworth (ed.), *The Old Testament Pseudepigrapha: Vol. 1* [New York: Doubleday, 1983], pp. 5–89 [5–7]). The passages on which I will focus (*1 Enoch* 46–48; 62–63) are part of the Book of Similitudes, the second section of *1 Enoch* (*1 Enoch* 37–71); this portion is only preserved in Ethiopic. Due to the lack of Qumran equivalents to *1 Enoch* 37–71, several scholars have suggested a possible later date. However, the general consensus agrees with the above assessment of the end of the first century BC or the early first century AD (James C. VanderKam, *An Introduction to Early Judaism* [Grand Rapids: Eerdmans, 2001], p. 110; Helyer, *Jewish Literature*, p. 385). Most scholars hesitate to attribute the book of Similitudes to a Christian author; at the most, the Similitudes are taken to be a Jewish reaction to the Christian interpretation of the "Son of Man." For a survey on the traditions in *1 Enoch*, see James C. VanderKam, *Enoch and the Growth of an Apocalyptic Tradition* (Washington: The Catholic Biblical Association of America, 1984).

5. See George W. E. Nickelsburg and James C. VanderKam, *1 Enoch: A New Translation* (Minneapolis: Fortress, 2004), pp. 3–6; Matthew Black, 'The Messianism of the Parables of Enoch: Their Date and Contribution to Christological Origins', in James H. Charlesworth (ed.), *The Messiah: Developments in Earliest Judaism and Christianity* (Minneapolis:

Dan. 7.9, 13-14	1 En. 46.1-3
(9) I kept looking Until thrones were set up, and the Ancient of Days took *His* seat; His vesture *was* like white snow, And the hair of His head like pure wool. His throne *was* ablaze with flames, Its wheels *were* a burning fire . . . (13) I kept looking in the night visions, And behold, with the clouds of heaven One like a Son of Man was coming, and He came up to the Ancient of Days and was presented before Him. (14) And to Him was given dominion, Glory and a kingdom, That all the peoples, nations, and *men of every* language Might serve Him. His dominion is an everlasting dominion Which will not pass away; And His kingdom is one Which will not be destroyed.	(1) At that place, I saw the One to whom belongs the time before time.* And his head was white like wool, and there was with him another individual, whose face was like that of a human being. His countenance was full of grace like that of one among the holy angels. (2) And I asked the one—from among the angels—who was going with me, and who had revealed to me all the secrets regarding the One who was born of human beings,† "Who is this, and from whence is he who is going as a prototype of the Before-Time?"‡ (3) And he answered me and said to me, "This is the Son of Man, to whom belongs righteousness, and with whom righteousness dwells."

Notes

* Isaac, '1 (Ethiopic Apocalypse of) Enoch', provides the following alternative translations in a foot-note: "Head of days," "Chief of days," "he who precedes time," "the Beginning of days," "the First of days," "he who is of primordial days," "the Antecedent of time" (Isaac, '1 [Ethiopic Apocalypse of] Enoch', p. 34, n. 46a).

† Charles translates this figure as "Son of Man" (R. H. Charles, '1 Enoch' in R. H. Charles (ed.), *The Apocrypha and Pseudepigrapha of the Old Testament in English* [Vol. 2; Oxford: Clarendon, 1913]).

‡ Charles, '1 Enoch', translates this last phrase "why he went with the Head of Days?"

The rest of *1 Enoch* 46 narrates how the Son of Man figure will "depose the kings from their thrones and kingdoms" (46.4-5), because they "do not extol the name of the Lord of the Spirits" (46.6). Rather, these kings or kingdoms judge "the stars of heaven, they raise their hands (to reach) the Most High . . . They manifest all their deeds in oppression . . . And their devotion is to the gods which they have fashioned with their own hands . . . Yet they like to congregate in his houses and (with) the faithful ones"[6] (46.7-8). The above picture, which depicts lawless nations that per-

Fortress, 1992), pp. 145–68 (146–48); James C. VanderKam, 'Righteous One, Messiah, Chosen One, and Son of Man in 1 Enoch 37–71', in James H. Charlesworth (ed.), *The Messiah: Developments in Earliest Judaism and Christianity* (Minneapolis: Fortress, 1992), pp. 169–91 (174–75); John J. Collins, *The Scepter and the Star: The Messiahs of the Dead Sea Scrolls and Other Ancient Literature* (New York: Doubleday, 1995), pp. 177–82. G. K. Beale has demonstrated the above interdependence in his dissertation (Beale, *The Use of Daniel in Jewish Apocalyptic Literature and in the Revelation of St. John* [Lanham: UPA, 1984], pp. 96–106).

6.   Isaac provides an alternate reading, 'possibly more correctly', in the footnote: 'they persecute the houses of his congregations and the faithful . . .' (Isaac, '1 [Ethiopic Apocalypse of] Enoch', p. 35, n. 46t).

secute the saints, resembles the circumstances in Daniel under which the Son of Man appears (Daniel 7) and the final restoration occurs (Daniel 11–12).

The fact that *1 Enoch* 46 expands on the Daniel imagery is also evident from chs 47–48. In *1 En.* 47.3, after the supplication of the saints for deliverance (47.1-2) we have another strong allusion to Dan. 7.9-10:

Dan. 7.9-10	1 En. 47.3
(9) I kept looking Until thrones were set up, and the Ancient of Days took *His* seat; His vesture *was* like white snow, And the hair of His head like pure wool. His throne *was* ablaze with flames, Its wheels *were* a burning fire. (10) A river of fire was flowing and coming out from before Him; Thousands upon thousands were attending Him, and myriads upon myriads were standing before Him; The court sat, and the books were opened.	(3) In those days, I saw him — the Antecedent of Time, while he was sitting upon the throne of his glory, and the books of the living ones were opened before Him. And all his power in heaven above and his escorts stood before Him.

The Son of Man and the Antecedent of Time also appear in 48.2, where the Son of Man receives a name.[7] The context of 48.2 speaks of the restoration of the saints (48.1) along with the judgment of the kings of the earth (48.8-10). Then, after a short description of the wisdom of the "Elect One" (*1 Enoch* 49) and his mercy and judgment (*1 Enoch* 50),[8] *1 En.* 51.1-2, like Dan. 12.2, speaks about the resurrection of the dead: "In those days, Sheol will return all the deposits which she had received and hell will give back all that which it owes. And he shall choose the

---

7.   The "Son of Man" is here described as that Messianic figure that will arise in the end-time for the redemption of God's people. For more information on the background of the "Son of Man" figure, see Black, 'Messianism', pp. 145–68; VanderKam, 'Righteous One', pp. 169–76; Collins, *Scepter*, pp. 177–82; idem, *Daniel*, pp. 79–80; Nickelsburg and VanderKam, *1 Enoch*, pp. 3–6; and William Horbury, 'Messianism in the Old Testament Apocrypha and Pseudepigrapha', in John Day (ed.), *King and Messiah in Israel and the Ancient Near East: Proceedings of the Oxford Old Testament Seminar* (JSOTSup, 270; Sheffield: Sheffield Academic Press, 1998), pp. 422–27.

8.   Both *1 En.* 48.2 and 49.2 speak of the "Son of Man" (48.2) or the "chosen one" (49.2) being the one "in the presence of the Lord of the Spirits." Also, both texts are followed by an allusion to the Servant in Isaiah. The former (48.2) is followed by a phrase, which alludes to Isa. 42.6-7: "He is the light of the gentiles and he will become the hope of those who are sick in their hearts" (*1 En.* 48.4b). Notice also the reference to the "chosen one" in 48.6. The later text (49.2) is followed by a description of the spirit of wisdom, similar to that in Isa. 11.2: "In him dwells the spirit of wisdom, the spirit which gives thoughtfulness, the spirit of knowledge and strength" (49.3). Notice also the parallel between the judging in *1 En.* 49.4 and Isa. 11.3-4. These allusions to Isaiah are significant, since they attribute a Messianic sense to the "Son of Man" figure. For more information on the interconnections of *1 Enoch* with the books of Daniel and Isaiah see Nickelsburg and VanderKam, *1 Enoch*, pp. 3–6; Black, 'Messianism', pp. 155–61; and VanderKam, 'Righteous One', pp. 170–76).

righteous from among (the risen dead), for the day when they shall be selected and saved has arrived."

By intentionally calling to mind the above Danielic imagery, the author of the Similitudes[9] identifies the time of his narrated story with the time of the final judgment, the restoration of the saints and the resurrection of Dan. 12.2. The fact that the author has in mind a specific time of fulfillment or era of restoration is evident from the recurring phrase "in those days" (47.1, 3; 48.8; 50.1; 51.1, 3, 4), as well as the reference to an appointed "day" or "days" in *1 En.* 47.2; 48.8, 10; 51.2. More importantly, the author uses the Danielic phrase "at that hour" (Dan. 12.1) in *1 En.* 48.2, saying: "At that hour, that Son of Man was given a name, in the presence of the Lord of the Spirits, the Before-Time."[10] The broader context of this hour is related to the time of the Danielic judgment and the opening of the books (47.3; 48.8-10), the description of the Ancient of Days sitting on his throne (46.1; 47.3), the coming of the Son of Man to vindicate God's people (46.1-5; 48.2, 6, 10),[11] and the final resurrection (51.1). Therefore, one may suggest that *1 Enoch* 46–48 expounds on the end-time era as it is found in Daniel, and specifically alludes to the "time" or hour of Dan. 12.1.

However, one could object to the above suggestion by arguing that the phrase "at that hour" does not really represent an intentional allusion to the Danielic hour. Indeed, had the author had the Danielic hour in mind, one would expect that he would have mentioned it more often[12] or used it at a more appropriate place, such as the allusion to the Danielic resurrection in 51.1. Also, the fact that the author repeatedly uses the term "day" and "days" instead of "hour" or "time" could indicate that the Danielic hour is not in his mind.

While this objection seems reasonable, nevertheless, the author does use the phrase "in that hour" directly linked to the "Son of Man" in 48.2, in the midst of a context that strongly alludes to the Danielic passages (as noted above). Even if the specific use of the term "hour" were not an intentional allusion by the author,

---

9. Even though the final product of the Similitudes may be the work of a redactor, I will be referring to this final redactor as the "author" of the Similitudes.

10. This specifically recalls the coming of the Son of Man to the Ancient of Days in Daniel 7. *1 Enoch* 48.2 has been characterized as an enthronement moment of the Son of Man (cf. also *1 En.* 49.2-4; 61.8; 62.2).

11. The deliverance of God's people through the mediatory role of the Elect One/Son of Man has possibly been developed in *2 Enoch*, where the deliverer is Melchizedek. For suggestions as to how *2 Enoch* expands on the themes of *1 Enoch*, see Charles A. Gieschen, 'The Different Functions of a Similar Melchizedek Tradition in *2 Enoch* and the Epistle to the Hebrews', in Craig A. Evans and James A. Sanders (eds), *Early Christian Interpretation of the Scriptures of Israel* (JSNTSup, 148; Sheffield: Sheffield Academic Press, 1997), pp. 364–79 (368–69); George W. E. Nickelsburg, *Jewish Literature between the Bible and the Mishnah* (Minneapolis: Fortress, 2005), pp. 185–88; Helyer, *Jewish Literature*, p. 379.

12. For example, there is no explicit reference to a future time in *1 En.* 69.26–71.17, which also contains several allusions to the book of Daniel (for the allusions, see Beale, *Use of Daniel*, pp. 108–112).

it would still represent a specific future hour or era in which the author of the Similitudes understands the Danielic visions to take place. The author of the Similitudes, like Daniel, projects the fulfillment of the Danielic visions to a specific future hour or era.

We now turn to *1 En.* 62.3, where another reference to an appointed "day" of judgment is explicitly mentioned. The context of *1 Enoch* 62–63 expounds on this "day of judgment," which will be a time of restoration and vindication for the saints (62.13). More specifically, *1 En.* 62.2-5 echoes the judgment throne of Dan. 7.9-10, especially since the notion of God sitting "on the throne of his glory" to implement judgment is mentioned twice (62.2, 3):

Dan. 7.9-10, 13	1 En. 62.2-5
(9) I kept looking Until thrones were set up, and the Ancient of Days took *His* seat; His vesture *was* like white snow, And the hair of His head like pure wool. His throne *was* ablaze with flames, Its wheels *were* a burning fire. (10) A river of fire was flowing and coming out from before Him; Thousands upon thousands were attending Him, and myriads upon myriads were standing before Him; The court sat, and the books were opened . . . (13) I kept looking in the night visions, And behold, with the clouds of heaven One like a Son of Man was coming, and He came up to the Ancient of Days and was presented before Him.	(2) The Lord of the Spirits has sat down on the throne of his glory,* and the spirit of righteousness has been poured out upon him . . . (3) On the day of judgement, all the kings, the governors, the high officials, and the landlords shall see and recognize him — how he sits on the throne of his glory, and righteousness is judged before him . . . . (4) Then pain shall come upon them as on a woman in travail with birth pangs — when she is giving birth (the child) enters the mouth of the womb and she suffers from child bearing. (5) One half portion of them shall glance at the other half; they shall be terrified and dejected; and pain shall seize them when they see that Son of Man sitting on the throne of his glory.

Note
* Whether this "Son of Man" refers to a human or a celestial being is debated. The issue has become more complicated since some scholars have suggested that the terms "Son of Man" and "chosen one" refer to two different beings. For a defense of the heavenly origin of the "Son of Man," as well as the identification of the two figures, see Black, 'Messianism', pp. 146–55.

The picture of the woman in birth pangs could be thematically parallel to the "time of distress such as never occurred since there was a nation until that time" (Dan. 12.1). This Danielic "time of distress" alludes to Jer. 30.7, where the imagery of the woman in birth pangs is also used (Jer. 30.6; cf. Isa. 26.17). In the same Enochic context, the Son of Man appears as God's chosen agent for implementing judgment and bringing life (cf. the Son of Man in 62.5-9, 14; 63.9, 11, 14), just as in *1 Enoch* 46–48.[13] The Danielic imagery is reinforced at the end of ch. 62, where

13. The reading "has sat down on the throne" can also be rendered "seated him upon the throne," which would then describe the enthronement of the Servant Son of Man by the Lord

reference is made to the resurrection of the dead: "The righteous and elect ones shall rise from the earth and shall cease being of downcast face. They shall wear the garments of glory" (62.15).

The "day of judgement," as it has been described above, is also referred to as the "day of hardship and tribulation" for the godless rulers (63.8), at which "time" (63.10), although they will understand their omission, it will be too late. The above references to a specific "day" or "time" of judgment for all governors and kings (which also includes the restoration and the resurrection of the saints) probably allude to the Danielic end-time era at which the Son of Man will execute judgment and in which the resurrection will take place. The author of the Similitudes explicitly refers to "those days" (47.1, 3; 48.8; 50.1; 51.1, 3, 4), "that day" (62.3, 13),[14] and "that hour/time" (48.2; 63.10) possibly in order to 1) suggest that the narrated events will take place at an "appointed time," determined by God; and 2) to create a sense of future expectation concerning the fulfillment of these events. Moreover, a third reason may be that he wants to provide a common temporal reference with the events described in Daniel. This is not improbable, since, as we have already shown, it is precisely these Danielic events on which the author expounds.

b. *3 Enoch*
In *3 Enoch* (or the Hebrew Apocalypse of Enoch)[15] an allusion to the Danielic hour is even more explicit than in *1 Enoch* 48 and 62. While the book of *3 Enoch*, due

of the Spirits. Indeed, the phrase that follows, "the spirit of righteousness has been poured out upon him," makes more sense with the new reading. In agreement with this rendering are Nickelsburg and VanderKam, *1 Enoch*, p. 79; and, with a small variation, Matthew Black, *The Book of Enoch or 1 Enoch: A New English Edition with Commentary and Notes, in Consultation with James C. VanderKam, with an Appendix on the 'Astronomical' Chapters (72–82) by Otto Neugebauer* (SVTP, 7; Leiden: Brill, 1985), pp. 59, 235. If this rendering stands correct, then *1 En.* 62.2 would parallel the phrasing in *1 En.* 61.8, which reads: "He placed the Elect One on the throne of glory."

14. The references to the "day" may be an echo to the Danielic "day." The LXX of Dan. 12.1 translates three out of the four occurrences of עת with the Greek word ἡμέρα (the first עת is translated as ὥρα). Moreover, the LXX has used the words ἡμέρα and ὥρα together in Dan. 12.13, which indicates the semantic proximity of the two words in the mind of the translator (none of these terms appear in the MT, while only ἡμέρα appears in Theodotion). See also the phrase "latter days" in Dan. 2.28; 10.14 and the LXX of Dan. 2.29, 2.45; 11.20, as well as the eschatological use of "day" in Dan. 8.26; 12.11; and 12.12.

15. The date of *3 Enoch* has been debated. Suggestions have varied from as early as the late first century AD (H. Odeberg, *3 Enoch* [New York, KTAV, 1973]) to no earlier than the tenth century AD (Milik, *The Books of Enoch*). The current consensus seems to be that, while the book contains early traditions, the final editorial work was done somewhere in the fifth or the sixth century AD. There is no doubt that the book was written in Hebrew and that it originates from a Jewish compositor. The authorial perspective of the book is through the eyes of Rabbi Ishmael (the book is pseudepigraphically assigned to him) who lived in AD 132. For

to its date of composition, cannot possibly provide a background for the Gospel of John, it nevertheless stands as part of the Jewish tradition that elucidates early Jewish texts and themes, especially as they relate to the Danielic hour (e.g. texts in Daniel, *1 Enoch*, and *2 Enoch*).[16]

3 Enoch 30.2 contains a marked quotation from Dan. 7.10, introduced by the phrase "it is written":

Dan. 7.10; 12.1	3 En. 30.2
(7.10) A river of fire was flowing and coming out from before Him; Thousands upon thousands were attending Him, and myriads upon myriads were standing before Him; The court sat, and the books were opened. (12.1) Now at that time (ובעת) Michael, the great prince who stands *guard* over the sons of your people, will arise. And there will be a time of distress such as never occurred since there was a nation until that time; and at that time (ובעת) your people, everyone who is found written in the book, will be rescued.	. . . the Prince of the World, who speaks in favor of the world before the Holy One, blessed be he, every day at the hour (בשעה)* when the book is opened in which every deed in the world is recorded, as it is written, "A court was held, and the books were opened."

Note
* See Alexander, '3 (Hebrew Apocalypse of) Enoch', pp. 244–45.

In the context of *3 En.* 30.2, the author has described the Danielic court as "the Great Law Court" that "sits in the height of the heaven of Arabot" (30.1) and has specifically mentioned an hour in which the books will be opened. The term "hour" may be taken literally to denote the daily hour at which the heavenly Sanhedrin council meets;[17] however, the term "hour" may also be taken metaphorically to represent an eschatological era, in which God's judgment will be exercised daily.[18]

more information on the composition of the book, see P. Alexander, '3 (Hebrew Apocalypse of) Enoch' in James H. Charlesworth (ed.), *The Old Testament Pseudepigrapha: Vol. 1* (New York: Doubleday, 1983), pp. 223–315 (225–29); and Evans, *Ancient Texts*, p. 31.

16. For the relationship between *3 Enoch* and early Jewish traditions, see Alexander, '3 (Hebrew Apocalypse of) Enoch', pp. 245–51.

17. The construction שעה can be translated as "short time" or hour (see the Aramaic equivalents in Dan. 3.6, 15; 4.16, 30; and 5.5). Ludwig Koehler and Walter Baumgartner, *The Hebrew and Aramaic Lexicon of the Old Testament* (Vol. 5; Leiden: Brill, 2000), pp. 2000–1.

18. The eschatological nature of the hour in *3 En.* 30.2 is suggested by the following considerations. 1) This hour occurs in the context of the Holy One sitting in the heavens and presiding in the 'Great Law Court' (30.1). Notice especially the description of the Holy One in 28.7: "When the Holy One, blessed be he, sits in judgement on the throne of judgement, his garment is white like snow, the hair of his head is as pure wool, his whole robe shines like a dazzling light and he is covered all over with righteousness as with a coat of mail" (an allusion to the Ancient of Days in Dan. 7.9). 2) The hour is specifically linked to the time when "the book is opened," which implies a context of judgement, presumably the final judgement (30.2). Notice that this judgment takes place "on the third day," which is specifically the day

According to this latter reading, the hour at which the books are opened spans "days."[19] The choice between temporal terms such as "hour" and "day" may serve to place an emphasis on the fact that this time is predetermined: the more particular and restrictive the temporal indicator becomes,[20] the more it communicates the "set" nature of this time or era.

The above parallel between *3 En.* 30.2 and Dan. 7.10 and 12.1 indicates that the Jewish author may have considered the Danielic hour as the era in which the books are opened. In this case, the author presents the eschatological hour of judgment as having been inaugurated in the heavenly realms.

Later, in *3 En.* 35.4, while the same theme of the final judgment continues, Dan. 7.10 is quoted again, only this time in full:[21]

Dan. 7.10	3 En. 35.4
A river of fire was flowing and coming out from before Him; Thousands upon thousands were attending Him, and myriads upon myriads were standing before Him; The court sat, and the books were opened.	. . . as it is written, "A thousand thousand waited on him, ten thousand times ten thousand stood before him. A court was held and the books were opened."

Immediately after this quotation, the text reads, "when the time (or 'hour', וּבשעת) comes to say 'Holy'" (35.5), which relates the Danielic judgment to the anticipation of a specific time.[22] The reference to a specific time continues in 35.6, which begins with the phrase "at that time" or better "at that hour" (באותה שעה); the verse speaks of God's discipline "until they accept the yoke of the kingdom." This reminds the reader of the hour mentioned before (30.2), in which hour the books are opened.

of resurrection in Hos. 2.2-3 (quoted in 28.10). 3) The hour is especially connected with the time of the eschatological judgment and opening of the books in Dan. 7.10 (30.2), and this is further indicated with the use of the introductory formula "it is written" (cf. also the quotations of Dan. 4.17 and 4.10-11 in *3 En.* 28.9 and 28.4 respectively). 4) The text in which the hour of judgment occurs (30.1-2) parallels the eschatological judgment descriptions in 31.1-2 and 32.1-2 (Alexander, '3 (Hebrew Apocalypse of) Enoch', p. 284), both of which quote from Isaiah — Isa. 16.5 and 66.16 respectively — the latter of which clearly speaks of the final judgment in the midst of a new creation. 5) Finally, Dan. 7-10 is quoted again in *3 En.* 35.4 within the context of judgment.

19. Notice the expression "every day at that hour" in 30.2.

20. For example, one uses hour instead of "day," or "day" instead of "era."

21. Notice also the allusion in *3 En.* 35.2 of Dan. 10.6.

22. The recitation of "Holy" may refer to the daily worship of Yahweh as he sits on his throne (cf. *3 En.* 18.7; 19.6; 38.1; 39.1; 40.1-2). This would correspond well to the "every day" references, especially in *3 En.* 28.7 and 30.2. The author certainly has in mind a daily exercise of worship. However, the text does not invite us to understand this daily worship apart from God's redemptive-eschatological framework. One can even detect an inaugurated eschatology, since the very reason for the recitations is the ultimate submission of all to God (cf. *3 En.* 35.6; also, notice the judgment on those who fail to recite in 40.3; 47.2).

Another probable allusion to the Danielic "time" (Dan. 12.1) occurs in *3 En.* 44.10, where one sees Michael interceding for the saints:

Dan. 12.1	3 En. 44.10
Now at that time (וּבָעֵת הַהִיא) Michael, the great prince who stands *guard* over the sons of your people, will arise. And there will be a time of distress such as never occurred since there was a nation until that time; and at that time your people, everyone who is found written in the book, will be rescued.	Then the Holy One, blessed be he, said to them: 'Abraham, my friend, Isaac, my chosen one, Jacob, my firstborn, how can I save them at this time (הִיא) from among the nations of the world?' Thereupon Michael, the Prince of Israel, cried out and lamented in a loud voice, saying, 'Lord, why do you stand aside?'

It appears likely that the author of *3 Enoch* speaks about the expectation of an eschatological "time" or "hour" that echoes the end-time references in Daniel.

c. *4 Ezra*

The book of *4 Ezra* also speaks of a future "time" in the midst of Danielic allusions.[23] While *4 Ezra* is composed of seven visions, I consider only the first three, and I specifically address the references to Daniel as they relate to the eschatological era in these visions.[24] The portrait of this eschatological era is gradually perfected in the eyes of the reader.

---

23. *Fourth Ezra* is the Jewish part of 2 Esdras (chs 3–14) that belongs to the Apocrypha. *4 Ezra* was probably written towards the end of the first century AD and reflects the Jewish hermeneutic of the time. The book divides into seven sections (visions) and its genre falls into the apocalyptic. See Evans, *Ancient Texts*, p. 34; Nickelsburg, *Jewish Literature*, pp. 287–94; Helyer, *Jewish Literature*, pp. 392–96; and B. M. Metzger, 'The Fourth Book of Ezra', in James H. Charlesworth (ed.), *The Old Testament Pseudepigrapha: Vol. 1* (New York: Doubleday, 1983), pp. 517–59 (520–23). The Latin text can be found in Robert L. Bensly, *The Fourth Book of Ezra, the Latin Version Edited from the MSS* (Cambridge: Cambridge University Press, 1895).

24. The book of *4 Ezra* has numerous allusions to Daniel elsewhere in the book (see the multiple Danielic references in *4 Ezra* 11–12 as noted at the end of this section); however, the description of the eschatological era is more prominent in the first three visions, where, as we will see, the concept of a final hour or "time" is coupled with Danielic allusions. The choice of the first three visions is validated by the fact that these visions compose a unity, since they portray the same structural pattern (see Michael E. Stone, *Fourth Ezra* [Hermeneia; Minneapolis: Fortress, 1990], pp. 24, 50–51). For the literary unity of the whole book of *4 Ezra*, see especially Earl Breech, 'These Fragments I Have Shored Against My Ruins: The Form and Function of 4 Ezra', *JBL* 92 (1973), pp. 267–74; Michael E. Stone, 'Coherence and Inconsistency in the Apocalypses: The Case of "The End" in 4 Ezra', *JBL* 102 (1983), pp. 229–43; and Alden L. Thompson, *Responsibility and Evil in the Theodicy of IV Ezra* (SBLDS, 29; Missoula: Scholars, 1977). See also the commentaries by J. M. Myers, *1 and 2 Esdras* (AB, 42; Garden City: Doubleday, 1974), pp. 119–21; R. J. Coggins and M. A.

In the first vision of the book of *4 Ezra*, the author introduces us to the time of the end. More specifically, in *4 Ezra* 4.26-27, the author initiates a discussion concerning the "end" of the present age, "because this age is hastening swiftly to its end" (*quoniam festinans festinat saeculum pertransire*).[25] This "end'" is characterized by evil and "sadness and infirmities" (4.27). While this present age has produced much ungodliness, this production will exist only "until the time of threshing comes" (4.30). If there is a delay in this "time of threshing," it is only for the sake of the righteous (4.39).[26] However, this delay does not entail an *ad-hoc* plan. Like a pregnant woman whose nine months have been completed and who cannot keep the child within her any longer, so also will be the end of this age, it will come in its appropriate time (4.40-42).[27] The author specifically speaks about the "appointed times" (*temporibus*),[28] at which the promises to the righteous will be fulfilled (4.27).

The author insists on the specifics of the "time" of the end by presenting us with Ezra's question of how much "more time is to come" (*plus quam praeteriti*) in *4 Ezra* 4.44-46 (cf. Dan. 12.12-13). In response, the angel in the dialogue speaks about the signs that will come before the end, most of which include unrighteousness and chaos (5.1-13).[29] In this section, the author uses two phrases familiar to the Old Testament:[30] "the days are coming" (*dies venient* in 5.1) and "at that time" (*in illo tempore* in 5.12), the latter of which may allude to Dan. 12.1.[31]

Knibb, *The First and Second Books of Esdras* (CBC; Cambridge: Cambridge University Press, 1979); and Stone, *Fourth Ezra*, pp. 14–21.

25. The word "end" has appeared before in *4 Ezra* 3.14, concerning the revelation of the end of times to Abraham. Stone has well developed the theme of the "end" in *4 Ezra*, especially as it relates to messianic and eschatological themes in *4 Ezra* (Stone, "'The End" in 4 Ezra', pp. 238–42; and idem, *Features of the Eschatology of IV Ezra* [HSS; Atlanta: Scholars, 1989], pp. 83–97). Also, for the theme of the "two ages" in *4 Ezra*, see Stone, *Fourth Ezra*, pp. 92–93.

26. For the hastening of the "times" and the sense of an appointed time, see also *2 Bar.* 20.1 and 1QM I, 11-13 (for the later, see my comments on pp. 74–76).

27. Cf. *2 Bar.* 30.2-4 (see comments on pp. 68–69). Myers also characterizes this period as the "time of judgement-salvation" (Myers, *1 and 2 Esdras*, p. 183).

28. The phrase "latter days" is translated as *novissimis temporibus* in the Vulgate of Dan. 2.28. The exact form *temporibus* is also used in the Vulgate of Dan. 11.6, 14.

29. Stone has recognized the literary unity of *4 Ezra* 5.1-13 and has also identified four oracular parts within this section: 1) Cosmic signs (5.4b-5); 2) Eschatological ruler (5.6-7); 3) Chaos (5.8b-9b); and 4) Loss of wisdom (5.9c-11) (Stone, *Fourth Ezra*, pp. 106–7).

30. Notice also the similar utilization of "signs" in the Old Testament as the expectation of the end of historical periods (apocalyptic language) in S. B. Frost, *Old Testament Apocalyptic* (London: Epworth, 1952), pp. 248–50.

31. The phrase "at that time" occurs twice in Dan. 12.1. The Latin translation for these occurrences is *in tempore autem illo* and *in tempore illo* respectively. As we have already noted in the preceding chapter, the phrase "at that time" (בָּעֵת הַהִיא) also occurs with eschatological overtones in the OT in Joel 4.1; Mic. 3.4; Zeph. 1.12; 3.19-20; Jer. 3.17; 4.11; 8.1; 31.1; 33.15; 50.4, 20; and Ezek. 21.30, 34.

The former phrase introduces an era in which "those who dwell on earth shall be seized with great terror, and the way of truth shall be hidden, and the land shall be barren of faith" (5.1), while the latter describes a time when "men shall hope but not obtain; they shall labor but their ways shall not prosper" (5.12). The above usage of "time" language indicates the author's intent to create awareness of a future appointed "time" concerning the end of this age. While the references to the "end" set up the eschatological tone for the rest of the book, the emphasis on the specific "time" of the end illustrates the significance of this topic to the author of *4 Ezra*.

How does this emphasis on the "time" of the end relate to the Danielic eschatological hour? Are there any indications that the author intentionally links this "time" with the Danielic visions?

In the second vision of the book of *4 Ezra*, when the author actually describes the end of the age, he specifically alludes to Dan. 7.10 and 12.1 and connects these allusions to the image of the woman in labor (cf. Jer. 30.6-7; Isa. 26.17 and 66.7-9). The following phrases portray the author's train of thought: "show your servant the end of your signs (6.12) . . . the word concerns the end (6.15) . . . Behold, the days are coming (6.18) . . . the books shall be opened . . . and women with child shall give birth to premature children . . . and these shall live and dance" (6.20-21).[32] Moreover, the author speaks of a terrible war in 6.24 and of God's salvation and the end of the world in 6.25-26.[33] The whole section begins with the following question: "What will be the dividing of the times? Or when will be the end of the first age and the beginning of the age that follows?' (6.7) Here, the author is concerned about the dividing of the "times," namely the dividing of the two ages, which is also the beginning of the new eschatological era.[34] Having described these "coming" days as a time of both judgment and life (6.20-21), the author concludes with a picture that echoes that of Dan. 12.1:

32. The reference to the opening of the books is a strong allusion to Dan. 7.10 (Metzger, 'Fourth Book of Ezra', p. 535; Stone, *Fourth Ezra*, p. 170). Notice also the opening of the books in *1 En.* 47.3 (see chart on p. 55).

33. This section also specifically speaks of God's visitation (6.18), which in *4 Ezra* denotes God's coming to execute judgment (see Stone, '"The End" in 4 Ezra', p. 231 n. 9) or the eschatological coming of God (W. Harnisch, *Verhängnis und Verheißung der Geschichte: Untersuchungen zum Zeit- und Geschichtsverständnis im 4. Buch Esra und in der syr. Baruchapokalypse* [FRLANT, 97; Göttingen: Vandenhoeck & Ruprecht, 1969], p. 308). Moreover, the section of *4 Ezra* 6.17-26 has been connected to the messianic kingdom, although within the broader eschatological time reference (Stone, '"The End" in 4 Ezra', p. 234; and idem, *Fourth Ezra*, p. 169).

34. Stone has defined well the "end" in *4 Ezra*, as "the decisive point" within a broader eschatological sequence or "the decisive turning point of history" (Stone, '"The End" in 4 Ezra', pp. 239, 241). This definition of the "end" allows for the concept of the division of times or ages as it appears in the book of *4 Ezra*.

Dan. 12.1	4 Ezra 6.24
Now at that time (*in tempore autem illo*)* Michael, the great prince who stands *guard* over the sons of your people, will arise. And there will be a time (*tempus*) of distress such as never occurred since there was a nation until that time (*tempus*); and at that time (*in tempore illo*) your people, everyone who is found written in the book, will be rescued.	At that time (*in illo tempore*)† friends shall make war on friends like enemies, and the earth and those who inhabit it shall be terrified, and the springs of the fountains shall stand still, so that for three hours they shall not flow.

Notes
* According to the Latin Vulgate.
† The exact phrase *in illo tempore* only occurs three times in *4 Ezra* (5.12; 6.24; and 13.23), all of which appear in the context of Danielic allusions.

The significance of the above Danielic echo in the context of other Danielic thematic allusions is that the author of *4 Ezra* intentionally links the end-time with the Danielic events. Notice, for example, the mention of war in 6.24, which is reminiscent of the war language in Dan. 7.21 and 11.35-38. Undoubtedly, the author of *4 Ezra* expounds the Danielic ideas through his own interpretative lenses. Nonetheless, the Danielic allusions or echoes should not be restricted to include only the events described in Daniel; they should also include the Danielic "time" of the end, since the author has made this explicit in both *4 Ezra* 5.1 and 6.24.[35]

More intertextual connections to Daniel appear in the third vision of *4 Ezra*, where the author relates God's Messiah to the ideas of suffering, resurrection, judgment and the becoming like stars (although he does not do this in the immediate context, but in the broader context of the vision):

Dan. 12.2-3	4 Ezra 7.29, 32, 97, 125
And many of those who sleep in the dust of the ground will awake, these to everlasting life, but the others to disgrace and everlasting contempt. And those who have insight will shine brightly like the brightness of the expanse of heaven, and those who lead the many to righteousness, like the stars forever and ever.	. . . my son the Messiah shall die (7.29)* . . . the earth shall give up those who are asleep in it (7.32) . . . they are to be made like the light of the stars (7.97) . . . shall shine more than the stars (7.125) . . .

Note
* So also Metzger, 'Fourth Book of Ezra', p. 538; Stone, *Fourth Ezra*, p. 219. Cf. also the resurrection *1 En.* 51.1, on which see my comments on pp. 55–56.

The above phrases in *4 Ezra* certainly allude to the resurrection in Dan. 12.2-3.[36]

35. *Fourth Ezra* 6.24 alludes to *4 Ezra* 5.1, in the context of determining the "time" of the end: "Behold, the days are coming when those who dwell on earth shall be seized with great terror, and the way of truth shall be hidden, and the land shall be barren of faith" (5.1).

36. Stone's comment on *4 Ezra* 7.29 is that, "a remarkable verbal parallel, with a

Indeed, the language of sleep for the dead is characteristic of Dan. 12.2, and the last two phrases (7.97 and 7.125), although somewhat removed from the explicit reference to the resurrection, both refer to a resurrected life after death, since their immediate contexts speak, respectively, about "being incorruptible" and about a "paradise" being revealed.

The above allusions occur again in *4 Ezra* 7.37-38, which also alludes to the judgment and resurrection scene in Dan. 12.2:

Dan. 12.2	*4 Ezra 7.37-38*
And many of those who sleep in the dust of the ground will awake, these to everlasting life, but the others to disgrace and everlasting contempt.	Then the Most High will say to the nations that have been raised from the dead, "Look now and understand whom you have denied whom you have not served, whose commandments you have despised! Look on this side and on that; here are delight and rest, and there are fire and torments!" Thus he will speak to them in the day of judgement.

The double destiny of the resurrected people in the midst of the eschatological judgment is characteristically Danielic, since Dan. 12.2 is the only place in the Hebrew Bible that has a double resurrection in mind.[37] Notice also the context of *4 Ezra* 7.37-38, which describes eschatological judgment,[38] and which is especially linked to the broader eschatological idea of the "end-time" age. More specifically, *4 Ezra* 7.32-33 reads, "and the earth shall give up those who are asleep in it, . . . and the Most High shall be revealed upon the seat of judgement"; also, *4 Ezra* 7.39-44 states that "he will speak to them on the day of judgement — a day that has no sun or moon or stars . . . but only the splendor of the glory of the Most High, by which all shall see what has been determined for them."[39]

The above Danielic allusions appear within the literary section of *4 Ezra* 7.26-44.[40] The significance of these Danielic allusions for our study becomes evident when one notices how this whole passage begins: "For behold, the time will come (*enim tempus veniet*), when . . ." (*4 Ezra* 7.26). The author specifically refers to a "time"

somewhat different sense, may be observed in Dan. 9.26" (Stone, *Fourth Ezra*, p. 216 n. 59). Myers believes that the reference to the "son" is probably a "Christian tampering" (Myers, *1 and 2 Esdras*, p. 253).

37. The resurrection in *4 Ezra* 7.37-38, like in Daniel, follows a final judgment.

38. Stone notes that the section of *4 Ezra* 7.26-44 presents a good exposition for the eschatological view of the author of *4 Ezra* (Stone, '"The End" in 4 Ezra', p. 230). On the eschatology of *4 Ezra* see J. Keulers, 'Die eschatologische Lehre des vierten Esrabuches', *BibS* 20.2–3 (1922), pp. 1–204; and Stone, *Eschatology*.

39. The explicit reference to the Messiah (7.29-40) also makes this age a messianic era (so also Myers, *1 and 2 Esdras*, p. 253). Therefore, in *4 Ezra*, the messianic era is linked to the end of the present age.

40. Except for *4 Ezra* 7.97 and 125.

that is expected to come. Thus, we find within the Jewish tradition the expectation of an eschatological "time," a time that is especially linked to the fulfillment of the Danielic promises.[41] Later on, within the broader context of the above Danielic allusions, the author describes this eschatological "time" with the phrases "in the last days" or "in the last times," especially in *4 Ezra* 7.77, 84, 87, 95: "for you have a treasure of works laid up with the Most High; but it will not be shown to you until *the last times*" (7.77); "they shall consider the torment laid up for themselves in *the last days*" (7.84); "they shall utterly waste away in confusion and be consumed with shame, and shall wither with fear at seeing the glory of the Most High before whom they sinned while they were alive, and before whom they are to be judged in *the last times*" (7.87); "they understand the rest which they now enjoy . . . and the glory which awaits them in *the last days*" (7.95) (cf. also *4 Ezra* 12.9, 21, 23, 28). The same phrase ("last days") also appears in Dan. 2.28, 29, 45, and Dan. 10.14, and though this phrase appears elsewhere in the OT, the expressions of Daniel are more likely in mind because of the other surrounding Daniel allusions.

The references to "the last times" and "the time of the end" in *4 Ezra* 12.9, 21, 23, 28 are also used in the midst of other Danielic allusions and echoes. The phrases specifically read: "for you have judged me worthy to be shown the end of the times and the last events of the times (*temporum finem et temporum novissima*)" (12.9); "two of them [kings] shall perish when the middle of its time (*tempore medio*) draws near; and four shall be kept for the time (*in tempore*) when its end approaches (*adpropinquare tempus eius ut finiatur*); but two shall be kept until the end (*in finem*)" (12.21); "in its last days (*in novissimis*) the Most High will raise up three kings, and they shall renew many things in it, and shall rule the earth and its inhabitants more oppressively than all who were before them" (12.23-24); "but he [one of the kings] also shall fall by the sword in the last days (*in novissimis*)" (12.28).

In the broader context of the above phrases, notice especially the description of the beast in *4 Ezra* 11.36-46, the Messiah in 12.32, the day of judgment in 12.34, and the teaching of the wise in 12.38.[42] The concept of the coming of the eschatological days also appears in *4 Ezra* 13.29, the context of which speaks about the "last days" (*in novissimis diebus* in 13.18, *in novissimo* in 13.20), the time of the Son's day

---

41. There are two possible backgrounds for the word "time" in *4 Ezra* and especially the phrase "last times" (cf. 6.34). First, the word "time" may be derived from the Qumran material, specifically from 1QS IV, 16-17 and 1QpHab 7.7, 12 (suggested by Stone, *Eschatology*, pp. 53–54). Second, it may be an expansion of the Danielic "time" as it appears in Dan. 2.28; 8.17, 19; and 9.27. Due to the following indications, the latter option seems more probable: 1) The Qumran texts cited above are probably influenced by the book of Daniel and possibly borrowed the concept of "time" from Daniel (see my comments on pp. 71–74); 2) As argued above, the book of *4 Ezra* occasionally alludes to Daniel, and, thus, it is not improbable that the author had the Danielic "time" in mind; 3) The emphasis on the "end" in *4 Ezra* resembles the emphasis on the "end" in Daniel; 4) The references to a messianic kingdom in *4 Ezra* resemble the messianic kingdom in Daniel 7.

42. For the Danielic background of *4 Ezra* 11–12 see Beale, *Use of Daniel*, pp. 112–29.

(*tempore* in 13.52), the "end of the times" (*et temporum finem* in 14.5), and the two parts and a half (14.11-12).[43] Though the specific reference to hour does not occur in *4 Ezra*, the idea of the "latter days" and other end-time references from Daniel do occur, including the expression "at that time" from Dan. 12.1.

d. *2 Baruch*

The eschatological language continues in *2 Baruch*, a book that greatly relies on *4 Ezra*.[44] While *2 Baruch* was written a few years later than *4 Ezra*,[45] and also probably later than the Gospel of John, its expansion on the eschatological themes of *4 Ezra*, especially as they relate to the Danielic end-time and the messianic era, reveals the Jewish interpretation of these themes and of Daniel around AD 100.[46] The following brief references to *2 Baruch* aim to strengthen the case that some of the eschatological expectations for an end-time within Judaism were influenced by the Danielic visions and the eschatological "time" therein.

The book of *2 Baruch* contains allusions to Daniel, as well as references to the notion of eschatological "time." First, let us review the following allusion:

Dan. 7.9-10	*2 Bar. 24.1-2*
(9) I kept looking Until thrones were set up, and the Ancient of Days took *His* seat; His vesture *was* like white snow, And the hair of His head like pure wool. His throne *was* ablaze with flames, Its wheels *were* a burning fire. (10) A river of fire was flowing and coming out from before Him; Thousands upon thousands were attending Him, and myriads upon myriads were standing before Him; The court sat, and the books were opened.	(1) For behold, the days are coming, and the books will be opened in which are written the sins of all those who have sinned . . . (2) And it will happen at that time that you shall see, and many with you, the long-suffering of the Most High . . .

43. For the Danielic association of the "man" rising out of the sea in *4 Ezra* 13, see again Beale, *Use of Daniel*, pp. 129–44.

44. For the interdependence of *4 Ezra* and *2 Baruch*, see Thompson, *IV Ezra*, pp. 121–55; Gwendolyn B. Sayler, *Have the Promises Failed? A Literary Analysis of 2 Baruch* (SBLDS 72; Chico: Scholars, 1984), pp. 123–34; Tom W. Willett, *Eschatology in the Theodicies of 2 Baruch and 4 Ezra* (JSPSup, 4; Sheffield: Sheffield Academic Press, 1989); and Stone, *Fourth Ezra*, pp. 36–43.

45. The Book of *2 Baruch* was probably written around AD 100 or sometime early in the second century AD (A. F. J. Klijn, '2 [Syriac Apocalypse of] Baruch', in James H. Charlesworth (ed.), *The Old Testament Pseudepigrapha: Vol. 1* [New York: Doubleday, 1983], pp. 615–52 [616–17]; Evans, *Ancient Texts*, p. 36; Helyer, *Jewish Literature*, p. 423).

46. For the social setting behind the book of *2 Baruch*, see J. Edward Wright, 'The Social Setting of the Syriac Apocalypse of Baruch', *JSP* 16 (1997), pp. 81–96, who argues that the contents of *2 Baruch* reflect the personal experiences of the Jewish author in the midst of social and religious distress.

The opening of the books clearly alludes to Dan. 7.9-10;[47] however, the author of *2 Baruch* continues in reference to this judgment moment and says that "at that time" the Most High will suffer. While in Daniel it is the Son of Man who suffers (implicitly), in *2 Baruch* it is God himself. Nevertheless, the phrase "at that time" is used to depict the time of judgment and suffering, and it is possible that the phrase has been borrowed from Dan. 12.1, where the "book" is also mentioned.

This is probably the case, since the same phrase ("at that time") is used elsewhere in *2 Baruch* in relation to the Danielic resurrection. In particular, notice how the language in Dan. 12.1-2 is used in *2 Bar.* 30.1-5:

Dan. 12.1-2	*2 Bar. 30.1-5*
(1) Now at that time Michael, the great prince who stands *guard* over the sons of your people, will arise. And there will be a time of distress such as never occurred since there was a nation until that time; and at that time your people, everyone who is found written in the book, will be rescued. (2) And many of those who sleep in the dust of the ground will awake, these to everlasting life, but the others to disgrace and everlasting contempt.	(1) And it will happen after these things when the time of the appearance of the Anointed One has been fulfilled and he returns with glory, that then all who sleep in hope of him will rise. (2) And it will happen at that time that those treasuries will be opened in which the number of the souls of the righteous were kept, and they will go out and the multitudes of souls will appear together, in one assemblage, of one mind. And the first ones will enjoy themselves and the last ones will not be sad. (3) For they know that the time has come of which it is said that it is the end of times.* (4) But the souls of the wicked will the more waste away when they shall see all these things. (5) For they know that their torment has come and that their perditions have arrived.

Note
* Notice also the reference to the consummation of times in *2 Bar.* 29.8. The author here introduces the period at which the Messiah will reign and will also return to heaven with glory (Willett, *Theodicies*, p. 116). For an eschatological overview of *2 Baruch*, see Willett, *Theodicies*, pp. 112–20.

Notice how the passage in *2 Bar.* 30.1-5 makes reference to the concept of time: "the time of the appearance of the Anointed One" (30.1); "at that time" (30.2); and "the time has come of which it is said that it is the end of times" (30.3).[48] All of these references can be traced back to Daniel (Dan. 8.17 ["the time of the end," לְעֶת־קֵץ]; Dan. 8.19 ["appointed time of the end," לְמוֹעֵד קֵץ]; and Dan. 12.1 ["at that time," וּבָעֵת הַהִיא]),[49] especially since the "appearance of the anointed one" causes the resurrection of "all who sleep in hope of him" (*2 Bar.* 30.1), which certainly echoes the

47. See also Sayler, *Promises*, p. 58; Rivka Nir, *The Destruction of Jerusalem and the Idea of Redemption in the Syriac Apocalypse of Baruch* (Atlanta: SBL, 2003), p. 122.

48. The phrase "end of time" (עַד־עֵת קֵץ) appears in Dan. 12.4 and 9, which makes this allusion even stronger (cf. also Dan. 11.35).

49. This particular "time" is the "consummation of time" in 29.8, which in the immediate context is described as the age in which the earth will yield its fruit, the hungry will enjoy

reference to "those who sleep" in Dan. 12.2. Also, the context of the resurrection in Dan. 12.2 places this resurrection "at that time," just as *2 Bar.* 30.2 reads. Moreover, the description of the fate of the two groups, the righteous in 30.2 and the wicked in 30.4-5, resembles the destiny of the two groups in Dan. 12.2.[50] The author, thus, intentionally alludes to the resurrection in Daniel, which would also establish an allusion to the "time" in Dan. 12.1-2.

Another reference to the Danielic resurrection appears in *2 Bar.* 42.8, where the author writes: "And dust will be called, and told, 'Give back that which does not belong to you and raise up all that you have kept until its own time'". The term "dust" represents the realm of the dead and is connected with the idea of resurrection in Isa. 26.19 and Dan. 12.2.[51] The author of *2 Baruch* interprets the above OT passages — either one of them or both — in an eschatological sense, as is evident from the reference to the time of the end in 42.6 and the eternality of the new resurrected era in 44.12-13.

The Danielic resurrection is also called to mind in *2 Bar.* 50.2, where the author again makes an explicit link with the phrase "at that time":[52]

Dan. 12.1-2	2 Bar. 50.2
(1) Now <u>at that time</u> Michael, the great prince who stands *guard* over the sons of your people, will arise. And there will be <u>a time</u> of distress such as never occurred since there was a nation until <u>that time</u>; and at <u>that time</u> your people, everyone who is found written in the book, will be rescued. (2) And many of <u>those who sleep</u> in the dust of <u>the ground</u> (MT: אֲדָמָה, LXX and Theodotion: γῆ) will awake, these to everlasting life, but the others to disgrace and everlasting contempt.	For <u>the earth</u> will <u>surely</u> give back <u>the dead</u> at <u>that time</u>.*

Note
* Cf. Murphy, *Second Baruch*, pp. 60–63.

themselves, and the *manna* will come again from on high (29.5-8). Moreover, this eschatological "time" is linked with the renewal of the temple and creation in 32.1-7.

50. *Second Baruch* is strong in asserting that the world is divided in two groups. Notice the description of the two groups or worlds in *2 Bar.* 42.7 in terms of "corruption" and "life." As Murphy has noted, "in 42.7, the ontological difference between the two worlds has been expressed anthropologically" (Frederick J. Murphy, *The Structure and Meaning of Second Baruch* [SBLDS, 78; Atlanta: Scholars, 1985], p. 55). For an analysis of this dualism in *2 Baruch*, see Murphy, *Second Baruch*, pp. 31–67.

51. *Second Baruch* 42.8 appears within the literary section of *2 Bar.* 35.1–47.2 (according to Willett, *Theodicies*, pp. 81–84). Notice the multiple Danielic allusions in this section (specifically in *2 Bar.* 36–42) as observed by Beale, *Use of Daniel*, pp. 144–53.

52. Four passages in *2 Baruch* explicitly describe the resurrection (*2 Bar.* 23.4-5; 30.1-5; 42.7-8; 50.1–52.7), three of which allude to Daniel with explicit references to a "time." The resurrection in *2 Bar.* 23.4-5 is mentioned only to emphasize its predestined nature, and so, it is referred to in passing (see also Willett, *Theodicies*, p. 119).

The fact that *2 Bar.* 50.2 alludes to Daniel is strengthened by the reference to the fulfillment of "those things which have been spoken of before" (50.4). Moreover, notice the double destination of the two groups (the righteous and the wicked) in 51.1-3.[53] In addition, the fact that the righteous "will be changed . . . from light to the splendor of glory" (51.10) and their excellence will be "greater than that of the angels" (51.12) resembles the transformation of the saints in Dan. 12.3.[54] Finally, this is a "time" that the righteous have chosen, a "time of which the end is full of lamentations and evils" (51.16), which is also reminiscent of the time of distress in Dan. 12.2.[55]

The author of *2 Baruch* explicitly communicates his awareness that the eschatological resurrection will happen "at that time."[56] Surely, this is a future time that depicts the eschatological era of restoration and raises the anticipation of the reader.

The question must be asked: Why would the author of *2 Baruch* employ such Danielic language to describe the end-time? First, the references to the Danielic "time" indicate a specific hermeneutical awareness in Judaism, that is, the fact that the eschatological era is conceptually linked to the prophesied end-time in Daniel. Second, the Danielic "time" does not merely communicate the eschatological nature of the events described; it also creates awareness and an expectation that these events *will* come at the appointed time. By alluding to the end-time in Daniel, the author likely wants to emphasize the certainty of the coming end. Finally, the Danielic eschatological events of judgment and resurrection are not to be perceived apart from the eschatological time frame within which these events occur. If not anything else, *2 Baruch* once again demonstrates the idea that the Jewish authors did not hesitate to link the Danielic ideas of judgment and resurrection with the eschatological "time" as depicted in Daniel. As in *4 Ezra*, though the precise allusion to Daniel's OG hour is absent in *2 Baruch*, allusions to Daniel's latter-day expressions do occur, including the phrase "at that time" from Dan. 12.1.

53. Another reference to those who sleep in the dust appears in *2 Bar.* 11.4, again as an allusion to Dan. 12.2 (Nir, *Redemption*, pp. 158–59).

54. See also Nir, *Redemption*, p. 162.

55. The same "time" is again referred to as "at that time" in *2 Bar.* 52.2.

56. Notice also the passage in *2 Bar.* 68.1-8, which contains the phrases, "there will come a time" and "after a short time," which appear in a context concerning distress. This passage follows the fall of Zion in 67.6 and the boastful king of Babylon in 67.7-8. Nevertheless, both Zion and the temple are restored in 68.5. Moreover, in *2 Bar.* 83.6-7, the author refers to "the ends of the times" and "judgment." Notice also the judgment language in 83.2-3 in relation to the "times" in 83.1. Even if one would argue that the use of "time" in conjunction with Danielic allusions was an influence of Christian ideas, my overall argument of this book — namely that John intentionally alluded to the Danielic "time" — is still strengthened, since this reference to the Danielic "time" is evident in such later extrapolations.

III. *The Use of the Danielic Hour in the Qumran Documents*

a. *1QS (Rule of the Community)*

The only explicit references to an appointed time in 1QS appear in Col. IV (4Q257 v), v. 20, "until the time appointed for the judgment [is] decided," and v. 25, "until the appointed end and the new creation."[57] Already from 1QS III, the author has distinguished between the sons of justice (or sons of truth) and the sons of deceit (1QS III, 19–21). The contrast also exists between the Prince of Lights,[58] who has dominion over all the sons of justice, and the Angel of Darkness, whose dominion extends over the corruptive deeds of the sons of deceit, "in compliance with the mysteries of God, until his moment (קצו)" (1QS III, 23).[59] The Angel of Darkness will also cause affliction and grief to the sons of light, and he will cause them to fall (1QS III, 23-24). The text specifically speaks about the "times of distress" (צרותם מועדי in 1QS III, 23).

The above distinction between the two groups continues in 1QS IV, where the sons of truth are promised blessings and eternal life, while the sons of deceit await torture and eternal damnation. Notice the similarity of the phrasing concerning the destiny of the two groups:

1QS IV, 6-8	*1QS IV, 11-13*
And the reward (ופקודת) of all those who walk in it will be healing, plentiful (רוב) peace in a long life, fruitful offspring with all everlasting blessings, eternal (עולמים) enjoyment with endless life (בחיי), and a crown of glory with majestic raiment in eternal (עולמים) light.	And the visitation (ופקודת) of all those who walk in it will be for an abundance (רוב) of afflictions at the hands of all the angels of destruction, for eternal (עולמים) damnation by the scorching wrath of the God of revenges, for permanent terror and shame (וחרפת) without end with the humiliation of destruction by the fire of the dark regions.

57. Leaney suggests a composition date of about 100 BC (A. R. C. Leaney, *The Rule of Qumran and Its Meaning: Introduction, Translation, and Commentary* [Philadelphia: Westminster, 1966], pp. 113–16). See also F. M. Cross, *The Ancient Library of Qumran* (London: Duckworth, 1958), p. 89.

58. The term "prince" could be a reference to an angel. If this is the case, then the text echoes the defense of Michael in Dan. 12.1 (Leaney, *Rule*, p. 148).

59. I have used the Hebrew text in the study edition of Martinez-Tigchelaar, *Dead Sea Scrolls*. The appointed moment of God refers to the time when Belial will dominate over God's people, after which his fall will lead to the messianic reign (cf. 1QS I, 17). Charlesworth translates קצו with "his end" (James H. Charlesworth (ed.), *Rule of the Community and Related Documents* [The Dead Sea Scrolls: Hebrew, Aramaic, and Greek Texts with English Translations, Vol. 1; Tübingen: Mohr (Siebeck), 1994], pp. 14–15). According to Koehler-Baumgartner, the Hebrew word קצ appears with the meaning of "time, length of time, period" in the DSS (*HALOT*, 3:1118).

The mention of the "visitation" refers to God's visitation of the world at the time of the end, when he will judge all people (cf. 1QS IV, 18-19, 26). The distinction of the people into two groups, as well as the double destination of these groups, is reminiscent of the double destination in Dan. 12.2, "these to everlasting life, but the others to disgrace and everlasting contempt." Apart from the distinction of the two groups and the appearance of an "eternal" destiny in both cases, the connection between 1QS and Daniel is further strengthened by the fact that 1QS uses the words of Dan. 12.2, "life" (לְחַיֵּי) and "disgrace" (or "shame," לַחֲרָפוֹת), to describe the destiny of the two groups (see the use of the same words in the chart above, p. 71).

Moreover, the identification of the sons of truth with the "light" (1QS, IV 8), as well as with the "spirit of knowledge" and "of concealment concerning the truth of the mysteries of knowledge" (1QS IV, 4, 6),[60] parallels the description of the wise, who will "shine brightly" (Dan. 12.3) and will gain understanding (Dan. 12.10), probably concerning the mysteries of God (cf. Dan. 2.18-19, 27-30, 47).[61]

Therefore, when the author of 1QS speaks about the dividing of the people into two groups at the appointed time (cf. 1QS IV, 25-26), he probably alludes to the Danielic division of the groups in the time of the end (Dan. 12.2). Indeed, according to 1QS, at the above appointed time of judgment "(then), God will refine, with his truth, all man's deeds, and will purify for himself the structure of man . . . in order to instruct the upright ones with knowledge of the Most High, and to make understand the wisdom of the sons of heaven" (1QS IV, 20-22). The author here intentionally picks up the wording from Daniel 12 (cf. also 11.32, 35), where the time of the end is described as a time when "many will be purged, purified and refined . . . and those who have insight will understand" (Dan. 12.10). Notice also how Dan. 11.33 mentions that "those who have insight among the people will give understanding to the many," as well as Dan. 12.3, which refers to "those who lead the many to righteousness."

While the author of 1QS primarily describes the historical present, he does so by qualifying it through the lenses of the eschatological judgment as it appears in Daniel. According to the author, the two divisions that will appear at the time of the end already exist in the present, because God has sorted the people into "equal parts":[62]

1QS IV, 16-17	1QS IV, 25
For God has sorted them into equal parts until the last time (כיא אל שמן בד) (בבד עד קץ אחרון) and has put an everlasting loathing between their divisions	For God has sorted them into equal parts until the appointed end (כיא בד בבד) (שמן אל עד קץ נחרצה) and the new creation (ועשות חדשה)

---

60. The mission of concealment seems to be in contrast with the mission of the Servant in Isa. 42.3, whose mission is to reveal and make known (P. Wernberg-Moller, *The Manual of Discipline: Translated and Annotated with an Introduction* [Leiden: Brill, 1957], p. 79).

61. Cf. Leaney, *Rule*, pp. 67–68, 152.

62. Wernberg-Moller examines the probability of this distinction being derived from Gen. 3.15 (Wernberg-Moller, *Manual*, pp. 84–85).

Now compare the above references to "time" and "appointed end" with the following Danielic texts:[63]

Dan. 9.26	Dan. 11.35-36
Then (וְאַחֲרֵי) after the sixty-two weeks the Messiah will be cut off and have nothing, and the people of the prince who is to come will destroy the city and the sanctuary. And its end (וְקִצּוֹ) will come with a flood; even to the end (וְעַד קֵץ) there will be war; desolations are determined (נֶחֱרָצֶת).	And some of those who have insight will fall, in order to refine, purge, and make them pure, until the end time (עַד־עֵת קֵץ); because it is still to come at the appointed time. Then the king will do as he pleases, . . . and he will prosper until (עַד) the indignation is finished, for that which is decreed (נֶחֱרָצָה) will be done.

It is evident from the above parallelism between 1QS IV, 16-17 and 1QS IV, 25 that the "last time" refers to the time that God has appointed for judgment and re-creation,[64] the appointed time of the end.[65] Indeed, in the succeeding verses, in 1QS IV, 16-17, the author qualifies this "time" as follows:

Dan. 11.35	1QS IV, 18-20
And some of those who have insight will fall, in order to refine, purge, and make them pure, until the end time (עַד־עֵת קֵץ); because it is still to come at the appointed time (לַמּוֹעֵד).*	God, in the mysteries of his knowledge and in the wisdom of his glory, has determined an end (קֵץ) to the existence of injustice and on the appointed time (וּבְמוֹעֵד) of the visitation he will obliterate it forever. Then truth shall rise up forever (in) the world, for it has been defiled . . . until the time appointed (עַד מוֹעֵד) for the judgement decided (נחרצה).

Note
* For other intertextual connections between the Old Testament and 1QS, see Sarianna Metso, 'The Use of Old Testament Quotations in the Qumran Community Rule', in Frederick H. Cryer and Thomas L. Thompson (eds), *Qumran between the Old and New Testaments* (JSOTSup, 290; Sheffield: Sheffield Academic Press, 1998), pp. 217–31.

The author displays an obvious awareness of the eschatological "time" in Daniel 8–12, time that relates to the last days (Dan. 10.14), results in purification

63. The combination of the words עד and קץ also appear in Dan. 11.45; 12.4, 6, 9, two of which have עַד־עֵת קֵץ.

64. The reference to the new creation echoes texts such as Isa. 43.19; 65.17; and 66.22.

65. For a discussion on the "end of days" in Qumran, see John J. Collins, 'Teacher and Messiah? The One Who Will Teach Righteousness at the End of Days', in Eugene Urlich and James VanderKam (eds), *The Community of the Renewed Covenant: The Notre Dame Symposium on the Dead Sea Scrolls* (Notre Dame: University of Notre Dame Press, 1994), pp. 193–210 (195–202).

(Dan. 12.10), involves a new creation (Dan. 12.2-3), and includes the separation of the people into two groups (Dan. 12.2).

Evidently, the author of 1QS displays an awareness of an appointed time of judgment and new creation; he relates this future hope to the present battle between truth and injustice in a way that forces the reader to take a stand. On the one hand, the certainty of the coming of the eschaton is an established presupposition; on the other hand, the author goes beyond this future hope to argue that what will happen in the end has already begun in the present. People should identify themselves with one of the two eschatological groups and live their present lives in accordance with their destiny. The author picks up the Danielic eschatological picture in order to address the contemporary situation, as well as to generate an awareness of God's plan so that the people will evaluate the role of their lives within that plan.[66]

b. *1QM (War Scroll)*

The Danielic hour also occurs in the first column of the *War Scroll* (1QM I), as well as in 1QM XV–XIX.[67] Scholars generally agree that 1QM I makes extensive use of Daniel.[68] Indeed, the connections between the two texts are apparent, since the author employs Danielic language to describe the eschatological war in 1QM.[69] Since most scholars already acknowledge the explicit allusions to the eschatological war in Daniel 11–12, I focus on whether this section also alludes to the Danielic "time" of the end. The first column of the *War Scroll* mentions the eschatological "time" (קץ, מועד,עת) in 1QM I, 4, 5, 8, 11, and it also refers to this same period with the word "day" (יום) in 1QM I, 9, 10, 11, 12.

The first use of the word "time" refers to the time of Belial (1QM I, 4), God's final adversary, and indicates how even Belial acts according to God's assigned plan: "in his time, he will go out with great rage to wage war against the kings of the north, and his anger wants to exterminate and cut off the horn of Israel" (1QM I, 4). The word used here is קץ, which generally means "time" or "period of time," except when used in the phrase אין קץ (literally, "no time") in which case it means "end."[70] The exact rendering "in his time" (ובקצו) in 1QM I, 4 resembles the

---

66. Notice also the following phrases in Daniel: "to the appointed time of the end" (לְמוֹעֵד קֵץ) in Dan. 8.19; "the end is still to come at the appointed time" (כִּי־עוֹד קֵץ לַמּוֹעֵד) in Dan. 11.27; and "until the end of time" (עַד־עֵת קֵץ) in Dan. 11.35, 12.4, 9.

67. The date of 1QM has been placed somewhere between the later part of the 1st century B.C. and the first century AD (Philip R. Davies, *1QM, the War Scroll from Qumran: Its Structure and History* [Rome: Biblical Institute Press, 1977], p. 90; So also Yigael Yadin, *The Scroll of the War of the Sons of Light Against the Sons of Darkness* [Oxford: Oxford University Press, 1962], pp. 244–46).

68. Collins, *Scepter*, pp. 159–60; idem, *Apocalypticism in the Dead Sea Scrolls* (New York: Routledge, 1997), pp. 99–100; Beale, *Use of Daniel*, pp. 42–66.

69. Notice, for example, the war against Edom, Moab, and Ammon (1QM I, 1; Dan. 11.41), the enemy of Kittim (1QM I, 2, 4, 6, 9, 12; Dan. 11.30), the attack from the north (1QM I, 4; Dan. 11.40, 44), etc.

70. See the entry in Koehler-Baumgartner, *HALOT.*

rendering "his end" (קצו) in Dan. 11.45, which makes possible an allusion to Daniel. However, since in 1QM I, 4 the word קץ is better translated "time" and not "end," the allusion may very well be to the "time" as it appears in Dan. 11.35, 40. Indeed, in Dan. 11.35, 40, the Danielic story has God's final adversary acting according to God's appointed plan.[71]

The remaining three occurrences of "time" (1QM I, 5, 8, 11) provide a clearer case for an allusion to the Danielic "time." More specifically, these instances state that "this is a time of salvation for the nation of God and a period of rule for all the men of his lot, and of everlasting destruction for all the lot of Belial" (1QM I, 5); also, "in the time of God, his exalted greatness will shine for all the eternal times" (1QM I, 8); and finally, "it will be a time of suffering for all the nation redeemed by God" (1QM I, 11). The words that are used are עת (1QM I, 5, 11) and מועד (1QM I, 8),[72] both of which are Hebrew, not Aramaic, words for "time" in the Old Testament. The same words are used interchangeably in Daniel 8–12 to describe the time of the end, which is both a time of salvation and a time of distress. In 1QM I, 5 particularly, this "time" (עת) is a "time of salvation for the nation of God and a period of rule for all the men of his lot, and for everlasting destruction for all the lot of Belial." This description well captures the receiving of the kingdom in Dan. 7.22, "and the time arrived when the saints took possession of the kingdom," as well as the resurrection in Dan. 12.2, "these to everlasting life, but the others to disgrace and everlasting contempt." (Notice the use of עת in Dan. 12.1, which points to the time of salvation and resurrection of the saints.)[73]

Moreover, 1QM I, 8 speaks of God's appointed time (thus the use of מועד), at which time God's "exalted greatness will shine for all the eternal times." This is in accordance to the shining of the sons of justice who will "shine to all the edges of the earth" (1QM I, 8) which echoes the shining in Dan. 12.3. However, this appointed time for glory corresponds to the "determined" day for battle and destruction (I, 9-10), the "day of the calamity" (I, 12), which is also described as a "time of distress":

71. Davies' structure of 1QM I suggests that 1QM I, 4 falls into the second stage of the final war (Davies, *1QM*, pp. 115–19).

72. For an extensive treatment of the use of these terms in the Bible and Qumran, see Gershon Brin, *The Concept of Time in the Bible and the Dead Sea Scrolls* (Leiden: Brill, 2001). However, Brin does not deal with the eschatological or apocalyptic connotations that these words have in their respective contexts.

73. The "time" in Dan. 7.22 is probably the same "time" that appears in Dan. 12.1, since the latter vision expands on the former and both accounts describe similar events (judgment and restoration).

Dan. 12.1	1QM I, 11-12
Now at that time Michael, the great prince who stands *guard* over the sons of your people, will arise. And there will be a time of distress (עת צָרָה) such as never occurred since there was a nation until that time; and at that time your people, everyone who is found written in the book, will be rescued.	The sons of light and the lot of darkness shall battle together for God's might . . . on the day of the calamity. It will be a time of distress (עת צרה) for all the nation redeemed by God. Of all their sufferings, none will be like this, hastening till eternal redemption is fulfilled.

One can hardly deny the allusion here, since there is a lexical reproduction of the phrase "time of distress" (עת צרה). Also, the description of the distress as one that has never occurred before is characteristically Danielic (Dan. 12.1; cf. also Jer. 30.7).[74] Finally, in both cases, the distress is followed by the redemption of the saints.[75]

In 1QM XV–XIX,[76] the eschatological battle is retold, this time in more detail, as the author attempts to encourage the faithful for the coming battle. Besides the specifics of the war, the author once again makes sure to place the war within the Danielic eschatological time frame. The description of the battle begins with another reference to the "time of distress" (עת צרה) (1QM XV, 1), and throughout the section the author refers seven times to the eschatological "time" (1QM XV, 5, 6 [מועד]; 1QM XV, 12 [קץ]; 1QM XVI, 3 [ביום ההואה]; 1QM XVII, 5 [מועד]; 1QM XVIII, 3 [בעת ההיאה]; and 1QM XVIII, 10 [מועד]). The description of the battle adds more allusions from Daniel than 1QM I: 1) the reference to Michael (1QM XVII, 6-7; Dan. 12.1);[77] 2) the suffering of the saints as a time of testing (1QM XV, 1; XVI, 15; XVII, 1-2, 9; Dan. 7.21; 11.35; 12.1); 3) the mention of the mysteries of God (1QM XVI, 11, 16; XVII, 9; Dan. 2.28-30); and (4) the possession of "everlasting redemption" (1QM XV, 1-2; XVIII, 11; Dan. 7.14, 18, 27; 12.2-3).[78]

I have already noted that the eschatological battle described in 1QM I (as well as 1QM XV–XIX) contains numerous Danielic allusions, which have already been

---

74. See also James M. Scott, 'Geographic Aspects of Noachic Materials in the Scrolls at Qumran', in Stanley E. Porter and Craig A. Evans (eds), *The Scrolls and the Scriptures: Qumran Fifty Years After* (JSPSup, 26; Sheffield: Sheffield Academic Press, 1997), pp. 368–81 (378).

75. While the resurrection is not specifically mentioned, one may assume that it is implied ("eternal redemption"). For the use of the resurrection concept in Qumran, see Emile Puech, 'Messianism, Resurrection, and Eschatology at Qumran and in the New Testament', in Eugene Urlich and James VanderKam (eds), *The Community of the Renewed Covenant: The Notre Dame Symposium on the Dead Sea Scrolls* (Notre Dame: University of Notre Dame Press, 1994), pp. 235–56 (246–56).

76. For the literary unit of 1QM XV–XIX, see Davies, *1QM*, pp. 20–23.

77. John J. Collins, 'The Expectation of the End in the Dead Sea Scrolls', in Craig A. Evans and Peter W. Flint (eds), *Eschatology, Messianism, and the Dead Sea Scrolls* (Grand Rapids: Eerdmans, 1997), pp. 74–90 (87).

78. Notice especially the use of Dan. 12.1, 3 in 1QM XVII, 6-7.

noted by other scholars.[79] One should not overlook that it is within these contexts that the above references to the eschatological "time" of judgment and salvation appear. In this light, it is likely that when the author refers to the appointed time of the end, he does so having in mind the Danielic "time."

c. *4QFlor (Florilegium)*

The 4Q Florilegium briefly comments on passages regarding the theme of eschatology.[80] In general, the author deals with the various phases of the end-time, such as the reconstruction of the temple, the rise of the Messiah, the final battle with Belial, and the distress of the saints. The relevance of the document to our study consists in the fact that the text refers to the eschatological time of distress immediately before quoting from the book of Daniel.[81]

More specifically, the author speaks of a "time of trial" (עת המצרף in 4QFlor 1 II, 3, 24, 5, 1) from which only a remnant will survive (4QFlor 1 II, 3, 24, 5, 2). This will be the case, because the righteous will remain faithful to the law,[82] "as is written in the book of Daniel, the prophet: 'The wicked act wickedly . . . and the just . . . shall be whitened and refined and a people knowing God will remain strong'" (4QFlor 1 II, 3, 24, 5, 3).[83] The quotation is a combination of Dan. 12.10 and 11.32 (cf. also Dan. 11.35), which makes the "time" of the trial in line 1 an allusion to the "time" of distress in Dan. 12.1.[84]

---

79. There are also a few fragments that represent parts of 1QM and use the Danielic theme of God's "mysteries." See 4Q491 8–10 II, 11: "according to the mysteries of God"; 4Q491 11 II, 9: "in accordance with God's mysteries"; and 4Q491 11 II 13: "for from of old you heard in the mysteries of God," of which the last two come from a scroll that represents 1QM XVI, 3-14; XVII, 10-14. (Also, see 4Q495 2, which corresponds to 1QM XVIII, 9-12; 4Q496 3 I, which corresponds to 1QM I, 4-9; and 4Q496 2+1 I, which corresponds to 1QM I, 11-17.) For the use of "mystery" in the Jewish literature, see Benjamin L. Gladd, *Revealing the Mysterion: The Use of Mystery in Daniel and Second Temple Judaism with Its Bearing on First Corinthians* (Berlin: Walter de Gruyter, 2008).

80. The document is also known as 4Q174 or 4QEschMidr (Midrash on Eschatology). For a short description and bibliography, see Evans, *Ancient Texts*, pp. 100–101. For an extensive treatment, see George J. Brooke, *Exegesis at Qumran: 4QFlorilegium in Its Jewish Context* (JSOTSup, 29; Sheffield: JSOT Press, 1985).

81. Only two explicit quotations have been identified in Qumran: 4QFlor 1 II, 3, 24, 5, 3 and 11QMelch 2.18 (James C. VanderKam, 'Apocalyptic Tradition in the Dead Sea Scrolls and the Religion of Qumran', in John J. Collins and Robert A. Kugler (eds), *Religion in the Dead Sea Scrolls* [Grand Rapids: Eerdmans, 2000], pp. 113–34 [117–18]).

82. So also Peter W. Flint, 'The Daniel Tradition at Qumran', in Craig A. Evans and Peter W. Flint (eds), *Eschatology, Messianism, and the Dead Sea Scrolls* (Grand Rapids: Eerdmans, 1997), pp. 41–60 (60).

83. Collins, 'End', p. 79.

84. Brooke has also noticed the preoccupation of the author with the time of trial, as well as the connection of the "time" to Daniel. Brooke also notices that both Dan. 12.10 and 11.35 connect to Psalm 2 through the word שׂכל (Brooke, *Exegesis*, p. 124).

The context that precedes this Danielic quotation comments on the "son of iniquity" (4QFlor 1 I, 21, 2, 1), as well as the war with Belial (4QFlor 1 I, 21, 2, 7–9). Moreover, it extensively interprets the "last days" along the lines of various eschatological themes.[85] One cannot escape noticing that the "last days" is the time frame in which the Danielic events also take place.[86] Indeed, the line directly preceding the aforementioned reference to Daniel's "time of trial" refers to "the last days" (4QFlor 1 I, 21, 2, 19). The context following the Danielic quotation speaks of "the time when Belial will open . . . upon the house of Judah difficulties to persecute them" (4QFlor 4, 3-4), which again echoes the Danielic time of the end, when the righteous will be persecuted (Dan. 11.33-35; 12.1, 10).

Consistent with the other Jewish texts studied, the author of 4QFlor demonstrates an awareness of the eschatological "time" from Daniel and the themes that pertain to this "time." The above review of the Jewish tradition demonstrates that one cannot detach the eschatological Danielic events (distress, final judgment, resurrection) or motifs (Son of Man, Michael, glorification, trial) from the Danielic hour or "time," at which these events take place. Indeed, the Jewish authors did not merely expound on the Danielic events and motifs, but also developed the concept of the Danielic final "time" in a way that generated an expectation for God's final act. Even in places where the term "hour" or "time" is absent and other Danielic themes emerge, one can confidently claim that the concept of the eschatological "time," "age," or "era" conceptually underlies the discourse in these texts.

IV. *Conclusion*

As we noted in the introduction to this chapter, the purpose of this survey has been to demonstrate that there exists a conceptual connection between the eschatological "time" and the Danielic eschatological themes of judgment and restoration in early Judaism. The evidence surveyed in this chapter demonstrates that such a connection is probable in various sections of the Jewish exegetical tradition.

If this is the case, then this survey shows that, 1) even before John, already in the Jewish tradition there is an anticipation of the fulfillment of the Danielic eschatological "time"; 2) in some instances, particularly in the DSS, there is even this inaugurated notion of the eschatological era (already-and-not-yet fulfillment); 3) this end-time expectation is linked to the Danielic eschatological events of judgment and resurrection; and 4) the connection between the hour in Daniel and the

---

85. The "last days" is the period in which the temple will be rebuilt (4QFlor 1 I, 21, 2, 2), the "branch of David" will rise together with the "Interpreter of the Law" (4Flor 1 I, 21, 2, 11-12), and God will provide rest from all enemies, especially from the sons of Belial (4QFlor 1 I, 21, 2, 7). The "last days" will also be the period for avoiding idolatry (4QFlor 1 I, 21, 2, 15-16; quoting Isa. 8.11 and Ezek. 44.10), and it reflects the eschatological war described in Ps. 2.1 (4QFlor 1 I, 21, 2, 18-19).

86. For a discussion on the meaning of the "last days" in 4QFlor and Qumran in general, see Brooke, *Exegesis*, pp. 175–78.

Danielic eschatological themes was familiar to the Jews, and therefore, John's use of hour in connection to the end-time judgment and resurrection would not have been perceived as unique.

THE OT BACKGROUND OF THE
ESCHATOLOGICAL HOUR IN JOHN 4.21, 23

I. *Introduction*

The purpose of this chapter is to explore the eschatological nature of the hour (ὥρα) in Jn 4.21, 23, and examine the thematic features to which it connects. As we will see, the use of hour in John 4, in contrast to the uses in John 5, 12, and 16, employs the fewest lexical connections to Daniel.[1] Nevertheless, this is an eschatological hour that relates to themes similar to those found in Jewish apocalyptic writings and the book of Daniel. Moreover, John does use Danielic language in this context, and this hour refers to the same eschatological moment throughout the whole gospel. Being the first significant instance of the hour in his gospel,[2] John prepares his readers by qualifying this hour eschatologically, without necessarily revealing all that he knows about the hour. In his initial development of the hour, he has connected it to the building of the new temple and the coming of the Messiah. The purpose of this chapter is to bring to the fore the eschatological nature of the hour in John 4.21, 23, to identify the themes to which it relates, and to observe how these themes may parallel thematic emphases in Daniel.

II. *The Immediate Context of John 4.21, 23*

In the first chapter of John's gospel, the reader is introduced to the themes of creation and new creation as being intrinsically related to Jesus's mission (through the language of light, life, and birth; Jn 1.1-18) and to Jesus's identity as the king of

---

1.   There are some uses of ὥρα that apparently do not have an eschatological or Danielic link (Jn 4.6, 52-53; 5.35; 11.9; 19.14, 27). I do not examine these uses. Moreover, the use of ὥρα in Jn 2.4; 7.30; 8.20; 13.1; 16.2, 4; 17.1 is conceptually linked to the eschatological hour in Jn 4.21, 23; 5.25, 28; 12.23, 27; 16.21, 25, 32 and will be referred to as needed in connection to these latter texts. In the light of the following study in John, it may be that these other uses are to be best viewed within the conceptual framework of the uses about to be studied.

2.   Although see also Jn 2.4, where the hour is mentioned but not defined.

Israel (Jn 1.19-51). Following this, the two incidents in John 2 describe the beginning of Jesus's ministry and mission, a mission that includes the coming of the hour (2.4) and the reestablishment of the temple through Jesus's own resurrection from the dead (2.19-22).

Furthermore, the literary section of Jn 2.23–4.42 contains two of Jesus's personal encounters, one with Nicodemus (Jn 2.23–3.36) and one with the Samaritan woman (4.1-42). Both incidents should be seen in conjunction to each other, since both expound on John's emphasis so far. In the former story, John employs new creation language (light, eternal life, birth), while the latter story mentions the coming of the hour in relation to the removal of the physical temple.

As part of the latter story, the word ὥρα occurs in Jn 4.21, 23, which reads, "an hour is coming when neither in this mountain nor in Jerusalem will you worship the Father . . . But an hour is coming, and now is, when the true worshipers will worship the Father in spirit and truth." These two occurrences appear within the literary section that narrates the dialogue between Jesus and the Samaritan woman (Jn 4.7-26). The dialogue focuses mainly on two themes, *living water* (4.7-15) and *worship* (4.19-26), although scholars typically do not explain how the transitional section about the Samaritan's husband (4.16-18) relates to what precedes and follows. Whether this transitional section alludes to the five gods of Samaria (idolatry)[3] or refers to the woman's disobedient lifestyle (immorality),[4] its purpose relates to what follows, namely the introduction of the topic of worship and the woman's recognition of Jesus's identity as "prophet" (4.19) or "Messiah" (4.25).[5] Therefore, the shift in the dialogue occurs in 4.16, dividing the passage into two sections,[6]

---

3.   Representative proponents of this view are C. K. Barrett, *The Gospel According to St. John: An Introduction with Commentary and Notes on the Greed Text* (London: SPCK, 1967), p. 235; and C. H. Dodd, *The Interpretation of the Fourth Gospel* (Cambridge: Cambridge University Press, 1958), p. 313.

4.   Several scholars prefer the literal interpretation, which either exposes the moral deficiency of the Samaritan woman (e.g. Raymond E. Brown, *The Gospel According to John* [AB, 29; New York: Doubleday, 1966], p. 171; Rudolf Schnackenburg, *The Gospel According to St. John* [3 Vols; New York: Crossroad, 1987], p. 433) or reveals Jesus's prophetic ability (e.g. Barnabas Lindars, *The Gospel of John* [NCB; Grand Rapids: Eerdmans, 1982], p. 186; Herman Ridderbos, *The Gospel of John: A Theological Commentary* [Grand Rapids: Eerdmans, 1997], pp. 158–62; Francis J. Moloney, *The Gospel of John* [SP, 4: Collegeville: Liturgical, 1998], p. 127).

5.   An alternate interpretation of this text exists, which argues that the fact that Jesus meets the Samaritan woman at the well and mentions her husbands depicts him as the new bridegroom (for this view see Jocelyn McWhirter, *The Bridegroom Messiah and the People of God* [Cambridge: Cambridge University Press, 2006], pp. 58–76). This view is attractive because it relates the references about the woman's husbands to Jesus's identity, which is one of the main concerns of the passage.

6.   Other scholars have observed a twofold emphasis in the structure (e.g. Moloney, *John* [1998]; Brown, *Gospel According to John,* I).

one that deals with the reception of the *living water*, and another that addresses the proper *worship* of the Father.

However, as different or separate as these two themes may seem, they also constitute two parts of the same whole. In other words, Jesus's conversation with the Samaritan woman, rather than addressing two separate issues, may be centering on one main theme: the creation of the new temple. The absence of the word "temple" from the passage should not confuse us, since the idea of temple is clearly present in the text, especially in 4.20-21. In his monograph, Stephen T. Um has argued extensively in favor of this interpretation, and I will reiterate some of his arguments in the following section.[7] Basically, the argument states that the flowing of the living water represents the garden-temple motif,[8] which is here complemented with a delocalized (universalized) form of worship. In this case, one should view the dialogue as forming a unified argument, and also the hour as being related both to the offering of the living water and the de-localization of worship.

In favor of this reading, I will mention only a few of the common elements between the two main parts of the dialogue (4.9-15 and 4.19-26). First, the division between Jews and Samaritans that is mentioned at the beginning of the first section (4.9) is replicated at the beginning of the second section (4.20-22), but in the latter centers on the temple worship.

Jn 4.9	*Jn 4.20-22*
Therefore the Samaritan woman said to him, "How is it that you, being a Jew, ask me for a drink, since I am a Samaritan woman?" For Jews have no dealings with Samaritans.	"Our fathers worshiped in this mountain, and you people say that in Jerusalem is the place where men ought to worship". Jesus said to her, "Woman, believe me, the hour is coming when neither in this mountain nor in Jerusalem will you worship the Father. You worship what you do not know; we worship what we know, for salvation is from the Jews."

7.   Stephen T. Um, *The Theme of Temple Christology in John's Gospel* (New York: T&T Clark, 2006); See also G. K. Beale, *The Temple and the Church's Mission: A Biblical Theology of the Dwelling Place of God* (NSBT; Downers Grove: InterVarsity, 2004).

8.   For arguments towards the suggestion that the garden of Eden represents a temple, see Beale, *Temple*, pp. 66–80; Gordon J. Wenham, 'Sanctuary Symbolism in the Garden of Eden Story', in Richard S. Hess and David Toshio Tsumura (eds), *'I Studied Inscriptions from Before the Flood': Ancient New Eastern, Literary, and Linguistic Approaches to Genesis 1–11* (Winona Lake: Eisenbrauns, 1994), pp. 399–404; Margeret Barker, *The Gate of Heaven: The History and Symbolism of the Temple in Jerusalem* (London: SPCK, 1991), pp. 63–103; Terje Stordalen, *Echoes of Eden: Genesis 2–3 and Symbolism of the Eden Garden in Biblical Hebrew Literature* (CBET, 25; Leuven: Peeters, 2000), pp. 111–38; and Donald W. Parry, 'Garden of Eden: Prototype Sanctuary', in Donald W. Parry (ed.), *Temples of the Ancient World: Ritual and Symbolism* (Salt Lake City: Deseret, 1994), pp. 126–51. Additional studies are cited in Richard M. Davidson, *Flame of Yahweh: Sexuality in the Old Testament* (Peabody: Hendrickson, 2007), pp. 47–48, n. 133.

Second, while Jesus refers to the significance of his identity in the first section (4.10, 14), this identity is also revealed at the end of the second section (4.25-26), as the following chart indicates:

Jn 4.10	Jn 4.25-26
Jesus answered and said to her, "If you knew the gift of God, and who it is who says to you, 'Give me a drink', you would have asked him, and he would have given you living water."	The woman said to him, "I know that Messiah is coming, he who is called Christ; when that one comes, he will declare all things to us". Jesus said to her, "I who speak to you am he."

Third, the combination of water (4.13-14) and spirit (4.23-24) is elsewhere used by John in reference to a new creational experience (see especially the new birth in Jn 3.5 and the outpouring of the Spirit in Jn 7.38-39).[9] As I have already mentioned, the flowing waters in 4.13-14 may represent the eschatological motif of the restoration of the temple, in which God's river will flow to distribute life.[10] This idea fits well with Jesus's negative assessment of the present form of worship on "this mountain" and in "Jerusalem" (4.20-21), both of which clearly refer to the hand-made temples.

The above interconnections should direct the reader in treating the dialogue in John 4.7-26 as a whole. One cannot fully understand Jesus's reference to the spring of living water apart from his comments on the temple worship, and vice versa. Therefore, in my examination of the hour, I will consider Jn 4.7-26 to be the immediate context in which this hour appears and by which this hour should be interpreted.

III. *The Eschatological Use of Hour in John 4.21, 23*

The double reference to the hour in 4.21, 23 relates directly to the beginning of a new era in history, when God's worship will be transformed (4.21, 23). Scholars generally agree that this new era is an eschatological one.[11] The new type of worship

---

9. See especially the argument made by Wai Yee Ng, *Water Symbolism in John: An Eschatological Interpretation* (StudBL, 15; New York: P. Lang, 2001).

10. See the argument on pp. 84–90 in support of this understanding.

11. E.g. George R. Beasley-Murray, *John* (WBC, 36; Waco: Word Books, 1987), p. 61; Craig S. Keener, *The Gospel of John: A Commentary* (Peabody: Hendrickson, 2003), p. 617; Lindars, *John*, p. 188. See also Alan R. Kerr, *The Temple of Jesus' Body: The Temple Theme in the Gospel of John* (Sheffield: Sheffield Academic Press, 2002), p. 188; Paul M. Hoskins, *Jesus as the Fulfillment of the Temple in the Gospel of John* (Eugene: Wipf and Stock, 2006), p. 144. Carson characterizes the shift as a "salvation-historical turning point" (D. A. Carson, *The Gospel According To John* [PNTC; Grand Rapids: Eerdmans, 1991], p. 224); Aune views the worship in the as Spirit as "a proleptic experience of eschatological existence" (see David E. Aune, *The Cultic Setting of Realized Eschatology in Early Christianity* [NovTSsup, 28;

is clearly contrasted to the traditional, cultic form of worship. Raymond Brown speaks about a replacement of the temple:

> Jesus is speaking of the eschatological replacement of temporal institutions like the Temple . . . In ii 21 it was Jesus himself who was to take the place of the Temple, and here it is the Spirit given by Jesus that is to animate the worship that replaces worship at the Temple.[12]

The transformed worship will not take place in hand-made temples, nor will it be confined by locality, but it will be done "in Spirit and truth" (4.23). A transformation of worship, however, requires the transformation of the temple itself, since Jesus's words about worshiping "in Spirit and truth" imply universal access to God's presence.

In order to gain a better understanding of the hour, I first examine the hour in conjunction to the eschatological transformation of the temple. Then I examine the possibility for this hour to refer to Daniel. The purpose is to find out whether this hour, within this context and the context of the whole gospel, recounts the Danielic hour.

a. *The Hour in Relation to the New Temple*

The hour (ὥρα) in Jn 4.21, 23 should not be viewed solely in connection to a transformed worship. Within his discussion with the Samaritan woman (4.7-26), Jesus is probably making a single argument, employing new creational temple language throughout. The new era represented by the term "hour" should also involve the giving of the "living water" with its subsequent result of "eternal life" (4.10, 14). A transformed worship cannot occur without the transforming power of the "living water."

La Potterie and Kerr have recognized the above hermeneutical link between the "Spirit and truth" in 4.23 and God's gift of "living water" in 4.10.[13] While they identify the Mosaic Law as the source of the living water, Kerr makes clear that the "living water" specifically refers to the Spirit. Other scholars have also argued that the flowing of the living water in Jn 4.10, 14 represents the Old Testament description of waters coming out of the temple, or even, possibly, relates to the garden-temple imagery. More specifically, in developing the temple Christology in the Fourth Gospel, Um has convincingly shown that the Edenic depictions in the Old Testament and Jewish literature closely associate life and water, so that water represents the source of life.[14]

Leiden: Brill, 1972], pp. 12–16); and VanGemeren has generally described the Spirit as the agent of restoration (VanGemeren, 'Restoration', pp. 81–102).

12. Brown, *Gospel According to John*, I, p. 180.

13. I. de la Potterie, *La vérité dans Saint Jean: Tome II* (AnBib, 74; Rome: Editrice Pontifico Istituto Biblico, 1999), pp. 684–87; Kerr, *Temple*, pp. 189–91.

14. Genesis 2.9 reads, "Now a river flowed out of Eden to water the garden; and from

The idea of water as a symbol for giving life is not unique to Jesus.[15] Rather, it appears elsewhere in the Old Testament and Jewish literature, in close association with the temple motif.[16] As a background to Jn 4.10-14, it has been generally acknowledged that the theme of *living water* derives from specific Old Testament texts that explicitly connect it to the temple.[17] The most relevant of these texts are Ezek. 47.1-12; Zech. 14.8; and Joel 3.18 [LXX; 4.18 in MT], all of which reflect images of the eschatological restoration. Ezekiel, in describing the new temple, specifically states:

> Then he brought me back to the door of the house; and behold, water was flowing from under the threshold of the house toward the east, for the house faced east. And the water was flowing down from under, from the right side of the house, from south of the altar . . . And it shall come to pass, that every animal of living and moving creatures, all on which the river shall come,

there it divided and became four rivers." Notice how the river was "to water" all the trees, including the tree of life in 2.9. Compare this river with the river in Ps. 46.4; 65.9. Um also cites *2 En.* 8; *Apoc. Abr.* 21; 1QH XVI, 4-26; *Jos. Asen.* 2.17-20 (Um, *Temple*, pp. 27–55).

15. Several scholars have seen the plausibility of water symbolizing life. For example, Ng, *Water*; Brown, *Gospel According to John*, I, p. 179; Schnackenburg, *John*, p. 427; Keener, *John*, pp. 604–605; Goppelt, 'ὕδωρ', *TDNT* 8:314–33. In defense of the water symbolizing life (eternal life), especially as it appears in the Old Testament prophetic texts, see Um, *Temple*, pp. 20–67; Beale, *Temple*, pp. 196–97; John A. Dennis, *Jesus' Death and the Gathering of True Israel* (Tübingen: Mohr Siebeck, 2006), pp. 177–78; and also Carson, *John*, pp. 218–19; and Andreas J. Köstenberger, *John* (BECNT; Grand Rapids: Baker Academic, 2004), p. 150.

16. Several scholars have argued that the idea of water in Jn 4.10, 14 represents the notion of revelation (Torah/wisdom). However, these scholars mostly base their arguments on the later rabbinic sources, and not on the Old Testament or earlier Jewish texts. Representatives of this view are Jones, *Water*; Birger Olsson, *Structure and Meaning in the Fourth Gospel: A Text-Linguistic Analysis of John 2.1-11 and 4.1-42* (Lund: CWK Gleerup, 1974), p. 214; H. Odeberg, *The Fourth Gospel* (Amsterdam: B. R. Grüner, 1974), pp. 150–68; S. Pancaro, *The Law in the Fourth Gospel: The Torah and The Gospel, Moses and Jesus, Judaism and Christianity According to John* (NovTSup, 42; Leiden: Brill, 1975), pp. 473–77; and Gail R. O'Day, *Revelation in the Fourth Gospel: Narrative Mode and Theological Claim* (Philadelphia: Fortress, 1986). While it may be true that Jesus's words portray a midrashic effort to combine two motifs in one (water as both life and revelation), the idea of water as life seems to prevail in the Fourth Gospel (especially Jn 3.5; 4.14; 7.37-39). See Um for the multiple texts in the Old Testament and early Jewish literature that attest to the use of "water" as a symbol leading to life (Um, *Temple*, pp. 133–67). A representative sample of the texts he mentions are Isa. 12.3; 26.19; 35.5-7; 41.17-19; 58.11; Ezek. 47.1-12; Joel 3.18; Zech. 8.12; 14.8 and *2 En.* 8.2; *Apoc. Ab.* 21.6; *Jos. Asen.* 2.20; 1QH XVI, 4-21.

17. See Leon Morris, *The Gospel According to John* (Grand Rapids: Eerdmans, 1995), p. 231; Carson, *John*, pp. 218–19; Beale, *Temple*, p. 196; Andreas J. Köstenberger, 'John', in G. K. Beale and D. A. Carson (eds), *Commentary on the New Testament Use of the Old Testament* (Grand Rapids: Baker, 2007), pp. 415–512 (438).

shall live: and there shall be there very many fish; for this water shall go
thither, and it shall heal them, and they shall live: everything on which the
river shall come shall live . . . And on the banks, on both sides of the river,
there will grow all kinds of trees for food. Their leaves will not wither, nor
their fruit fail, but they will bear fresh fruit every month, because the water
for them flows from the sanctuary. Their fruit will be for food, and their
leaves for healing.

(Ezek. 47.1, 9, 12; emphasis mine)

While the reference in Ezekiel may be the strongest,[18] Zech. 14.8 also states that
"living waters will flow out of Jerusalem," and Joel 3.18 confirms, "A spring will go
out from the house of the Lord." We notice especially how the latter phrase occurs
"in that day" (Joel 3.18) and in association to "that time" in Joel 3.1 (LXX, 4.1 in
MT).[19] These Old Testament references attest to the idea of water flowing from the
end-time temple, an idea that is probably present in Jn 4.10, 14, in connection to
the coming hour. The presence of an Old Testament background to the theme of
water in John is also evident from Jesus's own words in 7.38, where he introduces
the idea of "streams of living water" with the phrase, "as the scripture has said."
    The image of water as a life-giving symbol flowing from the temple is not foreign
to the New Testament, but is also depicted in the book of Revelation (Rev. 7.15, 17;
21.6; 22.1).[20] One may even argue that the hour in John 4 involves the inauguration
of a new temple the culmination of which is described in the book of Revelation.
As Carson phrases it,

> The Apocalypse concludes with a vision of the consummated kingdom, the
> new Jerusalem, in which there is no temple to be found, "because the Lord
> God Almighty and the Lamb are its temple" (Rev. 21.22). The fulfillment of
> that vision has not yet arrived in its fullness. Even so, Jesus insists, through
> his own mission the hour was dawning when the principal ingredients of that
> vision would be set in operation, a foretaste of the consummation to come.[21]

In Revelation 7, the picture concerns the "springs of the water of life" (7.17) that
apparently exists in the temple (ἐν τῷ ναῷ in 7.15) and will be enjoyed as an
eschatological blessing. In 21.6, the "alpha and omega" says that he will give "to
the one who thirsts from the spring of the water of life without cost" (ἐγὼ τῷ διψῶ
ντι δώσω ἐκ τῆς πηγῆς τοῦ ὕδατος τῆς ζωῆς δωρεάν); later, this water appears to

---

18. Ezekiel 47.1-12 describes the new temple in Jerusalem by alluding to the Garden of
Eden and says, "water was flowing from under the threshold of the house toward the east"
(47.1).

19. See the discussion on these texts in OT chapter, pp. 17–19.

20. See the comments in G. K. Beale, *The Book of Revelation: A Commentary on the
Greek Text* (NIGTC; Grand Rapids: Eerdmans, 1999), pp. 440–41.

21. Carson, *John*, p. 226.

be identified with the river that flows from the throne of God (22.1), which exists in the midst of the eschatological garden-temple of Rev. 21.10–22.5. The language used in these verses (quite similar to Jn 4.14) shows that the image of water flowing from a spring (as the gift of life) has been used elsewhere in the New Testament in relation to God's temple, representing an eschatological reality.

This understanding of water language in John 4 corresponds well with the idea of Jesus being the new temple as depicted in other parts of the gospel.[22] Jesus's words after the episode of the cleansing of the temple (2.13-22) make it clear — at least to John after the resurrection — that Jesus's body will constitute the new temple of God.[23] The reference to Jesus's resurrection from the dead in 2.21-22 is clearly connected to the notion of the temple. The verb ἐγείρω appears for the first time in this passage. Later, it will be used in reference to the resurrected life that both the Father and the Son give (Jn 5.21), to the resurrection of Lazarus (Jn 12.1, 9, 17), and to Jesus's resurrection (Jn 21.14).[24]

Precisely because Jesus is the temple he can also be the source of water and eternal life (Jn 4.14; cf. Jn 5.21, 24-29; 7.37-39). Jesus's words in 4.10 seem to underscore this thought, that is, to relate the symbol of water to Jesus's identity: "If you knew the gift of God,[25] *and who it is who says to you*, 'Give me a drink', you would have asked him, and he would have given you living water" (emphasis mine). It is through Jesus — the new temple — that one can receive water and quench her/his thirst. Again, in 4.14, Jesus associates the symbol of water with the notion of eternal life, both of which have their source in Jesus: "whoever drinks of the water that I will give him shall never thirst; but the water that I will give him will become in him a well of water springing up to eternal life."[26] With Jesus being the

22. The argument has repeatedly been made that Jesus is depicted as the new temple in the Gospel of John. Apart from Um, *Temple*; and Beale, *Temple*; see Kerr, *Temple*; Hoskins, *Temple*. See also U. Busse, 'Die Tempelmetaphorik als ein Beispiel von implizitem recurs auf die biblische Tradition im Johannesevangelium', in C. M. Tuckett (ed.), *The Scriptures in the Gospels* (BETL, 131; Leuven: Leuven University Press, 1997), pp. 395–428; and Sandra M. Schneiders, 'The raising of the new temple: John 20.19-23 and Johannine ecclesiology', *NTS* 52 (2006), pp. 337–55.

23. Before this, in Jn 1.14, the Word becomes flesh and he tabernacles among us (καὶ ἐσκήνωσεν ἐν ἡμῖν). This is probably an allusion to Ezek. 37.27, where God promises that he will tabernacle among his people (καὶ ἔσται ἡ κατασκήνωσίς μου ἐν αὐτοῖς) as part of the promises of restoration. Later on, in Jn 1.51, Jesus is portrayed as the one on whom the angels of God are "ascending and descending on the Son of Man" (this saying introduces a combined allusion to Gen. 28.12 and Dan. 7.13). The latter image points to the idea of Jesus being the locus of God's presence and revelation, that is, the new temple of God.

24. In all the above references, the word νεκρός accompanies the verb, which suggests that John has in mind Isa. 26.19.

25. The "gift of God" most likely refers to God's Old Testament promise of the Spirit, which also represents life (cf. Ezek. 37.5-6, 9-10, 14).

26. Interestingly, the "well of water springing to eternal life" in Jn 4.14 resides in the believer, which could indicate that the believer will also become a temple of God.

new temple out of which springs the "living water," it is not surprising to see John, in the broader context of the gospel, identifying the coming hour (of transformed worship) with Jesus's own hour of death and resurrection (Jn 4.2; 7.30; 8.20; 13.1); this death and resurrection inaugurates the new temple (2.21-22). In fact, Jesus's death is directly identified with "destroying" Israel's temple (Jn 2.19), and his resurrection is viewed as rebuilding the new temple (Jn 2.19-22).

In his conversation with the Samaritan woman, Jesus combines the above emphasis on the new temple with the idea of universal access to God. First, Jesus offers the living water to a Samaritan woman (non-Jewish), and second, the worship of the Father is de-localized (or even de-nationalized). The nullification of ethnic distinctions gives access to the presence of God (the temple) to all people. It may not be a coincidence that in Jn 12.20 the Greeks who come to worship (ἵνα προσκυνήσωσιν) at the feast eventually end up seeing Jesus.[27] This last element of universality resembles the expansion of the temple in the OT to include all peoples.[28]

Jesus's reference to Israel's temple being destroyed and interrupted of its worship has precedent in Daniel, where the end-time hour involves the destruction of the sanctuary and the cessation of sacrifices (Dan. 8.12-13; cf. Dan. 9.26-27; 12.11). Although this will be done by God's adversary, it will also function as God's act of wrath upon the people's disobedience, indicating the "end" of this age (Dan. 8.19) and the inauguration of a new age to come (Dan. 12.2). God will also use this period of destruction of the traditional cultic system to refine his people (Dan. 12.10) and to transform their existence (Dan. 12.2-3). In fact, the final outcome of the eschatological battle as it is described in the vision of Daniel 7 includes the universal worship of all peoples. When the Son of Man appears to receive the kingdom in Dan. 7.13-14, then "all the peoples, nations and languages will serve (λατρεύω) him" (7.14).[29] Within the broader context of the book of Daniel, this will occur at the eschatological hour of God's appearance to judge and to vindicate (Dan. 12.1-3).

The Johannine synthesis of water, worship, messianic agent, and eschatological hour occurs in the Jewish tradition in *1 En.* 48.1-5 (cf. also 1QS IV, 21 in context[30]),

---

27. The verb προσκυνέω appears 11 times in the Fourth Gospel: 9 times in John 4, once in 9.38 and once in 12.20. Notice that Jesus's reply to the request is: "The hour has come for the Son of Man to be glorified" (12.23). See my comments on pp. 136–37 on the use of hour in John 12.

28. E.g. Isa. 54.2-3; Jer. 3.16-18. Even if the "Greeks" are only Jews from the diaspora, they probably represent in some way the areas from which they come.

29. If not synonymous, the verbs λατρεύω and προσκυνέω in Daniel have parallel meanings. See their use in Dan. 3.12, 14, 18, and especially in Dan. 3.95 (μὴ λατρεύσωσι μηδὲ προσκυνήσωσι) and 6.27 (προσκυνοῦντες καὶ λατρεύοντες τῷ θεῷ). The phrase in Dan. 7.14 probably alludes to Dan. 3.7 for contrast. After the vision in ch. 2, the idea of worship becomes prominent in Daniel 3, where the verb προσκυνέω appears 11 times in relation to worshiping the golden image of Nebuchadnezzar. Daniel 3.7 states that "all the peoples, nations and languages fell down and worshiped (προσκυνέω) the golden image."

30. 1QS IV, 21 mentions the sprinkling of water in close association to an eschatological hour. The immediate context describes the eschatological battle between the sons of truth

which has borrowed the concept of the end-time hour from Daniel.[31] In *1 En.* 48.1-5, the idea of quenching one's thirst as the ultimate realization of worship is linked to the arriving of the Son of Man in the presence of the Ancient of Days (cf. Dan. 7.13-14) at an eschatological hour:

> Furthermore, in that place I saw the fountain of righteousness, which does not become depleted and is surrounded completely by numerous fountains of wisdom. All the thirsty ones drink (of the water) and become filled with wisdom. Then their dwelling places become with the holy, righteous, and elect ones. At that hour, that Son of Man was given a name, in the presence of the Lord of the Spirits, the Ancient of Time; even before the creation of the sun and the moon, before the creation of the stars, he was given a name in the presence of the Lord of the Spirits. He will become a staff for the righteous ones in order that they may lean on him and not fall. He is the light of the gentiles and he will become the hope of those who are sick in their hearts. All those who dwell upon the earth shall fall and worship before him; they shall glorify, bless, and sing the name of the Lord of the Spirits.
>
> (*1 En.* 48.1-5; emphasis mine)

Clearly, the above text has been influenced by Dan. 7.13-14.[32] The broader context of this passage mentions the final judgment and the opening of the books (47.3; 48.8-10), the Ancient of Days sitting on his throne (46.1; 47.3), the coming of the Son of Man to vindicate God's people (46.1-5; 48.2, 6, 10), and the final resurrection (51.1). One may safely suggest that *1 Enoch* 46–48 expands on the end-time era as it is found in Daniel, and specifically alludes to the *time* or *hour* of Dan. 12.1.[33] At this hour the people will quench their thirst and worship God. It is interesting that the above text views "*all* the thirsty ones" to be drinking and "*all* those who dwell upon the earth" to be worshiping, which parallels the universal element of worship in Dan. 7.14 and Jn 4.21, 23 (notice also the fact that the Son of Man is "a light to the gentiles").

The combined existence of these themes in the Jewish tradition indicates that the

and sons of deceit (light and darkness), the final outcome of which has been determined by God. More specifically, part of this outcome will be that God "will sprinkle over him [man] the spirit of truth like purifying water" (1QS IV, 21). The particular event will occur at the "last time" (1QS IV, 17), "the time appointed for the judgement decided" (1QS IV, 20), or "the appointed end and the new creation" (1QS IV, 25). At several points, the text alludes to the Danielic division between the eternal life and eternal damnation (cf. Dan. 12.1-2), on which see the discussion in my chapter on the Jewish Literature.

31. See the relevant comments on these texts on pp. 55–57, 71–74.

32. It has also been influenced by Isa. 49.6, 10: "I will make you as a light for the nations, that my salvation may reach to the end of the earth . . . They will not hunger or thirst, nor will the scorching heat or sun strike them down; For he who has compassion on them will lead them and will guide them to springs of water."

33. See my comments on *1 Enoch* 46–48 on pp. 53–57.

eschatological hour had been linked to the outpouring of the Spirit, the coming of the Son of Man, and the time for universal worship even before the writing of the Fourth Gospel. These were further understood to be connected with the Danielic prophecies about a final judgment and resurrection. John's use of hour as the time of fulfillment of the eschatological expectations could well have in mind the Jewish and Danielic references to a similar eschatological hour.

In brief, I have argued that the hour in John 4.21, 23 relates both to the notion of worship (4.21-24) and the notion of water that gives life (4.10, 14). These two ideas constitute a single thematic unit, since they both relate to the establishment of the new, eschatological, temple of God. The water being connected to the idea of the new temple is significant for viewing this water in relation to the abolition of the traditional temple-worship in Jn 4.21 and the introduction of the proper worship in Jn 4.23-24. In other words, the coming of the eschatological hour in Jn 4.21, 23, does not merely refer to the abrogation of the traditional mode of worship, but to the establishment of the new order of worship, the erection of the new temple.

The fact that the thematic elements of water, temple-worship (including the destruction of the temple and interruption of its worship), Messiah, and hour, are not absent from the Jewish tradition or from Daniel indicates that Jesus's words are in agreement with, if not influenced by, the apocalyptic traditions of the time. While at this point, a specific allusion to the Danielic hour in John 4 is not discernable, John uses the notion of hour in an eschatological sense and does so in relation to themes that parallel the broader Jewish apocalyptic thought, including Daniel. In my opinion, it is possible even within the context of John 4 to show that John had in mind the Danielic hour (Dan. 12.1).

b. *Hints for a Danielic Hour in John 4.21, 23*

Initially, one should realize that in the OT the word ὥρα occurs with an eschatological sense only in the book of Daniel. The uniqueness of the eschatological ὥρα in Daniel narrows down considerably the options for a possible background.

Moreover, within the context — or timeframe — of this eschatological hour in Jn 4.21, 23, Jesus mentions that the kind of water he gives will become in the believer "a well of water springing up to eternal life (εἰς ζωὴν αἰώνιον)" (4.14).[34] The exact phrase "unto eternal life" (εἰς ζωὴν αἰώνιον) is probably taken from Dan. 12.2 (εἰς ζωὴν αἰώνιον), which, as with hour, is the only place in the Hebrew and Greek Bible (OG and TH) that this phrase is to be found.[35] There, Daniel speaks of a literal

---

34. The phrase "eternal life" is central to the whole gospel, since John reiterates the idea in Jn 3.16, 36; 5.24; 6.40, 47, 54 (cf. 4.14; 6.27; 10.28; 12.25; 17.2-3).

35. While not all of the Johannine instances of "eternal life" intentionally allude to Daniel, all of them carry the resurrection idea as part of their meaning. This is probably because the phrase was initially used by Daniel, and it has thus acquired significance from its Danielic context. However, whenever this phrase is used in association with other Danielic words or themes, the probability exists for John to be intentionally alluding to the resurrected life in Dan. 12.2. Note the use of "eternal life" in 2 Macc. 7.9 and *Pss. Sol.* 3.12.

resurrection from the dead, with some going to eternal life and others to eternal contempt. For John, also, *eternal life* constitutes the new creational life associated with the notions of light (new creation) and birth (resurrected new life). Indeed, the notion of *eternal* life is not solely linked to an indefinite period of time, but involves the quality of life at hand. This latter meaning has probably been acquired due to the Danielic use of the phrase within the context of the final resurrection.

The combined use of *hour* and *eternal life* in John 4, in relation to the eschato-logical existence of the new temple and the idea of Jesus as the coming Messiah (4.25-26), may point to the intentional use of hour to refer to the new (eschatolo-gical) era prophesied by Daniel. The combination of *hour* and *eternal life* appears in the OT only in Dan. 12.1-2, and this same combination also appears in Jn 5.24-25; 12.23, 25; and 17.1-2, all of which relate to a Danielic background.[36] If one assumes that John has borrowed the later idea, *eternal life*, from Daniel,[37] then his use of the eschatological hour in the same context should alert one to a possible connection.

There is a further indication that the combined use of *eternal life* and *hour* in John 4 introduce the new era of resurrected life. The two themes of *water* (welling up to eternal life in 4.14) and *Spirit* (representing the mode of worship in the coming hour in 4.21-24) appear elsewhere in the gospel in close relation to new creational life.[38] One occurrence would be that in Jn 3.5, where Jesus speaks about the neces-sity of the new birth being through "water and Spirit" (ἐξ ὕδατος καὶ πνεύματος).[39] Another occurrence would be that in Jn 7.37-39, where in similar language to 4.14,

36. Cf. also 1 Jn 2.18, 25. See my comments on Jn 5.24-25; 12.23, 25; and 17.1-2, on pp. 108–15, 130–31 and 157–58 respectively.

37. In fact, Jesus viewed his entire conversation with the Samaritan woman under the perception of him giving her eternal life. This is implied in Jn 4.34, 36, where Jesus com-ments on his conversation with the woman in terms of doing "the will of him who sent me" (τὸ θέλημα τοῦ πέμψαντός με in 4.34) and "gathering fruit for eternal life" (εἰς ζωὴν αἰώνιον in 4.36). Interestingly, the former phrase (τὸ θέλημα τοῦ πέμψαντός με) appears in the exact form in three other places in John: The first instance is in John 5.30, where the work there specifically refers to the Danielic resurrection as it is alluded to in 5.28-29 (notice also the use of the eschatological hour in 5.28). The other two instances are in John 6.38-40, where Jesus explicitly relates the will of his Father with the notions of resurrection and "eternal life": "For this is the will of my Father, that everyone who looks on the Son and believes in him will have eternal life (ζωὴν αἰώνιον), and I myself will raise him up on the last day" (6.40). According to the above interpretative connections, Jesus viewed his conversation with the Samaritan woman through the lenses of the Danielic final resurrection and "eternal life." Within this eschatological framework, the references to the eschatological hour seem appropriate.

38. See the discussion in Gary T. Manning, Jr., *Echoes of a Prophet: The Use of Ezekiel in the Gospel of John and in Literature of the Second Temple Period* (JSNTSup, 270; New York: T&T Clark International, 2004), pp. 172–97.

39. Manning has argued for an OT background to Ezek. 36.25-27 (Manning, *Prophet*, pp. 186–89). Note that the context of Ezekiel is one of resurrection (Ezek. 37.1-14). See also Linda Belleville, 'Born of Water and Spirit: John 3.5', *TJ* 1 (1980), pp. 125–41.

Jesus speaks about water and the quenching of thirst in relation to the outpouring of the Spirit: "If anyone is thirsty, let him come to me and drink. He who believes in me, as the scripture said, 'From his innermost being will flow rivers of living water.'" The flowing of the *living* water refers to the impartation of life by the Spirit. John's immediate comments make plain the connection with the Spirit: "this he spoke of the Spirit, whom those who believed in him were to receive; for the Spirit was not yet given, because Jesus was not yet glorified" (7.39).[40] In commenting on Jn 4.10, Köstenberger makes a similar point: "In John's Gospel Jesus is identified explicitly with the Creator and Life-giver (5.26), and he dispenses the gift of 'living water', later unveiled as the Holy Spirit (7.37-39)."[41]

It has been argued that the reference to the Spirit in the phrase "in Spirit and Truth" in Jn 4.23 assumes the creative activity of this Spirit to beget from above (3.5),[42] thereby pointing to the new creational activity of God in the hour to come.[43] The relation of these concepts to God's creational activity is not foreign to the idea of temple in John, since Jesus has already defined the new temple in terms of resurrection from the dead (2.19-22).

One should not be surprised, then, to see how John has carefully chosen identical wording in describing the hour of the new temple-worship in John 4 and the hour of the resurrection from the dead in John 5. In both cases, the phrases "an hour is coming and now is" and "an hour is coming" are used in a similar manner, almost as if the act of true worship parallels the act of "hearing" (and rising from the dead):

Jn 4.21, 23	*Jn 5.25, 28*
ἔρχεται ὥρα καὶ νῦν ἐστιν, ὅτε . . . προσκυνήσουσιν (4.23)	ἔρχεται ὥρα καὶ νῦν ἐστιν ὅτε . . . ἀκούσουσιν (5.25)
ἔρχεται ὥρα ὅτε . . . προσκυνήσετε (4.21)	ἔρχεται ὥρα ἐν ᾗ . . . ἀκούσουσιν (5.28)

The parallels in the chart suggest that John does not have two distinct hours in mind, but that they are one and the same, at which the establishment of the new temple-worship *and* the resurrection will take place. The fact that this hour alludes to the eschatological hour in Dan. 12.1 will wait to be shown in my next chapter, where John becomes much more explicit concerning the Old Testament background of this eschatological moment in Jn 5.25, 28.

---

40. The idea that the Spirit had not yet come because Jesus was not yet glorified corresponds well with the reference to Jesus's hour a few verses earlier, where it is said that "his hour had not yet come" (7.30). The hour is directly connected to the glorification of Jesus in Jn 12.23, 27-28 and 17.1.

41. Köstenberger, 'John', p. 438.

42. See Brown, *Gospel According to John*, I, p. 180.

43. There is little doubt that the outpouring of the Spirit exists in the Old Testament as a promise for the eschaton ("last days").

IV. *Conclusion*

In this chapter, I have examined the use of hour in Jn 4.21, 23, and its immediate connection to the eschatological theme of the new temple. Since scholars have already argued that the imagery of the water in 4.10, 14 represents the Old Testament and Jewish notion of a river flowing out from the new eschatological temple, I have treated the two main themes of our passage, water and worship, as referring to the same idea of the establishment of the new temple. This interpretation is consistent with the fact that Jesus is portrayed as the new temple elsewhere in the Gospel of John (Jn 1.14, 51; 2.19-22) and explains why Jesus is portrayed as the source of the water of eternal life in Jn 4.10, 14.

Moreover, the thematic emphasis of our passage is consistent with other Jewish apocalyptic texts, and the book of Daniel, contexts that employ the hour as the eschatological moment of fulfillment. These parallels point to a possible influence in the use of language or the combined use of themes in close proximity in John 4. Certainly, within the specific Jewish worldview, the combined presence of such words and themes in John 4 qualifies the hour as an eschatological moment of fulfillment.

Furthermore, one could even argue for a possible connection with Daniel from the specific use of *eternal life* (4.14), a phrase that in the Greek or Hebrew Old Testament only occurs in Dan. 12.2. If one also adds the fact that an eschatological hour does not occur anywhere else in the Old Testament except in the book of Daniel, one may begin to think that John — or Jesus — could possibly have borrowed the concept of the eschatological hour from Daniel. This suggestion is consistent with the Johannine emphasis on resurrection and the identical parallels of the hour expressions in Jn 4.21, 23 with those found in Jn 5.25, 28. Of course, John has not yet fully revealed the identity of the eschatological hour; he has only prepared the reader by qualifying this hour eschatologically and by connecting it with themes that echo eschatological Old Testament expectations similar to those found in the book of Daniel. The conclusion that a Danielic background stands behind the hour in John 4 is pointed to further from an analysis of the use of hour in Jn 5.25, 28, to which I now turn.

THE OT BACKGROUND OF THE
ESCHATOLOGICAL HOUR IN JOHN 5.25, 28

I. *Introduction*

In Jn 5.19-30, Jesus unfolds several key themes that add significantly to the emphasis of the whole book. Jesus's response to the Jews provides us several clues regarding his own identity, such as the origin of his deeds, his relationship to the Father, his relationship to OT prophecies, the ability to give life, and the authority to judge. In addition, Jesus identifies himself as both the Son of Man and the Son of God, and he speaks about the Father as the one who has sent him. Most of these themes appear throughout John's gospel and are characteristically Johannine. It is not insignificant that the hour appears precisely among these themes. In the discussion that follows, my argument is that the Johannine hour in John 5.19-30 has sufficient common features with the Danielic hour to establish the probability of an allusion to Dan. 12.1.

II. *The Preceding Context: John 4.43–5.18*

The pericope of Jn 5.19-30 is part of a larger literary unit, namely Jn 4.43–5.47, which constitutes its immediate context. The unit begins with the healing of the official's son and is followed by the healing of the invalid man by the pool of Bethesda.[1]

---

1.   Most contemporary scholars see the healing story in 4.43-54 as an *inclusio* to the miracle in Cana in 2.1-11. If this is the case, the healing story in 4.43-54 has little connection — or no connection — to the healing story in 5.1-16, the latter of which would then begin a new literary unit (e.g. A. J. Köstenberger, *John* [BECNT; Grand Rapids: Baker Academic, 2004], p. 166; D. A. Carson, *The Gospel According To John* [PNTC; Grand Rapids: Eerdmans, 1991], pp. 233–40; C. S. Keener, *The Gospel of John: A Commentary* [2 Vols; Peabody: Hendrickson Publishers, 2003], pp. 628–34; Andrew T. Lincoln, *The Gospel According to Saint John* [BNTC; London: Continuum, 2005], p. 183; John Ashton, *Understanding the Fourth Gospel* [Oxford: Oxford University Press, 1991], p. 291). However, I agree with Dodd's view that argues for the literary unity of the two healing stories and the introductory function of these stories to Jesus's discourse in 5.19-47 (C. H. Dodd, *The Interpretation of the Fourth Gospel* [Cambridge: Cambridge University Press, 1958], pp. 318–20).

The two stories serve as an introduction to Jesus's discourse in Jn 5.19-47, in which he concentrates on the identity of the Son. Therefore, the stories should function as a starting point for revealing Jesus's identity. Common to both stories is the recounting of a healing miracle.

In the former incident, the official's son who is mortally ill (Jn 4.47, 49) is healed through Jesus's words. The emphasis in this healing is placed on two elements. First, the passage underscores Jesus's words: "Your son will live." This phrase is repeated three times in the narrative (Jn 4.50, 51, 53). Second, the passage emphasizes the precise hour that the son was healed; the son was healed at the same hour ([ἐν] ἐκείνῃ τῇ ὥρᾳ) that Jesus spoke the words. The word "hour" is also repeated three times in the same narrative (Jn 4.52-53). It is likely that John here introduces Jesus's authority to give life in connection to the theme of hour in prospect of 5.25, 28-29, where the Son's voice effects the resurrection from the dead in the hour to come. Although the reference to the hour in 4.52-53 and also the resurrection of the official's son are not eschatological in any direct sense, they might anticipate, nevertheless, the hour and the resurrection in 5.25, 28-29.

In the latter incident, the invalid man lying next to the pool of Bethesda is again healed by Jesus's words. Jesus says to this man: "Stand up (ἔγειρε), pick up your mat and walk," and the man is immediately healed (Jn 5.8-9). The verb ἐγείρω has already been used three times in reference to Jesus's resurrection (Jn 2.19-22), and it is later used metaphorically to refer to the resurrection of Lazarus (Jn 12.1, 9, 17) and of Jesus (Jn 21.14). The verb here may also mean "to stand up," as it is also used in Jn 7.52; 11.29; and 13.4. However, its close association with Jn 5.21 may indicate that John uses the word with a double reference in mind, something that is not uncommon in John. The emphasis in this story is the fact that Jesus worked a miracle on the Sabbath. In John's gospel, Jesus's persecution by the Jews begins at this point, in Jn 5.16, and it is due to Jesus's act of healing on the Sabbath day, since no person had the authority to work on the Sabbath except God. Jesus seizes this opportunity to expound on his identity and authority in view of his relationship to the Father.

While the two stories (4.43-54 and 5.1-16) serve as an introduction to Jesus's exposition on his identity and mission in 5.19-47, the second story introduces the following question to the reader: What authority gives Jesus the right to work on a Sabbath? It is precisely to this issue that Jesus responds in John 5.17, by saying, "My Father is still working, and I also am working." An editorial comment explains that Jesus's response gave further ground for persecution, since he was claiming God to be his own Father and thus making himself equal to God (Jn 5.18).[2] How did Jesus make himself to be equal to God? Morris argues that Jesus claimed God

---

2. For an analysis of the juridical nature of the scene, see Martin Asiedu-Peprah, *Johannine Sabbath Conflicts as Juridical Controversy* (WUNT, 132; Tübingen: Mohr [Siebeck], 2001). Also, for an examination of the phrase "equal to God," see Wayne A. Meeks, 'Equal to God', in Robert T. Fortna and Beverly R. Gaventa (eds), *The Conversation Continues: Studies in Paul and John* (Nashville: Abingdon, 1990), pp. 309–21.

to be his own Father "in a special sense,"[3] and this was precisely what prompted the conclusion of equality with God. Had Jesus claimed God to be the Father of all, Jesus's claim would not have caused any suspicion. But Jesus claimed God to be *his own* Father in a particular way, and this relationship placed him in a privileged position with respect to God.[4]

As true as this understanding may be, Jesus asserts another thing: that he works *along with* God towards the same goal,[5] thus having similar prerogatives, such as the right to work on the Sabbath.[6] It is not incidental to the narrative that Jesus performs this miracle on a Sabbath rather than any other day. The Sabbath miracle is significant to the rest of Jesus's exposition, for by performing the miracle on a Sabbath Jesus makes the following twofold claim: 1) My work is divinely authorized, since God alone has authority over the Sabbath; and 2) My work is identified with God's salvific work, since God, within the seventh-day rest, is working toward the restoration of humanity.[7] Jesus intentionally heals on a Sabbath because his work is divinely authorized and also is identified with God's salvific work.[8]

---

3.   L. Morris, *The Gospel According to John* (Grand Rapids: Eerdmans, 1995), pp. 274–75.

4.   Hunter argues that the saying "my Father and I" seemed a rebellious statement in the ears of the Jews, making Jesus equal to the Father. However, Jesus's reply intends to show that he is not rebellious, but obedient (A. M. Hunter, *The Gospel According to John* [Cambridge: Cambridge University Press, 1965], p. 57).

5.   However, the unity that Jesus claims to have with the Father is ontological, as well as functional. Jesus's argument is not merely a functional one, namely about what he does: "I do what the Father does" (cf. 5.19); rather, Jesus's argument is primarily an ontological one, namely about who he is: "I am one with the Father." As Ridderbos says, "it is the grand goal of the Fourth Gospel to trace the miracle of Jesus's work to the miracle of his person and to bring out that *because* he is the Christ, the Son of God, he gives life to everyone who believes in him" (H. Ridderbos, *The Gospel of John: A Theological Commentary* [Grand Rapids: Eerdmans, 1997], p. 195).

6.   For Jews, work on the Sabbath was a sole prerogative of God, and no one was thought to be equal to God in this regard (Exod. 15.11; Isa. 46.5; Ps. 89.8); see Raymond E. Brown, *The Gospel According to John* (AB, 29; New York: Doubleday, 1966), pp. 216–17.

7.   Indeed, the idea of God being at work, although apparently in contrast with the seventh day of rest (Gen. 2.3; Exod. 20.11), is attested elsewhere in the OT (Brown, *Gospel According to John*, I, p. 217; Dodd, *Interpretation*, pp. 320–24). Brown provides further evidence that the Jews linked God's work with the giving of life. He cites Rabbi Johanan (TalBab, *Taanith*, 2a), who refers to God's work in three areas: 1) providing rain (Deut. 28.12); 2) giving birth (Gen. 30.22); and 3) raising the dead (Ezek. 37.13) (Brown, *Gospel According to John*, I, p. 217). Moreover, in Ps. 43.2 (LXX; 44.1 in MT) and Ps. 73.12 (LXX; 74.12 in MT), God is said to have worked for Israel's past deliverance and continues to be working for Israel's future vindication. Also, in Job 33.29, God is working toward the giving of life and the saving from death (Job 33.23-28). The above traditions reinforce the view that Jesus's words in Jn 5.17 refer to God's prerogative of restoring his people in the eschaton, which includes the resurrection, as 5.19-30 makes clear.

8.   Hanson has proposed that the wording in Jn 5.17 may have been influenced by Hab. 1.5: "Look among the nations! Observe! Be astonished, wonder (θαυμάσατε θαυμάσια)!

III. *The Structure of John 5.19-30*

John 5.19-30 is structured in a chiastic pattern, which reveals the emphasis of the passage and clarifies Jesus's argument.[9] Vanhoye has well argued for the presence of a chiastic pattern in this passage. Brown also noticed the existence of duplications in this passage, but did not detect the rhetorical force of these duplications, especially as they relate chiastically to each other.[10]

A closer look at the parallels of the passage will reveal its chiastic structure. First, Jesus twice states his inability to act apart from the Father (5.19, 30). Then he underscores the result of astonishment (5.20, 28) at the fact that the Son gives life — just as the Father does — and has received authority to judge (5.21-22, 26-27). Finally, he repeats the idea of receiving life through the hearing of the Son's voice (5.24, 25); the hearing of the voice and the reception of life is also mentioned in Jn 5.28-29 as a parallel to the greater works that cause the people's amazement (5.20). Consequently, the chiastic pattern of John 5.19-30 has the following structure:

Because I am doing something (ἔργον ἐγὼ ἐργάζομαι) in your days, you would not believe if you were told." (Hanson, *Prophetic Gospel*, pp. 70–71). Notice the phrase "I am working" (κἀγὼ ἐργάζομαι) in Jn 5.17 and the use of "wonder" (θαυμάζω) in Jn 2.20, 28.

9. X. Leon-Dufour, 'Trois chiasmes johanniques', *NTS* 7 (1960–61), pp. 249–55 (253–55), and A. Vanhoye, 'La composition de Jn 5, 19-20', in André de Halleux (ed.), *Melanges B. Rigaux* (Gembloux, Belgium: Duculot, 1970), pp. 259–74, also see a chiasmus in the passage. The structure that I am defending agrees with that of Vanhoye.

10. Brown notes the following parallels between 5.19-25 and 5.26-30:

    21 // 26   The power of life shared by Father and Son.
    22 // 27   The power of judgemnt shared by Father and Son.
    20 // 28   The reaction of surprise.
    25 // 28   An hour is coming (and is) when the dead will hear the Son's voice.
    25 // 29   Those who have done right shall live.
    19 // 30   The Son does nothing by himself. He sees what he must do.

Brown concludes that the latter part of the passage is an editorial addition that reiterates much of the first part of the passage (Brown, *Gospel According to John*, I, p. 219).

John 5.19

  ἀμὴν ἀμὴν λέγω ὑμῖν,

(a) <u>οὐ δύναται ὁ υἱὸς ποιεῖν ἀφ' ἑαυτοῦ οὐδὲν</u>

 John 5.20

  ὁ πατὴρ . . . δείξει αὐτῷ ἔργα μείζονα τούτων

 (b) <u>ἵνα ὑμεῖς θαυμάζητε.</u>

  John 5.21-22

  (c) <u>ὥσπερ γὰρ ὁ πατὴρ ἐγείρει τοὺς νεκροὺς καὶ ζῳοποιεῖ,</u>
    <u>οὕτως καὶ ὁ υἱὸς οὓς θέλει ζῳοποιεῖ</u>
    οὐδὲ γὰρ ὁ πατὴρ κρίνει οὐδένα, ἀλλὰ τὴν <u>κρίσιν</u> πᾶσαν <u>δέδωκεν</u> τῷ
    υἱῷ

   John 5.24

    Ἀμὴν ἀμὴν λέγω ὑμῖν

   (d) ὅτι <u>ὁ τὸν λόγον μου ἀκούων</u> . . . <u>ἔχει ζωὴν</u> αἰώνιον καὶ . . .
     μεταβέβηκεν ἐκ τοῦ θανάτου <u>εἰς τὴν ζωήν.</u>

   John 5.25

    ἀμὴν ἀμὴν λέγω ὑμῖν
    ὅτι ὥρα ἔρχεται καὶ <u>νῦν</u> ἐστιν

   (d') ὅτε οἱ <u>νεκροὶ ἀκούσουσιν τῆς φωνῆς</u> τοῦ υἱοῦ τοῦ θεοῦ καὶ
     <u>οἱ ἀκούσαντες ζήσουσιν.</u>

  John 5.26-27

  (c') <u>ὥσπερ γὰρ ὁ πατὴρ ἔχει ζωὴν ἐν ἑαυτῷ,</u>
    <u>οὕτως καὶ τῷ υἱῷ ἔδωκεν ζωὴν ἔχειν ἐν ἑαυτῷ.</u>
    καὶ ἐξουσίαν <u>ἔδωκεν</u> αὐτῷ <u>κρίσιν</u> ποιεῖν ὅτι υἱὸς ἀνθρώπου ἐστίν

 John 5.28-29

 (b') <u>μὴ θαυμάζετε τοῦτο,</u>
   ὅτι ὥρα ἔρχεται
   ἐν ᾗ πάντες οἱ ἐν τοῖς μνημείοις ἀκούσουσιν τῆς φωνῆς αὐτοῦ
   καὶ ἐκπορεύσονται οἱ τὰ ἀγαθὰ ποιήσαντες <u>εἰς ἀνάστασιν ζωῆς</u>

John 5.30

(a') <u>οὐ δύναμαι ἐγὼ ποιεῖν ἀπ' ἐμαυτοῦ οὐδέν·</u>

An interpretative summary of the chiasm would appear as follows:

(a)   5.19 – The Son depends on the Father

   (b)   5.20 – The Son's greater works cause the amazement of the Jews

      (c)   5.21-22 – The Father has given life and judgment to the Son

         (d)   5.24 – The Son's voice causes resurrection

         (d˙)   5.25 – The Son's voice causes resurrection

      (c˙)   5.26-27 – The Father has given life and judgment to the Son

   (b˙)   5.28 – The Jews are instructed not to be amazed

(a˙)   5.30 – The Son depends on the Father

The above chiastic pattern becomes more discernable when one notices the striking linguistic parallelisms that John employs:

Jn 5.19	*Jn 5.30*
ὁ υἱὸς οὐ δύναται ποιεῖν ἀφ' ἑαυτου οὐδὲν	οὐ δύναμαι ἐγὼ ποιεῖν ἀπ' ἐμαυτοῦ οὐδέν
Jn 5.20	*Jn 5.28*
ἵνα ὑμεῖς θαυμάζητε	μὴ θαυμάζετε τοῦτο
Jn 5.21-22	*Jn 5.26-27*
ὥσπερ γὰρ ὁ πατὴρ ἐγείρει τοὺς νεκροὺς καὶ ζῳοποιεῖ, οὕτως καὶ ὁ υἱὸς οὓς θέλει ζῳοποιεῖ. τὴν κρίσιν πᾶσαν δέδωκεν τῷ υἱῷ	ὥσπερ γὰρ ὁ πατὴρ ἔχει ζωὴν ἐν ἑαυτῷ, οὕτως καὶ τῷ υἱῷ ἔδωκεν ζωὴν ἔχειν ἐν ἑαυτῷ. καὶ ἐξουσίαν ἔδωκεν αὐτῷ κρίσιν ποιεῖν
Jn 5.24	*Jn 5.25*
Ἀμὴν ἀμὴν λέγω ὑμῖν ὅτι ὁ τὸν λόγον μου ἀκούων καὶ πιστεύων τῷ πέμψαντί με ἔχει ζωὴν αἰώνιον	ἀμὴν ἀμὴν λέγω ὑμῖν ὅτι . . . οἱ νεκροὶ ἀκούσουσιν τῆς φωνῆς τοῦ υἱοῦ τοῦ θεοῦ καὶ οἱ ἀκούσαντες ζήσουσιν.

The emphasis in the above chiasmus is placed on the fact that the voice of the Son will cause resurrection from the dead (5.24-25). The following structural features make apparent that John's primary argument involves the Son's voice raising the dead: first, the idea of receiving life after hearing the Son's voice is placed at the center of the chiastic structure in Jn 5.24-25 (d–d'); also, the double repetition of the hearing of the voice in 5.24-25 is reinforced with the double use of the introductory ἀμὴν ἀμὴν λέγω ὑμῖν formula; the same idea of hearing the voice is further developed in 5.28-29 by alluding to the resurrection in Daniel:[11]

---

11. I will expound on this allusion later in discussion of vv. 28-29.

Jn 5.25	Jn 5.28-29
the hour is coming (ἔρχεται ὥρα) and now is, when the dead will hear the voice (ἀκούσουσιν τῆς φωνῆς) of the Son of God, and those who hear (οἱ ἀκούσαντες) will live (ζήσουσιν).	the hour is coming (ἔρχεται ὥρα), in which all who are in the tombs will hear His voice (ἀκούσουσιν τῆς φωνῆς αὐτοῦ) and will come forth; those who did the good deeds to a resurrection of life (ζωῆς)

Furthermore, the fact that the Son has authority both to give life and to judge, in Jn 5.21-22 and 5.26-27 (c–c'), is the very reason that the voice of the Son causes resurrection life in Jn 5.24 and 5.25; and finally, Jn 5.28 involves the only imperative in the passage (μὴ θαυμάζετε), which likely makes the hearing of the Son's voice in 5.28 the climax of Jesus's argument.

Granted that my suggested emphasis is correct, namely the Son's voice causing the resurrection from the dead, what does this emphasis signify? What is the explicit argument that Jesus makes in light of the above chiasmus and thematic emphasis? The significance of Jesus's statement that the Son's voice will cause the resurrection from the dead relates to the inaugurated fulfillment of the Danielic prophecies. The development of Jesus's reasoning may be formed in the following way:

Jn 5.19	The Son's work depends on what the Father does
Jn 5.20	The Son's work will cause the amazement of the people
Jn 5.21-22	The Son's work is to give life and to judge
Jn 5.24	Whoever hears *my* voice and believes in *my* Father has eternal life and escapes judgment
Jn 5.25	The hour for the dead to hear the voice of the Son and live is now beginning to be fulfilled
Jn 5.26-27	The Son of Man has received authority to give life and to judge
Jn 5.28-29	The hour for the dead to hear the voice of the Son and live will be consumated
Jn 5.30	*My* work depends on what the Father says

Note that Jesus proceeds from identifying the *Son's work* as that which brings life and judgement (in 5.19-23) to the assertion that the hour of the *Son's work* has arrived and will be finally consummated as the fulfillment of the Danielic prophecy (in 5.25-29).[12] Therefore, the chiastic structure of the passage underscores Jesus's main point that his works satisfy the divine, prophetic utterances, and they do so at the appointed hour.

---

12. Apart from the passage's chiastic pattern, the division of the above two sections is also apparent from the following observation: Jesus shifts from talking about himself in the third person (5.19-23 and 5.25-29) to the use of first-person pronouns in 5.24 and 5.30.

IV. *The Danielic Use of Hour in John 5.19-30*

Jesus's reply in Jn 5.19 expands on what Jesus previously said about his work in 5.17: "My Father is still working, and I also am working."[13] This is evident from the parallel notions of relating the works of the Father to himself, which exist both in 5.17 and 5.19-23. Moreover, the same word ἀπεκρίνατο is used to introduce both responses. Jesus's second response serves only to clarify his initial statement,[14] especially because the Jews understood this claim as one that asserts equality with God (5.18). Consequently, the purpose of Jesus's response, starting from 5.19, is to clarify his relationship to the Father, to call attention to the works of the Father as the eschatological works of salvation and judgment, which the Son also does, and to conclude that he is the unique Son of God, Israel's representative king, and the coming Messiah. The following exposition shows that Jesus interpreted his mission in light of the Danielic Son of Man and that the hour in John 5.25, 28 is a probable allusion to Dan. 12.1.

a. *John 5.19*

Jesus begins with a statement concerning his dependency on the Father.[15] Jesus introduces his statement with a formula, ἀμὴν ἀμὴν λέγω ὑμῖν, which also occurs in 5.24 and 5.25. What is the function of this formula? The formula appears 25 times in the Gospel of John and nowhere else in the NT, which makes it an exclusively Johannine expression.[16] It is possible that John uses the phrase merely for the purpose of emphasis.[17] However, after a closer look at the 25 occurrences, a case can be made that the phrase is used as a literary device to signal an intention to explain, enlighten, or correct a misunderstanding. In most of the 25 instances, the double ἀμὴν formula follows some kind of unbelief, misunderstanding, doubt, or puzzlement.[18] Therefore, John may have found a literary device that answers a broad

---

13. Ridderbos, *John*, p. 191.

14. For a comprehensive treatment of Jesus's works, see Peter W. Ensor, *Jesus and His Works: The Johannine Sayings in Historical Perspective* (WUNT, 85; Tübingen: Mohr [Siebeck], 1996).

15. Dodd has argued for the presence of a hidden proverb in Jn 5.19. C. H. Dodd, 'A Hidden Parable in the Fourth Gospel', in C. H. Dodd, *More New Testament Studies* (Manchester, England: Manchester University Press, 1968), pp. 30–40. Also Mark W. G. Stibbe, *John* (Sheffield: Sheffield Academic Press, 1993), p. 78. However, Beasley-Murray argues otherwise (Beasley-Murray, *John*, p. 75), and Ridderbos provides additional reasons for the improbability of the presence of a proverb here (Ridderbos, *John*, pp. 192–93).

16. In the OT, the double amen functions as an affirmative response to a statement, which is usually an exaltation of God. Cf. Pss. 41.14; 72.19; 89.53; 106.48.

17. For a good discussion on the 25 occurrences of the double ἀμὴν sayings, see R. Alan Culpepper, 'The AMHN AMHN Sayings in the Gospel of John', in Robert B. Sloan and Mikeal C. Parsons (eds), *Perspectives on John: Method and Interpretation in the Fourth Gospel* (NABPRSS, 11; New York: Mellen, 1993), pp. 57–102.

18. In Jn 1.51, the double ἀμὴν formula follows Nathaniel's conception of Jesus and

spectrum of unbelief, puzzlement or misunderstanding. In this case, the presence of the double ἀμὴν formula stresses the opposition between the Jews and Jesus that the passage has already introduced (Jn 5.16, 18).[19]

The repetition that is involved in Jesus's reply may, at first, appear redundant. However, the repetition of the statement is surely emphatic and enables John to form the following chiasm, which further highlights Jesus's dependency on the Father:

	Jn 5.19
A	the Son can do nothing of his own accord
B	but only what he sees the Father doing.
B'	For whatever the Father does,
A'	that the Son does likewise.

Therefore, the γὰρ in 5.19 is best seen as either a negation-affirmation[20] or as an explanation.[21] In either case, whether the repeated phrase moves from the negative to the positive or simply serves as an explanation, the repetition is emphatic. Jesus intends to clarify his statement, "the Son can do nothing on his own, except what he sees the Father doing," with the statement, "whatever the Father does, the Son does likewise." While the γὰρ could possibly be causal (or inferential), this is less probable, since the two parts of the verse essentially assert the same thing; their content is nearly identical.

Therefore, Jesus's initial response to the Jews, concerning their opposition to Jesus's claim that his works are equal to God's, is the following: I do what the Father does. However, the work that Jesus sees the Father doing (5.19) is to give

---

serves as a further expansion or explanation of this conception. In Jn 3.3, 5, 11, it follows Nicodemus' misunderstanding of Jesus's mission and identity. In Jn 5.19, 24, 25, it follows the Jews' unbelief and opposition. In Jn 6.26, 32, 47, 53, as well as in Jn 8.34, 51, 58, it follows the unbelief of the Jewish crowd, their challenging questions, and their puzzlement with Jesus's sayings. In Jn 10.1, 7, it addresses the unbelief of the Pharisees. In Jn 12.24, it addresses the misunderstanding of the Greeks and his disciples. In Jn 13.16, 20, 21, it does not seem to address a specific misunderstanding; however, one could argue that Jesus's intention is to enlighten the general misunderstanding that the disciples had about his mission. In Jn 13.38, the double ἀμὴν formula follows Peter's misguided commitment. In Jn 14.12, it follows Philip's puzzlement about seeing the Father. In Jn 16.20, 23, the phrase could introduce an explanation for the disciples' puzzlement concerning the "little while." In Jn 21.18, the formula follows Peter's puzzlement concerning Jesus's three questions on Peter's love.

19. Furthermore, the use of the double ἀμὴν formula in 5.19, 5.24, and 5.25, supports the structure of the passage as I have argued earlier: Jesus defines "the Son's work" in 5.19-23, makes a personal application in 5.24, and then, in 5.25-30, argues that this work fulfills the Danielic prophecies.

20. Brown, *Gospel According to John*, I, p. 218.

21. The γὰρ of 5.19 is the first out of four that occur in 5.19, 20, 21, and 22. The determination of the function of each γὰρ makes Jesus's argument more explicit. The logical function of each γὰρ need not be the same; rather, each γὰρ should be examined independently.

life and to judge (5.21-22 and 5.26-27), which makes Jesus's claim of dependence on the Father only the starting point of his argument. Eventually, what Jesus really intends for his audience to understand is that the Father has given him authority to give resurrection life and to execute end-time judgment, and that such authority constitutes the inaugurated fulfillment of the eschatological prophecies.

b. *John 5.20*

In Jn 5.20, Jesus provides the reason why the Son does the works of the Father (5.19). The Son does the works of the Father *because* the Father loves the Son and shows him all that he does.[22] Most scholars agree with this interpretation, since they translate the second γὰρ as causal (5.20). God demonstrates his love for the Son by granting him the authority to bring about divine works. The two conjunctions (καὶ) introduce the results of God's love, namely, the showing of the divine works to the Son. The Father shares his works with the one he loves. Moreover, the extent of the Father's love is so great, that he will disclose to the Son even greater works (than physical healings).[23] Jesus asserts that the Father will show the Son these greater works "in order that" (ἵνα) the Jews may be amazed. Jesus has already said that Nathaniel will see greater things (Jn 1.50), and he later promises the disciples that they will do even greater things than Jesus (Jn 14.12).[24] However, what kind of amazement will these greater works cause?

The verb θαυμάζω probably carries a negative connotation, rather than a positive one.[25] Jesus does not imply that the Jews will be impressed and believe, but rather that they will be astonished and alarmed.[26] Within the Gospel of John, the word θαυμάζω is used six times (Jn 3.7; 4.27; 5.20, 28; 7.15, 21), and in every case it relates to a misunderstanding of Jesus's teaching or the work to which he is commissioned.[27] (This understanding points further to the earlier suggestion that the double

---

22. John has already established that the Father loves the Son in Jn 3.35, which reads: "The Father loves the Son and has placed all things in his hands."

23. It is possible, here, to interpret the Father's love as a covenantal love.

24. Both Jn 1.50 and 14.12 are connected to a double ἀμὴν.

25. The OT uses θαυμάζω in this manner; for example see Ps. 47.6-7 (LXX; 48.5-6 in MT); Isa. 52.5; and Dan. (TH) 8.27. The same is also the case in several NT occurrences (e.g. Mt. 9.8 and Lk. 8.25). Note also that in Aelius Aristides 50.17, a healing work is described as an "amazing work of God."

26. The idea of amazement is also found in Isa. 52.15, which describes the lifting up and glorification of the Isaianic servant (Isa. 52.13), and which serves as the context behind the Isaianic quotation in Jn 12.38.

27. The amazement in the Gospel of John is especially linked to a misunderstanding of Jesus's works and words. In Jn 3.7, the amazement is about the new birth that Jesus has mentioned to Nicodemus and which generates new life. In the immediate context, Jesus relates this new life with his own mission to be lifted up on the cross (Jn 3.14-15). In John 4.27, the disciples are puzzled (or perplexed) because Jesus speaks with a Samaritan woman. By engaging himself in a conversation with the Samaritan woman, Jesus brings light and new life to this woman, who seems to have found the truth in Jesus. In Jn 7.15, the Jews are amazed

ἀμὴν is typically a response to unbelief, misunderstanding, doubt, or puzzlement). Note especially Jn 7.21, which reads, "I did one deed, and you all marvel" (ἐν ἔργον ἐποίησα καὶ πάντες θαυμάζετε), and refers to the healing incident in 5.1-16.

Granting that the Father has disclosed his works to Jesus (5.20), and assuming the validity of our proposal that Jesus employs a Danielic eschatological prophecy to qualify his work in Jn 5.28-29 (as I argue below), we have an initial indication here that Jesus may have claimed to be doing God's eschatological work of salvation. Indeed, in the immediate context of Jn 5.20b, the greater works do seem to bring about the eschaton, especially if one interprets these greater works to consist of the judgment and resurrection in 5.21-22 and 5.26-27. The amazement of the Jewish people is not justified, because God had foretold these works. This is precisely Jesus's point in 5.28, in which he instructs the Jews not to be amazed because God had foretold the hour at which the eschatological resurrection of the dead would take place.

c. *John 5.21-22*

My assertion that the greater works are those of effecting judgment and giving life becomes even more certain if one takes the third γὰρ in 5.21 as causal. This conjunction would then introduce the basis for the people's amazement in 5.20. Why would the people be amazed? Because, just as the Father gives life to the dead, so also the Son will give life to the dead (5.21). The Son's ability to raise the dead, therefore, constitutes the greater works of 5.20b. Indeed, the chiastic structure of the passage supports this connection, since both Jn 5.21-22 and 5.26-27 (c–c') are linked with the people's amazement (notice the parallel construction ὥσπερ γὰρ . . . οὕτως καὶ . . .):

Jn 5.20b-22	Jn 5.26-28a
and he will show him greater works than these, so that you will marvel (ἵνα ὑμεῖς θαυμάζητε).	
For just as (ὥσπερ γὰρ) the Father raises the dead and gives them life, even so (οὕτως καὶ) the Son also gives life to whom he wishes.	For just as (ὥσπερ γὰρ) the Father has life in himself, even so (οὕτως καὶ) he gave to the Son also to have life in himself;
[For not even the Father judges anyone,] but he has given all judgement to the Son,	
	and he gave him authority to execute judgement, [because he is the Son of Man]
	Do not marvel (μὴ θαυμάζετε) at this

at Jesus's teaching, which he claims to have learned from the Father (7.16), and, finally, in Jn 7.21, the amazement is due to the incident of the healing of the invalid man in Jn 5.1-16, and, therefore, relates to the amazement in Jn 5.20, 28.

The Jews believed that the giving of life was a prerogative of God alone (Deut. 32.39; 1 Sam. 2.6; 2 Kgs 5.7; Hos. 6.2). The reference to life here is to a literal resurrection from the dead,[28] since first, Jesus uses the noun νεκρός to describe the condition of the one who receives life, and second, John often uses the verb ἐγείρω elsewhere in the gospel to refer to a physical/literal resurrection (Jn 2.19-22; 12.1, 9, 17; 21.14). Moreover, the Father's ability to give life and to judge is reminiscent of God's end-time activity to bring about the resurrection.[29]

The idea of a physical resurrection is not unique to the NT. Jesus's words in Jn 5.21 betray an allusion to Isa. 26.19 and possibly to Ezek. 37.9,[30] both of which speak of a resurrection from the dead.[31] Isaiah 26.19 is likely the background here. The only place in the OT (LXX) where both the words ἐγείρω and νεκρός occur is in Isa. 26.19, which reads: "Your dead (οἱ νεκροί) shall live (ἀναστήσονται), their corpses (οἱ ἐν τοῖς μνημείοις) shall rise (ἐγερθήσονται)."[32] The allusion becomes clearer in conjunction with the language used in Jn 5.28-29. The exact phrase that John employs to describe the dead in 5.28, οἱ ἐν τοῖς μνημείοις, is used nowhere in the OT in relation to the idea of resurrection, except in Isa. 26.19.[33] The following chart illustrates the connection:

28. A literal resurrection encompasses both the physical and the spiritual aspects of a resurrection.

29. See Lincoln, *John*, p. 203.

30. Ezekiel 37.9 may be in mind, especially with its use of the words νεκρός and ζάω ("breathe upon these dead people [νεκρούς], that they may live [ζησάτωσαν]"), and the use of the word μνῆμα ("tomb") in 37.12. Later, we will see how Ezekiel 37 may also lie behind the language used in Jn 5.24, 28-29. Allusions to Isaiah and Ezekiel, especially in conjunction with a suggested Danielic background (Dan. 7.13-14; 12.1-2), appear in other Johannine passages as well. For example, John alludes to Ezek. 1.1 and Dan. 7.13 in Jn 1.51 (Manning, *Prophet*, pp. 150–60). Also, John alludes to Ezek. 36.25-27 and Isa. 44.3 in Jn 3.5 (Ibid., pp. 186–89) and to Dan. 7.13 in Jn 3.13-14. Moreover, the quotations of Isa. 53.1 and 6.10 in Jn 12.38, 40, appear in the context of several Danielic allusions in Jn 12.23, 31, 34 (for the Danielic allusions, see my comments on John 12, pp. 126–35).

31. The Nestle-Aland text (NA[27]) has also proposed Deut. 32.39; 1 Sam. 2.6; 2 Kgs 5.7; and Hos. 6.2 as possible allusions to Jn 5.21. The above set of verses validates the Jewish tradition that Yahweh was the sole giver and taker of life. He had the authority and the power to kill and to give life. Undoubtedly, the content of these verses constitutes the general background behind Jn 5.21; Jesus's words must have relied on the knowledge of such a tradition. However, one needs further evidence to validate a direct and conscious allusion by John.

32. Isaiah 26.19 is also alluded to in 4Q521, which describes the coming Messiah as the one who shall revive the dead. For the suggestion of this allusion, see Craig A. Evans, 'Jesus and the Dead Sea Scrolls', in Peter W. Flint and James C. VanderKam (eds), *The Dead Sea Scrolls After Fifty Years: A Comprehensive Assessment* (Vol. 2; Leiden: Brill, 1999), pp. 585–88. Note also the comments in Tanna Daba Eliyyahu ER 22, which associates the resurrection in Isa. 26.19 with the "days of the Messiah" (so also in Midr. Psalms 18.11). The resurrection in Isa. 26.19 has been also interpreted to take place 'in the future life' (Pirqe R. El. 34).

33. The word ἐγείρω refers to the healing of Jn 5.8. In fact, the entire discourse on the

Isa. 26.19	Jn 5.21, 28-29
Your <u>dead</u> <u>will</u> <u>live</u> (ἀναστήσονται οἱ νεκροί); their <u>corpses</u> (οἱ ἐν τοῖς μνημείοις) <u>will rise</u> (ἐγερθήσονται). You who lie in the dust, awake and shout for joy, for your dew is as the dew of the dawn, and the earth will give birth to the departed spirits.	(5.21) For just as the Father <u>raises the dead</u> (ἐγείρει τοὺς νεκροὺς) and <u>gives them life</u> (ζῳοποιεῖ), even so the Son also <u>gives life</u> (ζῳοποιεῖ) to whom he wishes. (5.28-29) Do not marvel at this; for the hour is coming, in which all <u>who are in the tombs</u> (οἱ ἐν τοῖς μνημείοις) will hear His voice, and will come forth; those who did the good deeds <u>to a resurrection</u> (εἰς ἀνάστασιν) of life, those who committed the evil deeds <u>to a resurrection</u> (εἰς ἀνάστασιν) of judgement.

If indeed Isa. 26.19 — and also possibly Ezek. 37.9 — is the background for Jn 5.21, we must examine the implications: not only does Jesus claim to have access to the same prerogatives as the Father, but he also claims that his works have initiated the process through which the Isaianic promises of restoration will be fulfilled. Jesus is the realization of the Isaianic restoration; he is about to lead the captives free by effecting the resurrection foretold. This allusion to the OT resurrection, in 5.21, 28-29 provides additional evidence that the central point in Jesus's answer actualizes the OT promises through the Son's works in the coming hour (5.28-29).

In 5.22, John provides an additional reason for the people to be amazed: the Father judges no one, but has given all judgment to the Son.[34] Therefore, the last γὰρ of the four is probably a sequential one and exists to reinforce the third γὰρ (5.21). The image of the Son receiving authority to judge also appears in 5.27, which probably alludes to Dan. 7.13-14.[35] Although one could easily challenge the claim to a Danielic background in 5.22, one can hardly deny its presence in 5.27, since the only passage in the OT where the Son of Man receives authority to judge is in Dan. 7.13-14 (the probability of this allusion in relation to the Son of Man will be discussed further under 5.27).

Dan. 7.13-14	Jn 5.22, 27

resurrection in 5.19-30 interprets the healing of the invalid man. Haenchen writes: "The reader whose eyes have been opened comes to know, in verse 24, that in causing the lame man 'to rise up' there is merely an allusion to the real resurrection" (Ernst Haenchen, *John 1: A Commentary on the Gospel of John, Chapters 1–6* [Philadelphia: Fortress, 1984], p. 253).

34. The giving of life in 5.21 is set in the context of eschatological judgment. Lincoln, *John*, p. 203.

35. In the creation narrative of Genesis 1–2, God gives to humans authority to rule over the earth (Gen. 1.26), and then God rests from all work on the seventh day, the Sabbath (Gen. 2.2-3). Also, the use of "Son of Man" in Dan. 7.13 may echo the human Adam who had received authority to rule as the representative of humanity. If this is the case, then the Son of Man may be given all authority in Jn 5.21-22, 26-27 because he is the Danielic Son of Man who also represents humanity as the second Adam.

and behold, with the clouds of heaven one like a Son of Man (υἱὸς ἀνθρώπου) was coming, and he came up to the Ancient of Days . . . and to him was given authority (ἐδόθη αὐτῷ ἐξουσία) . . . His authority (ἡ ἐξουσία αὐτοῦ) is an everlasting authority (ἐξουσία) which will not pass away; and his kingdom is one which will not be destroyed.	(5.22) For not even the Father judges anyone, but he has given (δέδωκεν) all judgement to the Son (5.27) and he gave him authority (ἐξουσίαν ἔδωκεν αὐτῷ) to execute judgement, because he is the Son of Man (υἱὸς ἀνθρώπου).

Therefore, Jesus's argument begins to take on an eschatological tone: Jesus is the messianic figure who has come to bring forth life and judgment.[36] On the one hand, this claim is Jesus's defense concerning the healing that he did on the Sabbath. In this regard, Jesus argues that his work is divinely authorized and hence *justified* to take place on a Sabbath; also, he argues that his work is restorative — identified with God's salvific work — and hence also *suitable* to take place on the Sabbath. On the other hand, the above claim is Jesus's comment on the significance of this healing, namely that the healing was merely a sign for something greater. Indeed, Jesus has just said that greater works will be seen, works that will involve the resurrection of the dead and the coming of the final judgment.

Jesus's claim that these eschatological events are part of what he does may have posed a problem for those who held that the resurrection of the dead belongs to the final end of history. This was indeed the general expectation of the Jews; however, Jesus now claims that the works of the resurrection and judgment have become a present reality in his mission. Brown has rightly noted that these works of Jesus comprise the substance of the Johannine hour, which is now here.[37] Beasley-Murray also agrees that Jesus has brought "the life of the new age to the present one; likewise he mediates its corollary of judgement in this time (cf. 9.39-41; 12.31-32)."[38] Undeniably, in 5.21-22, John emphasizes the present realization of the eschatological life and judgment.[39] The point made is that Jesus embodies the role of the eschatological judge.

d. *John 5.23*
The purpose (ἵνα) for the giving of life and judgment to the Son (5.20-21) is "in order for all to honor the Son, even as they honor the Father" (5.23). In a similar instance of rejection by the Jews, in Jn 8.49, the Jews dishonor Jesus by identifying

---

36. See also *1 En.* 69.27, where the Son of Man also functions as judge in allusion to Daniel.

37. Brown affirms, "Judgement, condemnation, and passing from death to life are part of the hour, which is now here" (Brown, *Gospel According to John*, I, p. 219).

38. G. R. Beasley-Murray, *John* (WBC, 36; Waco: Word, 1987), p. 76.

39. However, as Barrett notes, "the judgement, like the resurrection, belongs both to the present and the future" (C. K. Barrett, *The Gospel According to St John: An Introduction with Commentary and Notes on the Greek Text* (London: SPCK, 1967), p. 217). This distinction between present and future will become more evident later, especially in Jn 5.25-29.

him with Satan. This means that their rejection of Jesus entails the rejection of God himself, precisely because the works of Jesus are the works of the Father. The Father has given Jesus authority over life and death in order that he would become the Father's sole representative on earth. Jesus has become the representative of God in the following ways: 1) his words and works represent God's voice and deeds; and 2) his audience's response with honor or rejection corresponds to the honor or rejection of God. One's stance before Jesus represents one's stance before God. John emphasizes this point by repeating it twice: once in the affirmative and once in the negative:

Jn 5.23a	*Jn 5.23b*
all will honor the Son even as they honor the Father	he who does not honor the Son does not honor the Father who sent him

Interestingly, this honor language also appears in Dan. 7.14 (וִיקָר), where the Ancient of Days, in addition to authority, also gives honor to the Son of Man. Here, we have a further hint before the clear allusion to Dan. 7.13-14 in Jn 5.27 that Jesus may have identified himself and his mission with the Danielic prophecies.[40]

Dan. (TH) 7.14	*Jn 5.22b-23*
And to him (αὐτῷ) was given (ἐδόθη) the dominion (ἡ ἀρχὴ), and the honor (ἡ τιμή), and the kingdom	but he has given (δέδωκεν) the judgement (τὴν κρίσιν) to the Son (τῷ υἱῷ), so that all will honor (τιμῶσι) the Son (τὸν υἱὸν) even as they honor (τιμῶσι) the Father. He who does not honor (μὴ τιμῶν) the Son (τὸν υἱὸν) does not honor (οὐ τιμᾷ) the Father who sent him.

Once again, John's reasoning has close affinities with that of Dan. 7.14; the Father has given all life, authority for judgement, and honor to the Son.

e. *John 5.24*

The second double ἀμὴν saying, in Jn 5.24, recapitulates Jesus's point from the preceding verses. Jesus provides a summary of what he has already said in 5.19-23 and also applies this statement to himself. Although the double ἀμὴν formula primarily serves as a literary device to readdress the initial issue (5.16, 18), its use here also summarizes what has been said so far (5.19-23): whoever listens to Jesus and believes in the one who sent him has life and escapes judgement. More specifically, Jesus relates what he has said so far about the *Son's work* to himself (note the shift from the third person to the first person).[41] Jesus is the one who has been given the

---

40. The connection may be more apparent in the Aramaic (especially since the noun שָׁלְטָן corresponds to the Greek word ἐξουσίαν in Jn 5.27).

41. In the discourse, Jesus twice moves from speaking about himself in the third person to the use of personal pronouns: from 5.19-23 to 5.24 and from 5.25-29 to 5.30.

authority to give life and to judge. Therefore, Jesus's argument, although essentially unchanged, has now become more explicit: his presence (his own words and works) enables one to possess eternal life and to avoid judgement. Personal belief in Jesus has eschatological effects.

Scholars have rightly observed that this verse contains the "essential Johannine kerygma."[42] This kerygma focuses on the reception of "eternal life," which is one of John's favorite phrases.[43] Indeed, John emphasizes the concept of eternal life, especially as it relates to faith. This is evident from the following parallel statements in John's gospel:

Jn 3.15	ἵνα πᾶς ὁ πιστεύων ἐν αὐτῷ ἔχῃ ζωὴν αἰώνιον
Jn 3.16	ἵνα πᾶς ὁ πιστεύων εἰς αὐτὸν μὴ ἀπόληται ἀλλ᾽ ἔχῃ ζωὴν αἰώνιον
Jn 3.36	ὁ πιστεύων εἰς τὸν υἱὸν ἔχει ζωὴν αἰώνιον
Jn 5.24	Ἀμὴν ἀμὴν λέγω ὑμῖν ὅτι ὁ τὸν λόγον μου ἀκούων καὶ πιστεύων τῷ πέμψαντί με ἔχει ζωὴν αἰώνιον
Jn 6.40	πᾶς ὁ θεωρῶν τὸν υἱὸν καὶ πιστεύων εἰς αὐτὸν ἔχῃ ζωὴν αἰώνιον
Jn 6.47	ἀμὴν ἀμὴν λέγω ὑμῖν, ὁ πιστεύων ἔχει ζωὴν αἰώνιον
Jn 6.54	ὁ τρώγων μου τὴν σάρκα καὶ πίνων μου τὸ αἷμα ἔχει ζωὴν αἰώνιον
Jn 11.25	ἐγώ εἰμι ἡ ἀνάστασις καὶ ἡ ζωή· ὁ πιστεύων εἰς ἐμὲ κα‡ν ἀποθάνῃ ζήσεται
Jn 20.31	ταῦτα δὲ γέγραπται . . . ἵνα πιστεύοντες ζωὴν ἔχητε ἐν τῷ ὀνόματι αὐτοῦ

However, the "eternal life" is an eschatological phrase derived from Daniel, since the only place in the OT (LXX) where the precise phrase "eternal life" occurs is in Dan. 12.2.[44] The Danielic eternal life refers to the resurrection life of the eschaton and constitutes the OT background behind the Johannine concept of "eternal life":

---

42. Beasley-Murray, *John*, p. 76; and R. Schnackenburg, *The Gospel According to St. John* (3 Vols; New York: Crossroad, 1987), p. 108.

43. The phrase "eternal life" appears 17 times in the Gospel of John (Jn 3.15, 16, 36; 4.14, 36; 5.24, 39; 6.27, 40, 47, 54, 68; 10.28; 12.25, 50; 17.2, 3) and six times in 1 John (1.2; 2.25; 3.15; 5.11, 13, 20). In the rest of the gospels, it appears 3 times in Matthew (Mt. 19.16, 29; 25.46), 2 times in Mark (Mk 10.17, 30), and 3 times in Luke (Lk. 10.25; 18.18, 30). In the LXX of the OT it appears only in Dan. 12.2.

44. The phrase also appears in the Greek translations of 2 Macc. 7:9; *4 Macc.* 15.3; and *Pss. Sol.* 3.12, two of which (2 Macc. 7.9; *Pss. Sol.* 3.12) clearly refer to the end-time resurrection of the dead. Other scholars have noticed the connection between the phrase "eternal life" and Dan. 12.1-2 in the Fourth Gospel (e.g., Ashton, *Fourth Gospel*, pp. 215–16, n. 22; and U. E. Simon, 'Eternal Life in the Fourth Gospel', in F. L. Cross (ed.), *Studies in the Fourth Gospel* (London: Mowbray, 1957), pp. 97–110).

Dan. 12.2	Jn 5.24
And many of them that sleep in the dust of the earth will awake (ἀναστήσονται), some to eternal life (εἰς ζωὴν αἰώνιον), and some to reproach and eternal shame.	Truly, truly, I say to you, he who hears my word, and believes him who sent me, has eternal life (ζωὴν αἰώνιον), and does not come into judgement, but has passed out of death into life (εἰς τὴν ζωήν).

The connection between the phrase "eternal life" and Dan. 12.2 is further strengthened by the fact that Matthew refers to the "eternal life" in contexts that allude to Daniel.[45] One could argue, of course, that the fact that "eternal life" originates in Daniel does not necessitate that the NT author has the context of Daniel in mind. This objection is valid, for the mere appearance of the same phrasing in two texts does not necessarily constitute an allusion to the OT text.

What first strongly points to such an allusion is that the phrase occurs nowhere else in the Greek OT. Second, the appearance of the phrase "eternal life" here is coupled with the rest of John's allusions to Daniel and the similar themes of honor, judgment, and resurrection. Moreover, in Jn 6.27, Jesus explicitly asserts that the Son of Man is the one who provides "eternal life" and, in the immediate context, he interprets "eternal life" as the resurrection that will take place in the last day (6.40, 54).[46] All of these together suggest that the phrase "eternal life" is taken directly from Dan. 12.2, which establishes yet another connection between Jn 5.19-30 and Dan. 12.1-2. Finally, we will see that Jn 5.28-29, which explicitly builds on 5.25, clearly alludes to Dan. 12.2.

Directly following the double ἀμὴν formula in 5.24 is "the one hearing my word and believing." In the OT, the notion of hearing is often used in the sense of obeying (e.g. Deut. 18.2, 13, 49; Ps. 80.12; Isa. 28.12, 23; 66.4; Jer. 49.21; Dan. 9.10-11, 14),[47] and this is also the case in John (e.g. Jn 8.43, 47; 9.27; 10.8, 16; 12.47; 18.37). Here, the act of hearing parallels the act of believing. The hearing of the divine voice is coupled with the notion of resurrection in Ezek. 37.4, 9-10, where God's breath revives the dead bones in Ezekiel's vision. In fact, Ezekiel 37 is the only place in the OT in which the hearing of the divine voice leads to a resurrection.[48] Notice the existence of the multiple lexical parallels between Ezekiel 37 and the context of Jn 5.24:

---

45. There is reference to the Son of Man coming in the clouds or the Son of Man effecting judgment (see Mt. 19.28-29; 25.31, 46).

46. Apart from Jn 5.24, 27 and 6.27 John closely relates the phrase "eternal life" to the Danielic Son of Man in the following passages: Jn 3.13-16; 6.53-54; and 12.23-25.

47. Barrett, *John*, p. 217.

48. We have already seen Ezek. 37.9 as a possible background for Jn 5.21. Here, John expands on this earlier connection.

Ezek. 37.4, 9-10, 12	Jn 5.21, 24, 25, 28-29
Again he said to me, Prophesy over these bones and say to them, "O dry bones, hear the word (ἀκούσατε λόγον) of the Lord." . . . Then He said to me, Prophesy to the spirit, prophesy, son of man, and say to the spirit, "Thus says (λέγει) the Lord, Come from the four winds, and breathe upon the dead (τοὺς νεκρούς), and they will live (ζησάτωσαν)." So I prophesied as he commanded me, and the spirit entered into them, and they lived (ἔζησαν), and stood on their feet, a very great congregation. . . . Therefore prophesy and say, Thus says (λέγει) the Lord; Behold, I will open your tombs (ὑμῶν τὰ μνήματα), and will bring you up out of your tombs (ἐκ τῶν μνημάτων), and will bring you into the land of Israel.	(5.21) For just as the Father raises the dead (ἐγείρει τοὺς νεκρούς) and gives them life (ζωοποιεῖ), even so the Son also gives life (ζωοποιεῖ) to whom he wishes. (5.24) Truly, truly, I say to you, he who hears my word (ὁ τὸν λόγον μου ἀκούων), and believes him who sent me, has eternal life (ζωήν), and does not come into judgement, but has passed out of death into life (τὴν ζωήν). (5.25) Truly, truly, I say to you, the hour is coming and now is, when the dead will hear the voice (οἱ νεκροὶ ἀκούσουσιν τῆς φωνῆς) of the Son of God, and those who hear will live (οἱ ἀκούσαντες ζήσουσιν). (5.28-29) Do not marvel at this; for the hour is coming, in which all who are in the tombs will hear his voice (οἱ ἐν τοῖς μνημείοις ἀκούσουσιν τῆς φωνῆς αὐτοῦ), and will come forth; those who did the good deeds to a resurrection of life (εἰς ἀνάστασιν ζωῆς), those who committed the evil deeds to a resurrection (εἰς ἀνάστασιν) of judgement.

In the preceding context of Jn 5.19-30, Jesus's word has performed two miracles (4.50; 5.8-9), indicating in action that his words are the source of life. These works indicate that the hour of resurrection is now here. John 5.24 emphasizes the present realization of resurrection,[49] especially with John's use of the perfect tense of μεταβαίνω: "but has passed (μεταβέβηκεν) from death to life."[50] However, one may reasonably say that the present possession of eternal life entails a future possession as well, and the present avoidance of judgment also applies to the final judgment. Barrett rightly makes a distinction between the present realization of events and the future realization, a distinction that is clearer, as we will see, between the present experience of the hour in 5.25 and its future expectation in 5.28.[51]

f. *John 5.25*

The hearing of the voice that leads to eternal life, in 5.24, constitutes the focal point of Jesus's response so far. However, Jesus's discourse continues the same theme in 5.25 by essentially repeating what has already been said in 5.24. Why is this so? The function of the double ἀμὴν formula in 5.25 may help us understand the apparent repetition. As I have already noted, the double ἀμὴν formula is a literary device

49. Ridderbos, *John*, p. 197.
50. Note the parallelism with 1 Jn 3.14.
51. Barrett, *John*, p. 218.

that probably signals an explanation for a prior misunderstanding. In this particular instance, it is used to further Jesus's clarification on the initial issue (5.16, 18) and to recapitulate the argument so far (5.19-24). What Jesus has implicitly affirmed will now be made explicit. In fact, I will argue that Jesus's climactic point in 5.25-30 has to do with prophecy and fulfillment.

Jesus, in 5.25, repeats the assertion of the preceding verse (5.24) in order to further his argument, which will eventually defend the validity of the assertion. Indeed, Jesus's argument might be constructed as follows:

Jn 5.19-23	The Son does only what the Father does, which is to give life and to judge, since the Father has shown everything to the Son.
Jn 5.24	Whoever hears my voice and believes my Father has eternal life and escapes judgement.
Jn 5.25-29	The fact that the hearing of the voice of the Son results in life should not amaze anyone, because this had been foretold in Daniel.
Jn 5.30	I do only what the Father says, which is the divine will.

In other words, Jesus's argument may be paraphrased as follows: Now that I have revealed to you that whoever hears my voice has eternal life (5.24), you should be able also to discern that the hour is coming, and is now here, when the dead will hear the voice of the Son and live; this is the hour of the resurrection from the dead (5.25-29). One notices that although the statement in 5.25 is somewhat repetitious of that in 5.24, John's rephrasing in 5.25 adds a few elements that make the argument more explicit.

Jn 5.24	*Jn 5.25*
Truly, truly, I say to you,	Truly, truly, I say to you, the hour is coming, and is now here, when
he who hears my word, [and believes him who sent me]	the dead will hear the voice of the Son of God,
has eternal life, [and does not come into judgement, but has passed out of death into life].	and those who hear will live.

Verse 25 adds the constructions ἔρχεται ὥρα καὶ νῦν ἐστιν, οἱ νεκροί, τῆς φωνῆς τοῦ υἱοῦ τοῦ θεοῦ, and the verb ζήσουσιν, the combination of which introduces the hour when the voice of the Son of God will cause the resurrection from the dead.

The title "Son of God" identifies Christ with the promised king of Israel, the Messiah, who is expected to establish God's kingdom at the eschaton. Similarly, John elsewhere understands the title "Son of God" as a royal or messianic title in

Jn 1.49 (king);[52] 11.27 (Messiah); and 20.31 (Messiah).[53] In the OT, several messianic prophecies also relate the "Son" title to royalty (cf. 2 Sam. 7.12-14; Ps. 2.7; and Ps. 110.1). However, within the context of Daniel, the kingdom is given rather to the Son of Man and to Israel (Dan. 7.13-14; 22; 27).

Concerning the word νεκρός, every instance of it in John relates to the notion of resurrection (Jn 2.22; 5.21, 25; 12.1, 9, 17; 20.9; 21.14).[54] In the OT, this word relates to the notion of resurrection only in Isa. 26.19 and Ezek. 37.9.[55] Therefore, by using the word νεκρός in 5.25, John reiterates the language of Jn 5.21 and echoes the resurrection passages of Isa. 26.19 and Ezek. 37.9-10.[56] In 5.25, John probably has in mind a spiritual resurrection, distinct from the physical resurrection in 5.28-29.[57] It may be that 5.25 describes the spiritual resurrection of the present age, while 5.28-29 describes the physical resurrection of the age that is to come. Indeed, most scholars have contended for the spiritual nature of the resurrection in 5.25.[58] As Barrett has phrased it, "John distinguishes between the present spiritual resurrection and the future bodily resurrection."[59]

However, the above distinction — as scholars have observed it — is not a sharp one, for John probably sees both the spiritual and the physical aspects of the final resurrection as two sides of the same coin, hence also the parallel between 5.25 and

52. See Seyoon Kim, *'The "Son of Man"' as the Son of God* (WUNT, 30; Tübingen: Mohr [Siebeck], 1983).

53. Ashton relates the designation "Son of God" to various Jewish and Samaritan traditions concerning the coming of the Prophet-King (Ashton, *Fourth Gospel*, pp. 292–303).

54. Note especially that Jesus's voice raises Lazarus from the dead in Jn 12.17 (τὸν Λάζαρον ἐφώνησεν ἐκ τοῦ μνημείου καὶ ἤγειρεν αὐτὸν ἐκ νεκρῶν), a verse that resembles the language in Jn 5.21, 25, and 28.

55. For the background of Isa. 26.19 and Ezek. 37.9-10, see also my discussion on Jn 5.21, 24.

56. Manning has adequately argued for the background of Isa. 26.19, Ezek. 37.4, 9, 12; and Dan. 7.14; 12.2 in Jn 5.25-28 (Manning, *Prophet*, pp. 160–71). See also Köstenberger, 'John', in G. K. Beale and D. A. Carson (eds), *Commentary on the New Testament Use of the Old Testament* (Grand Rapids: Baker, 2007), pp. 442–43.

57. The hour in 5.25 is portrayed as if it is a present reality. The references in Jn 12.23; 13.1; 17.1 (ἦλθεν or ελήλυθεν) also indicate the present reality of the hour. There, it refers to the suffering of Jesus (Barrett, *John*, p. 198).

58. Most scholars have noticed that the emphasis of the phrase "an hour is coming and is now here" presupposes a spiritual resurrection in 5.25. On the contrary, the phrase "an hour is coming", in 5.28, implies a future, physical, resurrection. This distinction is based on the distinction between an inaugurated eschatology in 5.25 and a future eschatology in 5.28-29. See Lincoln, *John*, p. 204; Ridderbos, *John*, pp. 199–201; Stibbe, *John*, pp. 78–79; Ben Witherington III, *John's Wisdom: A Commentary on the Fourth Gospel* (Louisville, Ky.: Westminster John Knox, 1995), p. 143. Bultmann also embraces the two eschatologies of 5.25 and 5.28-29, but for a different reason: he believes that 5.28-29 is a later redaction that sought to address possible eschatological misunderstandings (Rudolf Bultmann, *The Gospel of John: A Commentary* [Philadelphia: Westminster, 1971], pp. 260–62).

59. Barrett, *John*, p. 218. So also Beasley-Murray, *John*, p. 77.

5.28-29.[60] As Carson states, "the resurrection life for the physically dead in the end time is already being manifest as life for the spiritually dead."[61] In my opinion, both the spiritual and the physical resurrection should be seen as literal resurrections. In 5.25, then, Jesus would be speaking of a literal resurrection from the dead, that is, a literal spiritual resurrection, which inaugurates the resurrection in 5.28-29.[62] For this reason, the Johannine hour contains both resurrections, which also makes the hour an era — rather than a single moment in time — signifying God's eschatological act. Jesus's deeds and words comprise this act of God that has commenced the hour of life and judgment.

In Jesus's words, the actualization of the resurrection from the dead (as foretold in Isa. 26.19 and Ezek. 37.9-10) is combined with the Johannine hour. Other possible references to an eschatological hour in the Fourth Gospel appear in Jn 2.4; 4.21, 23; 5.25, 28; 7.30; 8.20; 12.23, 27; 13.1; 16.2, 4, 21, 25, 32; and 17.1.[63] This hour appears to be an eschatological one due to its eschatological signification given by John.

A closer look at the above occurrences of ὥρα in John suggests that, at the very least, this hour recounts several eschatological conditions. The Johannine hour inaugurates an era in which there will be no need for a physical temple (Jn 4.21, 23), the dead will be resurrected (Jn 5.25, 28), Jesus's disciples will be persecuted (Jn 16.2, 4), and special revelation will become available (Jn 16.25). However, it is also the hour of Jesus's death, which paradoxically also represents Jesus's glory (Jn 7.30; 8.20; 12.23, 27; 13.1; 16.21; 17.1). It is not accidental that John has related the hour of Jesus's death to the hour of eschatological conditions for the disciples. Indeed, it is Jesus's death that will remove the need for a physical temple (Jn 2.19-22), lead to the resurrection from the dead (Jn 21.14), become the cause for further persecution (Jn 15.18-25), and lead to the special revelation of the Spirit (Jn 14.25-26; 16.7, 13). Therefore, it appears that Jesus's death and resurrection inaugurates the hour of the new eschatological era. For Jesus, this eschatological hour begins to be realized in his ministry and at the cross, while, for the disciples, it is realized as they relate to Jesus's death and resurrection (by acquiring new life and by being persecuted).

Moreover, the immediate context of John 5.19-30 reveals the eschatological character of the Johannine hour. John identifies this hour with that moment — or era — in which the final judgment and resurrection will take place. This can only be the hour of the eschaton.

---

60. A spiritual resurrection can be regarded as part of a literal resurrection. This interpretation is incompatible with a resurrection that is merely noetic or metaphorical, since a literal spiritual resurrection presupposes that the spiritually dead people are literally dead in their spirit, and that a spiritual resurrection literally revives their dead spirit.

61. Carson, *John*, p. 256.

62. For a different view, see Hunter, *John*, p. 59.

63. Brown has also grouped these verses and argues that they depict an hour with a significant referent (Brown, *Gospel According to John*, I, p. 517). Keener also lists these verses and ascribes to them a tendency towards a realized eschatology (Keener, *John*, p. 507).

Finally, the eschatological character of the Johannine hour becomes even more evident when one takes into account its Danielic background. The question, however, needs to be asked: does the hour in Jn 5.25, 28 relate at all to the hour in Dan. 12.1-2? A connection between the two hours is probable, when one considers the following factors concerning the Danielic hour: first, it relates to the time of the resurrection of the eschaton (Dan. 12.2), which resembles the resurrection found in Jn 5.28-29. Secondarily, in context, the hour also relates to three additional notions: 1) the Son of Man figure (Dan. 7.13), who is also mentioned in Jn 5.27; 2) the final judgment (Dan. 7.13-14; 8.25e; 12.1-2), which appears in Jn 5.22, 24, and 27; and, 3) "eternal life" (Dan. 12.2), which is found in Jn 5.24.

This should not be perceived as coincidence, namely that John relates the above themes within the confines of an hour with similar characteristics to the Danielic hour, since the only eschatological hour in the whole OT is the one that appears in the book of Daniel. Indeed, the word ὥρα in Dan. 8.17, 19; 11.35, 40, 45; 12.1, 13, pertains not only to the time of final judgment (Dan. 7.13-14; 8.25e; 12.1-2) but also to the eschatological hour of resurrection from the dead (Dan. 12.1-2), which are the two primary themes that Jesus emphasizes in Jn 5.19-30. John naturally links the theme of eschatological hour to the final resurrection in Jn 5.28-29, since the two (hour and final resurrection) probably have their source in Daniel.

The description of the hour as *coming but also now here* (5.25) may point to an inaugurated fulfillment of the final resurrection in Dan. 12.2. Jesus emphasizes that the spiritually dead may hear his voice and "live," that is receive "eternal life" (5.24). The fact that the hour is also yet to come indicates that the resurrection of the dead awaits a future fulfillment to be consummated. This future installment is described in the resurrection reference of 5.28-29, according to which the hour has not yet arrived.

The allusion to the Danielic eschatological hour in John 5.25, 28 has been acknowledged by other scholars, especially in view of the hour's association with the resurrection in 5.28-29 (on which see the following comments). Ferraro, Beale, and Frey are the ones to have suggested an influence from Daniel, while others have also mentioned the parallel.[64] The validity of the allusion to the Danielic hour will be confirmed later with the examination of hour in 5.28-29.

g. *John 5.26-27*

The coming of an hour when the dead will hear the Son's voice and live (5.25) is grounded in the Father's having given authority over life and judgment to the Son (5.26-27). The above connection is due to the causal γὰρ, in 5.26.[65] The giving of life

---

64. G. Ferraro, *L' "ORA" Di Cristo Nel Quarto Vangelo* (Rome: Herder, 1974), p. 150; Beale, "'Last Hour' in 1 Jn 2.18'; and Frey, *Eschatologie III*, pp. 382–84. See also Beutler, *Judaism and Jews*; and B. Pitre, *Jesus, the Tribulation, and the End of the Exile* (Tübingen: Mohr [Siebeck], 2005), pp. 482, 495–96, 498.

65. Note the similar construction ὥσπερ γὰρ . . . οὕτως . . . in Jn 5.21. These two occurrences are the only ones in John. Elsewhere in the NT the construction appears 9 times (Mt.

in 5.26 parallels the giving of life in 5.21, which has now become resurrected life, due to the immediate context (5.25, 28-29).[66] Van der Watt has concluded that the phrase ζωὴ αἰώνιος "must be regarded as the primary and basic expression, while ζωὴ (alone) is used without any semantic difference."[67]

It has been widely held that John 5.27 alludes to the Danielic Son of Man in Dan. 7.13. Specifically, this allusion is indicated from the fact that the designation "Son of Man" is anarthrous in both Jn 5.27 and Dan. 7.13.[68] Moreover, the use of the words ἐξουσία, δίδωμι, and κρίσις, appear both in Jn 5.27 and in Dan. 7.13-14 (cf. Dan. 7.26-27), in which the Son of Man receives authority to judge.[69] Note the following parallels:

12.40; 24.27, 37; Lk. 17.24; Rom. 5.19; 6.19; 1 Cor. 11.12; 15.22; Jas 2.26). In all of the above verses, the γὰρ is causal, except for the two occurrences in Romans, which may be also taken as inferential or sequential. It is interesting to note that all the four references in Matthew and Luke mention the Son of Man.

66. The fact that the Father has given life to the Son is not necessarily restricted to the period after the incarnation. The Son had life in himself even before the incarnation (Jn 1.4). The giving of life in Jn 5.26 may reflect what is generally considered as the "eternal genera-tion of the Son" (for this, see Carson, *John*, pp. 256–57). In this context, the Son's prerogative to have life in himself results in his authority to impart resurrection life to the believer.

67. J. G. van der Watt, 'The Use of 'ΑΙΩΝΙΟΣ in the Concept ΖΩΗ 'ΑΙΩΝΙΟΣ in John's Gospel', *NovT* 31 (1989), pp. 217–28.

68. The "Son of Man" phrase appears in the OT also in: Num. 23.19; Judg. 8.16; Ps. 8.5; 143.3; Job 16.21; 25.6; Sir. 17.30; Jer. 2.6; 27.40; 28.43; 30.12; 30.28.

69. In Dan. 7.26-27, it is the people of God that receive authority; however, this people of God, in the context of Daniel 7, is the interpretation of the Son of Man that appears in Dan. 7.13, so that the "saints" and the "Son of Man" are identified with each other. Indeed, the latter part of Daniel 7 (vv. 15-28) provides the interpretation for the vision narrated in the first part (vv. 1-14). On the one hand, the Son of Man is given everlasting authority (ἐξουσία; שָׁלְטָן) and a kingdom (βασιλεία; מַלְכוּ) that will never be destroyed (7.14). Also, he appears to be the one to execute God's judgment on behalf of the righteous (7.22; see charts note on p. 117). On the other hand, when judgment is carried out, the kingdom is given to the saints (7.22, 27). However, not only do the saints receive an everlasting kingdom (τὴν βασιλείαν; מַלְכוּ), but they also possess a universal authority (τὴν ἐξουσίαν; שָׁלְטָן). Therefore, both the Son of Man and the saints are given the same kingdom and similar authority. In both cases the same verb (δίδωμι; יהב) is used to denote this giving. This strongly indicates a corporate representation: the Son of Man functions as the representative of the saints (see the discussion in E. Lucas, *Daniel* (AOTC; Downers Grove: InterVarsity, 2002), pp. 185–87).

Dan. 7.13-14, 22, 26-27	Jn 5.27
(7.13-14) I kept looking in the night visions, and behold, with the clouds of heaven one like a Son of Man (υἱὸς ἀνθρώπου) was coming, and he came up to the Ancient of Days and was presented before him. And to him was given authority (ἐδόθη αὐτῷ ἐξουσία), and all the nations of the earth according to posterity and all honor was serving him. And his authority (ἡ ἐξουσία αὐτοῦ) is an everlasting authority (ἐξουσία) which will not pass away; and his kingdom is one which will not be destroyed. (7.22) until the Ancient of days came, and he gave judgement (τὴν κρίσιν ἔδωκε)[1] to the saints of the Most High; and the time arrived, and the saints possessed the kingdom. (7.26-27) And the judgement (ἡ κρίσις) has sat, and they will remove his authority and will decide to defile it and destroy it completely. And he gave (ἔδωκε) the kingdom and the authority (τὴν ἐξουσίαν) and the greatness of the kingdoms that are under the whole heaven to the saints of the Most High to reign over an everlasting kingdom, and all authorities will be subjected to him (αὐτῷ) and obey him (αὐτῷ)	and he gave him authority (ἐξουσίαν ἔδωκεν αὐτῷ) to execute judgement (κρίσιν), because he is the Son of Man (υἱὸς ἀνθρώπου).

Note
* This phrase can either mean "judgment was given to the saints" (as dative indirect object) or "judgment was passed on the saint's behalf" (as dative of advantage). See G. K. Beale, *The Book of Revelation: A Commentary on the Greek Text* (NIGTC; Grand Rapids: Eerdmans, 1999), p. 997, for a preference of the latter rendering. Both understandings of the phrase support the proposed allusion: in the former instance, the saints receive authority to judge because the Son of Man has received such authority in Dan. 7.13-14 (in this case, the connection with Jn 5.27 is in the word ἔδωκεν); in the latter instance, the Son of Man passes judgment on the enemy, again, in accordance with 7.13-14 (in this case, the connection with Jn 5.27 is in the word ποιεῖν).

Although some scholars in the past have doubted a Danielic allusion here — suggesting that it refers to Jesus as a "man" or "human" — many scholars today have affirmed a connection with Daniel based on the contextual themes, which point to an apocalyptic interpretation of the Son of Man.[70] In fact, this should now probably be considered the general consensus.

The movement from the Son of God (5.25) to the Son of Man (5.27) should not be taken as an indication that the two titles are synonymous.[71] Rather, John probably intends to describe Jesus as the Son of God, who is *also* the Danielic Son of Man. He wants to move his readers from an understanding of Jesus as the royal Messiah, the Son of God, to the royal figure of the Son of Man. Martyn has rightly

70. Moloney remains one of the few that still insists on this being a reference to Jesus as only a human being (Francis J. Moloney, *The Gospel of John: Text and Context* [BIS, 72; Leiden: Brill, 2005], pp. 66–92). For a good discussion on the background of the "Son of Man," see Lindars, *Jesus*; Kim, *Son of Man*; Burkett, *Son of the Man*; Idem, *Debate*.

71. J. Louis Martyn, *History and Theology in the Fourth Gospel* (Louisville: John Knox, 2003), p. 128 n. 193. Although it is possible that the two titles are synonymous — so Martyn argues — it is improbable that this is so (Ashton, *Fourth Gospel*, pp. 339–40).

recognized a movement in John from the Mosaic prophet to the Son of Man motif.[72] John's previous use of the Son of Man title has portrayed this movement: In 1.51, while Nathaniel understands the Messiah to be the Son of God and the king of Israel, Jesus qualifies this understanding with a Son of Man saying. Also, in 3.13-14, John links the Son of Man both with Moses and with the lifting up of the Isaianic servant.[73]

Therefore, John purposefully uses the royal title "Son of God" to refer to the expected Messianic king and prophet (Deut. 18.18), and then proceeds to qualify this expectation with the apocalyptic "Son of Man" figure. In doing this, John interprets Jesus's coming to the world, not merely as the prophet and king, but rather as the ultimate royal judge who has come to end the world as it presently exists. By identifying Jesus with the Danielic Son of Man, John suggests that the ultimate eschaton has entered into history (Dan. 8.17, 19; 11.40, 45; 12.1), that the kingdom of this world will be judged (Dan. 7.10-12, 22, 26), and that God's people will receive the everlasting kingdom of God (Dan. 7.14, 18, 22, 27).

What is, therefore, Jesus's argument in 5.26-27? Jesus argues that the hour of the resurrection has come (5.25) *because* the Son, to whom the Father gave life and authority to judge, *is* the Danielic Son of Man, who was prophesied to be given authority to judge (with the implicit notion that those not condemned will be given life).[74] Already from these verses, Jesus implies that the resurrection he has spoken about is the eschatological resurrection from Dan. 12.2. John further expands the above argument by explicitly referring to the final resurrection of Dan. 12.2 in Jn 5.28-29. He associates the fact that Jesus is the Son of Man (Dan. 7.13) with the reality that Jesus will bring into effect the final resurrection (Dan. 12.2).

h. *John 5.28-29*

In 5.28, Jesus begins his statement with the imperative: μὴ θαυμάζετε τοῦτο. The antecedent to which the pronoun τοῦτο probably refers is Jesus's ability to give life and to judge as the Son of Man. Out of the 44 times that the pronoun τοῦτο occurs in John's gospel, 36 clearly refer to an antecedent. However, in five instances, τοῦτο refers to something that follows, which is introduced by ὅτι (Jn 5.16, 18; 10.17;

---

72. Martyn, *Fourth Gospel*, pp. 101–43. Martyn has argued that John qualifies or supplements the prophetic Messianic figure of Jesus with the Danielic Son of Man (Ibid., pp. 125–30).

73. Note the similar comments by Ridderbos, *John*, pp. 92–93, 136–37, 200. Kim has argued for Jesus's self-designation as both "Son of God" and "Son of Man" (Kim, *Son of Man*). Within the Jewish tradition, we have the identification of the Danielic Son of Man with the designation of Son of God (4Q 243). Kim also suggests that the following NT passages indicate a similar connection between the titles "Son of God" and "Son of Man": Mt. 25.31-46; Mk 2.10; 8.27–9.10; 13.26-27; 14.61-62; Lk. 9.26; 22.54-77 (Kim, *Son of Man*, pp. 1–4).

74. Keener also argues that the allusion to the Danielic Son of Man in 5.27 best explains Jesus's authority here (Keener, *John*, p. 654).

12.18, 39).[75] Could it be that τοῦτο, in Jn 5.28, also refers to that which follows, since it is followed by ὅτι clause? Both options are possible. Indeed, neither the grammar nor the syntax provide us any clear direction: on the one hand, one can translate the phrase, "Do not be amazed at what I have just said, because . . ."; on the other hand, one can also translate it as, "Do not be amazed at the following, namely that . . .". If a decision should be made, it needs to be made on the basis of Jesus's overall argument; the best option is that which best explains the logical relationships and parallel structures within the passage.

After examining the logical relationships that exist within Jn 5.19-30, I have concluded that the most reasonable option is to take τοῦτο as referring to its antecedent.[76] First, in 5.28, whatever option one adopts, the referent of τοῦτο causes the people's amazement. However, we have already seen that the cause of the people's amazement is that the Son has been granted life and authority to judge (5.21-22), which is reiterated in 5.26-27. Second, the phrase "do not be amazed at this" anticipates an explanation, a rationale about why the people should not be amazed. The conjunction ὅτι ("because . . .") best serves this rationale; otherwise, one would seem to have to find this rationale in the beginning of v. 30, which would make it rather distant. Third, the chiastic structure of Jn 5.19-30 makes better sense if the amazement is linked to the preceding verses, rather than to the following section. Finally, it makes perfect sense for John to explain one Danielic allusion (5.27) with another (5.28-29). Therefore, it appears likely that τοῦτο refers to the antecedent in vv. 26-27.

In this case, Jesus would be saying, "Do not be amazed that the Son has been given authority to resurrect and to judge as the Danielic Son of Man (5.26-27), because the hour is coming when the Danielic resurrection will come to pass (5.28-29)." The people should not be amazed, because God had foretold that these things would happen.[77] Jesus's argument implies the Danielic prophecy and its fulfillment.

It is apparent from the following parallels that Jn 5.28-29 is based on and repeats the core of what has already been said in 5.24 and 5.25.

---

75. Once it is introduced by an ἵνα.

76. So also Ridderbos, *John*, p. 201; Haenchen, *John*, 1:253.

77. Dahl comes to a similar conclusion concerning the argumentative function of the Danielic allusion in Jn 5.28-29; however, he fails to see the direct connection between 5.28-29 and 5.26-27, especially since he does not view the "Son of Man" reference in 5.27 to be an apocalyptic figure (Nils A. Dahl, "'Do Not Wonder!' John 5.28-29 and Johannine Eschatology Once More', in Robert T. Fortna and Beverly R. Gaventa (eds), *The Conversation Continues: Studies in Paul and John* (Nashville: Abingdon, 1990), pp. 322–36.

Jn 5.24	Jn 5.25	Jn 5.28-29
Truly, truly, I say to you ('Αμὴν ἀμὴν λέγω ὑμῖν ὅτι)	Truly, truly, I say to you ('Αμὴν ἀμὴν λέγω ὑμῖν ὅτι)	
	the hour is coming (ἔρχεται ὥρα), and is now here, when	Do not marvel at this; for the hour is coming (ἔρχεται ὥρα), in which
he who hears (ὁ ἀκούων) my word, [and believes him who sent me]	the dead will hear the voice (ἀκούσουσιν τῆς φωνῆς) of the Son of God,	all who are in the tombs will hear his voice (ἀκούσουσιν τῆς φωνῆς αὐτοῦ),
has eternal life (ζωὴν), and does not come into judgement (κρίσιν), but has passed out of death into life (ζωὴν).	and those who hear will live (ζήσουσιν).	and will come forth; those who did the good deeds* to a resurrection of life (εἰς ἀνάστασιν ζωῆς), those who committed the evil deeds to a resurrection (εἰς ἀνάστασιν) of judgement (κρίσεως).

Note
* The resurrection in Jn 5.28-29 appears to be based on works, not faith. Does this statement contradict John's emphasis on having faith? Hodges has correctly argued that the phrase "those who have done good" does not refer to any meritorious works; rather it is an absolute statement that describes those who have been transformed into a new life. Indeed, the phrase "those who have done good" categorizes all believers into one group, which excludes the bearing of imperfection or the existence of variation in the "good" of each individual (Zane C. Hodges, 'Those Who Have Done Good—John 5.28-29', *BSac* [1979]: pp. 158–66).

While John also employs language similar to the resurrection description in Isa. 26.19 (as we argued earlier),[78] the Danielic text stands more clearly in the foreground, since the phrasing in John 5.28-29 closely resembles the Danielic text (although John has probably combined the two texts, Isa. 26.19 and Dan. 12.2). So close is the resemblance with Dan. 12.1-2, that one could even argue the plausibility of a quotation, since John's depiction of a double resurrection is unique to Dan. 12.2.[79] Observe particularly that ὥρα is part of the allusion, which confirms our earlier conclusion in 5.25 that ὥρα was the end-time hour from Daniel.

78. See the discussion and relevant chart earlier in this chapter. We have also suggested a possible background of Ezek. 37.9-10, 12 for the hearing language in Jn 5.24, 25, 28. The NA[27] mentions Isa. 26.19, Ezek. 37.12 and Dan. 12.2 as possible allusions in Jn 5.28-29.
79. Although we have seen that the double resurrection repeatedly occurs in early Judaism in dependence on Dan. 12.2.

Dan. 12.1-2	Jn 5.28-29
Now at that hour (ὥραν) . . . many of them that sleep in the dust of the earth will awake (ἀναστήσονται), some to (οἱ μὲν εἰς) eternal life (ζωὴν), and some to (οἱ δὲ εἰς) reproach and eternal shame.	Do not marvel at this; for the hour (ὥρα) is coming, in which all who are in the tombs will hear his voice, and will come forth; those who did the good deeds to (οἱ . . . εἰς) a resurrection of life (ἀνάστασιν ζωῆς), those who committed the evil deeds to (οἱ δὲ . . . εἰς) a resurrection (ἀνάστασιν) of judgement.

As I have already argued, the saying in 5.28-29 forms the climactic point of the pericope at hand (5.19-30), expanding on the central point of the chiasm in 5.24-25.[80] The climax of Jesus's reasoning involves the following elements: 1) The resurrection of the eschaton will be executed by Jesus; 2) apart from being the Son of God, the Messiah, Jesus is also the Danielic Son of Man who will bring the world to its end; 3) as predicted, the resurrection will result in both eternal life and eternal judgment in the hour to come.

While in Jn 5.25 this same resurrection is portrayed as a present reality, in Jn 5.28-29 the resurrection is yet to come. These should not be perceived as two separate events. Although some scholars have considered John's emphasis to be merely on a realized eschatology, we have already seen that most scholars have distinguished between an inaugurated or realized and a future eschatology in Jn 5.25 and 28-29.[81] Indeed, it is most likely that John views the resurrection of Dan. 12.2 as both inaugurated in Jesus's time (5.24, 25)[82] and to be consummated at his return (5.28-29).[83] In both cases, John refers to the same eschatological event. Moreover, in both resurrection references (5.24-25 and 28-29), John alludes to Isa. 26.19 and Dan. 12.2 (and possibly Ezek. 37.9-10, 12), which indicates that John is thinking of them as the realization of the same OT prophetic event.

John relates the resurrection fulfillment of Dan. 12.2, quoted in Jn 5.28-29, with the coming hour (cf. 5.25). In the immediate context, he has portrayed Jesus as the Son of Man who effects judgment (5.27), gives eternal life (5.24), and resurrects

---

80. Jesus's argument culminates in vv. 28-29: "Do not be amazed at what I have just said, because the hour is coming when the Danielic resurrection will take place."

81. See the discussion on pp. 111–15.

82. The eschatological resurrection has been literally or actually inaugurated within the believer; hence John's use of language such as "new life," "new birth," "light," and "resurrection," in relation to the believer.

83. Van der Watt has proposed yet another suggestion. He has argued that the resurrection in Jn 5.28-29 refers to the final resurrection of "the people living *before* the incarnation" of Christ. It is a resurrection that applies to those that were already dead at the time of Jesus. On the other hand, the resurrection in Jn 5.25 refers to the spiritual resurrection of "those who live and still live after the incarnation" (J. G. van der Watt, 'A New Look at John 5.25-9 in the Light of the Use of the Term "Eternal Life" in the Gospel According to John', *Neot* 19 [1985], pp. 71–86).

people from the dead (5.25) — all within the parameters of the Johannine hour. While some may find it still possible that John does not have the Danielic hour in mind, it is more likely to say that he does, since along with mentioning of the hour in Jn 5.28, John alludes to Daniel three times in 5.22-24 and twice in 5.27 and 5.28-29.[84]

i. *John 5.30*

Jesus's statement in 5.30 forms an *inclusio* with his statement in 5.19. The statement in 5.30, however, has greater rhetorical effect, since Jesus here talks about himself in the first person. What Jesus began to say from the beginning about the Son, he now applies to himself. However, there is another difference between 5.19 and 5.30. While the former claims that the Son does what he *sees* the Father doing, the latter asserts that Jesus does what he *hears* the Father saying. Is this difference accidental?

On the one hand, one should not make a sharp distinction between the seeing and hearing. Ultimately, they both result in the same works (ποιεῖν) and they both relate to the same source (τὸν πατέρα). Whether Jesus sees or hears the Father, he recognizes the same authoritative instructions. On the other hand, one cannot help noticing that the Son *sees* the Father in 5.19, because the Father is described to be at work in 5.17, 19-20. Similarly, the *hearing* in 5.30 also has a close referent, which is the will of God. Where is this will of God to be found? Later in the same gospel, in 6.38-40, the will of God is defined in reference to the resurrection of the last day.

Jn 5.30	Jn 6.38-40
I can do (ποιεῖν) nothing on my own initiative. As I hear, I judge; and my judgement is just, because I do not seek my own will, but the will of him who sent me (τὸ θέλημα τὸ ἐμὸν ἀλλὰ τὸ θέλημα τοῦ πέμψαντός με).	For I have come down from heaven, not to do (ποιῶ) my own will, but the will of him who sent me (τὸ θέλημα τὸ ἐμὸν ἀλλὰ τὸ θέλημα τοῦ πέμψαντός με). This is the will of him who sent me (τὸ θέλημα τοῦ πέμψαντός με), that of all that he has given me I lose nothing, but raise it up on the last day. For this is the will of my Father (τὸ θέλημα τοῦ πατρός μου), that everyone who beholds the Son and believes in him will have eternal life, and I myself will raise him up on the last day.

John's use of the same language in 5.30 and 6.38-40 (τὸ θέλημα τὸ ἐμὸν ἀλλὰ τὸ θέλημα τοῦ πέμψαντός με) indicates that Jesus is speaking about the same thing, namely the end-time resurrection. In fact, Jesus employs the same wording in 4.34 to explain to the disciples that his food is to do the will of the one who sent him (τὸ θέλημα τοῦ πέμψαντός με), which in context bears fruit unto eternal life (εἰς ζωὴν αἰώνιον, in 4.36).[85] It is evident from the above parallel that, for John, the will of

---

84. The word *hour* is connected to the resurrection of the dead also in Midr. Psalms 17.13. Note especially the phrase "in the hour of the awakening of the dead" and the reference to Isa. 26.19.

85. The word θέλημα also appears in Jn 1.13 to convey that those who believe will be born through God's will (this relates to the second birth described in John 3).

the Father is linked to the promise of eternal life and the resurrection of the last day. Therefore, in 5.30, Jesus probably *hears* the Father's will as it is inscribed in the Danielic prophecy mentioned in 5.28-29. Jesus seeks to do the Father's will, which is expressed in Dan. 12.1-2. This observation further enhances my suggestion that Jesus centralizes his argument around the eschatological prophecy in Dan. 12.2.

V. *Conclusion*

After having secured a Danielic connection in Jesus's discourse in Jn 5.19-30, the proposal that the Johannine hour in 5.25, 28 has its source in Daniel gains force. Let us review once more the data that has led us to this conclusion. First, the phrase ζωὴ αἰώνιος in John 5.24 alludes to the OG/TH of Dan. 12.2, which refers to the resurrection that will take place in the eschaton.[86] We have also seen that the receiving of authority to judge by the Son (in Jn 5.22, 24, and 27) alludes to Dan. 7.13-14, 26-27, where the Ancient of Days gives the Son of Man (or Israel) the authority to effect the final judgment. The additional description of the Son receiving honor in Jn 5.23 further recalls the image of Dan. 7.14, where honor is given to the Son of Man. Moreover, the explicit reference to the Son of Man in relation to judgement in Jn 5.27, clearly alludes to the apocalyptic Son of Man in Dan. 7.13. Furthermore, several scholars agree that the reference to a double resurrection in Jn 5.28-29 alludes to the eschatological resurrection in Dan. 12.2. Another connection between Jn 5.19-30 and Daniel is the fact that both texts utilize language from the same OT references to resurrection, namely Isa. 26.19 and possibly Ezek. 37.9-10, 12. These latter OT texts serve as background for both Jn 5.21, 25, 28-29 and Dan. 12.2.

Within this context (Jn 5.19-30), John mentions the coming of an hour that has close affinities with the hour in Daniel; both hours (in Jn 5.25, 28 and in Dan. 12.1-2) are eschatological and specifically refer to a final judgment and a final resurrection. In the Johannine context, this eschatological hour is perceived as inaugurated in 5.25 and consummated in 5.28-29.

The above observations show that Jesus spoke about the imminent coming of judgment and resurrection life only as these were foretold in the OT, and especially as they were described in Daniel within the confines of the eschatological hour. We will show in the following chapters that an additional number of significant occurrences of ὥρα elsewhere in John are rooted in Daniel and are used in an eschatological sense (as in Daniel 8–12); these instances are similar to the uses we have seen in Jn 4.21, 23 and 5.25, 28.

---

86. John also relates the phrase to the resurrection of the eschaton in Jn 6.40, 54.

THE OT BACKGROUND OF THE
ESCHATOLOGICAL HOUR IN JOHN 12.23, 27

I. *Introduction*

While we have seen that earlier passages from the Fourth Gospel reflect the Danielic background of the Johannine hour, the use of hour in Jn 12.23, 27 further relates the Johannine eschatological hour to Danielic themes and reflects a Danielic backdrop. In this chapter, I will investigate the possible allusions to the book of Daniel that exist in Jn 12.20-36 and relate to the eschatological hour in the Fourth Gospel.

II. *The Immediate Context of John 12.23, 27*

Since the coherence of Jn 12.20-36 has been argued elsewhere, I will not attempt a defense for it here.[1] Instead, I will present the structure of Jn 12.20-36, as it has already been proposed by La Potterie and Moloney.[2] The structure of the passage involves a parallelism between Jn 12.23-30 and 12.31-36a (see chart on p. 125), which strengthens the literary coherence in Jn 12.20-36. I present the proposal of La Potterie in such a way as to make this parallelism apparent:

---

1.   Several scholars have treated Jn 12.20-36 as a literary unity, being derived from a singular source: C. H. Dodd, *Historical Tradition in the Fourth Gospel* (Cambridge: Cambridge University Press, 1963), pp. 366–69, 338–43. Ignace de la Potterie, 'L'exaltation du Fils de l'homme (Jn 12.31-36)', *Greg* 49 (1968), pp. 460–78 (461–62); Schnackenburg, *John*, 2.380–81; Kiyoshi Tsuchido, 'Tradition and Redaction in John 12.1-43', *NTS* 30 (1984), pp. 609–19; Johannes Beutler, 'Greeks Come to See Jesus (John 12.20f)', *Bib.* 71 (1990), pp. 333–47; Ashton, *Fourth Gospel*, p. 494. See also the discussion in Francis J. Moloney, *The Johannine Son of Man* (BSRel, 14; Rome: LAS, 1978), pp. 161–64.

2.   De la Potterie, 'L'exaltation du Fils de l'homme', pp. 461–62; Francis J. Moloney, *The Gospel of John* (SP, 4; Collegeville: The Liturgical Press, 1998), p. 352. Neyrey has also noticed the pattern of "Statement–Misunderstanding–Clarification" that occurs in two parallel cycles within Jn 12.27-36 (Jerome H. Neyrey, S. J., *The Gospel of John* [NCBC; Cambridge: Cambridge University Press, 2007], p. 219).

	Jn 12.23-30	Jn 12.31-36a
A	A first revelation (12.23-28a): the hour of glorification for the Son of Man	A second revelation (12.31-32): the judgment of the world and the lifting up of Jesus
B	The revelation is explained by a heavenly voice (12.28b)	The revelation is explained by the narrator (12.33)
C	The crowd misunderstands (12.29)	The crowd misunderstands (12.34)
D	Jesus explains further (12.30)	Jesus explains further (12.35-36a)

The coming of the Greeks to see Jesus in Jn 12.20-22 introduces the whole passage. Also, Jesus's departure in John 12.36b is a deliberate reaction to the misunderstanding of the Jews and enhances the relevance of the OT quotations in 12.37-43, which deal with the rejection of the Jews.

Of particular importance to the hour, as well as to the argument of the passage, is the revelation-explanation motif as it appears in A and B above. More particularly, the revelation-explanation motif that appears in Jn 12.23-28, concerning the glorification of the Son of Man, presents the following chiasm:

(a)   The hour has come for the Son of Man to be glorified (12.23)

  (b)   The necessity of Jesus's death (12.24-26)

(a')   Jesus commits himself to the hour of glorification (12.27-28)

The response to the above revelation is the misunderstanding by the crowd (12.29) and Jesus's further explanation (12.30).

Following the first revelation, the subsequent revelation-explanation motif in Jn 12.31-33 further clarifies the hour of glorification:

(a)   The time of judgment: The judgment of the world has come, and the ruler of this world will now be driven out (12.31)

(b)   The time of salvation: The lifting up of Jesus will cause all people to be drawn to him (12.32)

(c)   Jesus's exaltation: explained as his death on the cross (12.33)

Once again, a misunderstanding by the crowd (12.34) and Jesus's further explanation (12.35-36a) follows this second revelation.

If this assessment of the passage is correct, then the hour of glorification and suffering (12.23-28) incorporates the judgment of the world and the drawing of all people (12.31-32). Jesus's emphasis in the former section (12.23-30) is placed on the present realization of this hour. Both verses in which ὥρα occurs (12.23, 27) affirm that this hour has arrived or is at hand (ἐλήλυθεν in 12.23 and ἦλθον in 12.27).

Moreover, John's comment in 12.33 explicitly relates Jesus's lifting up (or the hour of glorification) to the cross. As in Jn 5.19-30, we have reference to the mission of the Son of Man (12.34), while John 12 also mentions the "ruler of this world" (12:31), the "Messiah" (12.34), and the "children of light" (12.36). In the rest of this chapter, I intend to show that the double identification of the hour with the concepts of "judgement" and "salvation" has been influenced in general by the context of Dan. 7.13-14 and in particular by Dan. 12.1-2.

III. *The Danielic Background of Hour in John 12.23, 27*

The proposed allusion understands the use of hour in John 12.23, 27 as a reference to the hour in Dan. 12.1. Specifically, Dan. 12.1 reads:

> And at that hour (ὥρα in OG) Michael the great prince will stand up, that stands over the children of your people: and there will be a time of distress, such distress as has not been from the time that there was a nation on the earth until that time: at that time your people will be lifted up (ὑψωθήσεται in OG), even every one that is written in the book.

Before evaluating the probability of this allusion, one must first consider whether the allusion is even possible. If a literary connection between the hour in Jn 12.23, 27 and Dan. 12.1 exists, one would expect the Danielic motifs of judgment and deliverance to somehow relate to Jn 12.20-36.

It is evident from Jn 12.23 that the Johannine hour is closely associated with the glorification of the Son of Man.[3] We have already examined the connection between the Son of Man figure and the hour in Jn 5.27-29 and have concluded that the use of the hour there alludes to Dan. 12.1.[4] Why would John relate the eschatological hour to the glorification of the Son of Man in John 12?[5]

---

3.   While scholars in the past have considered the references to the Son of Man as references to "humanity" or a "human being," many scholars today have affirmed the connection with Daniel based on the contextual Johannine themes, which point to an apocalyptic interpretation of the Son of Man. Moloney, who still argues for the former view, is one of the exceptions to the above consensus (Moloney, *The Gospel of John: Text and Context* [BIS, 72; Leiden: Brill Academic Publishers, 2005], pp. 66–92). For the background of the "Son of Man," see Lindars, *Jesus Son of Man: A Fresh Examination of the Son of Man Sayings in the Gospels* (London: SPCK, 1983); D. Burkett, *The Son of the Man in the Gospel of John* (JSNTSup, 56; Sheffield: Sheffield Academic Press, 1991); idem, *The Son of Man Debate: A History and Evaluation* (SNTSMS, 107; Cambridge: Cambridge University Press, 1999).

4.   Notice the loose quotation of Dan. 12.2 in Jn 5.28-29, as well as the reference to the eschatological hour in Jn 5.25, 28.

5.   Before we examine the glorification motif, one may object to the proposal of linking the hour with the Danielic Son of Man. The argument may be raised that although the use of "Son of Man" in Jn 12.23, 34 may be a deliberate allusion to Dan. 7.13, the hour is still absent from Daniel 7. While this may be true, nevertheless, the hour is mentioned in

It seems plausible that John followed the OG (not TH) interpretation of Dan. 12.1, which describes the saints as being "lifted up" (ὑψωθήσεται) in the same manner as the servant in Isaiah is "lifted up" (Isa. 52.13). Perhaps influenced by the latter passage in Isaiah, John semantically relates the words δοξάζω and ὑψόω. However, as is evident from Jn 12.20-36, he has added to both words the notion of suffering:

Jn 12.23-24	Jn 12.32-34
The hour has come for the Son of Man (ὁ υἱὸς τοῦ ἀνθρώπου) to be glorified (δοξασθῇ). Truly, truly, I say to you, unless a grain of wheat falls into the earth and dies (ἀποθάνῃ), it remains alone; but if it dies (ἀποθάνῃ), it bears much fruit.	And I, if I am lifted up (ὑψωθῶ) from the earth, will draw all men to myself. But he was saying this to indicate the kind of death (θανάτῳ) by which he was to die (ἀποθνήσκειν). The crowd then answered him . . . how can you say, the Son of Man (τὸν υἱὸν τοῦ ἀνθρώπου) must be lifted up (ὑψωθῆναι)?

Scholars rightly agree that the use of the "lifting up" language is not incidental for John; it specifically alludes to Isa. 52.13.[6] The suffering of Jesus is elsewhere described as the suffering of the servant in Isaiah,[7] which indicates that John may have borrowed the idea of royal suffering from Isaiah 53.[8]

However, it is not less incidental that all five occurrences of ὑψόω in John's gospel directly associate the "lifting up" motif with the Son of Man (Jn 3.14; 8.28; 12.32; 12.34). If along with the "lifing up" of the servant in Isa. 52.13 John has in mind the "lifting up" of the saints in Dan. 12.1, then the Son of Man is naturally destined to be lifted up and the eschatological hour by consequence pertains to the glorification of the Son of Man (Jn 12.23, 27).[9]

Dan. 12.1 (cf. esp. the LXX), where the saints seem to attain some sort of glorification (cf. Dan. 12.1-3). One must keep in mind that the saints of Daniel 12, according to the context of Daniel 7, interpret the Son of Man figure, since the saints are identified with the Son of Man in Daniel 7, as we have seen in the discussion of Jn 5.24-30. Therefore, the hour mentioned in Dan. 12.1 is likely connected to or a development of the time of suffering and vindication of the saints in Daniel 7.

   6.   See C. K. Barrett, *The Gospel According to St John: An Introduction with Commentary and Notes on the Greek Text* (London: SPCK, 1967), p. 356; Raymond E. Brown, *The Gospel According to John* (AB, 29; New York: Doubleday, 1966), p. 478; B. Lindars, *The Gospel of John* (NCB; Grand Rapids: Eerdmans, 1982), p. 157; A J. Köstenberger, *John* (BECNT; Grand Rapids: Baker Academic, 2004), p. 128; A. T. Lincoln, *The Gospel According to Saint John* (BNTC; New York: Continuum, 2005), p. 352.

   7.   E.g. the use of the paschal lamb imagery in Jn 1.29 and 19.36.

   8.   Block has recently proposed that the suffering servant in Isaiah represents a suffering king (Daniel Block, 'My Servant David: Ancient Israel's Vision of the Messiah', in Richard S. Hess and M. Daniel Carroll R. [eds], *Israel's Messiah in the Bible and the Dead Sea Scrolls* [Grand Rapids: Baker, 2003], pp. 17–56 [27–28, 43–49]).

   9.   See p. 126n. 5 (and p. 116n. 69) for an explanation as to why the Son of Man should be identified with or incorporated to the saints in Dan. 12.1-2.

According to the comparison table below, John has probably combined the two separate traditions, the one coming from Isaiah and the other from Daniel.[10]

Isa. 52.13	Dan. 7.13-14; 12.1-3	Jn 12.23, 32-34
Behold, my servant will understand (συνήσει), and be lifted up (ὑψωθήσεται), and glorified (δοξασθήσεται) exceedingly.	(7.13-14) and behold, with the clouds of heaven one like a Son of Man (υἱὸς ἀνθρώπου) was coming, and he came up to the Ancient of Days . . . and to him was given authority (12.1-3) And at that hour (ὥραν) . . . and on that day the whole people will be lifted up (ὑψωθήσεται), every one that is written in the book. . . . And those who understand (οἱ συνιέντες) will shine like the brightness of the sky.	(12.23) And Jesus answered them, saying, The hour (ἡ ὥρα) has come for the Son of Man (ὁ υἱὸς τοῦ ἀνθρώπου) to be glorified (δοξασθῇ). (12.32-34) And I, if I am lifted up (ὑψωθῶ) from the earth, will draw all men to myself. But he was saying this to indicate the kind of death by which he was to die. The crowd then answered him . . . how can you say, the Son of Man (τὸν υἱὸν τοῦ ἀνθρώπου) must be lifted up (ὑψωθῆναι)? Who is this Son of Man (ὁ υἱὸς τοῦ ἀνθρώπου)?

Let us consider the significance of this comparison.[11] First, a probable connection is introduced between the "lifting up" of Isa. 53.12 and the LXX of Dan. 12.1. This connection is strengthened by the fact that the people who suffer and are "lifted up" in Dan. 12.1 are called οἱ συνιέντες in Dan. 12.3, a language that reflects the wording describing the servant in Isa. 52.13 (συνήσει ὁ παῖς μου). The OG of Dan. 12.1 may have been influenced by the resurrection language in Isa. 26.19.

Whatever the influence may be, the fact remains that in Dan. 12.1-3, the saints — along with the Son of Man — are depicted along the lines of the servant in Isaiah. Consequently, the combination of both the Danielic Son of Man and the suffering servant in John 12 should not surprise.[12] While John's identification of the words

10. The combination of the two specific sources (Isaiah and Daniel) is not foreign to John, since we have encountered it elsewhere in the gospel. For example, notice that Jesus's words in Jn 5.24-29 betray an allusion to the resurrection in Isa. 26.19 and Dan. 12.2 (and possibly to Ezek. 37.9). The only place in the OT (LXX) where both the words ἐγείρω and νεκρός occur is in Isa. 26.19, which reads: "Your dead (οἱ νεκροί) shall live (ἀναστήσονται), their corpses (οἱ ἐν τοῖς μνημείοις) shall rise (ἐγερθήσονται)." Also, the word μνημεῖον — not to mention the phrase οἱ ἐν τοῖς μνημείοις — is used nowhere in the OT in relation to the idea of resurrection, except in Isa. 26.19, and John uses this exact phrasing (οἱ ἐν τοῖς μνημείοις) in conjunction with the resurrection from the dead in Jn 5.28. However, within the same passage (Jn 5.25-29), one finds several allusions to Daniel, including the strong allusion to Dan. 12.2 in Jn 5.28-29 (see my comments on Jn 5.19-30, pp. 101–23).

11. Beutler has argued for more Isaiah allusions in John 12. See Johannes Beutler, 'Greeks Come to See Jesus', pp. 333–47.

12. John may be using the word ὑψόω ("to lift up") as a double entendre, in reference

δοξάζω and ὑψόω may have originated in Isaiah, the idea that the Son of Man will be the one glorified or lifted up, being absent from the rest of the Old Testament, can only have its origin in connecting Dan. 7.13 with 12.1.[13]

The combination of the Son of Man with the hour as an allusion to Daniel is enhanced by the fact that the Son of Man is to *suffer* and *be lifted up*; which adds another common element between Jn 12.20-36 and Dan. 12.1-3, one that cannot be easily dismissed.[14] Indeed, the fact that the Son of Man suffers by way of being lifted up in Jn 12.20-36 (esp. vv. 24, 27, 33) corresponds well with the Son of Man being the representative of the suffering saints in Daniel 7, as well as in Dan. 12.1-3, in which context the saints suffer and are being lifted up (Dan. 7.21 and 11.35; 12.1).

Scholars have discerned that immediately after Jesus's speech in Jn 12.23-33 (about the glorification of the Son of Man in terms of death and by way of being lifted up), the people respond with a misunderstanding concerning the role of the Son of Man (12.34): "We have heard from the law that the Messiah remains forever. How can you say that the Son of Man must be lifted up? Who is this Son of Man?"[15] The people's expectation of the Messiah to "remain forever" may be found in Ps. 89.36,[16] but Hoskyns has also argued that the concept of the Son of Man's eternal reign may also derive from Dan. 7.13-14,[17] which would make sense in the present context. Jesus's mention of the glorification of the Son of Man in Jn 12.23 is reminiscent of the authority and glory that the Son of Man receives in Dan. 7.13-14. However, Jesus proceeds to explain the role of the Son of Man in

to both Isa. 52.13 and Dan. 12.1. This is not unusual in John, since he has used the same word elsewhere as a double entendre: the word ὑψόω in Jn 3.14 refers to both Isa. 52.13 and Num. 21.8-9.

13. The phrase "lifted up from the earth," as it is used in Jn 12.32, has the connotation of deliverance "from the earth." The phrase ἐκ τῆς γῆς appears elsewhere in John's gospel only in Jn 3.31, with a negative sense. While the phrase at times signifies an earthly origin, in the LXX, the same phrase occasionally takes a redemptive sense, alluding to the exodus event (cf. Exod. 1.10; 3.8; 6.1, 11; 7.2; 12.33; Isa. 63.11). For a proposal for the redemptive character of the "lifting up," see John W. Romanowsky, '"When the Son of Man Is Lifted Up": The Redemptive Power of the Crucifixion in the Gospel of John', *Hor* 32 (2005), pp. 100–16.

14. Beasley-Murray connects the "lifting up" with the hour by associating both with the cross (G. R. Beasley-Murray, *John* (WBC, 36; Waco: Word, 1987), pp. 46–47).

15. Ridderbos rightly notes that the inquiry here is not so much about the identity of the Son of Man, as it is about his nature ("what kind of Son of Man are you speaking of," in H. Ridderbos, *The Gospel of John: A Theological Commentary* (Grand Rapids: Eerdmans, 1997), p. 441, n. 206).

16. Psalm 89.36 reads, "his seed will endure forever" (τὸ σπέρμα αὐτοῦ εἰς τὸν αἰῶνα μενεῖ).

17. E. C. Hoskyns, *The Fourth Gospel* (London: Faber & Faber, 1947), p. 427. See also, Lindars, *John*, p. 434. Van Unnik explores all the possible options and sides with Ps. 89.36 (W. C. Van Unnik, 'The Quotation from the Old Testament in John 12.34', *NovT* 3 [1959], pp. 174–79; cf. also Gilliam Bamfylde, 'More light on John XII 34', *JSNT* 17 [1983], pp. 87–89).

terms of death (12.24-25) and also by alluding to the "lifting up" of the suffering servant in Isaiah (12.32). Even if the people employed the eternal Messianic reign in Ps. 89.36 to launch their argument, they must have at least related this eternal reign with the Son of Man figure in Dan. 7.13-14, since both parts of their question revolve around this figure.

In addition to the notion of being "lifted up," John qualifies the eschatological hour with the word κρίσις in Jn 12.31. We have already encountered the association of the eschatological hour with the notion of judgment in Jn 5.22, 24, 27, 29 and have concluded that the combination of the Son of Man with the notion of judgment specifically derives from Dan. 7.13, 22. More specifically in Jn 12.31, we have the defeat by judgment of the "ruler of this world." In the wider context of the gospel, this ruler is identified with Satan or the Devil.[18] John presents Satan as God's final adversary, who will be judged and defeated on the cross (cf. 12.33). This "ruler" echoes the arrogant "king" in Dan. 7.8, 11 and the insolent "king" in Dan. 11.36-45,[19] the former of which is destroyed in the context of God's judgment and the latter defeated within the context of a cosmic battle.[20] In Dan. 10.13, 20-21; 12.1,[21] the word ἄρχων is used to describe angelic beings that entangle themselves in cosmic battles, particularly the eschatological battle that will eliminate God's final adversary (Dan. 12.1).[22]

Another Danielic theme would be the mention of "eternal life" in Jn 12.25.[23] Indeed, according to Dan. 12.2, the phrase refers to the final resurrected state of the saints, which will be attained only after the suffering of the saints and the final cosmic battle eliminating God's enemy (see Dan. 12.1 in connection to Dan. 11.40-45). This ties well with John's emphasis in John 12, where only those that "die" (12.24) or "hate their lives" (12.25) will end up securing "eternal life."[24] While I do not

18. See the short survey of the phrase "ruler of this world" in Judith L. Kovacs, "'Now Shall the Ruler of This World Be Driven Out": Jesus' Death as Cosmic Battle in John 12.20–36', *JBL* 114 (1995), pp. 227–47 (229–31).

19. See also the use of ἄρχων in Isa. 16.4-5 and Ezek. 7.27; 38.2-3; 39.1.

20. Kovacs has argued for Jn 12.20-36 being a text that alludes to apocalyptic cosmic battles (Kovacs, 'Cosmic Battle', pp. 227–47).

21. Possibly also in Dan. 11.5, 18.

22. This corresponds well with 1 Jn 2.18-25, where the notion of the eschatological hour is similarly linked with the battle against God's adversary and the possession of "eternal life" (see my comments on 1 Jn 2.18-25, pp. 163–67).

23. The phrase "eternal life" is central to the whole gospel, since John reiterates the idea in Jn 3.16, 36; 5.24; 6.40, 47, 54 (cf. 4.14; 6.27; 10.28; 12.25; 17.2-3). The exact phrase is probably taken from Dan. 12.2, which is the only place in the Hebrew and Greek Bible where it can be found. There, Daniel speaks of a literal resurrection from the dead, others unto eternal life and others unto eternal contempt. The phrase "eternal life" is related to the Danielic Son of Man in the following passages: Jn 3.13-16; 5.24, 27; 6.27; 6.53-54; and 12.23-25. See especially the discussion on Jn 5.24-28 above.

24. For the authenticity of Jn 12.24, see Peter W. Ensor, 'The Authenticity of John 12.24', *EvQ* 74 (2002), pp. 99–107.

suggest that the mere reference to the phrase "eternal life" alludes to Dan. 12.2 everywhere it occurs in the NT, I do propose that when "eternal life" appears in a context with other lexical allusions to Dan. 12.1-3, the probability is that the phrase carries the meaning of the Danielic resurrection. The proposal is reinforced by the close combination of the themes "judgment" and "salvation" in 12.31-32. As in Jn 5.28-29, and especially Dan. 12.1-2, the eschatological hour involves both the final vindication and the final judgment.

Finally, Jesus's last response in Jn 12.35-36 deserves a brief mention. The phrase ἔτι μικρὸν χρόνον communicates the need for an immediate positive response to Jesus as the "light."[25] However, the brevity of time in the broader context of the gospel also corresponds to the brevity of the tribulation that Jesus is about to face.[26] The shortness of the final distress appears in texts such as Isa. 26.16, 20; 54.7-8, where the word μικρὸν is used in relation to the eschatological judgment and resurrection. The brevity of suffering is also implied in Dan. 7.25, where the saints will be "handed over" (παραδοθήσεται) to the insolent king for a limited time (ἕως καιροῦ καὶ καιρῶν καὶ ἕως ἡμίσους καιροῦ).

Indeed, the specific language on the brevity of time introduces the important distinction between light and darkness. The people are exhorted to "walk" or "believe" in the light. The dualism involves a decision involving either upholding the light or siding with the darkness. Such dualism is found in the Qumran texts to communicate the immediacy and necessity of taking sides before the nearing judgment. Jesus's exhortation to become "sons of light" (12.36) especially shares the thinking in Qumran with respect to sons of light and sons of darkness fighting in an eschatological war.[27] As Kovacs has argued, the conflict between light and darkness is an eschatological conflict that refers to a cosmic battle.[28] Daniel envisions this battle as one between the Son of Man and the insolent king in Dan. 7.13, 24-25 or between Michael and God's last enemy in Dan. 11.40–12.3. It seems that Jesus views himself as participating in this eschatological battle (cf. 12.31) and thus exhorts the people to take sides. If this assessment is correct, then Jesus would naturally have spoken about the coming hour by alluding to the hour of the eschatological battle in Dan. 11.35, 40, 45; and especially 12.1, all of which refer to the final battle (Dan. 11.35, 40, 45) or the final tribulation (Dan. 12.1).

The above combination of lexical and thematic elements in Jn 12.20-36 makes the proposal for an allusion to Daniel probable. The references to 1) the Son of Man, 2) the "lifting up" motif, 3) the judgment of the "ruler" of this world, and 4) the acquiring of "eternal life," all in connection with 5) the eschatological hour and 6) within an atmosphere of cosmic battle, attest to a probable Danielic influence.

---

25. It is clear from Jn 1.3-9; 8.12; 9.5 that, according to John, Jesus is the light.

26. The brevity of time is elsewhere mentioned in Jn 7.33; 13.33; 14.19; 16.16-19. The link between the brevity of time and Jesus's tribulation is more obvious in Jn 16.16-19, where an emphasis is placed on the meaning of the word μικρὸν (see my comments on p. 148).

27. See 1QS 1.9; 2.16; 3.13, 20-25; 4.11; and 1QM 1.1-13.

28. Kovacs, 'Cosmic Battle', pp. 227–45.

Nevertheless, there is an additional argument to be made, which relates to the tradition that lies behind the text in Jn 12.20-36. To this argument we now turn.

IV. *The Hour in John 12.23, 27 and the Gethsemane Tradition*

Apart from the direct associations of the Johannine hour with the Danielic motifs in Jn 12.20-36, the text invites us to interpret the hour along the tradition of the Gethsemane episode.[29] The passage in Mk 14.34-36, 41 strongly resembles the Johannine description of Jesus's agony: in both texts Jesus is troubled in his soul (Mk 14.34; Jn 12.27), he entertains the option of being delivered from the distress (Mk 14.35; Jn 12.27), he chooses to follow his destiny by praying to the Father (Mk 14.36; Jn 12.28), and he announces that the hour has come (Mk 14.41; Jn 12.23, 27). In this light, it is probable that Jn 12.20-36 has been influenced by the Synoptic tradition, which would also open the possibility of a Johannine borrowing of the hour from Mark.[30] However, the multiple attestation of the hour strongly suggests that the hour tradition is probably traced back to Jesus.[31]

Why would Jesus — and subsequently the early church — use the idea of a coming hour? Where did the idea of an eschatological ὥρα come from? The Synoptic tradition provides hints or evidence that the eschatological hour has a Danielic background. The Danielic identity of the hour that Jesus mentions in the Gethsemane episode (Mk 14.35, 41) is evident in two places.

First, Mark's eschatological hour has previously been mentioned and defined in Mk 13.11, 32, a context that makes multiple references to Daniel.[32] Notice the mention of wars and the coming of the "end" (13.7-8, 13), as well as the use

---

29. The debate concerning the relationship between John and the synoptic gospels is long and complex (see the discussion in D. Moody Smith, *John Among the Gospels: The Relationship in Twentieth Century Research* [Columbia: University of South Carolina Press, 2001]; see also Adelbert Denaux, ed., *John and the Synoptics* [BETL, 101; Leuven: Leuven University Press, 1992]). Discussion on the particular relationship between John and Mark can be found in Ian D. Mackay, *John's Relationship with Mark: An Analysis of John 6 in Light of Mark 6–8* (Tübingen: Mohr [Siebeck], 2004), pp. 9–54. Even more specifically, concerning the relationship of Jn 12.20-36 with the Gethsemane tradition in the synoptic gospels, see Raymond E. Brown, 'Incidents that are Units in the Synoptic Gospels but Dispersed in St. John', *CBQ* 23 (1961), pp. 143–60 (143–48).

30. Notice the use of the eschatological hour in the Synoptic tradition: Mt. 24.36, 44, 50; 25.13; 26.45, 55; Mk 13.11, 32; 14.35, 41; Lk. 22.53.

31. So also C. S. Keener, *The Gospel of John: A Commentary* (2 Vols; Peabody: Hendrickson Publishers, 2003), p. 508; C. A. Evans, *Mark 8.27–16.20* (WBC, 34B; Dallas: Word, 2002), p. 411.

32. While some have argued that the passion narrative in Mark 14 corresponds to a first fulfillment of the predictions in Mark 13 (e.g. R. H. Lightfoot, *The Gospel Message of St. Mark* [Oxford: Clarendon, 1958], pp. 52–53), others argue that Jesus's trial functions only as a model for how the disciples should act when the trials of Mark 13 arrive (Adela Yarbro Collins, *Mark* [Hermeneia; Minneapolis: Fortress, 2007], p. 678). Whatever the case may be,

of constructions such as δεῖ γενέσθαι (Mk 13.7; cf. Dan. 2.28), ὁ ὑπομείνας εἰς τέλος (Mk 13.13; cf. Dan. 12.12), and τὸ βδέλυγμα τῆς ἐρημώσεως (Mk 13.14; cf. Dan. 11.31; 12.11), which are characteristically Danielic. Also, the time of distress in Mk 13.19 ("those days will be a time of tribulation such as has not occurred since the beginning of the creation which God created until now, and never will") clearly alludes to the distress in Dan. 12.1.[33] More importantly, though, notice Mark's quotation in 13.26 of Dan. 7.13: καὶ τότε ὄψονται τὸν υἱὸν τοῦ ἀνθρώπου ἐρχόμενον ἐν νεφέλαις μετὰ δυνάμεως πολλῆς καὶ δόξης. Clearly, the context of Mark 13 invites us to interpret the hour in light of its use in Daniel 11–12.[34] The agony and distress of Gethsemane looks forward to the hour of battle and deliverance, namely the hour of the cross. One may even dare to compare Jesus's agony in Gethsemane with the "time of anguish, such as has never occurred since nations first came into existence" (Dan. 12.1)![35]

Second, the idea of "handing over" features prominently in Mk 14.10-11, 18, 21, 41-42, and it is directly connected to the eschatological hour as it is mentioned in the Gethsemane passage. More specifically, Mk 14.41 reads: ἦλθεν ἡ ὥρα, ἰδοὺ παραδίδοται ὁ υἱὸς τοῦ ἀνθρώπου εἰς τὰς χεῖρας τῶν ἁμαρτωλῶν. Pitre has recently suggested that the notion of "handing over" in Mk 14.41 has been influenced by Dan. 7.25 (LXX).[36] In addition, he further suggests that the hour in this verse pertains to the eschatological Danielic hour. His argument relies on the common use of the verb παραδίδωμι and of the phrase εἰς τὰς χεῖρας by both Mk 14.41 and Dan. 7.25.

Dan. 7.13, 25	Mk 14.41
(7.13) and behold, with the clouds of heaven one like a Son of Man (υἱὸς ἀνθρώπου) was coming	the hour has come; behold, the Son of Man (ὁ υἱὸς τοῦ ἀνθρώπου) is being delivered (παραδίδοται)
(7.25) and they will be delivered (παραδοθήσεται) into his hand (εἰς τὰς χεῖρας αὐτοῦ) for a time, times, and half a time.	into the hands (εἰς τὰς χεῖρας) of sinners.

my argument relies on the assumption that the hour in Mk 14.41 derives its eschatological sense from the use of hour in Mk 13.32.

33. This Danielic time of distress alludes to the distress in Jer. 30.7. The same distress is also brought up in Jn 16.21, 33, again in association with the eschatological hour (see my comments on pp. 154–57).

34. This is in agreement with other scholars who have linked the hour in Mk 13.32 with the Danielic hour. See especially, Raymond E. Brown, *The Death of the Messiah* (Vol. 1; New York: Doubleday, 1999), p. 168; Evans, *Mark 8.27–16.20*, p. 411; and recently B. Pitre, *Jesus, the Tribulation, and the End of the Exile* (Tübingen: Mohr [Siebeck], 2005), p. 482.

35. This may be hinted at by the reference of the great tribulation in Mk 13.19, which clearly alludes to the tribulation in Dan. 12.1. Pitre argues that the hour of Gethsemane alludes to the time of the great tribulation in Dan. 12.1 (Pitre, *Tribulation*, pp. 482–85).

36. Ibid., pp. 482–85.

Moreover, the mention of the Son of Man in Mk 14.41 makes the allusion all the more probable, as well as the reference to the hour, which also corresponds to the word καιρός in Dan. 7.25. This would be consistent with the Danielic emphasis found throughout Mark 13, especially since that same chapter reiterates the hour (Mk 13.11, 32), refers to the Son of Man (Mk 13.26), and utilizes the "handing over" language (Mk 13.9, 11-12).

How does the above tradition in Mark inform our reading of Jn 12.20-36? First, even if the two accounts do not represent the same event, the fact that both texts refer to Jesus's agony or distress before the cross makes it possible that they also both refer to the same hour. Second, by observation we notice that there exists a similar Danielic emphasis behind the Gethsemane episode in Mark as we also find in Jn 12.20-36. This similar emphasis points toward the possibility that John may have followed Mark in his interpretation of the hour. As most scholars would acknowledge, John was probably aware of Mark's text or the tradition reflected in that text and, therefore, knew of Mark's Danielic emphasis on the hour. This would explain well the Danielic emphasis that exists in Jn 12.20-36, as we have shown it to exist above. However, are there any indications in John's gospel that his hour is of a similar kind to the hour in Mark? I believe we have enough evidence in John's gospel to posit it.

In Jn 13.2, 11, 21, the word παραδίδωμι describes Judas' "handing over" of Jesus. When the moment comes for Judas to leave, Jesus emphatically exclaims: νῦν ἐδοξάσθη ὁ υἱὸς τοῦ ἀνθρώπου (Jn 13.31, see below for translation). By saying this, Jesus alludes to the hour of glorification in Jn 12.23 and thus confirms that the hour of Jesus's glorification includes his "handing over" to Satan.[37]

Jn 12.23	Jn 13.31
The hour (ἡ ὥρα) has come for the Son of Man (ὁ υἱὸς τοῦ ἀνθρώπου) to be glorified (δοξασθῇ).	Now (νῦν) is the Son of Man (ὁ υἱὸς τοῦ ἀνθρώπου) glorified (ἐδοξάσθη), and God is glorified (ἐδοξάσθη) in Him.

The hour at which Jesus had come and which caused him great distress (12.27), the hour at which he would be glorified and at which he would be lifted up (12.23, 32), is also the hour at which he is handed over by Judas (13.31). John clearly associates the "handing over" motif with the eschatological hour.

This connection becomes even clearer when one notices that Jesus's distress in his inner being occurs, first, when he confronts the coming of the eschatological hour in John 12.27, and, second, when he confronts the fact that he will be "handed over" in Jn 13.21.[38] On the one hand, the cause of the distress is the "hour," while, on the other hand, the cause of the distress is his being "handed over."

37. Notice that in Dan. 7.25 the saints — who interpret the figure of the Son of Man in the vision of Dan. 7.13-14 — are "handed over" to the insolent king.

38. Jesus is distressed one more time in the gospel in Jn 11.33.

Jn 12.27-28	Jn 13.21, 31
Now (νῦν) my soul has become troubled (τετάρακται); and what shall I say, "Father, save me from this hour?" But for this purpose I came to this hour. Father, glorify (δόξασον) your name. Then a voice came out of heaven: "I have glorified (ἐδόξασα) it, and will glorify (δοξάσω) it again."	(13.21) When Jesus had said this, he became troubled (ἐταράχθη) in spirit, and testified and said, Truly, truly, I say to you, that one of you will deliver me.

(13.31) Now (νῦν) is the Son of Man (ὁ υἱὸς τοῦ ἀνθρώπου) glorified (ἐδοξάσθη), and God is glorified (ἐδοξάσθη) in Him. |

Both of the above texts make use of the adverb νῦν to refer to the hour of distress. This νῦν clearly points to the Johannine hour, the hour of Jesus's glorification.

These observations indicate that John's hour is not much different from the hour in Mark. Rather, the two "hours" match at many points, as we have shown. Most importantly, their association with common Danielic motifs makes it more probable for John to have aligned himself with Mark's Danielic interpretation of the hour, especially since they both speak of Jesus's agony or distress before the cross.

V. *The Hour in John 12.23, 27 as the Fulfillment of a Preceding Expectation*

Apart from the presence of Danielic themes in the immediate context and the association of the Johannine hour with that in Mark due to the Gethsemane tradition, the interpretation of the hour in Jn 12.23, 27 is also affected by the broader context and overall argument of the gospel. Certainly, the eschatological hour is a theme that develops particularly within the Fourth Gospel.[39] Apart from the passing first reference in John 2.4, we have seen that the eschatological hour features more prominently in Jn 4.21, 23 and Jn 5.25, 28. The next significant reference occurs in Jn 12.23, 27, after a double mention that the hour has not yet arrived (7.30; 8.20).[40] Intra-textual connections lead us to interpret the hour in John 12 in light of the hour in John 4 and 5.

Indeed, every mention of the eschatological hour in John includes the verb "to come" (ἔρχομαι), either to denote that the hour "is coming," or "has not yet come," or "has come."[41] This creates an intra-textual prophetic expectation/fulfillment motif that culminates with Jesus's glorification on the cross (12.23; 13.1; 17.1). Therefore,

39. Note the observations by Brown, *Gospel According to John*, I, p. 517.
40. The hour in Jn 7.30 and 8.20 is likely a reference to Jesus's hour of crucifixion, which is also the time of his glorification (in light of Jn 12.20-36). John's explanation that this hour has not yet arrived links this hour with the references in 2.4; 4.21, 23; 5.25, 28, and shows an intentional theological development in John of the eschatological hour.
41. All, with the exception of John 2.4, which uses the synonymous word ἥκω. See Jn 4.21, 23; 5.25, 28; 7.30; 8.20; 13.1; 16.2, 4, 21, 25, 32; 17.1.

while John 12.23 introduces the arrival of the eschatological hour, the hour references in John 4 and 5 provide the substance of what is expected to be fulfilled.

First, the hour in Jn 4.21, 23 concerns the eschatological time when worship
(προσκυνέω) of the Father will become proper and de-localized. It may not be accidental that our passage begins in 12.20 with a few Greeks that have gone up to the
feast for worship (προσκυνέω). The hour of Jesus's glorification somehow relates
to the Greeks' coming to worship.[42] The Greeks that have come to see Jesus are
probably Jews from the diaspora. In the wider context of Jn 11–12, these Greeks
of diaspora "may invoke the Isaianic notion of Gentiles flocking to God in the end
times."[43] These Greeks likely are associated with the Gentile regions from which they
come, regions that were also promised to be gathered at the time of Israel's restoration. This is suspected by the reference to the ingathering of the dispersed Israel
in Jn 11.47-52.[44] The hour at which God's worship will be de-localized (Jn 4.21,
23) is the hour at which God's worship will be universalized. John further hints at
the proximate reconstitution of worship by stating that the Greeks sought to "see"
Jesus (12.21).[45]

This "seeing" reminds the reader of Jesus's invitation to "come and see" in
Jn 1.39, which entails a believing response on the part of the disciples. This may
also explain why we find Philip and Andrew leading the Greeks to Jesus (12.22),
since these two also appear in Jn 1.40, 43 as Jesus's followers.[46] Similarly, John
associates the act of "seeing" with the act of "believing" elsewhere in his gospel.[47]
In our context the inability to "see" is specifically linked to unbelief in the Isaianic
quotation in Jn 12.40: "lest they see with their eyes." The inability to believe is

---

42. Apart from John 4 and 12, the only other reference of worship (προσκυνέω) in the
Gospel of John is in 9.38, where the blind man worships Jesus.

43. Köstenberger, *John*, p. 377, who also cites Isa. 42.2 and 49.6. See also Lincoln, *John*,
p. 348. In addition, see also Isa. 66.18-21.

44. The notion of ingathering of the dispersed Israel is of particular importance to the
whole argument, since it relates with the end of exile. The end of exile, the restoration, and the
gathering of true Israel is a prominent theme in the prophets, and so also in Daniel. For more
information on this theme, see J. A. Dennis, *Jesus' Death and the Gathering of True Israel*
[Tübingen: Mohr (Siebeck], 2006), who argues that Jesus's death directly relates to Israel's
restoration according to OT expectations. See also Pitre, *Tribulation*. Draper also connects
the reference to the "seed" in Jn 12.24 with the coming of the Greeks in Jn 12.20 to denote
the return of the diaspora (Jonathan A. Draper, 'Holy Seed and the Return of the Diaspora in
John 12.24', *Neot* 34 [2000], pp. 347–59).

45. The parallel made here is between the purpose of the Greeks' coming (ἵνα
προσκυνήσωσιν ἐν τῇ ἑορτῇ) and their actual action (θέλομεν τὸν Ἰησοῦν ἰδεῖν).

46. In the context of Jn 1.39, John mentions Andrew and Philip by name, and Philip
becomes the intermediator that brings Nathaniel to Jesus. John may specifically mention
Philip and Andrew in Jn 12.22 in order to make the connection between the two chapters
clear.

47. See especially Jn 9.37-39, where Jesus's words on "seeing" reflect the blind man's
ability to "see," as well as his act of worship. See also Jn 11.40.

mentioned three times in 12.37-39, before it is compared with the inability to "see" in 12.40. John appears to use the verb "to see" in Jn 12.21 in order to communicate the willingness of the Greeks to believe. There is probably an identifiable reason why Jesus responds to the Greeks' desire to "see" by saying that the "the hour has come." The reason appears to be that within the Gospel of John, this hour has been defined as the moment at which the worship of God will be reshaped, delocalized, even universalized (Jn 4.21, 23).

Furthermore, we have the use of hour in Jn 5.25, 28. This hour concerns the eschatological time when judgment and resurrection will take place. The following lexical parallels between Jn 5.19-30 and 12.20-36 are enough to support a literary dependence between the two passages. First, of course, is the idea of an hour (ὥρα) that is either coming (ἔρχεται in 5.25, 28) or has come (ἐλήλυθεν in 12.23; cf 12.27), especially in relation to the Son of Man (υἱὸς τοῦ ἀνθρώπου in 5.27 and 12.23, 34). The combination of the words "hour" (ὥρα), "son" (υἱὸς), and "glory/glorify" (δόξα; δοξάζω) can only be found in John 5 (vv. 25, 27-28, 41, 44) and John 12 (vv. 23, 27-28, 34),[48] as well as in John 17.1, 5. Moreover, the word νῦν occurs in clear association to the eschatological hour in John 5.25 and 12.27, 31.[49] The word κρίσις is common in both texts (Jn 5.22, 24, 27, 29 and 12.31), as well as the phrase "eternal life" (ζωὴν αἰώνιον in Jn 5.24 and 12.25). Also, the mention of "honor" appears in Jn 5.23 and 12.26. Finally, the themes of judgment and salvation appear in close association with the eschatological hour especially in Jn 5.28-29 and 12.31-32.

Already in Jn 5.19-30 we have the expectation of an eschatological hour. When the time comes for the arrival of this hour (12.23), one expects to find the anticipated events fulfilled. While there may still be some development in the meaning of the hour, it is logical to assume that the hour in John 5 and 12 consistently refers to the same thing. This is evident, first, because of the internal pattern "the hour is coming"/"the hour has come" and use of "now" (νῦν) that implies fulfillment, and second, because of the common literary features and themes that both contexts share. On this basis, one may argue that if the hour in Jn 5.25, 28, alludes to Daniel, then it probably also functions the same in Jn 12.23, 27.

Thereupon, one should not be surprised to see the hour being contextually linked to the concepts of judgment (Jn 12.31) and deliverance (Jn 12.32), both of which appear in Daniel 7 and 12 respectively. This association has already been established in Jn 5.21-22, 26-27, where both the Son of Man (5.27) and the hour (5.25, 28) are explicitly linked to the themes of judgment and resurrection.

The existence of an internal "anticipation/fulfillment" pattern in John does not exclude the existence of an external, textual source of expectation. As true as it may be that the expectation of the hour has been generated from within the gospel itself, one should not exclude the possibility that the expectation of this hour extends even outside the Gospel of John. Of course, in this case, one needs to ground the

---

48. Notice also the thematic emphasis of the glory that comes from man, which is common to Jn 5.41 and Jn 12.41.

49. Cf. also Jn 4.23; 16.21-22; 17.1, 5.

existence of such an expectation of an hour in other texts,[50] one of them arguably being Daniel. As I have mentioned before, the only possible OT text with reference to an eschatological hour is the book of Daniel (LXX),[51] which also introduces other eschatological (or non-eschatological) motifs found in the Gospel of John.[52] Both John and the various Jewish texts studied in ch. 3 independently develop the eschatological hour and time of Daniel 8–12.

VI. *Additional Considerations*

The above arguments for a Danielic background behind the hour in Jn 12.23, 27 seem sufficient to establish the probable influence of Daniel in John's writing. When all of these arguments are considered together, the probability increases that John had in mind the eschatological hour of Daniel. The case, however, can be further strengthened when one considers the broader context of John 10–12.

The passage of John 12.20-36 is placed within the broader thematic emphasis on kingship in John 10–12. Beginning with John 10, Jesus is described as the Shepherd, which, as most scholars have noticed, alludes to the royal Davidic role in Ezekiel 34, 37. As the Good Shepherd, Jesus decides to lay down his own life for the sheep (Jn 10.11, 15), which raises the question: Where does John ground the idea of a suffering Messianic figure? How does he justify the fact that the eternal "king" will die?

The story continues in John 11, where Jesus exercises his authority to give life (cf. Jn 5.19-30) and thus proves himself to be the Messiah (Jn 11.27). The end of the chapter describes Jesus's death as the event through which God's people will be gathered again into one (Jn 11.51-52), which anticipates the coming of the Greeks (Jews from diaspora) to Jesus in Jn 12.20. This ingathering of the tribes of Israel alludes to the Davidic expectations in Ezekiel 37. John 12 begins with a story that may signify Jesus's anointing as king (Jn 12.1-8), especially since the story that follows describes Jesus's entering into Jerusalem in fulfillment of OT royal prophecies (Jn 12.12-19). In fact, the phrase "king of Israel" (12.13) has been added, which further indicates John's emphasis. After this, our passage speaks prominently of the hour at which the Son of Man will be glorified, which, if my proposal is correct, alludes to the Son of Man's reign and glorification in Daniel 7 and 12.

These observations suggest that John may have combined several royal or

---

50. See my third chapter, which is on the Jewish exegetical tradition concerning the Danielic hour.

51. We have already seen that the Greek term for hour appears 53 times in the OT (LXX) and 13 times in Daniel (LXX), 9 of which are clearly eschatological.

52. Some of these motifs would be the reference to the "Son of Man" (Dan. 7.13), the constant use of the phrase "eternal life" (which only occurs in Dan. 12.2 in the OT), the ideas of judgment (Daniel 7) and resurrection (Dan. 12.2), the concept of distress (Dan. 12.1), and the defeat of God's final adversaries (Dan. 7.11-12; 11.45). All of these occur within the boundaries of the eschatological hour in Daniel (see the LXX of Dan. 8.17, 19; 9.21; 11.35, 40, 45; 12.1, 13).

Messianic traditions (Psalm 89; Isaiah 53; Ezekiel 34, 37; Daniel 7, 12) — one of which may have been the Danielic Son of Man who receives the kingdom — to describe Jesus's mission on the cross as the moment of his enthronement and glorification.[53]

VII. *Conclusion*

Granted the validity of the Johannine allusion to the Danielic hour, let us consider the significance of this allusion, especially in the context of Jn 12.23, 27. The allusion to the Danielic hour indicates that John 12 views this hour as being fulfilled in the death and resurrection of Jesus.[54] In the Danielic context, this hour is the hour of the final judgment, the hour of the eschatological battle and suffering, and the hour of deliverance. Jesus's death on the cross brought about this eschatological hour, the end-time moment, when all of these events will take place. Therefore, by connecting the Johannine hour to the one in Daniel, one realizes that Jesus's ministry — especially his death and resurrection — is the eschatological act of God. The fact that the hour has come announces that the final eschaton has been inaugurated.

---

53. Similar traditions have been combined elsewhere in the Fourth Gospel (e.g. Jn 5.24-29).

54. The resurrection is in mind due to the description of Jesus's glorification in 12.23-25, which includes both death and life. It is typical for John to use double entendre throughout his gospel, and so also should be the case here with the use of "to glorify" and "to be lifted up" (as in 12.32).

THE OT BACKGROUND OF THE
ESCHATOLOGICAL HOUR IN JOHN 16.16-33

I. *Introduction*

The examination of the use of hour in Jn 4.21, 23; 5.25, 28; and 12.23, 27, has disclosed strong indications that the Johannine hour may allude to Dan. 12.1. The gospel continues with the use of the eschatological hour in John 16, to which we now turn. In order to investigate the use of hour in John 16 and the possible allusion to Daniel, I will first explicate the eschatological nature of the hour and then argue how this hour may relate to Daniel. The former will bring forth the eschatological focus of the passage and will illuminate the significance of hour within this eschatological locus.

The text on which I focus is the literary unit of Jn 16.16-33. Within this passage, there are three occurrences of hour: the first is linked to the woman bearing a child; the second relates to the plain explication of truth; and the third is connected to the scattering of the disciples. As I will show, each of the above images relates to OT texts such as Isa. 26.17 and 66.7; and Zech. 13.7. These textual echoes expose the eschatological connotation of Jesus's words and qualify the hour as an eschatological moment.

We will then observe that this eschatological hour is very similar to that in Daniel, and, in conjunction with other lexical parallels, I will argue for a probable allusion to Dan. 12.1-2. However, since Jn 16.16-33 belongs to the broader context of the Farewell Discourse, it is essential that we begin by addressing Jesus's words in this context.

II. *The Context of John 16.16-33*

John 16.16-33 is part of the larger context of the Farewell Discourse in John (13.1–17.36).[1] The discourse begins with a reference to Jesus's approximate hour

---

1. In what follows, I have divided John 13–16 in sections that basically follow the divisions in A. J. Köstenberger. Similar divisions also appear in G. R. Beasley-Murray.

of departure from this world ("Jesus knew that his hour had come [ἦλθεν αὐτοῦ ἡ ὥρα] to depart from this world and go to the Father" in 13.1). In context, this hour has been defined in Jn 12.23, 27 as the eschatological moment of Jesus's death and glorification (see my comments on the previous chapter on John 12). Therefore, one may view the whole of Jesus's discourse as related to Jesus's hour of departure.

Indeed, the discourse begins in the upper room, where Jesus washes the feet of his disciples, and Judas is identified as the one who delivers Jesus to the enemy (13.1-30). Jesus's reference to his glorification (13.31-32) and his going away (13.33) instigates Peter's question, 'Lord, where are you going?' as well as his declaration that he would follow Jesus to his death. Peter had not perceived the place where Jesus was going. In John 14, Jesus begins to explain to the disciples what he meant by 'going away' (Jn 14.1-5). In doing this, Jesus has to explicate the relationship between the Father, the Son and the Spirit (14.8-14) and then explain that his departure will result in the coming of the Spirit (14.15-31). It is not a coincidence that at the end of both of these sections (14.1-14 and 14.15-31) Jesus explicitly tells his disciples that he is going to the Father (14.12, 28). Jesus intends to clarify that his ultimate destination is not death but the Father (as mentioned in 13.1).

In John 15, as he speaks after a small interval (14.30-31), Jesus still addresses the issue of his departure, only now with an emphasis on the disciples. The true vine metaphor (15.1-10) intends to communicate the significance of Jesus's new commandment of love (15.11-17). At the center of these verses stand Jesus's words, "These things I have spoken to you so that my joy may be in you, and that your joy may be made full" (15.11). This joy stands in contrast to the disciples' inner distress at the prospect of Jesus's death (see Jn 14.1). The whole phrase reveals Jesus's intention to change the perspective of the disciples, especially in their understanding of the coming hour of distress.

The following sections deal with the persecution of the disciples (15.18–16.4a), and the work of the Spirit that is to come (16.4b-15). The hour first appears in 16.2 and refers to the disciples' future persecution: "They will make you outcasts from the synagogue, but the hour is coming (ἔρχεται ὥρα) for everyone who kills you to think that he is offering service to God." The time frame here is clearly in the future, since immediately after this Jesus refers to the same hour as something to be expected: "but I have said these things to you so that when their hour comes . . ." (16.4a; ὅταν ἔλθη ἡ ὥρα αὐτῶν). In 16.4b-6, Jesus again explains the reason for his words: "I did not say these things to you from the beginning, because I was with you. But now I am going to him who sent me; yet none of you asks me, 'Where are you going?' But because I have said these things to you, sorrow has filled your heart." Not only does Jesus speak to the disciples because he is departing, but also because the disciples' misunderstanding of this departure has caused them grief in their hearts. Their grief may have even been deepened by Jesus's reference to the coming hour of their own persecution. Jesus responds by telling them, first, that they were not seeking to find out Jesus's actual destiny,[2] and second, that his departure is

---

2. Jesus rebukes the disciples for not asking where he is going in 16.5. While Peter had

to their advantage, since following this departure the Spirit will come to the disciples (16.7-15). While the disciples are warned that they will face hatred, persecution and death (15.18–16.4a), they are also promised the help of the Spirit (16.4a-15).

Having come closer to our text, it is now time to outline the basic structure of Jesus's words in 16.16-24 and 16.25-33, respectively. The former passage begins with Jesus reaffirming his departure, but only for a little while, for the disciples will see him again (16.16). This "little while," along with the disciples' constant misunderstanding of Jesus's words (16.17-18), opens up the topic of the nature of the distress (16.20-22), the joy that will follow (16.22, 24), and the privilege of prayer (16.23-24, 26).[3] The following is a basic outline of Jn 16.16-24:

Jn 16.16	Jesus speaks about the "little while" (16)
Jn 16.17-18	The disciples respond by not understanding the saying about the "little while" (17a, 18), and
	The disciples do not understand what "going to the Father" means (17b)
Jn 16.19-24	Jesus discerns the disciples' inquiry (ἐρωτᾶν) and responds (19):
	1. Joy will follow a temporary grief (20-22, introduced by ἀμὴν ἀμὴν λέγω ὑμῖν)
	2. "In that day" the disciples will have no queries (οὐκ ἐρωτήσετε οὐδέν) (23a)
	3. Intimate prayer will make this joy fulfilled (23b-24, introduced by ἀμὴν ἀμὴν λέγω ὑμῖν)

The following section (16.25-33) deals with a final interaction between Jesus and the disciples, which further reveals the disciples' inability to comprehend Jesus's words. Initially, Jesus speaks about the coming hour in which he will speak plainly (16.25) and expands on the concept of intimate prayer, which will become a privilege "in that day" (16.26). This hour and this "day" have clearly not yet come. He then becomes more specific by telling them that as he left the Father to come into this world, he will now leave this world to go with the Father (16.28). The disciples misunderstand all three things that Jesus has said: they perceive Jesus's words to be plain already (16.29), they speak as if the day with "no questions" has arrived (16.30a), and their belief narrowly focuses on Jesus's first coming, rather than on his departure to the Father (16.30b). Jesus questions the foundation of their "belief" by essentially saying that, for the disciples, the present hour will not be one of faith but of desertion (16.32; "The hour is coming, indeed it has come, when you will

---

asked such a question in 13.36, he did so with the understanding of Jesus's going to death. This has filled the disciples' hearts with grief rather than joy. However, Jesus has tried to explain to his disciples that his destiny is not death but life (resurrected life) with the Father. Jesus rebukes the disciples because the disciples do not seek to find Jesus's actual destiny (Francis J. Moloney, *The Gospel of John* [SP, 4; Collegeville: The Liturgical Press, 1998], p. 439).
    3.   Notice also the final peace that will prevail in the midst of the distress in 16.33.

be scattered, each one to his home, and you will leave me alone"). In summary, the following is a brief outline of Jn 16.25-33:

Jn 16.25-28	Jesus explains to the disciples:
	1. In the coming hour, Jesus will speak plainly (25)
	2. "In that day," the disciples will experience the intimacy of prayer (26-27)
	3. As Jesus has come to the world from the Father, so he will also leave this world to go to the Father (28)
Jn 16.29-30	The disciples misunderstand:
	1. Jesus's words are plain already (29)
	2. The day for "no questions" has arrived (30a)
	3. Their faith relies on Jesus's first coming alone (30b)
Jn 16.31-32	Jesus responds:
	1. He points out a deficiency in the disciples' faith (31)
	2. He refers again to the coming hour, which is the present time for the disciples, and redefines it as one of desertion, not of faith (32)
Jn 16.33	(Therefore), Jesus has spoken these words so that the disciples may have peace and courage in the midst of a world that produces distress.

Finally, at the end of the discourse, Jesus turns to the Father and prays a high-priestly prayer that focuses on the Son (17.1-5), on the disciples (17.6-19), and on those who will believe (17.20-26). The hour once again features prominently in the very first words of Jesus's prayer to the Father in 17.1: "Father, the hour has come" (πάτερ, ἐλήλυθεν ἡ ὥρα).

III. *The Eschatological Nature of Hour in John 16.16-33*

a. *The Hour of the Woman Bearing a Child: John 16.21*

The first occurrence of hour in our passage (16.16-33) occurs in connection to the woman bearing a child. Jesus employs the image of birth to convey the temporary nature of distress and the expected joy to come. More specifically, he says, "When a woman is in labor, she has pain, because her hour has come (ἦλθεν ἡ ὥρα αὐτῆς). But when her child is born, she no longer remembers the anguish because of the joy of having brought a human being into the world" (16:21). This image has been borrowed from Isa. 26.17 and 66.7-9:

> As the pregnant woman approaches the time to give birth, she writhes and cries out in her labor pains, thus were we before you, O Lord.
>
> (Isa. 26.17)

> Before she travailed, she brought forth; before her pain came, she gave birth to a boy. Who has heard such a thing? Who has seen such things? Can a land be born in one day? Can a nation be brought forth all at once? As soon as Zion travailed, she also brought forth her sons. "Shall I bring to the point of

> birth and not give delivery?" says the LORD. "Or shall I who gives delivery
> shut the womb?" says your God.
>
> (Isa. 66.7-9)

The image of the woman in labor has eschatological overtones and thus qualifies the hour as the eschatological moment at which God's promises to Israel will come to pass.

Isaiah 26 has been identified as part of the broader context of Isaiah 24–27. The broader context concerns God's judgment on the nations and the restoration of his people.[4] Isaiah 26 presents Judah's song of petition to God to save and restore peace to his people. There is also reference to the broadening of Israel's land (Isa. 26.15). While Isaiah 26 may indeed form a prayer, it is nevertheless part of a prophetic announcement for the future of Israel.[5] Therefore, the content of Judah's petition is part of a broader prophetic proclamation, which has eschatological overtones.

One of the eschatological indications is the use of the image of a woman bearing a child. The image can be found elsewhere in Isaiah, in 49.21, 54.1 and 66.7. Here, the image of the woman bearing a child is compared with the Israelites, who have failed to bear fruit for God. It is a simile that pictures the Israelites' failure to succeed in bringing peace and salvation to their own land; thus, God's people are compared to a false pregnancy.[6] The image conveys the short distress that the Israelites are facing, a distress that is attributed to God.[7]

This distress is evident in Isa. 26.16, which reads, "O Lord, in distress they sought you; they poured out a whispered prayer when your discipline was upon them" (יְהוָה בַּצַּר פְּקָדוּךָ צָקוּן לַחַשׁ מוּסָרְךָ לָמוֹ). The rendering of this verse is difficult, since the LXX translates צָקוּן ("to pour out") as a noun (צָקוּן).[8] This results in the Greek

---

4. Some have titled Isaiah 24–27 the "Apocalypse of Isaiah." See Brian Doyle, *The Apocalypse of Isaiah Metaphorically Speaking: A Study of the Use, Function and Significance of Metaphors in Isaiah 24–27* (BETL, CLI; Leuven: Leuven University Press, 2000); and R. E. Clements, *Isaiah 1–39* (NCB; Grand Rapids: Eerdmans, 1987), p. 196. Watts disagrees with this structure, as he has structured Isaiah according to the different generations in history. He has also suggested a chiastic structure that exists in chs 23–27, which is centered on Isa. 25.6. See J. D. W. Watts, *Isaiah 1–33* (WBC, 24. Dallas: Word, 1998).

5. Eissfeldt has identified this song as a prayer rather than a national lament, while Sweeney thinks of Isaiah 26 as a "communal complaint song" (Marvin A. Sweeney, *Isaiah 1–39: With an Introduction to Prophetic Literature* [FOTL, 17; Grand Rapids: Eerdmans, 1996], p. 341). Isaiah 26.7-19 especially forms a literary unit with strong eschatological content. For the unity of these verses see Dan G. Johnson, *From Chaos to Restoration: An Integrative Reading of Isaiah 24–27* (JSOTSup, 61; Sheffield: Sheffield Academic Press, 1988), pp. 70–71.

6. Clements, *Isaiah*, p. 216.

7. In Isa. 66.9, God is the cause of the pregnancy and the one who brings the woman to her hour of labor (see also Isa. 45.7). Moreover, in Isa. 26.16, the distress is caused by God's judgment. The rendering of this latter verse has been disputed, especially because of the third person plural.

8. For a detailed examination of the complexity of the verse and the proposed solutions see J. N. Oswalt, *The Book of Isaiah: Chapters 1–39* (NICNT; Grand Rapids: Eerdmans, 1986),

rendering ἐν θλίψει μικρᾷ ("with small affliction"). Nevertheless, most scholars understand 26.16 to refer to Israel's distress, either at the present time or in the past. They take צַר to mean "distress" and מוּסָר to mean "discipline."[9] Watts also sees a reference to distress, but finds this distress to refer either to the enemies of God or to the few unfaithful within Israel.[10]

Isaiah 26.16 seems to have the following chiastic pattern, which is common to poetry (cf. 26.1). If this is the case, then the poetical form of the verse clarifies its obscure meaning.

A In distress		בַּצַּר
	B they sought you	פְּקָדוּךָ
	B' they poured out a prayer	צָקוּן לַחַשׁ
A' (when) your discipline (was) on them[11]		מוּסָרְךָ לָמוֹ

pp. 483–84 n. 42; Doyle, *Apocalypse*, pp. 307–8, n. 78–82; J. Alec Motyer, *The Prophecy of Isaiah: An Introduction and Commentary* (Downers Grove: InterVarsity, 1993), pp. 217–18, n. 2.

9.   Some of these scholars are Clements, *Isaiah*; Doyle, *Apocalypse*; Oswalt, *Isaiah*; Motyer, *Isaiah*; B. S. Childs, *Isaiah* (OTL; Louisville: Westminster John Knox, 2001); and Hans Wildberger, *Isaiah 1–27: A Continental Commentary* (Minneapolis: Fortress, 1997). However, Sweeney translates צַר as "enemy" and takes the whole verse to refer to God's enemies, not Israel. Although this interpretation is further supported by the third person plural of the verb פְּקָד, it stretches the meaning of words such as צַר (enemy) and לַחַשׁ (spell).

10. See comments by Watts in his Isaiah commentary. The obscurity of the verse lies on two factors: first, the meaning of the word צָקוּן, which also affects the meaning of the words פְּקָד and לַחַשׁ; second, the explanation of the third person plural that is found in פְּקָד. I believe that it is the latter factor—the third person plural of פְּקָד—that has led scholars to disagree about the meaning of the word צָקוּן. Nevertheless, the word צָקוּן is by itself also difficult to understand. One can take the word צָקוּן either as a verb (צָקוּן) or as a noun (צָקוּן). On the one hand, most scholars consider the word to be a verb, from the root צוּק, and so render it either "to constrain" or "to pour out" (as in BDB). On the other hand, the LXX translates the word as a noun. Oswalt follows the LXX translation, which renders the word ἐν θλίψει ("in straits") (see Oswalt, *Isaiah*, pp. 483–84). However, the most probable meaning is "to pour out," which is in agreement with most of the commentators (see Clements, *Isaiah*; Doyle, *Apocalypse*; Motyer, *Isaiah*; Childs, *Isaiah*; and Sweeney, *Isaiah*). Although the LXX has translated צָקוּן as a noun, this can be explained by the apparent obscurity of the verse or a possible tendency by the translator to emphasize Israel's distress. Moreover, the MT pointing favors a verb (and there is no Kethib-Qere reading; see also 1QIsaᵃ), and the word לַחַשׁ can hardly make any sense this way if צָקוּן is taken as a noun (Oswalt has translated לַחַשׁ as "bowed down" or "humbled," following the Akkadian meaning, but this is not persuasive. There is no compelling reason to deviate from the meaning of the word in Hebrew. Also, when the word appears in Isa. 3.3, Oswalt renders it according to its regular Hebrew meaning).

11. The petitioner uses the third person plural to distinguish himself from Israel's past misdoings that required God's discipline. Interpreted along the lines of Motyer, *Isaiah*, pp. 217–18. See discussion in W. March, 'The Study of Two Prophetic Compositions in Isaiah 24.1–27.1' (unpublished dissertation; Union Theological Seminary, 1966), pp. 142–44.

Isaiah 26.16 stresses that within the context of distress, prayer becomes vital. The emphasis of the LXX on the distress (as we saw above), although inappropriate for the meaning of the MT, indicates the significance of the distress in the song. One could argue that the distress of the people has become the basis for their petition in 26.16. When the petition ends, God's people are urged to hide for a little while until God's wrath is over (26.20). Notice how the LXX uses the word μικρός both in 26.16 and in 26.20 to indicate the shortness of the distress.

Israel undergoes distress because she has borne no fruit for God. The image of the woman bearing a child in Isa. 26.17-18 shows that although God has brought Israel to a moment of labor, Israel gave birth to nothing. The image itself is an oxymoronic event: when a woman is in pain, at least she is in pain for the sake of a new life that is to be born; when Israel is in pain before God, she is in pain for nothing.[12]

The statement on the resurrection of the dead in Isa. 26.19 forms a sharp contrast with the inability of the Israelites to give birth to life: "Your dead will live, their corpses will rise. You who lie in the dust, awake and shout for joy, for your dew is as the dew of the dawn, and the earth will give birth to the departed spirits." The resurrection of Isa. 26.19 constitutes God's answer to Israel's barren state of being (26.17-18). It is the means by which the childless woman gives birth and God's people receive joy. Through the resurrection of the dead, the indignation will be removed (26.20) and God's people will be restored to life. This promise probably refers to both a national restoration of Israel and a physical resurrection of the individual.[13] As we have already seen, this text is later used by Daniel to portray the eschatological resurrection from the dead (Dan. 12.2).

The resurrection in Isa. 26.19 anticipates the eschatological turnover of the woman's barren state later in the same book. Even if the pains of Israel in Isa. 26.17-18 do not bear any child, the labor pains in Isa. 66.7-9 explicitly result in childbirth:

> Before she travailed, she brought forth; before her pain came, she gave birth to a boy. Who has heard such a thing? Who has seen such things? Can a land be born in one day? Can a nation be brought forth all at once? As soon as Zion travailed, she also brought forth her sons. 'Shall I bring to the point of birth and not give delivery?' says the LORD. 'Or shall I who gives delivery shut the womb?' says your God.
>
> (Isa. 66.7-9)

12. The LXX has a variation of 26.18. It reads: "we have conceived and have been in pain, and have brought forth the breath of your salvation, which we have brought upon the earth." This rendering gives a positive overtone to the song, almost as if the petitioner speaks from the point of view that is after the restored state. It may have been that the LXX translator had himself such a point of view. If this were the case from the translator's viewpoint, the restored state would be preceded by distress and discipline. This viewpoint arises from seeing 26.17-18 in the light of the promise of restoration in 26.19.

13. See my comments on Dan. 12.2 in my second chapter. So also Childs, *Isaiah*, p. 192.

God will make the pregnancy effective, and this will transform the mourning into joy (66.10, 14). Clearly the context of Isaiah 66 is eschatological, especially with reference to Israel's restoration after the exile and the reference to the new creation. Indeed, the mentioning of the new birth in 66.7-9 should be interpreted in the context of resurrection (66.14, "your bones will flourish like the new grass") and of the final judgemnt, glory, and restoration as it appears in 66.15-24. God's judgment (66.15-16) will result in the creation of the new heavens and new earth (66.22) and in the worship of God by all flesh (66.23). Within this context, the metaphor of the woman in labor that is used in Isa. 66.7-9 takes on an eschatological significance, especially since it is also reminiscent of Isa. 26.17.

Our attention to the image of a woman in labor in Isaiah 26 and 66 seeks to provide the backdrop for the use of the same image in Jn 16.21. Scholars have already identified Jn 16.21 as a reference to Isa. 26.17.[14] We already saw that the petition in Isaiah 26 functions in its context as a prophetic utterance for the final restoration of Israel; this petition is seen in Jn 16.21 to find its fulfillment in Jesus. Below, I provide a comparison between the LXX of Isaiah and the text of John. The LXX is chosen because the apparent similarities between the two texts indicate that John probably had the LXX in mind. First are indicated a few parallels that appear in the broader context of the Isaiah song and in the immediate context of Jn 16.21:

Isaiah 26	John 16
(26.1) In that day (τῇ ἡμέρᾳ ἐκείνῃ) this song will be sung in the land of Judah . . .	(16.23) In that day (ἐν ἐκείνῃ τῇ ἡμέρᾳ) you will not question me about anything. Truly, truly, I say to you, if you ask the Father for anything in my name (ἐν τῷ ὀνόματί μου), he will give it to you.
(26.13) O Lord our God, other masters besides you have ruled us; but through you alone we confess your name (τὸ ὄνομά σου).	(16.26) In that day (ἐν ἐκείνῃ τῇ ἡμέρᾳ) you will ask in my name (ἐν τῷ ὀνόματί μου), and I do not say to you that I will request of the Father on your behalf.

As the above chart indicates, the whole song in Isaiah 26 will become a reality "in that day" (26.1), just as the promises about prayer given in Jn 16.23, 26 will be fulfilled "in that day." Also, in both texts, the prayer involves the invocation of the Lord's and Jesus's names, respectively.[15] These observations are strengthened by the petition of prayer in Isa. 26.16, which occurs in the context of distress and awaits the final resurrection from the dead (26.19). If the image of the woman bearing a

---

14. Keener, *John*, p. 1045; D. A. Carson, *The Gospel According To John* (PNTC; Grand Rapids: Eerdmans, 1991), p. 544; Köstenberger, 'John', in G. K. Beale and D. A. Carson (eds), *Commentary on the New Testament Use of the Old Testament* (Grand Rapids: Baker, 2007), p. 496.

15. Notice also that peace is portrayed as the desired final outcome in both cases (Isa. 26.12; Jn 16.33).

child in Jn 16.21 alludes to Isa. 26.17, then Jesus's reference to prayer in Jn 16.23, 26 may take on the sense of the eschatological petition of his people within a distress produced by the world (16.33) and God's long-awaited response of deliverance. However, in order to substantiate this, we need to compare the texts for the proposed allusion between Isa. 26.17; 66.7-9; and Jn 16.17.

Isaiah 26	John 16
(26.16-17) O Lord, they sought you in distress (ἐν θλίψει); they remembered you in a short distress (ἐν θλίψει μικρᾷ), your discipline was upon them. As the pregnant woman approaches the time to give birth (τοῦ τεκεῖν), she writhes and cries out in her labor pains, thus were we before you, O Lord.	(16.16, 17, 19) A little while (μικρὸν), and you will no longer see me; and again a little while (μικρὸν), and you will see me.
(26.20) Come, my people, enter into your rooms and close your doors behind you; hide for a little while (μικρὸν) until the indignation of the Lord runs its course.	(16.21) Whenever a woman is in labor (τίκτῃ) she has pain, because her hour has come; but when she gives birth to the child, she no longer remembers the distress (τῆς θλίψεως) because of the joy that a child has been born into the world.

As one may observe from the above, Jesus employs an eschatological image — the woman in labor — that is surrounded by words and notions that are reminiscent of the texts in Isaiah.[16] Apart from the invocation of prayer in the Lord's name and the similar time frame of "that day," the two texts (Isaiah and John) are similar in other ways. First, the distress will be experienced only "for a little while." In both texts, the same word is used to indicate the shortness (μικρός) of the trial. Second, the pain of a woman ready to give birth (τίκτω) to a child is the prominent image used to describe the renewal that God will bring forth. In addition to the language of "giving birth," the eschatological image of a woman in labor is conceptually unique to Isaiah 26, 66 and John 16.[17] Third, the reference to the distress by both texts (θλῖψιν) indicates the state from which God will deliver his people. Fourth, the imminent death and resurrection of Jesus parallels the resurrection language in Isa. 26.19 (see especially Jn 5.25, 28-29).[18] Moreover, Jesus speaks of the joy that the disciples will experience because of his resurrection. This joy is linked with the

---

16. John seems to be depending partly on the MT (with his emphasis on prayer) and partly on the LXX (with his emphasis on the shortness of the distress). Both options provide sufficient ground for a connection. Possibly, John depends on a tradition that has incorporated both the MT and LXX here.

17. The reference in Mic. 4.9-10 is the next closest parallel. See also the woman in Rev. 12.1-2 (Beale, *The Book of Revelation: A Commentary on the Greek Text* (NIGTC; Grand Rapids: Eerdmans, 1999), p. 632).

18. It may be that the resurrection is not explicitly mentioned in John 16, but the idea is certainly implicit.

resurrection in Isa. 26.19 and is also mentioned in Isa. 66.14, from where John uses precisely the same phrase: καὶ χαρήσεται ὑμῶν ἡ καρδία.[19]

In light of the above indications, it is probable that John used Isaiah 26 and 66 to draw on language that was appropriate for Jesus's words. The allusion indicates the approximate time for prophetic fulfillment. While, on the one hand, the image of the woman bearing a child illustrates Jesus's point about joy replacing sorrow, on the other hand, it provides the OT backdrop by which one must understand what God is about to do with Jesus: the Isaianic prophecies concerning distress (or judgment) and resurrection from the dead (or new creation) are about to be fulfilled. This eschatological background to the words and concepts used in John 16 will certainly affect our understanding of the hour, since it has been planted within this eschatological imagery.

b. *The Hour of Understanding: John 16.25*

The second occurrence of hour in our passage (16.16-33) occurs in connection to the plain language that Jesus will use with the disciples, and thus, it will be a time of perfect understanding (16.23).[20] More specifically, Jesus says in 16.25, "I have said these things to you in figures of speech. The hour is coming (ἔρχεται ὥρα) when I will no longer speak to you in figures, but will tell you plainly of the Father." As Köstenberger notes, "'these things' in 16:25 most immediately refers to what Jesus is seeking to illustrate in 16:21',[21] that is, the image of the woman bearing a child. This is probable because of the word παροιμία ("figurative language") which describes what Jesus has already said. If this is the case, then the coming hour in 16.25 (ἔρχεται ὥρα) may also refer to the hour of labor (which, as we observed, represents the time of the eschatological judgment and resurrection).

However, in 16.25, the hour takes on an additional feature, that is, the time when there will be a plain communication of Jesus's words. Scholars agree that this plain communication of words relates to the Spirit's communication of truth as it is described in Jn 16.12-15. Both acts of communication (16.12-15 and 16.25) can be perceived as referring to either the same event or two consecutive, but similar

---

19. Jesus also uses the verb "to see" (ὄψεσθε) to indicate the means by which the disciples will receive joy (Jn 16.16, 17, 19, 22), which is the same exact verb used in Isa. 66.14 (and 66.18) in a similar manner.

20. The verb ἐρωτάω in 16.23 has been debated. The word can mean either "to ask a question" or "to request." Those that prefer the latter rendering do so on the basis of the immediate context, namely, the request of 16.23b-24. However, both the classical usage of the word and the broader context that has the disciples asking questions lead towards the former rendering of the word. Therefore, Jesus is saying that the disciples will no longer have the need to ask any questions. The reason for this absence of need may be traced back to the teaching of the Spirit in 16.12-13. Another reason could be that God's eschatological plan of tribulation and resurrection will be fulfilled and thus also revealed (16.19-20) (pace Keener, *John*, pp. 1046-47).

21. Köstenberger, *John* (BECNT; Grand Rapids: Baker Academic, 2004), p. 477. See also Moloney, *John* (1998), p. 453.

in nature, events.[22] Barrett correctly notes that the hour in 16.25 "is not that of the immediately following sentences, but of the period after the resurrection, when the Spirit is given."[23] Indeed, only when the Spirit teaches the disciples, will the disciples come to an understanding of the truth. Christ is, therefore, speaking of a new era of understanding.[24] However, how can it be that Jesus says that he is going to speak plainly about the Father? Is this not the task of the Spirit? Schnackenburg adequately answers this theological question in light of the disciples' understanding of Jesus's ministry. Before the death and resurrection of Christ, everything seems to be obscure in the eyes of the disciples.[25] After the cross and resurrection events, the disciples will be able to understand and believe. As Schnackenburg phrases it: "The 'ascent' or 'exaltation' of the Son of Man forces men even more powerfully to come to a decision regarding faith or unbelief (see 6.62; 8.28 19.37) . . . All Jesus's speaking on earth is here seen to be cryptic, even for the disciples who believe, and full revelation will only come in the future."[26] Most notably, Beasley-Murray states:

> [I]n the "hour" that is coming, i.e., following the hour of Jesus's suffering, he is to speak *plainly* of the Father. This can only signify his instruction mediated through the Spirit-Paraclete, as indicated in 16.12-15 . . . The threefold appearance of ἀναγγελεῖ in vv. 12-15 corresponds to the ἀπαγγελῶ of v. 25.[27]

The following comparison chart illustrates Beasley-Murray's point and makes the connection between Jn 16.12-15 and Jn 16.25 likely.

22. Carson, *John*, p. 547; Ridderbos, *John*, pp. 540–41; Keener, *John*, p. 1047; Frey, *Die johanneische Eschatologie III: Die eschatologische Verkundigung in den johanneischen Texten* (WUNT, 117; Tübingen: Mohr [Siebeck], 2000), p. 192; and Raymond E. Brown, *The Gospel According to John* (AB, 29A; New York: Doubleday, 1970), p. 735, who connects Jn 16.25 with 14.25-26.

23. C. K. Barrett, *The Gospel According to St John: An Introduction with Commentary and Notes on the Greek Text* (London: SPCK, 1967), p. 413.

24. See Köstenberger's comments in his commentary.

25. The fact that Jesus has spoken in obscure words may stand in analogy to the obscure nature of the prophetic words that Daniel has heard. In Dan. 12.8, the LXX uses the word παραβολή, a synonym to παροιμία, to describe the obscurity of the prophetic utterances of the book of Daniel. In Jn 16.25, Jesus probably intends to provide a contrast between the lack of clarity concerning God's prophetic words and the clear understanding that one will have in the coming hour.

26. Schnackenburg, *The Gospel According to St. John* (3 Vols; New York: Crossroad, 1987), p. 162.

27. Beasley-Murray, *John*, p. 287.

Jn 16.12-15	Jn 16.25
I have many more things to say to you (ὑμῖν λέγειν), but you cannot bear them now. But when he, the Spirit of truth, comes, he will guide you into all the truth; for he will not speak (οὐ λαλήσει) on his own initiative, but whatever he hears, he will speak (λαλήσει); and he will disclose to you (ἀναγγελεῖ ὑμῖν) what is to come. He will glorify me, for he will take of mine and will disclose it to you (ἀναγγελεῖ ὑμῖν). All things that the Father (ὁ πατὴρ) has are mine; therefore I said that he takes of mine and will disclose it to you (ἀναγγελεῖ ὑμῖν).	These things I have spoken to you (λελάληκα ὑμῖν) in figurative language; the hour is coming when I will no longer speak to you (οὐκέτι λαλήσω ὑμῖν) in figurative language, but will tell you (ἀπαγγελῶ ὑμῖν) plainly of the Father (τοῦ πατρὸς).

The slight difference that exists between the words ἀναγγέλλω and ἀπαγγέλλω should not discourage one from viewing these as parallel,[28] since the disclosure by the Spirit will also fulfill Jesus's promise. The fact that the Spirit speaks (ἀναγγέλλω) what he has already received from Christ (16.14) indicates that Jesus's promise to speak plainly (ἀπαγγέλλω) will be done through the Spirit. In Jn 4.25, the Samaritan woman also reveals that "when that one [the Messiah] comes, he will declare all things to us (ἀναγγελεῖ ἡμῖν ἅπαντα)," to which Jesus replies "I who speak to you am he" (4.26). Interestingly, this discussion also involves the coming hour (ἔρχεται ὥρα in 4.23).[29] Nevertheless, while in Jn 4.25-26 Jesus assumes the role of disclosing all things, in Jn 16.12-15, he explains that this will be done through the Spirit.

The above parallels indicate that the hour in Jn 16.25 pertains to the coming of a new age when the disciples will enjoy the disclosure of truth. The fact that this will be done through the Spirit connects this new age with the eschatological promises about the outpouring of the Spirit, which are also linked to prophetic understanding. Jesus's argument about the coming hour of clarity addresses the disciples' confusion regarding the appropriate meaning of the prophetic words in Isaiah and, as we will later see, Daniel.[30]

c. *The Hour of the Scattering of the Disciples: John 16.32*
The third reference to hour in our passage (16.16-33) relates to the scattering of the disciples and their desertion of Jesus. Jesus says to his disciples, "the hour is coming, indeed it has come (ἔρχεται ὥρα καὶ ἐλήλυθεν), when you will be scattered, each one to his home, and you will leave me alone. Yet I am not alone because the Father is with me" (16.32). This has been acknowledged to be a clear allusion to

---

28. The two words are synonyms or close in meaning (under the word-group of ἀγγέλλω), and they are treated as such in the theological dictionaries. Part of the meaning that this word-group may take is that of the pronouncement of prophetic fulfillment (see U. Becker and D. Müller, 'Proclamation, Preach, Kerygma', *NIDNTT* 3:44-46).

29. On the use of hour in Jn 4.21, 23, see my comments in the relevant chapter.

30. In Jn 16.21, John has probably combined an allusion to Isa. 26.17 with language borrowed from Dan. 12.1. See my argument later in this chapter.

Zech. 13.7.[31] In what follows, I will demonstrate the likelihood of the allusion and also clarify its significance in relation to the hour in Jn 16.32.

Zechariah 13.7 says: "Awake, O sword, against my shepherd, and against the man, my associate . . . Strike the shepherd that the sheep may be scattered; and I will turn my hand against the little ones'." Some scholars have situated Zech. 13.7-9 right after Zech. 11.17.[32] The major reasons for this decision are the reference to a sword in 11.17 and the reference to the worthless shepherd throughout the section of Zechariah 9–11. This view consequently sees the shepherd in 13.7 to be the same ineffective shepherd of 11.15.[33] However, Zech. 13.7-9 need not be misplaced.[34] The shepherd in 13.7 is not an ineffective shepherd, but one that is associated with Yahweh.[35] The function of the shepherd in Zech. 13.7-9 is different from the one mentioned in Zechariah 10–11. Moreover, while Zech. 10.2-3 and 11.15-17 focus on the ineffective shepherd, the primary focus of Zech. 13.7-9 is on the flock. As Petersen has noted: "In the second line of the poem, the author moves from the figure of the shepherd to his compatriots, which indicates that a sole shepherd is not the primary focus of attention."[36]

Although Zech. 13.7-9 is considered to be a poem, it has also been identified as a "prophecy of salvation."[37] Its context has certain eschatological overtones and the passage is literally positioned between two "on that day" sets of references in 12.1–13.6 and 14.1-21 (more specifically, in 12.3, 4, 6, 8, 9, 11; 13.1, 2, 4; and in 14.4, 6, 8, 9, 13, 20, 21). Smith correctly relates Zech. 13.7-9 to its immediate literary context and describes the passage as "an eschatological oracle of hope and

31. See the quotation in Mk 14.27 (Carson, *John*, p. 548). Among others, the allusion has been acknowledged by Köstenberger, *John*, p. 480; Lindars, *John*, p. 514; Beasley-Murray, *John*, p. 288; and Carson, *John*, p. 548.

32. See Rex Mason, *The Books of Haggai, Zechariah, and Malachi* (CBC; Cambridge: Cambridge University Press, 1977), p. 110; P. D. Hanson, *The Dawn of Apocalyptic: The Historical and Sociological Roots of Jewish Apocalyptic Eschatology* (Philadelphia: Fortress, 1979), pp. 338–39.

33. Hanson argues for this view. He believes that the shepherd of 13.7 is identified with the leader mentioned in 11.17. Hanson, *Apocalyptic*, pp. 338–53.

34. For a scholarly assessment of the view that places Zech. 13.7-9 right after 13.1-6, see David L. Petersen, *Zechariah 9–14 and Malachi: A Commentary* (OTL; Louisville: John Knox, 1995), pp. 129–32; Michael H. Floyd, *Minor Prophets: Part 2* (FOTL, 22; Grand Rapids: Eerdmans, 2000), pp. 538–40; Smith, *Micah-Malachi*; D. R. Jones, *Haggai, Zechariah, and Malachi* (TBC; London: SCM, 1962), pp. 168–69. See also the following German sources: K. Elliger, *Das Buch der zwölf kleinen Propheten, 2* (ATD, 25; Göttingen, 1964), p. 165; M. Saebø, *Sacharja 9–14: Untersuchungen von Text und Form* (WMANT, 34; Neukirchen-Vluyn, 1969), pp. 216–77.

35. See R. L. Smith, *Micah-Malachi* (WBC, 32; Dallas: Word, 1984), pp. 282–83.

36. D. L. Petersen, *Zechariah 9–14 and Malachi: A Commentary* (OTL; Louisville: John Knox, 1995), p. 130.

37. Smith, *Micah-Malachi*, p. 283; Floyd, *Minor Prophets*, p. 540.

salvation which will be fulfilled after a period of tribulation."[38] This eschatological context is significant for the interpretation of the text. Within this context, Zechariah refers to the day when God will come against his own people; he also speaks against the false prophets who will be revealed and ashamed "on that day" (13.1-6).

Zechariah 13.7 states that God will smite his shepherd with a sword, the consequences of which will be the scattering of the sheep, namely, God's people.[39] The image is reminiscent of God's eschatological wrath that will be poured on the Israelites. The purpose of this distress is for God to refine his people before the end (13.9). However, from within this distress, the people will call on God's name, and God promises to answer (13.9). Although the flock will be scattered and destroyed, it will be restored again. In summary, in Zech. 13.7, the people of God are situated in a context of judgment and distress, and prayer constitutes the means of restoration. As in Isaiah 26 (vv. 13, 16), Zechariah also refers to the "calling on Yahweh's name" as the means to establish a renewed relationship (Zech. 13.9).[40]

The idea of scattering God's people during the end-time is so unique to Zechariah in all of the OT, that the mere reference to the scattering of the disciples in Jn 16.32 establishes an allusion to Zech. 13.7. Both Zechariah and John speak of a distress, which will result in prayer (done in God's name), and both refer to an intimate relationship with God.[41] Moreover, distress seems to have a purpose in Zechariah, and so it does in John, at least from the perspective of the reader. The purpose of the distress in Zechariah is to refine and test the people of God. If John has seen and embraced the purpose of the distress in Zechariah, then not only will the distress in John lead to an intimate relationship with God, but it will also purify and refine the disciples. The distress can ultimately transform the disciples, first through the means of the cross (16.20-22) and then through the persecution of the world (16.1-4, 33). By using this allusion, Jesus communicates to the disciples the role that they will play in the unfolding of the eschatological promises.

This allusion uncovers the eschatological nature of the hour that is "coming and has already come" (16.32) and situates the disciples at the very moment of this eschatological fulfillment. It is clear that Jesus saw himself as the "smitten shepherd" and interpreted his ministry along the lines of this passage. In Mk 14.27, Jesus tells his disciples as they were on their way to the garden of Gethsemane, "You will all fall away; for it is written, I will strike the shepherd, and the sheep

---

38. Smith, *Micah-Malachi*, p. 283.

39. The striking of the king also occurs in Isa. 50.6 and Mic. 5.1.

40. Petersen, *Zechariah*, p. 132.

41. Notice that Zechariah 13 begins with the time designation "in that day" (ἐν τῇ ἡμέρᾳ ἐκείνῃ in Zech. 13.1), in which the people will call on God's name, and he will answer them (Zech. 13.9). This is parallel to the coming day of intimate prayer in Jn 16.23, 26. In Zechariah, the intimacy of God's relationship with his people is expressed through the covenantal formula (Zech. 13.9).

will be scattered."[42] John uses this OT text to identify a direct prophetic fulfillment, and in doing so, he expands the perimeter of the hour to include the realization of one more OT prophecy.

IV. *The Eschatological Hour in Relation to Daniel 12.1-2*

We have already examined the use of hour in Daniel and the eschatological connotations it takes up in this context of Dan. 12.1-2. The text there describes the concluding outcome of the battle narrated in the ending verses of Daniel 11. The phrase "at that hour" (κατὰ τὴν ὥραν ἐκείνην) in Dan. 12.1 refers to the time of the end in 11.40, 45, in which the insolent king attacks Israel and then dies. Also, the time of distress (θλίψεως) in 12.1 has been described in such a way as to allude to the image of a woman that is ready to bear a child (Jer. 30.6-7; cf. Isa. 26.16-17; Isa. 66.7-9). This "time" concerns the end-times, in that it defines the period of time that comes right before God's determined end. This period will conclude with resurrection from the tombs into eternal life for some and eternal disgrace for others. Through distress, God will bring about new life.

In order to have a clear picture of the possibility of an allusion to the Danielic hour in John 16, I provide the following chart, which compares the two texts.

Dan. 12.1	Jn 16.21, 25, 32-33
And at that hour (τὴν ὥραν ἐκείνην) Michael the great prince shall stand up, that stands over the children of your people; and there shall be a time of distress (θλίψεως), such as has not been from the time that there was a nation on the earth until that time; in that day (ἐν ἐκείνῃ τῇ ἡμέρᾳ) your people will be delivered, every one that is written in the book.	(16.21) Whenever a woman is in labor she has pain, because her hour (ἡ ὥρα αὐτῆς) has come; but when she gives birth to the child, she no longer remembers the distress (τῆς θλίψεως) because of the joy that a child has been born into the world. (16.25) These things I have spoken to you in figurative language; the hour (ὥρα) is coming when I will no longer speak to you in figurative language, but will tell you plainly of the Father. (16.32-33) Behold, the hour (ὥρα) is coming, and has already come, for you to be scattered, each to his own home, and to leave me alone; and yet I am not alone, because the Father is with me. These things I have spoken to you, so that in me you may have peace. In the world you have distress (θλῖψιν), but take courage; I have overcome the world.

A possible connection between the use of hour in Dan. 12.1-2 and Jn 16.21, 25, 32, mainly exists on the basis of two words: the word ὥρα and the word θλίψις. However, the combination of these two words in such close proximity (up to

---

42. See the comment made by Smith, who connects Zech. 13.7 to Jesus's disciples (Smith, *Micah-Malachi*, pp. 283–84).

3 verses) appears only in the above texts, in Daniel and in John, and nowhere else in the Old Testament, Jewish,[43] or New Testament literature. This makes the parallel unique and thus enhances the chances for an allusion. Moreover, the only two references of the word θλῖψις in the Fourth Gospel occur here, in John 16, and in both instances John closely attaches the notion of the hour (Jn 16.21 and 32-33). In addition to these indications, the common use of the phrase ἐν ἐκείνῃ τῇ ἡμέρᾳ ("in that day") in Dan. 12.1 and Jn 16.23, 26, further strengthens the presence of an allusion.[44]

If ὥρα is not an allusion to Daniel, then it would certainly be an exceptional coincidence. Rather, it makes more sense to conclude that John has probably used the words ὥρα and θλῖψις in order to allude to the final tribulation mentioned in Daniel. In doing this he also incorporates two images, one from Isaiah and one from Zechariah. In the first instance, John uses the words ὥρα and θλῖψις in association to the woman bearing a child (16.21). It is plausible that John interprets Jesus's reference to the Isaianic image of the woman bearing a child (16.21) as the θλῖψις in Dan. 12.1. The choice of words in Jn 16.21 may be intentional to that end:

> Whenever a woman is in labor she has pain, because her hour has come (ἦλθεν ἡ ὥρα); but when she gives birth to the child, she no longer remembers the anguish (τῆς θλίψεως) because of the joy that a child has been born into the world.

One should not be surprised that John combines allusions to Daniel and Isaiah, since he has done so elsewhere in the gospel.[45] Moreover, Dan. 12.1 itself alludes to the resurrection idea of Isa. 26.19.[46] Also, it describes the tribulation of the people by way of allusion to Jer. 30.6-7, where both Dan. 12.1 and Jer. 30.7 have the "time of distress" (עֵת צָרָה). In addition, Jeremiah's "time of distress" involves the description of a woman bearing a child.[47] This makes it all the more natural for John to combine

---

43. An exception would be the close association of "time" and "distress" (תצ צרה) in the *War Scroll*, 1QM I, 11-12; XV, 1, and the appearance of the phrase "time of trial" (עת המצרף) in 4QFlor 1 II, 3, 24, 5, 1. See also the phrase "times of distress" (מועדי צרותם) in 1QS III, 23. However, these are Hebrew, not Greek texts.

44. The exact phrase occurs 19 times in the prophetic literature, and only once in Daniel. The phrase "in that day" (16.23, 26) is eschatological language employed to fit the context of the eschatological joy, Jesus's resurrection, and the outpouring of the Spirit. It is extensively used in the Old Testament as a literary device that denotes prophetic utterance of the eschaton. Some of the usages in the OT would be as follows: Isa. 2.11, 17, 20; 4.2; 7.18; 10.27; 24.21; 27.1; Jer. 4.9; Hos. 2.16, 18; Joel 3.18; Amos 8.9; 9.11; Zeph. 3.16; and Zech. 14.4. The use of this phrase, however, in Dan. 12.1 together with the word ὥρα and θλῖψις points further to the latter being an allusion.

45. E.g. John 5.21, 25, 28-29.

46. See Bailey, 'Daniel 12.2 and Isaiah 26.19', pp. 305–308. Notice also the use of Isaiah 26 in Dan. 11.36–12.4 (see my comments on Daniel).

47. The tribulation in Dan. 12.1 refers to that in Jer. 30.6-7, where after employing the

(in Jn 16.21) the image of a woman in childbirth with the hour and tribulation of Dan. 12.1. John may intentionally use the word θλίψις in combination with the hour as an allusion to Daniel.

In a similar manner, John associates the Danielic hour with the scattering of the disciples in his clear allusion to Zech. 13.7. The effect in doing this is twofold: First, Jesus addresses the disciples' misunderstanding. The disciples cannot comprehend that Jesus's reference to the hour is still to come, an hour that includes both sorrow and joy, both tribulation and resurrected life; they think that the era Jesus talks about has already arrived (notice the double use of νῦν in the disciples' answer in 16.29-30). Jesus needs to employ an imagery that will explain the present hour (ἔρχεται ὥρα καὶ ἐλήλυθεν in 16.32) in terms of suffering and denial. The text from Zechariah serves this end, since it clarifies the hour for the disciples as one of tribulation.

Second, in connection to the above, the context of Zech. 13.7 brings to mind both the tribulation of the Messiah (shepherd) and the tribulation of his people (sheep). Along with Jesus's distress, the disciples will also undergo a period of tribulation. The allusion to Zechariah does not minimize the Danielic associations to the Johannine hour and "distress." On the contrary, it reinforces the idea that John's combined use of hour and "distress" refers to a time of tribulation for God's people similar to that in Daniel. The effect of the Zechariah allusion indicates that the Danielic hour of θλίψις (Dan. 12.1) incorporates both the representative of the people (Son of Man) and the people themselves.

In addition to the above, the two contexts in Daniel and in John employ similar thematic features. The hour in 16.2, 4 is one of opposition and persecution of the saints and the same can also be said of the hour in 16.32. This parallels the opposition against the people of God in Daniel, which is the dominant motif in connection to the hour (Dan. 11.35, 40; 12.1). Also, in Jn 16.20, the grief will be turned into joy, a picture that is best described with the pains of the woman that is in labor (16.21).[48] Just as this θλίψις will be turned into joy, so will the θλίψις in Daniel result in the resurrection of the dead, which is also the result in Isaiah 26 and 66 (in the latter, the result is new creation).

Through the use of allusion to Dan. 12.1, John depicts the realization of the Danielic hour of θλίψις and the subsequent resurrection. Since the combination of the two words, ὥρα and θλίψις, do not appear either in Isaiah or in Zechariah, but only occur in Dan. 12.1, one may conclude that John had the Danielic context in

image of "a woman in childbirth" (30.6) the author states: "Alas! For that day is great, there is none like it; and it is the time of Jacob's distress, but he will be saved from it" (30.7). Compare this with Daniel's description of tribulation, "such as has not been from the time that there was a nation on the earth until that time" (12.1). See also the image of the woman bearing a child in *1 En.* 62.4, in the context of which the Son of Man appears as God's chosen agent for implementing judgment and bringing life.

48. For the eschatological significance of this image, see Keener, *John*, p. 1045; L. Morris, *The Gospel According to John* (Grand Rapids: Eerdmans, 1995), p. 706; Brown, *Gospel According to John*, II, p. 732.

mind. Placed at the end of the Farewell Discourse, right before Jesus's death and resurrection, this makes good sense.

The allusion to Daniel becomes even stronger if one also considers Jesus's address to the Father in 17.1-2, in which address Jesus explicitly connects the hour to the authority of the Son to judge (cf. Dan. 7.14)[49] and to give eternal life (cf. Dan. 12.2).[50] Notice the multiple associations with Daniel 7 and 12 in the following chart:

Dan. 12.1-2 and 7.13-14	*Jn 16.32–17.2*
(12.1-2) and at that hour (τὴν ὥραν ἐκείνην) Michael the great prince shall stand up, that stands over the children of your people; and there shall be a time of distress (θλίψεως), such as has not been from the time that there was a nation on the earth until that time; at that time your people shall be delivered, every one that is written in the book. And many of them that sleep in the dust of the earth shall awake, some to eternal life (ζωὴν αἰώνιον), and some to reproach and eternal shame.	(16.32-33) Behold, an hour is coming (ἔρχεται ὥρα), and has already come, for you to be scattered, each to his own home, and to leave me alone; and yet I am not alone, because the Father is with me. These things I have spoken to you, so that in me you may have peace. In the world you have distress (θλῖψιν), but take courage; I have overcome the world.
(7.13-14) I beheld in the night vision, and, behold, one coming with the clouds of heaven as the Son of man (ὡς υἱὸς ἀνθρώπου), and he came on to the Ancient of days, and was brought near to him. And to him was given the authority (ἐδόθη αὐτῷ ἐξουσία), and all the glory (πᾶσα δόξα), and the kingdom; and all nations, tribes, and languages, shall serve him: his authority is an eternal authority (ἡ ἐξουσία αὐτοῦ ἐξουσία αἰώνιος), which shall not pass away, and his kingdom shall not be destroyed.	(17.1-2) Jesus spoke these things; and lifting up his eyes to heaven, he said, "Father, the hour has come (ἐλήλυθεν ἡ ὥρα); glorify your Son, that the Son may glorify you (δόξασόν σου τὸν υἱόν, ἵνα ὁ υἱὸς δοξάση σέ), even as you gave him authority (ἔδωκας αὐτῷ ἐξουσίαν) over all flesh, that to all whom you have given him (πᾶν ὃ δέδωκας αὐτῷ), he may give eternal life (ζωὴν αἰώνιον)."

We have already shown that the phrase "eternal life" is characteristically Danielic, since in the whole OT, it appears only in Dan. 12.2. The presence of the phrase "eternal life" in Jn 17.2, in the midst of other Danielic concepts (taken from Daniel 7), should influence our perception of the hour in the preceding context. Indeed, the fact that the phrase "eternal life" appears in the immediate context of the Johannine use of the words ὥρα and θλίψις (16.32-33), further indicates that this ὥρα and

49. Compare Dan. 7.14, καὶ ἐδόθη αὐτῷ ἐξουσία, with Jn 17.2, καθὼς ἔδωκας αὐτῷ ἐξουσίαν. In both texts it is the "Son" that receives authority.

50. Jesus receives authority to judge and give eternal life also in Jn 5.19-30, within the framework of the same eschatological hour. See my comments in the relevant chapter for the significance of Daniel in connection with these themes.

this θλίψις most probably derive from Dan. 12.1. Therefore, while Jesus's address in 17.1, "Father, the hour has come," may certainly refer to Jesus's death and resurrection, it most probably alludes to the fulfillment of the eschatological promises found in Daniel.

V. *Conclusion*

John uses ὥρα in John 16 with an eschatological sense. This is evident especially from its connection to two clear allusions, one to Isa. 26.17 and 66.7-9 in Jn 16.21 and the other to Zech. 13.7 in Jn 16.32. Both of these OT texts relate to the notion of tribulation, which appears to be a central emphasis in the words of Jesus. By means of allusion, John conveys the understanding that these OT prophetic pronouncements are about to be fulfilled. Moreover, the use of ἀπαγγέλλω in reference to the coming hour (16.25) could connote the explication of prophetic truth as it unfolds in fulfillment. The significance of the above OT background is twofold: first, it situates the hour within a text that alludes to OT eschatological pronouncements, and second, it qualifies this hour as the moment of eschatological tribulation.

Where did John get the idea of hour? As I have already mentioned, the only place in the OT where one may find an eschatological hour is the book of Daniel. Moreover, John's use of θλίψις in connection to the hour in Jn 16.21 and 32-33 (the only uses of θλίψις in the whole gospel) reinforces the likelihood for an allusion to Daniel. In fact, we have seen that the combination of the two words, ὥρα and θλίψις, is unique to Dan. 12.1 and Jn 16.21, 32-33, as it appears nowhere else in OT, Jewish, or NT literature.[51] Moreover, the use of hour in Jn 17.1, with its multiple Danielic associations, such as the Son receiving glory and also the authority to judge and give eternal life (cf. Dan. 7.13-14; 12.1-2), further enhances the suggestion of a Danielic background. In particular, the presence of the phrase "eternal life" in the immediate context of an hour of tribulation (ὥρα and θλίψις) indicates a probable connection with Daniel.

According to this interpretation, Jesus's (and John's) argument would be that the final hour of tribulation and resurrection, as it appears in Daniel, has arrived. While this hour certainly involves affliction, God's ultimate purpose is to lead his people to life. Jesus's destiny, his glorification, does not end with the cross, but with the many that God will glorify. This same glorified destiny also belongs to the disciples, but they, too, need first to walk a similar troubled path as their Lord who has blazed the trail before them.

---

51. Furthermore, the presence of the exact phrase ἐν ἐκείνῃ τῇ ἡμέρᾳ in Dan. 12.1 and Jn 16.23, 26 also points to the allusion, especially since both concern an eschatological period of tribulation. While this exact phrase occurs 29 times in the LXX (19 times in the prophetic literature), its presence in Jn 16.23, 26 likely derives from Dan. 12.1 because of the other Daniel 12 allusions in the immediate context.

The OT Background of the
Eschatological Hour in 1 John 2.18

I. *Introduction*

Having examined the OT background of the eschatological hour in the Fourth Gospel, I now turn to the first epistle of John, where the word hour also appears. The eschatological nature of the hour in 1 Jn 2.18 has been generally acknowledged, since the hour there is explicitly described as the "last hour." Just recently, Beale has suggested a possible Danielic background to this hour,[1] and this chapter will reflect many of his arguments. In what follows, I investigate the validity of this suggestion, namely, the likelihood of a Danielic background to the hour in 1 Jn 2.18. For this purpose, I focus on the immediate context of the hour, which is 1 Jn 2.18-27, examine literary features that possibly relate to Daniel, and reflect on the eschatological features of the broader context. In doing so, I attempt to provide even more support for Beale's proposal.

II. *The Literary Boundaries and Structure of 1 John 2.18-27*

Scholars have debated the boundaries of the literary unit in which 1 Jn 2.18 belongs, as well as the relation of this literary unit to its broader context. Here, I will briefly address the following two issues: (a) the end boundary of the literary unit of 1 Jn 2.18-27 (28 or 29) and the unit's relationship to the preceding context; and (b) the internal structure and argument of 1 Jn 2.18-27.

While there has been a debate concerning the ending boundary of 1 Jn 2.18-27 (28 or 29), the majority of scholars have sided with v. 27 as the most probable ending of our passage.[2] Those that argue for v. 28 being a suitable ending do so mainly for

---

1.   Carson points out that the initial suggestion came from Beale (D. A. Carson, '1–3 John', in G. K. Beale and D. A. Carson (eds), *Commentary on the New Testament Use of the Old Testament* (Grand Rapids: Baker, 2007), pp. 1064–65; G. K. Beale, 'The Old Greek of Daniel as a Background to the "Last Hour" in 1 Jn 2.18', (Read at the 'Greek Bible' Section at the Annual Meeting of the SBL in Boston, MA; November, 2008).

2.   The following are some representative scholars: Peter Rhea Jones, 'Structural

two reasons: a) a possible *inclusio* may exist in vv. 18 and 28, with the common references to the "little children," the adverb "now," and the common thematic emphasis on eschatology (the last hour in 2.18 and the coming of Christ in 2.28); and b) the exhortation in v. 28 to "remain in him" summarizes the argument of the preceding section. With respect to the first reason, Brown has rightly argued that the existence of parallel themes in vv. 18 and 28 does not necessarily suggest that v. 28 should be included in the preceding passage.[3] These common themes can equally be taken as two parallel introductions to two different sections (notice the eschatological emphasis in both 2.18-27 and 2.28–3.3). Concerning the second reason, one could similarly take the exhortation to "remain in him" as the springboard from which a new section begins. Moreover, v. 28 does not serve as a suitable ending, because v. 29 does not seem to be the best candidate for beginning a new section. Verse 29 lacks a literary marker that would indicate a break, since it begins with a conditional sentence ("if . . .").

The fact that v. 29 forms an awkward beginning may have led Smalley to include the verse as part of the present passage (2.18-29). Smalley begins with the conviction that v. 28 is part of the preceding context, and then, for no particular reason (other than v. 29 being a transition between two passages), he decides to attach v. 29 to the preceding unit. In my opinion, the best option remains that of the majority of scholars, who view the reference to the "little children" in v. 28 as marking the beginning of a new unit.[4]

Concerning the relationship of 2.18-27 with its preceding context, scholars again disagree, based on how one divides the whole epistle. For example, while Brown and Smalley prefer to link 2.18-27 with its preceding context,[5] Schnackenburg, Schunack, and Klauck view the passage in connection with what follows.[6] My

analysis of 1 John', *RevExp* 67 (1970), pp. 433–44; Raymond E. Brown, *The Epistles of John* (AB, 30; New York: Doubleday, 1982); Hans-Josef Klauck, 'Zur rhetorischen Analyse der Johannesbriefe', *ZNW* 81 (1990), pp. 205–24; idem, *Der erste Johannesbrief* (EKKNT, 23/1; Zurich: Benziger Verlag, 1991); John Christopher Thomas, 'The Literary Structure of 1 John', *NovT* 40 (1998), pp. 369–81; and Colin G. Kruse, *The Letters of John* (PNTC; Grand Rapids: Eerdmans, 2000).

3. Brown, *Epistles of John*, pp. 118–19.

4. With Brown, I concede that v. 28 (and probably 29) serves as a transitional verse from one unit to another (Brown, *Epistles of John*, p. 119).

5. Brown, *Epistles of John*, pp. 123–29; and Stephen Smalley, *1,2,3 John* (WBC, 51; Nashville: Thomas Nelson, 2007), pp. xxx–xxxi; So also C. H. Dodd, *The Johannine Epistles* (MNTC; London: Hodder and Stoughton, 1946); J. C. Coetzee, 'The Holy Spirit in 1 John', *Neot* 13 (1979), pp. 43–67; Jones, 'Structural analysis', pp. 433–44.

6. Rudolf Schnackenburg, *The Johannine Epistles: A Commentary* (New York: Crossroad, 1992); Gerd Schunack, *Die Briefe des Johannes* (ZBKNT, 17; Zurich: Theologischer Verlag, 1982); Klauck, 'Zur rhetorischen Analyse'; idem, *Der erste Johannesbrief*; see also J. A. du Rand, 'Studies in the Johannine Letters: A discourse analysis of 1 John', *Neot* 13 (1981), pp. 1–42; and D. Edmond Hiebert, 'An Expositional Study of 1 John: Pt 4, An Exposition of 1 John 2.18-28', *BSac* 146 (1989), pp. 76–93.

approach resembles more that of Marshall, Strecker, and Thomas,[7] who hesitate to force an external structure onto the text, especially when the text's internal features deny conformity to such structures. According to this latter approach, the transitional points in the epistle's main body (1.5–5.12) do not constitute major breaks in the argument, but smoothly represent a progression of the author's argument throughout. Even if one insists on seeing one or two breaks, these should not be considered major. In this case, one may view 2.18-27 as equally relating to the preceding and the following contexts.[8]

In addressing the present reality of the "last hour" in 1 Jn 2.18, the author takes up what has already been said in 2.17, which reads, "The world is passing away, and also its lusts; but the one who does the will of God abides forever." Already in 2.17, an emphasis is placed on inaugurated eschatology, since the world as we know it (through the "flesh," "eyes," and "living" in 2.16) has begun its course of dissolution. Also, those who are faithful to God have begun to experience an eternal state of being. The dissolution of the world and the eternal endurance of believers show the present time to be the "final hour." As we will see later, the author further relates this hour to those who have come to deceive.

The internal structure and argument of 1 Jn 2.18-27 is best viewed by allowing the text to speak for itself. The author's threefold address to the readers through the personal pronoun ὑμεῖς (2.20, 24, 27) points to a fourfold subdivision of the segment. Moreover, the fact that in vv. 20 and 27 the address includes the conjunction "and" (καὶ ὑμεῖς) indicates that the two first addresses (beginning with vv. 20 and 24) should be grouped together, while the third (2.27) should probably stand alone.

According to these structural indicators, the author begins this unit with his primary statement in 2.18-19, by saying that the last hour is here because the antichrists have appeared by separating themselves from the community. The author develops the argument by means of two personal addresses (ὑμεῖς). In his first address (2.20-23), the author attempts to explain the reasoning behind his evaluation of the antichrists in 2.18-19. His argument goes like this:

Premise 1	The readers (believers) have the anointing (2.20a)
Premise 2	The readers (believers) know the truth (2.20b-21)
Premise 3	Truth cannot be the source of lies (2.21c)

---

7. I. Howard Marshall, *The Epistles of John* (NICNT; Grand Rapids: Eerdmans, 1978); George Strecker, *The Johannine Letters: A Commentary on 1, 2, and 3 John* (Minneapolis: Fortress, 1996); and Thomas, 'Literary Structure', who proposes a chiastic macrostructure of 1 John with the following segmentations: 1.1-4; 1.5–2.2; 2.3-17; 2.18-27; 2.28–3.10; 3.11-18; 3.19-24; 4.1-6; 4.7–5.5; 5.6-12; 5.13-21. Thomas proposes that 3.11-18 is the center of the chiasm. See also Kruse, *Letters of John*. Du Rand has also noticed the cyclical pattern of the themes and motifs in the structure of 1 John ('Studies in the Johannine Letters', p. 35).

8. Notice how the editors of the Nestle-Aland New Testament have segmented the text: 1.5–2.17; and 2.18-27; and 2.28–3.24; and 4.1–5.12.

Premise 4	The one who denies Jesus as the Christ is a liar (2.22a)
Inferential Conclusion	The liar does not belong to us
Inferential Conclusion	The liar is the antichrist (2.22b)

In his second address (2.24-25), the author explains how the reader will distinguish himself to be a true member of the community, in contrast to the opponents of 2.18-22. If the apostates distinguished themselves as antichrists by not remaining in the community (2.19), then the believers will reveal their identity by having the truth remaining in them (or by remaining in him [Christ]; μένετε ἐν αὐτῷ in 2.27). The argument goes as follows:

Premise 1	That which you have heard must remain in you (2.24)
Premise 2	The promise (you have heard) is that of eternal life (2.25)
Inferential Conclusion	Eternal life must remain in you

The above argument explicitly relates the appearance of the antichrists at the last hour with one's possession of eternal life.[9] Having eternal life "in you" (ἐν ὑμῖν μενέτω, 2.24) has become the standard by which the true believer is to be distinguished from the antichrists. This is precisely the standard by which Israel is distinguished to be God's people in Dan. 12.2, namely, by means of receiving eternal life (see comments below).

For the conclusion, one should take vv. 26 and 27 together. While verse 26 is an inferential conclusion (based on 2.18-25) that summarizes the subject matter of the preceding (including περὶ τῶν πλανώντων ὑμᾶς), v. 27 provides the final overview of the reader's spiritual condition, as well as an exhortation to "remain in him." This final exhortation is the last inference of 2.18–27, and thus serves as its main point.

In the following, I have sketched an outline according to the above proposed structure:

Primary Statement	2.18	The final hour is here, since the antichrists have appeared.
	2.19	There is a distinction between those belonging to the community and those not belonging to the community.
First Explanation: How is the antichrist to be distinguished	2.20-23	*You* have the anointing; and, you have knowledge of truth; and, truth cannot be the source of lies. The one who denies that Jesus is the Christ is a liar. Therefore, the antichrist is a liar and denies both the father and the son.

---

9. Note also the eternal endurance in 2.17.

| Second Explanation: How is the believer to be distinguished | 2.24 2.25 | (*You*) Let that which you have heard from the beginning remain in you, so that you may remain in the son and in the father. The promise that you have received is that of eternal life. |
| Summary | 2.26- 27 | I wrote to you about those who deceive (that is, the antichrists). [Therefore], *You* have the anointing remaining in you, which has taught you the truth: on this basis, remain in Christ. |

III. *The Danielic Background of the Hour in 1 John 2.18*

A number of scholars have proposed the book of Daniel as part of a general background to the "last hour" in 1 Jn 2.18;[10] however, apart from Beale's specific proposal,[11] the case has not yet been made to examine the validity of an allusion, nor has anyone explored this idea to the fullest. One could possibly ask: if the reference to the "last hour" in 1 John alludes to Daniel, what are the implications for interpreting the epistle?

To begin with, however, we must first establish that the allusion is to the Danielic hour. In fact, in the case of 1 Jn 2.18, and after evaluating the evidence, one can easily conclude that a Danielic allusion is probable. In the following discussion, I examine the literary and thematic connections that link the Johannine hour to the eschatological hour in Daniel.

The first indication for an allusion is based on the following cluster of vocabulary shared by both Daniel and 1 John 2.

Dan. 8.19; 12.1-2 (OG)	*1 Jn 2.18, 25*
(8.19) He said, Behold, I am going to let you know what will occur at the last period (ἐπ᾽ ἐσχάτου) of the indignation, for it pertains to the appointed hour (εἰς ὥρας) of the end. (12.1-2) Now at that hour (τὴν ὥραν) Michael, the great prince who stands guard over the sons of your people, will arise . . . Many of those who sleep in the dust of the ground will awake, these to eternal life (εἰς ζωὴν αἰώνιον), but the others to disgrace and everlasting contempt.	(2.18) Children, it is the last hour (ἐσχάτη ὥρα); and just as you heard that antichrist is coming, even now many antichrists have appeared; from this we know that it is the last hour (ἐσχάτη ὥρα). (2.25) This is the promise which he himself made to us: eternal life (τὴν ζωὴν τὴν αἰώνιον).

10. See Carson, '1–3 John', who has registered agreement with Beale about a Danielic influence. In discussing the broad background of 2.18, Brown includes Dan. 8.17, 19 and refers to the OT use of the phrase "in the last of days" (*Epistles of John*, p. 331). With Brown, Klauck also mentions the phrase "last days" (Dan. 2.28; 10.14) as part of a general background to the "last hour" (Klauck, *Der erste Johannesbrief*, p. 147).

11. An SBL paper presentation (Beale, '"Last Hour" in 1 Jn 2.18').

The combination of the words "hour" and "last" in 1 Jn 2.18 may be the strongest indication that the Johannine hour refers to the eschatological hour in Daniel.[12] Both words are used in several places in Daniel to denote the period of time before the "end."[13] The word "hour" (ὥρα) is explicitly associated with the "end" (συντέλεια) in Dan. 8.19; 11.35; and 11.40.[14] Similarly, the word "last" (ἐσχάτος) is associated with a period of time (ἡμέρα) in Dan. 10.14.[15] Furthermore, the close association of the words ὥρα and ἐσχάτος, apart from an obviously non-eschatological and parabolic occurrence in Mt. 20.12, occurs only in 1 Jn 2.18 and Dan. 8.19.

The Danielic hour denotes the time of eschatological turmoil (Dan. 12.1), in which the end-time opponent persecutes and deceives the saints (Dan. 11.30–12.1) and which will lead up to the double resurrection of eternal life and eternal shame (Dan. 12.2). By coining the expression "last hour," the author of First John intends to allude to this eschatological trial, when God's enemy attempts to deceive God's people (cf. Dan. 8.25).

As we have seen in previous chapters, John alludes to the Danielic hour in his gospel with the phrase ὅτι ἔρχεται ὥρα καὶ νῦν ἐστιν (Jn 5.25; cf. 4.23). The hour there is one of final judgment and resurrection from the dead. Now, the author of 1 John applies the familiar Johannine terminology to the coming of the antichrist: ὅτι ἀντίχριστος ἔρχεται, καὶ νῦν ἀντίχριστοι πολλοὶ γεγόνασιν. By doing this, however, he concludes twice that the arrival of the antichrist denotes the arrival of the "final hour" (ἐσχάτη ὥρα ἐστίν). Like the inaugurated eschatology in Jn 5.25, the hour in 1 John is also *already and not yet*. The readers of 1 John live within the eschatological time frame of the end. Perhaps the closest parallel in John to the eschatological hour of 1 Jn 2.18 is Jn 16.32-33, where the hour refers to the trial of Jesus's followers.

The suggestion for a Danielic allusion in 1 Jn 2.18 is further strengthened by the fact that the author speaks of the promise of eternal life (ζωὴν αἰώνιον, in 2.25). In light of our assessment of the author's argument in 1 Jn 2.18-27 (see previous section), the idea of "eternal life" plays a significant part in this argument. It is by way of having eternal life that one may have the certainty of belonging to God's community (cf. 3.15). The message of "eternal life" was the one preached by both the apostles (1.2) and Christ (2.25), and it constitutes "what was heard from the

---

12. Beale has advanced a detailed argument for the combination of the two words (ὥρα and ἐσχάτος) and their use in Daniel. He specifically mentions such Danielic expressions as "time of the end," "appointed time," "last days," "at that hour," etc. (Beale, '"Last Hour" in 1 Jn 2.18').

13. I have already noted the eschatological use of the word ὥρα and the word ἐσχάτος in Daniel.

14. Beale argues that any association in Daniel of "last" + "hour" or "final" + "hour" likely serves as background to the "last hour" in 1 Jn 2.18 (Beale, '"Last Hour" in 1 Jn 2.18').

15. Some LXX mss (967 and 88-Syh) end Dan. 10.14 with the phrase "the hour is yet for days," instead of the usual "the vision is yet for days" (Beale, '"Last Hour" in 1 Jn 2.18').

beginning," which now remains in the believer (2.24; 5.11, 13). Indeed, the purpose of the whole epistle is to assure the readers of having eternal life (5.13).[16]

I propose that the phrase "eternal life" should be interpreted in light of its use in Dan. 12.2, especially since it appears in 1 Jn 2.25, only three verses before the author cautions the readers not to be ashamed (αἰσχύνομαι, in 2.28) at the final παρουσία of Christ. The combination of the phrase ζωὴ αἰώνιος and the word αἰσχύνη (or αἰσχύνομαι) appears only in the contexts of Dan. 12.2 (OG, TH); 1 Jn 2.25, 28; and Jude 13, 21.[17] Wherever the above vocabulary is combined, the author clearly has in mind the eschatological judgment and salvation, as is also confirmed by the reference in Jude. In 1 John, there is no doubt that the use of the verb αἰσχύνομαι refers to the final judgment. It is possible that this verb derives from the use of αἰσχύνη in Dan. 12.2, especially since 1 Jn 2.28 speaks about the second coming of Christ (ἐν τῇ παρουσίᾳ αὐτοῦ). The above three indicators (last hour, eternal life, and shame), along with the mention of the antichrist figure in 2.19, 22,[18] should be enough to establish a connection with Daniel.

The prominent theme that links the eschatological hour in Daniel with the Johannine "last hour" is that of God's final adversary. The terms used for the opposing forces in 1 John vary. More particularly, the term "antichrist" is explicitly linked to the last hour in 1 Jn 2.18.[19] The "evil one" (πονηρὸς) and the "devil" are also used as terms to depict the adversary (2.13-14; 3.8, 10; 5.18-19), and the term "world" is depicted as the realm which the "evil one" dominates (5.19) and in which the spirit of the antichrist works (4.3-4). Interestingly, the world is viewed as "passing away" (2.17), which also points to the final eschatological moment in which God's people will face the final enemy. Of the above terms, the term "antichrist" echoes the insolent king in Daniel.

Scholars agree that one should seek the tradition for the "antichrist" language in

---

16. The phrase "eternal life" appears both in the introduction (1.2; "and we have seen and testify and proclaim to you the eternal life") and the conclusion of the epistle, where it is connected to God's Son, Jesus Christ (5.20; "This is the true God and eternal life"). For the author of 1 John, "eternal life" represents the ultimate fulfillment of God's promise (2.25) and the standard by which one is classified within God's people (3.14-15; 5.12-13). While the phrase "eternal life" occurs 6 times in the epistle (1.2; 2.25; 3.15; 5.11, 13, 20), its equivalent "life" appears another 7 times (1.1, 2; 3.14; 5.11, 12, 16) and the verb "to live" occurs once in 1 Jn 4.9.

17. There is no other occurrence in the OT or the NT where the combination appears within a maximum range of 10 verses.

18. See my comments on the antichrist figure later, as this relates to Matthew, Mark, and 2 Thessalonians.

19. On the antichrist, see Stephen J. Nichols, 'Prophecy Makes Strange Bedfellows: On the History of Identifying the Antichrist', *JETS* 44 (2001), pp. 75–85; Roy Yates, 'The Antichrist', *EvQ* 46 (1974), pp. 42–50; Warren McWilliams, 'Interpretations of the Antichrist', *BI* (1990), pp. 50–53; Schnackenburg, *Johannine Epistles*, pp. 135–39; Brown, *Epistles of John*, pp. 333–37; Smalley, *1, 2, 3 John*, pp. 93–94.

the contexts of Matthew 24, Mark 13, and 2 Thessalonians 2.[20] The word "antichrist" parallels the designations "false Christ" and "false prophet" from the gospels, as well as the "man of lawlessness" from 2 Thessalonians. I need not enter into an extensive search of these passages in order to find Danielic quotations and allusions in them, since their close association to Daniel has been widely acknowledged.[21] The fact that all three sources contain multiple quotations and allusions to the book of Daniel indicates that the "antichrist" tradition goes back to God's final adversary in Daniel.[22]

In the book of Daniel, God's enemy may change faces (see the visions in Daniel 7, 8, and 10–12), but this is only until the final adversary arrives with whom the determining battle occurs. The adversary is described as one who utters "boastful words" (Dan. 7.11), and who speaks words "against the Most High" and wears down "the saints of the Most High" (Dan. 7.25). In Dan. 8.25, the same adversary "makes deceit prosper under his hand." Similarly, in Dan. 11.36, he does "as he wills" and he exalts himself and magnifies himself "above every god."[23] As Schnackenburg has noticed, this description fits well with the "man of lawlessness" in 2 Thessalonians 2 and also with the deception that will take place in the eschaton.[24] The notion of deception (πλανάω) appears as a threat in Matthew (24.4-5, 11) and Mark (13.5-6), as it is also present in 1 John (2.26; 3.7).[25]

20. See the chart of the three passages, along with Revelation, that Kruse provides in his commentary (Kruse, *Letters of John*, pp. 99–100).

21. On the Danielic influence of the context of Mt. 24.24, see R. T. France, *The Gospel of Matthew* (NICNT; Grand Rapids: Eerdmans, 2007), pp. 915–16. Lane notices a Danielic influence in the context of Mk 13.22 (William L. Lane, *The Gospel of Mark* [NICNT; Grand Rapids: Eerdmans, 1974], pp. 471–72). For the Danielic influence on 2 Thess. 2.1-4, see Charles Wanamaker, *The Epistles to the Thessalonians* (NIGTC; Grand Rapids: Eerdmans, 1990), pp. 246–48; and G. K. Beale, *1–2 Thessalonians* (IVPNT; Downers Grove: InterVarsity, 2003), pp. 203–11. So also Lars Hartman, *Prophecy Interpreted: The Formation of Some Jewish Apocalyptic Texts and of the Eschatological Discourse Mark 13 Par.* (CBNTS, 1; Lund, Sweden: Gleerup, 1966), whose argument is to connect the eschatological discourses in Mark, Matthew, and 2 Thessalonians primarily with Daniel (he also mentions 1 John on p. 237).

22. See also Beale, '"Last Hour" in 1 Jn 2.18'.

23. The emphasis on "sin" in 1 John, especially in view of the author's definition of sin as lawlessness in 3.4, adds another eschatological dimension that cannot be easily dismissed. Marshall rightly argues that the link of "sin" with "lawlessness" implies an action that places oneself "on the side of the devil and the antichrist . . . in opposition to God" (Marshall, *Epistles of John*, p. 176). The prospect of apostasy is an end-time act, and John probably views his opponents as participating in such an act (2.18-19). Colin G. Kruse, 'Sin and Perfection in 1 John', *ABR* 51 (2003), pp. 60–70. See also the useful article by Ignace de la Potterie, '"Sin is Iniquity" (1 Jn 3.4)', in I. de la Potterie and Stanislaus Lyonnet (eds), *The Christian Lives by the Spirit* (New York: Alba House, 1971), pp. 36–55; and the treatment of "the lawless one" in I. Howard Marshall, *1 and 2 Thessalonians* (NCB; Grand Rapids: Eerdmans, 1983), pp. 190–92.

24. Schnackenburg, *Johannine Epistles*, pp. 135–36.

25. Notice also the deception in 2 Thess. 2.3, 10-12.

In this section, we have noticed several lexical connections between 1 Jn 2.18-27 and the book of Daniel. First, I have shown how the lexical cluster of "last hour," "eternal life," and "to be ashamed" appears in both contexts. Furthermore, the idea of righteousness follows the argument in both texts (1 Jn 2.29 and Dan. 12.3). Finally, we have noted that the idea of an antichrist appearing in the "last time" echoes the insolent king of Daniel.

IV. *The Broader Eschatological Context of 1 John 2.18*

In addition to what has been said above, this section will investigate some additional eschatological themes and allusions that appear in the broader context of the epistle, and which relate to the proposed allusion to the Danielic hour.[26] The purpose of this section is to identify the eschatological focus of the broader context of 1 Jn 2.18, as well as to examine any further possible allusions to Daniel in the immediate context of 1 Jn 2.18-27.

The unit of 1 Jn 1.5–2.17 contains several eschatological notions that prepare the reader for the reference to the last hour in 2.18. Scholars have noticed that the contrasting themes of "light" and "darkness" in 1 Jn 1.5–2.11 resemble the cosmic battle between the forces of light and the forces of darkness as they are represented in Qumran.[27] We have encountered a similar emphasis in Jn 12.35-36 (see my comments on pp. 130–31). The author of the epistle, while addressing a conflict within the church of the late first century, does so by interpreting this conflict in terms of the final eschatological hour of trial. The contrast between light and darkness is reinforced by another contrast, that between truth and falsehood.

I have already discussed the extensive use of Danielic passages (particularly Dan. 12.2-3) in 1QS III and IV.[28] The document portrays the battle between the Prince of Lights and the Angel of Darkness, as well as the involvement of their respective sons. In 1QS IV, particularly, the sons of truth are promised eternal life, while the sons of deceit await torture and eternal damnation. The following chart shows the distinction of the two groups and their parallels with Dan. 12.2.[29]

---

26. While several attempts have been made to focus on the eschatology of 1 John, none of them seem to be comprehensive enough to elevate eschatology as the primary focus of the epistle. The exception to this may be Frey. See the following treatments: Wai Yee Ng, 'Johannine Eschatology as Demonstrated in First John' (unpublished thesis; Westminster Theological Seminary, 1988); Kurt Niederwimmer, 'Zur Eschatologie im Corpus Johanneum', *NovT* 39 (1997), pp. 105–16; and Frey, *Eschatologie III*.

27. E.g. see Schnackenburg, *Johannine Epistles*, p. 75; Smalley, *1, 2, 3 John*, pp. 18–19; Klauck, *Der erste Johannesbrief*, p. 82; Strecker, *Johannine Letters*, p. 26.

28. For the full argument, see pp. 71–74.

29. This chart also appears in the chapter dealing with the Jewish literature.

1QS IV, 6-8	1QS IV, 11-13	Dan. 12.2
And the reward (וּפְקוּדַת) of all those who walk in it will be healing, plentiful (רוֹב) peace in a long life, fruitful offspring with all everlasting blessings, eternal (עוֹלָמִים) enjoyment with endless life (בְּחַיֵּי), and a crown of glory with majestic raiment in eternal (עוֹלָמִים) light.	And the reward (וּפְקוּדַת) of all those who walk in it will be for an abundance (רוֹב) of afflictions at the hands of all the angels of destruction, for eternal (עוֹלָמִים) damnation by the scorching wrath of the God of revenges, for permanent terror and disgrace (וְחֶרְפַּת) without end with the humiliation of destruction by the fire of the dark regions.	Many of those who sleep in the dust of the ground will awake, these to eternal (עוֹלָם) life (לְחַיֵּי), but the others to disgrace (לַחֲרָפוֹת) and eternal (עוֹלָם) contempt. Those who have insight will shine brightly like the brightness of the expanse of heaven, and those who lead the many to righteousness, like the stars eternally (לְעוֹלָם) forever.

Apart from the references to the "light" and the "darkness," the relevance of the above chart for 1 John 2 becomes stronger when one notices that 1QS uses words that parallel (though do not allude to) Dan. 12.2, "eternal" (עוֹלָם), "life" (חַי), and "disgrace" (or "shame," חֶרְפָּה) to describe the destiny of the two groups. Moreover, the identification of the sons of truth with the "light" (1QS, IV 8), as well as with the "spirit of knowledge" (1QS IV, 4), parallels the combination of the words "light," "truth," and "to know" in 1 Jn 1.5–2.27. Finally, in 1QS IV, 16, the text reads: "For God has sorted them into equal parts until the last time." The eschatological battle between the sons of light (or truth) and the sons of darkness (or falsehood) occurs due to the twofold distinction that God has caused to exist until the "last time." The above parallels with 1QS enhance the eschatological nature of the author's broader argument in 1 John and strengthen the argument for the "last hour" (2.18) being not only eschatological but also an allusion to Daniel, since many of the parallel notions in 1QS are themselves parallel to or allude to Daniel.

The conflict between good and evil is also described in 1 Jn 2.13-14 by way of attaining a victory over the evil one. The overcoming of the evil one enhances the idea of warfare, only now the opponent is being summed up as one figure — the devil (cf. 3.8, 10). The theme of achieving victory over the evil opponents is resumed in the epistle, in 4.1-4 and 5.3-5, which indicates its significance for the author.

The opposing destinies of the world (and those attached to the world) and those who do God's will, as it occurs in 1 Jn 2.17, may also reflect the idea of the double destiny described in Dan. 12.2. Marshall mentions that the passing away of the world should be viewed in close association with the last hour in 2.18, which we have argued to be Danielic.[30] If this is the case, then "those who do God's will" in 2.17 may be identified with the "wise" and "those who turn many to righteousness"

30. Marshall, *Epistles of John*, pp. 147–48.

in Dan. 12.3. This identification is especially prompted by the fact that the glorification of these people lasts εἰς τὸν αἰῶνα (Dan. 12.3; cf. Dan. 12.7).[31]

Dan. 12.3 (OG)	1 Jn 2.17
Those who have insight will shine brightly like the brightness of the expanse of heaven, and those who stand firm on my words (τοὺς λόγους μου), like the stars forever (εἰς τὸν αἰῶνα) and ever.	The world is passing away, and also its lusts; but the one who does the will of God (τὸ θέλημα τοῦ θεοῦ) abides forever (εἰς τὸν αἰῶνα).

Therefore, the statement in 1 Jn 2.17, "whoever does the will of God abides forever," may naturally lead to the discussion of the "last hour" (2.18) and the promise of eternal life (2.25). These are all interconnected themes parallel to and, possibly, derived from the book of Daniel.

Finally, other eschatological themes that appear throughout the epistle also affect the overall picture. Such themes are the second coming of Christ (2.28–3.3), the final judgment (2.28; 4.17), the eschatological gift of joy (1.4), the forgiveness of sin (1.9; 2.2, 12), the indwelling of the Spirit (3.24; 4.1-6, 13; 5.6-8),[32] and the idea of passing from death to eternal life (3.14-15). All of these broader eschatological themes elsewhere in the broader context of 1 John show how naturally an allusion to Daniel's eschatological hour fits in 1 Jn 2.18.

V. *Conclusion*

After having examined the use of the hour in 1 Jn 2.18-27 and its relation to the book of Daniel, the existence of the Johannine allusion to the Danielic hour appears to be probable. The combined use of "last" (or "end") and hour in Daniel (8.19; 11.40, 45; cf. 12.1) indicates that the author of 1 John may have borrowed the Danielic idea of a "last hour," especially since such a combination appears in the OT only in Daniel. Moreover, the use of the Danielic notions of "eternal life" and "shame" in such close proximity points further to the allusion in 1 Jn 2.18.

Furthermore, I have attempted to establish the eschatological nature of the overall argument in 1 John 1–3. To this end, I have mentioned additional references elsewhere in the epistle of "eternal life," the eschatological battle between the "light" and the "darkness," the victory over the evil one, and the reference to the double destiny in 2.17. The presence of other eschatological themes such as the second coming of Christ and the forgiveness of sin also attest to the eschatological focus in the epistle. These eschatological themes show how fitting is an allusion to Daniel's end-time hour in 1 Jn 2.18.

---

31. We have encountered the phrase μένει εἰς τὸν αἰῶνα again in Jn 12.34 and have discussed the possibility of an allusion to Dan. 7.14: καὶ ἡ ἐξουσία αὐτοῦ ἐξουσία αἰώνιος ἥτις οὐ μὴ ἀρθῆ. See pp. 129–30 for relevant comments.

32. The references to the anointing in 1 Jn 2.20, 27 may also refer to the indwelling of the Spirit.

9

HERMENEUTICAL, THEOLOGICAL AND
BIBLICAL-THEOLOGICAL CONCLUSIONS

1. *The Johannine Use of the Danielic Hour*

In this book we have attempted to establish the probable existence of an allusion to Daniel in the Johannine use of hour. The use of the eschatological hour in the Johannine literature often in combination with other Danielic expressions and themes has led us to conclude that the allusion exists in several instances. In this final chapter, I summarize how we have arrived at this conclusion and draw the appropriate inferences. Moreover, I suggest possible implications that the Johannine use of the Danielic hour may have on the interpretation of the Fourth Gospel, on the development of a Christian anthropology, Christology, and eschatology, and also on the unfolding of salvation history. First, let us consider the argument that has brought us to this conclusion.

Initially, we saw how the notion of an eschatological time (עֵת) has been used in the OT, particularly within the expressions "in that time" and "time of distress." These expressions also appear in the book of Daniel and relate to the eschatological hour found in the OG of Daniel. The survey has shown that the Old Testament contains the concept of eschatological time and thus allows for the use of עֵת to refer to God's end-time intervening act.[1] More specifically, the phrase "in that time" (בָּעֵת הַהִיא) appears in contexts with eschatological language denoting the coming of an end-time era (see especially Joel 4.1; Zeph. 1.12; 3.19-20; Jer. 31.1; 33.15).[2] It is associated with such eschatological time references as the "day of the Lord" (Joel 2.1, 11; 3.4; 4.14; Zeph. 1.7, 10, 14; cf. Jer. 30.8; 31.6) and the "latter days" (Jer. 30.24; Mic. 4.1). In these particular OT contexts, the phrase "in that time" often denotes a time of judgment that is followed by Israel's final restoration through God's messianic figure. One may suggest that the above common use of

---

1. We have defined the "eschaton" as God's appointed time in history that introduces a distinct era in which reality as we know it has been transformed and whose results are irreversible; this eschatological time includes the "end" of God's enemies and also points to God's final goal for history and his people.
2. See also Mic. 3.4; and Jer. 3.17; 4.11; 8.1; 50.4, 20.

the phrase could have become by Daniel's time a *terminus technicus* referring to the "eschaton."

In addition, we have observed that the word עֵת has also been used in the OT in reference to the concept of distress (עֵת צָרָה). We specifically studied the instance in Jer. 30.7, which, aside from its historical application, also points to an eschatological tribulation that involves God's wrath (Jer. 30.23-24) and leads to a permanent restoration. The distress in Jer. 30.7 has been picked up by Daniel in Dan. 12.1, linking it with the phrase "in that time"[3] and connecting it with the end-time resurrection (Dan. 12.2). The above use of עֵת in the OT has shown that, even before Daniel, the prophets had developed an expectation concerning God's intervening act that is to inaugurate a new era for God's people.

In line with the use of eschatological "time" in the OT, the OG translates some of these Hebrew words in Daniel with ὥρα (8.17, 19; 11.35, 40, 45; 12.1). An emphasis is placed on God's final adversary who will stand in opposition to everything that God represents: he will destroy the sanctuary (8.11-13, 24; 9.26; cf. 12.11), persecute God's people (8.25; 11.35, 41), oppose the Prince of princes (8.25; 9.26-27), and exalt himself as god (8.11, 25; 11.36). However, he will come to an end without the intervention of human effort (8.25; 11.45). This defeat is apparently permanent and irreversible (Dan. 7.26). These events will take place within the parameters of the hour, which in the OG of Daniel represents an eschatological period.[4]

The appearance of the Son of Man (Dan. 7.13-14) or Michael (Dan. 12.1) establishes God's kingdom forever (Dan. 7.14, 18, 22, 27) and effects the eschatological resurrection of the dead (Dan. 12.2), some to eternal life and others to eternal disgrace. For OG Daniel, the expectation of this hour in 12.1 concerns the distant future (12.4).

The Danielic concept of an eschatological time and hour is later picked up in early Judaism. This is evident, since the concept of hour appears in the Jewish literature within contexts that allude to the Danielic end-time events ("time of the end," "judgement," "resurrection"). Therefore, within the Jewish tradition there exists an anticipation of the fulfillment of the Danielic eschatological time. In some instances (see the use in the DSS), there is even an inaugurated notion of this eschatological era (already-and-not-yet fulfillment). This use of hour in parts of the Jewish literature shows that a connection between the hour and other Danielic eschatological themes was familiar to the Jews, and therefore, the similar use of hour by John, especially in connection to the ideas of resurrection, judgment, and persecution, would not have been received as unusual.

Indeed, John has combined the hour (ὥρα) with eschatological expressions and themes that have their source in Daniel. While he does not fully disclose the Danielic associations to the hour from the beginning (Jn 2.4; 4.21, 23),[5] he never-

---

3.   The phrase "in that time" appears three times in the MT of Dan. 12.1.
4.   For the eschatological nature of this period, see the expressions in the MT, OG, and TH in Dan. 8.17, 19; 10.14; 11.35, 40, 45; 12.4.
5.   Though notice that John mentions the Danielic idea of "eternal life" in 4.14.

theless prepares the reader by relating the hour to the person of Jesus (2.4) and by further connecting it with themes that echo eschatological Old Testament expectations (4.21, 23).[6] The result is that Jesus's hour inaugurates the eschatological era.

In John 5, Jesus's discourse on judgment and resurrection life explicitly connects the hour to Danielic themes, thus directing the reader to view the coming hour in connection to the end-time prophecies in Daniel. Jesus associates himself with the Son of Man (5.27 = Dan. 7.13) who has been given authority to judge (5.22, 27 = Dan. 7.14) and to give eternal life (5.24 = Dan. 12.2). Moreover, the "son" will receive honor (5.23 = Dan. 7.14) and will bring about the eschatological resurrection from the dead (5.25, 28-29 = Dan. 12.1-2). All these are characteristically Danielic themes (Dan. 7.13-14; 12.2). The association of the coming hour with the above allusions and themes from Daniel shows us that, at least in this context, John perceives the hour to be the eschatological moment — or era — when the Danielic Son of Man will exercise judgment, give spiritual life, and resurrect the dead from their graves. John's deliberate description of the hour as both "coming" (4.21; 5.28) and "coming and now is" (4.23; 5.25) may signify that he viewed the Danielic eschatological era as having been inaugurated with Jesus, yet still awaiting its consummation in the future.

The suggestion that the use of hour in John 5.25, 28 alludes to the eschatological hour in Dan. 12.1 becomes even stronger when one considers that the word ὥρα appears with an eschatological sense nowhere else in the OT (LXX) apart from the book of Daniel. We have found that the above indications convincingly support the probability of a Johannine allusion to the Danielic hour in John 5.

Furthermore, in John 12, Jesus again speaks about the hour, which has now arrived (12.23, 27; 13.1) and concerns the time of Jesus's glorification. More specifically, Jesus connects the eschatological hour with his death and resurrection (12.24, 32-33), which will result in eternal life (12.25). This hour also involves the defeat of "the ruler of this world" (12.31), and it introduces a conflict between light and darkness (12.35-36).[7] One may argue that Jesus's death on the cross brought into existence an escalation of the Danielic eschatological hour, which had already been inaugurated by Jesus and in which the end-time battle takes place, God's final adversary is defeated, and the conflict between God and his opponents is resolved. By connecting the Johannine hour to the one in Daniel, one realizes that Jesus's ministry — especially his death and resurrection — is the eschatological act of God. John has employed the appropriate language to denote that the final hour has indeed begun to arrive.[8]

---

6.   These eschatological expectations concern the giving of "living water" (4.10, 14) and the renewal of worship (4.21-23), both of which contain the eschatological promises of the outpouring of the Spirit and the establishment of the end-time temple.

7.   This conflict has been described in terms of a cosmic battle (J. L. Kovacs, "'Now Shall the Ruler of This World Be Driven Out": Jesus' Death as Cosmic Battle in John 12.20-36', *JBL* 114 (1995), pp. 227–47.

8.   The mere mention of an eschatological hour that has *arrived* (Jn 12.23; 13.1; 16.32;

John continues with his use of hour in John 16, where the hour is associated with two more eschatological images, the pangs of a woman bearing a child (Isa. 26.17; 66.7-9) and the scattering of the sheep (Zech. 13.7). In their OT contexts, both of these images relate to the notion of tribulation, which appears to be a central emphasis in Jesus's words in John 16. By alluding to these OT eschatological images, John conveys the understanding that the specific prophetic pronouncements are about to be fulfilled. John's use of θλίψις ("distress") in connection to the hour in Jn 16.21 and 32-33 is likely intended to allude to the eschatological "distress" in Dan. 12.1. In fact, the combination of the two words, ὥρα and θλίψις, is unique to Dan. 12.1 and Jn 16.21, 32-33 (it appears nowhere else in the OT, Jewish, or NT literature). The suggestion that the hour in John 16 alludes to Daniel is further enhanced by John's language in Jn 17.1-2, which connects the hour with such Danielic themes as the Son receiving glory and the authority to judge and to give eternal life (see Dan. 7.13-14; 12.1-2).

Where could John have derived the idea of eschatological ὥρα, if not from Daniel? As we have reiterated earlier, the only place in the OT where one may find an eschatological hour is the book of Daniel, which makes it plausible that John may have had it in mind. In this case, Jesus has used the word ὥρα to argue that the final hour of tribulation and resurrection, as it is depicted in Daniel, has arrived. Jesus's death on the cross initiates the end-time affliction (both for him and the disciples), the distress that has never occurred since the beginning of all nations. However, while this hour may certainly involve great affliction, God's ultimate purpose is to lead his people to life.

A similar Danielic emphasis within the Fourth Gospel appears in 1 Jn 2.18 and its context, where the combined use of "last" and "hour" indicates that the author of 1 John probably borrowed the Danielic idea of a "last hour" (such a combination of "last" and "hour" appears in the OT only in Daniel). The "last hour" in 1 Jn 2.18 relates to the arrival of the antichrists, which is reminiscent of God's end-time battle with his final adversary (cf. Dan. 11.30–12.4) and the saints' tribulation and oppression at the hands of this adversary (Dan. 7.21, 25; 8.24-25; 11.33, 35, 41; 12.1, 10). The appearance of the antichrists in the Johannine community probably fulfills Jesus's predictions about the coming of false Christs (Mark 13 and Matthew 24), which are also associated with end-time themes borrowed from Daniel. The fact that 1 Jn 2.25 and 2.28 mention the Danielic ideas of "eternal life" and "shame," respectively (see Dan. 12.2), further points to the existence of an allusion to the Danielic hour in Jn 2.18. According to this proposal, the audience of 1 John lives within the timeframe of the eschatological oppression and deception by the end-time opponent prophesied in Daniel. This is a time in which those belonging to God distinguish themselves from the enemy by retaining possession of eternal life (1 Jn 2.24-25).

17.1) implies the existence of a preceding expectation for this hour. At the statement "the hour has come," the question naturally arises in the reader's mind, "which hour?" The existence of an eschatological hour in Daniel adequately satisfies the need for a preceding prediction, especially since the description of hour in Daniel fits well with the Johannine use of the same term.

Comparable to the use of hour in the Fourth Gospel and 1 John is the hour in the book of Revelation, which has also been argued by several scholars to have a Danielic background. The word ὥρα occurs 10 times in Revelation (3.3, 10; 9.5; 11.13; 14.7, 15; 17.12; 18.10, 17, 19), every instance of which relates to the idea of judgment. In Rev. 3.10, the word ὥρα designates the "hour of trial" that will come upon the whole earth, and Beale has argued for a probable allusion to the hour and tribulation of Dan. 12.1.[9] If the tribulation in 3.10 relates to the eschatological tribulation in Dan. 12.1 (as several other scholars have indicated),[10] it makes good sense to read the hour in 3.10 also as an allusion to the eschatological hour of Dan. 12.1, since the two notions are closely connected in the phrase "the hour of trial."[11]

Moreover, the phrase "the hour of his judgement has come" in Rev. 14.7 and the association of this hour with the fall of Babylon in the next verse (Rev. 14.8; "fallen, fallen is Babylon the great") has been identified as a probable allusion to the Danielic hour of judgment (cf. "the hour of his end will come" in Dan. 11.45; and "Babylon the great" in Dan. 4.30 (OG), the context of which Nebuchadnezzar is judged in "one hour" in Dan. 4.17).[12]

Finally, the use of the phrase "one hour" in Rev. 17.12; 18.10, 17, 19, has also been linked with Daniel, especially since the exact phrase is used in Dan. 4.17, 19.[13] Notice that the immediate context of the phrase "one hour" in Revelation (17.12; 18.10, 17, 19) employs characteristic Danielic expressions such as the reference to the "ten horns" (Rev. 17.12; cf. Dan. 7.7-8), the mentioning of the war against the saints (Rev. 17.14; cf. Dan. 7.21), the phrase "King of Kings" (Rev. 17.14; cf.

9. G. K. Beale, *The Book of Revelation: A Commentary on the Greek Text* (NIGTC; Grand Rapids: Eerdmans, 1999), p. 292. Note also the tribulation in Rev. 7.14 and the Danielic allusion there. It is plausible that the author of Revelation has the same eschatological tribulation (θλῖψις) in mind throughout the book (Rev. 1.9; 2.9, 10; 2.22; 7.14), which is also linked to the "hour of trial" in 3.10.

10. See Grant R. Osborne, *Revelation* (BECNT; Grand Rapids: Baker, 2002), p. 193; Robert H. Mounce, *The Book of Revelation* (NICNT; Grand Rapids: Eerdmans, 1998), p. 103; David E. Aune, *Revelation 1–5* (WBC, 52a; Nashville: Thomas Nelson, 1997), p. 239; and Stephen S. Smalley, *The Revelation to John: A Commentary on the Greek Text of the Apocalypse* (Downers Grove: InterVarsity, 2005), pp. 91–92.

11. This "hour of trial" resembles the hour of persecution for the disciples in Jn 16.2, 4, 32-33. Notice the use of ὥρα in Jn 16.2, 4, 32, and then Jesus's comment in 16.33: "in the world you have tribulation (θλῖψιν)."

12. Beale, *Book of Revelation*, pp. 752, 754–55; Osborne, *Revelation*, pp. 536–37. Osborne goes one step further and sees a parallel between the use of hour in Revelation and in the Fourth Gospel (Osborne, *Revelation*, p. 536). Smalley also implies a connection between the hour in Revelation and that in John's gospel (Smalley, *Revelation*, p. 363).

13. See Beale, *Book of Revelation*, 879. In agreement with Beale, commentators such as Osborne and Smalley also view the "one hour" in Dan. 4.17a, 19 OG as a plausible background for the "one hour" in Rev. 18.10 (Osborne, *Revelation*, p. 646; Smalley, *Revelation*, p. 452; cf. also David E. Aune, *Revelation 17–22* (WBC, 52c; Nashville: Thomas Nelson, 1998), pp. 997–98).

Dan. 4.37 LXX), and especially the use of "Babylon the great" (Rev. 17.5; 18.2, 10, 21; cf. Dan. 4.30 LXX; 4.27 in MT). In the midst of these Danielic allusions, it is natural for the author of Revelation to have used the Danielic designation for the time of judgment ("one hour") to denote the eschatological time of God's judgment on the ungodly (Babylon). It appears, therefore, that those scholars who have recognized a Danielic background to the use of hour in Revelation have done so on sufficient grounds.

In light of the above use of hour in the Johannine literature, one must arrive at the conclusion that an allusion to the Danielic hour in John is highly likely. Granted the validity of this suggestion, we will now explore some possible implications that this suggestion may have on our understanding of the Gospel of John, on the dogmatic areas of anthropology, Christology and eschatology, and on the biblical-theological concept of salvation history.

II. *Hermeneutical Implications for the Gospel of John*

The initial hermeneutical question to be asked regarding the use of hour in the Gospel of John is how, precisely, this hour fulfills the prophetic predictions in Daniel. I suggest that John probably views the hour as a direct fulfillment.[14] One might also argue for a stock-in-trade use;[15] however, this could only exist in a secondary sense. The option of direct fulfillment is more probable, since the Danielic hour to which John alludes concerns prophetic pronouncements about the eschaton, awaiting a future fulfillment. Indeed, most of the Daniel 7–12 descriptions are prophecies, some of which were at least partially fulfilled in the days between the fifth and the second century BC,[16] while the rest of the proclaimed events were expected to take place some time in the future, within the parameters of an eschatological hour.

It is precisely this hour that is being fulfilled in the life of Jesus. While the expression ἔρχεται ὥρα (Jn 4.21, 23; 5.25, 28; 16.2, 4, 32) may communicate the idea that this hour is yet to come (from Jesus's or even John's viewpoint), the simultaneous use of the phrase καὶ νῦν ἐστιν (Jn 4.23; 5.25; cf. also 12.23, 27; 13.1; 16.32; 17.1) betrays the inaugurated fulfillment of this eschatological era in the time of Jesus.

---

14. By *direct* fulfillment I mean the direct verbal fulfillment of the OT prediction to which the NT text refers. This would be distinguished from an *indirect* prophetic fulfillment, which would involve the typological kind of fulfillment of events or patterns. For the latter kind of fulfillment, see Leonhard Goppelt, *Typos: The Typological Interpretation of the Old Testament in the New* (Grand Rapids: Eerdmans, 1982), pp. 13–14.

15. A stock-in-trade-use is when a NT author uses an OT word or phrase not with the intention of alluding to a specific OT text, but due to the common use and wide acceptance of the word or phrase up to the NT author's time.

16. For example, note the prophecies concerning the rise and fall of the Persian and the Greek empires (Dan. 8.20-26).

There is an emphasis, therefore, in the Gospel of John on an inaugurated eschatology, one that is already-but-not-yet realized.[17]

Apart from the eschatological perspective that the notion of direct fulfillment may impart to the gospel, the Johannine use of the Danielc hour may also contribute to a fuller development of a Johannine theology of hour.[18] It has already been argued that the hour theme plays a central role in the theology of the gospel.[19] Indeed, John mentions Jesus's hour at the very beginning of Jesus's ministry (2.4) and also at the end, right before the Farewell Discourse (12.23, 27). Even within John's presentation of the Farewell Discourse, the hour is prominent at the beginning (13.1) and the end (16.32). In addition, Jesus's priestly prayer begins with reference to the hour, which has now arrived (17.1). In John's gospel, the ministry of Jesus, including his death and resurrection, is defined by the eschatological hour. Jesus inaugurates the fulfillment of the Danielic prophecies about the end-time victory over God's opponent and the final judgment and resurrection. John's emphasis on the Danielic notion of "eternal life" (Dan. 12.2) throughout his gospel verifies that Jesus has established God's eternal kingdom (Jn 3.3, 5; cf. Daniel 7) by imparting resurrection life to those who believe.[20] Moreover, the development of a Johannine theology that takes into consideration the use of the Danielic hour may cast further light on the eschatological outlook of the Johannine community.

III. *Theological Implications for Anthropology, Christology, and Eschatology*

Apart from the apparent implications for the Gospel of John, a Danielic understanding of the hour in the Fourth Gospel may contribute to other fields of dogmatic interest, such as the areas of anthropology, Christology, and eschatology. Of course, the proposed contribution intends to reinforce the already existing theological perspectives in these fields.

In the area of anthropology, the contribution of this study involves the suggestion that the final resurrection (in Dan. 12.2) has already begun. This notion of inaugurated eschatological fulfillment has ramifications for the biblical understanding of humanity, especially the new created humanity. If the hour of eschatological resurrection has arrived — as John repeatedly affirms — then those who believe have become a "new creation" by participating in the final resurrection. The fact that this participation involves the spiritual regeneration of the believer should not lead one to view this participation metaphorically; rather, the believer takes part in a literal,

---

17. This emphasis in the Gospel of John has already been acknowledged by many scholars.

18. This could possibly be expanded to include a biblical theology of eschatological time (in both OT and NT).

19. See for example, van der Merwe, ᵕ῟Ωρα', pp. 255–87.

20. It has already been suggested that the Johannine insistence on "eternal life" substitutes for the emphasis on God's kingdom in the synoptic gospels.

albeit spiritual, resurrection. The Johannine emphasis on spiritual birth (Jn 1.13; 3.3-8; cf. 8.41; 16.21) testifies to the development of an anthropological view of humanity based on the new creational act of resurrection. This understanding of new humanity as already (spiritually) resurrected may also affect other areas of theology, since it also bears on issues of salvation.

The use of the Danielic hour in the Gospel of John may also contribute to Christology, since Jesus is portrayed as the Son of Man who represents the church in her eschatological battle. The Pauline notion of being "in Christ" cannot be fully appreciated without a proper understanding of Jesus's role as the "head" of humanity, the representative of God's people. While in the person of Jesus one may certainly see the divine Word incarnate (Jn 1.14), one should not depreciate the human Jesus who intercedes for believers (Jn 17.9-26; cf. 1 Tim. 2.5). While the eternal Son may *eternally possess* the privilege of judging and giving life, the incarnate Christ *has received* this authority as the Son of Man, God's appointed king over humanity, to judge and give life. This means that, "in Christ," we have received the kingdom and eternal life, because, as our human representative, he first received the kingdom and eternal life.

Finally, the possible implications for eschatology are apparent. The fulfillment of the Danielic hour in the death and resurrection of Jesus signifies that the Danielic eschatological prophecies have begun their fulfillment in Jesus: Jesus satisfies the prophecy relating to the execution of judgment (Dan. 7.13-14, 22, 26-27 in Jn 5.22, 27), he fulfills the prophecy for the establishment of God's kingdom (Dan. 7.13-14, 22, 26-27 in Jn 5.22, 27), and above all, in Jn 5.25 (in relation to 5.28-29), Jesus fulfills the resurrection prophecy (Dan. 12.2), which leads to eternal life. The fact that the life, death, and resurrection of Jesus has served as the fulfillment of the Danielic hour does not exclude yet another fulfillment, or consummation, in the future; Jesus will certainly bring the Danielic prophecies to consummation (Jn 5.28-29). However, the arrival of the Danielic hour does lead us to the conclusion that the Danielic prophecies have been primarily applied with Jesus and continue their application with the church (Jn 16.2, 4, 32; 1 Jn 2.18). Through this initial fulfillment of the Danielic hour, one may also structure the pattern through which the final fulfillment will take place.

IV. *Biblical-Theological Implications for the Unfolding of Salvation History*

Our final thought relates to the biblical-theological notion of the history of salvation. If John has used the Danielic hour to indicate a direct fulfillment in the life of Jesus, this means that the eschaton has arrived. Jesus has initiated the "last hour," in which the church now lives (1 Jn 2.18). This eschatological observation has two possible implications with regard to God's history of salvation: first, it shifts the place and time of final judgment and resurrection from happening only at the end of history to being inaugurated at Jesus's first coming; and second, it identifies the life and work of Christ with the life and work of the church.

The first implication suggests that God has introduced the final judgment and resurrection within the course of history, beginning with the cross and resurrection of Jesus, and continuing with the justification and regeneration of the believer. The individual's response to the person and work of Jesus finalizes the verdict of God's final judgment (Jn 3.18-19; 5.24; 12.48) and places one into the realm of eternal life or death (Jn 5.24; 8.51). Salvation need not await the end of historical reality, but is available to those who seek it in the present. This shift of the place and time of the final events illuminates the salvation that God has brought in history and transforms the church's eschatological hope and expectations for the future. The period of the church is the time in which the people will become separated into two distinct groups: those who possess eternal life and those who do not.

Moreover, the fact that the Danielic eschatological hour has been expanded to include the church-age implies that the life and work of the church recapitulates the life and work of Jesus. While Jesus has certainly fought the eschatological battle and secured its final outcome, this battle still goes on due to the wordly existence of the community of God's people. Jesus's affliction by the world and his exposure to deceptive influences will be repeated in the life of the church (Jn 15.18–16.4); and his hour will become their hour (Jn 16.2, 4). We have seen how this conflict is portrayed in the context of the final hour in 1 Jn 2.18. God's people are called to live a continual death by detaching themselves from the world (1 Jn 2.15-17), and also to exhibit their genuine birth by possessing eternal life (1 Jn 2.24-25). Finally, the Danielic hour finds further fulfillment in the lives of those who have insight (Dan. 12.3), that is, those to whom Christ talks plainly (Jn 16.25) and who possess knowledge of the truth (1 Jn 2.21).

BIBLIOGRAPHY

Alexander, P., '3 (Hebrew Apocalypse of) Enoch', in James H. Charlesworth (ed.), *The Old Testament Pseudepigrapha: Vol. 1* (New York: Doubleday, 1983), pp. 223–315.

Allen, Leslie C., *The Books of Joel, Obadiah, Jonah and Micah* (NICOT; Grand Rapids: Eerdmans, 1976).

—*Ezekiel 1–19* (WBC, 28; Dallas: Word, 1994).

Altick, Richard D., and John J. Fenstermaker, *The Art of Literary Research* (New York: Norton, 1993).

Andersen, Francis I., and David Noel Freedman, *Hosea: A New Translation with Introduction and Commentary* (AB, 24; New York: Doubleday, 1980).

—*Amos: A New Translation with Introduction and Commentary* (AB, 24A; New York: Doubleday, 1989).

—*Micah: A New Translation with Introduction and Commentary* (AB, 24E; New York: Doubleday, 2000).

Ashton, John, *Understanding the Fourth Gospel* (Oxford: Oxford University Press, 1991).

Asiedu-Peprah, Martin, *Johannine Sabbath Conflicts as Juridical Controversy* (WUNT, 132; Tübingen: Mohr (Siebeck), 2001).

Aune, David E., *The Cultic Setting of Realized Eschatology in Early Christianity* (NovTSup, 28; Leiden: Brill, 1972).

—*Revelation 1–5* (WBC, 52a; Nashville: Thomas Nelson, 1997).

—*Revelation 6–16* (WBC, 52b; Nashville: Thomas Nelson, 1997).

—*Revelation 17–22* (WBC, 52c; Nashville: Thomas Nelson, 1998).

Bailey, Daniel P., 'The Intertextual Relationship of Daniel 12.2 and Isaiah 26.19: Evidence from Qumran and the Greek Versions', *TynBul* 51 (2000), pp. 305–08.

Baker, David W., *Nahum, Habakkuk, Zephaniah* (TOTC; Downers Grove: InterVarsity, 1988).

Baldwin, Joyce G., *Daniel: An Introduction and Commentary* (TOTC; Downers Grove: InterVarsity, 1978).

Balz, Horst, 'Johanneische Theologie und Ethik im Licht der "letzten Stunde"', in Wolfgang Schrage (ed.), *Studien zum Text und zur Ethik des Neuen Testaments: Festschrift zum 80. Geburtstag von Heinrich Greeven* (New York: Walter de Gruyter, 1986), pp. 35–56.

Bamfylde, Gilliam, 'More light on John 12.34', *JSNT* 17 (1983), pp. 87–89.

Barker, Margaret, *The Gate of Heaven: The History and Symbolism of the Temple in Jerusalem* (London: SPCK, 1991).

Barr, James, *Biblical Words for Time* (SBT, 33; Naperville: Alec R. Allenson, 1962).

Barrett, C. K., 'The Old Testament in the Fourth Gospel', *JTS* 48 (1947), pp. 155–60.

—*The Gospel According to St John: An Introduction with Commentary and Notes on the Greek Text* (London: SPCK, 1967).

Baumgarten, Albert I. (ed.), *Apocalyptic Time* (Boston: Brill, 2000).

Beale, G. K., *The Use of Daniel in Jewish Apocalyptic Literature and in the Revelation of St. John* (Lanham: UPA, 1984).

—*John's Use of Old Testament in Revelation* (JSNTSup, 166; Sheffield: Sheffield Academic Press, 1998).

—*The Book of Revelation: A Commentary on the Greek Text* (NIGTC; Grand Rapids: Eerdmans, 1999).

—'Questions of Authorial Intent, Epistemology, and Presuppositions and Their Bearing on the Study of the Old Testament in the New: A Rejoiner to Steve Moyise', *IBS* 21 (1999), pp. 152–80.

—*1–2 Thessalonians* (IVPNT; Downers Grove: InterVarsity, 2003).

—*The Temple and the Church's Mission: A Biblical Theology of the Dwelling Place of God* (NSBT; Downers Grove: InterVarsity, 2004).

—'The Old Greek of Daniel as a Background to the "Last Hour" in 1 Jn 2.18', (Read at the 'Greek Bible' Section at the Annual Meeting of the SBL in Boston, MA; November, 2008).

Beale, G. K., and D. A. Carson, *Commentary on the New Testament Use of the Old Testament* (Grand Rapids: Baker, 2007).

Beasley-Murray, George R., 'John 12.31–34: the Eschatological Significance of the Lifting Up of the Son of Man', in Wolfgang Schrage (ed.), *Studien zum Text und zur Ethik des Neuen Testaments: Festschrift zum 80. Geburtstag von Heinrich Greeven* (New York: Walter de Gruyter, 1986), pp. 70–81.

—*John* (WBC, 36; Waco: Word, 1987).

Becker, Jürgen, 'Wunder und Christologie: zum literarkritischen und christologischen Problem der Wunder im Johannesevangelium', *NTS* 16 (1970), pp. 130–48.

Becking, Bob, 'The Exile Does Not Equal the Eschaton: An Interpretation of Mic. 4.1-5', in F. Postma, K. Spronk, and E. Talstra (eds), *The New Things Eschatology in Old Testament Prophecy: Festschrift for Henk Leene* (Maastricht: Shaker, 2002), pp. 1–7.

Beetham, Christopher A., *Echoes of Scripture in the Letter of Paul to the Colossians* (BIS, 96; Leiden: Brill, 2009).

Belleville, Linda, 'Born of Water and Spirit: John 3.5', *TJ* 1 (1980), pp. 125–41.

Ben-Porat, Ziva, 'The Poetics of Literary Allusion', *PTL* 1 (1976), pp. 105–28.

Bensly, Robert L., *The Fourth Book of Ezra, the Latin Version Edited from the MSS* (Cambridge: Cambridge University Press, 1895).

Berkley, Timothy W., *From a Broken Covenant to Circumcision of the Heart: Pauline Intertextual Exegesis in Romans 2.17-29* (SBLDS, 175; Atlanta: Society of Biblical Literature, 2000).

Berlin, Adele, *Zephaniah: A New Translation with Introduction and Commentary* (AB, 25A; New York: Doubleday, 1994).

Beutler, Johannes, 'Greeks Come to See Jesus (John 12.20f)', *Bib* 71 (1990), pp. 333–47.

—'The Use of Scripture in the Gospel of John', in R. Alan Culpepper and C. Clifton Black (eds), *Exploring the Gospel of John: in Honor of D. Moody Smith* (Louisville: John Knox, 1996), pp. 147–62.

—*Studien zu den johanneischen Schriften* (SBAB, 25; Stuttgard: Bibelwerk, 1998).

—*Judaism and the Jews in the Gospel of John* (Rome: Editrice Pontificio Istituto Biblico, 2006).

Bezeugen, Christus, *Festschrift fur Wolfgang Trilling zum 65. Geburtstag* (ETS, 59; Leipzig: St. Benno-Verlag, 1989).

Black, Matthew, 'The Christological Use of the Old Testament in the New Testament', *NTS* 18 (1971), pp. 1–14.

—*The Book of Enoch or 1 Enoch: A New English Edition with Commentary and Notes* (SVTP, 7; Leiden: Brill, 1985).

—'The Theological Appropriation of the Old Testament by the New Testament', *SJT* 39 (1986), pp. 1–17.

—'The Messianism of the Parables of Enoch: Their Date and Contribution to Christological Origins', in James H. Charlesworth (ed.), *The Messiah: Developments in Earliest Judaism and Christianity* (Minneapolis: Fortress, 1992), pp. 145–68.

Blank, J., *Krisis: Untersuchungen zur johanneischen Christologie und Eschatologie* (Freiburg: Lambertus, 1964).

Blenkinsopp, Joseph, *Isaiah 56–6: A New Translation with Introduction and Commentary* (AB, 19B; New York: Doubleday, 2003).

Block, Daniel I., 'Beyond the Grave: Ezekiel's Vision of Death and Afterlife', *BBR* 2 (1992), pp. 113–41.

—*The Book of Ezekiel: Chapters 1–24* (NICOT; Grand Rapids: Eerdmans, 1997).
—*The Book of Ezekiel: Chapters 25–48* (NICOT; Grand Rapids: Eerdmans, 1998).
—'My Servant David: Ancient Israel's Vision of the Messiah', in Richard S. Hess and
    M. Daniel Carroll R. (eds), *Israel's Messiah in the Bible and the Dead Sea Scrolls* (Grand
    Rapids: Baker, 2003), pp. 17–56.
—'Preaching Old Testament Apocalptic to a New Testament Church', *CTJ* 41 (2006),
    pp. 17–52.
Borgen, P., 'The Place of the Old Testament in the Formation of New Testament Theology:
    Prolegomena and Response', *NTS* 23 (1976–1977), pp. 59–75.
Bream, H. N., 'No Need to be Asked Questions: A Study of John 16.30', in Boo Kiat Chang and
    Y. N. Han (eds), *Search the Scriptures* (Leiden: Brill, 1969), pp. 49–74.
Breech, Earl, 'These Fragments I Have Shored Against My Ruins: The Form and Function of
    4 Ezra', *JBL* 92 (1973), pp. 267–74.
Brin, Gershon, *The Concept of Time in the Bible and the Dead Sea Scrolls* (Leiden: Brill, 2001).
Brooke, George J., *Exegesis at Qumran: 4QFlorilegium in Its Jewish Context* (JSOTSup, 29;
    Sheffield: JSOT, 1985).
Brown, Colin (ed.), *New International Dictionary of New Testament Theology* (4 Vols; Grand
    Rapids: Zondervan, 1975-1985).
Brown, Raymond E., 'Incidents that are Units in the Synoptic Gospels but Dispersed in St.
    John', *CBQ* 23 (1961), pp. 143–60.
—*The Gospel According to John* (AB, 29, 29A; 2 vols; New York: Doubleday, 1966-70).
—*The Epistles of John* (AB, 30; New York: Doubleday, 1982).
—*The Death of the Messiah* (Vol. 1; New York: Doubleday, 1999).
Bruce, F. F., 'The Oldest Greek Version of Daniel', in H. A. Brongers, F. F. Bruce, *et al.* (eds),
    *Instruction and Interpretation: Studies in Hebrew Language, Palestinian Archeology and
    Biblical Exegesis* (Leiden: E. J. Brill, 1977), pp. 22–40.
—'Prophetic Interpretation in the Septuagint', in Robert P. Gordon (ed.), *The Place Is Too
    Small for Us: The Israelite Prophets in Recent Scholarship* (SBTS, 5; Winona Lake, Ind.:
    Eisenbrauns, 1995), pp. 539–46.
Brueggemann, Walter, *A Commentary on Jeremiah: Exile and Homecoming* (Grand Rapids:
    Eerdmans, 1998).
Bruns, J. Edgar, 'A Note on John 16.33 and 1 John 2.13-14', *JBL* 86 (1967), pp. 451–53.
Brunson, Andrew C., *Psalm 118 in the Gospel of John: An Intertextual Study on the New Exodus
    Pattern in the Theology of John* (WUNT, 158; Tübingen: Mohr (Siebeck), 2003).
Buchanan, G. W., 'Eschatology and the "End of Days"', *JNES* 20 (1961), pp. 188–93.
Bullock, C. Hassell, *An Introduction to the Old Testament Prophetic Books* (Chicago: Moody,
    2007).
Bultmann, Rudolf, *The Gospel of John: A Commentary* (Philadelphia: Westminster, 1971).
Burkett, Delbert, *The Son of the Man in the Gospel of John* (JSNTSup, 56; Sheffield: Sheffield
    Academic Press, 1991).
—*The Son of Man Debate: A History and Evaluation* (SNTSMS, 107; Cambridge: Cambridge
    University Press, 1999).
Busse, U., 'Die Tempelmetaphorik als ein Beispiel von implizitem recurs auf die biblische
    Tradition im Johannesevangelium', in E. Peters and Christopher Mark Tuckett (eds), *The
    Scriptures in the Gospels* (BETL, 131; Leuven, Belgium: Leuven University Press, 1997),
    pp. 395–428.
Buth, Randall, 'A More Complete Semitic Background for *bar-enasha*, "Son of Man"', in
    Craig A. Evans and James A. Sanders (eds), *Function of scripture in early Jewish and
    Christian tradition* (Sheffield: Sheffield Academic Press, 1998), pp. 176–89.
Caird, George B., 'Judgement and Salvation: An Exposition of John 12.31-32', *CJT* 2 (1956),
    pp. 231–37.
—*The Revelation of Saint John* (BNTC; Peabody, Mass.: Hendrickson, 1966).
—*The Language and Imagery of the Bible* (Grand Rapids: Eerdmans, 1980).

Caragounis, Chrys C., *The Son of Man* (Tübingen: Mohr (Siebeck), 1986).
—'The Kingdom of God in John and the Synoptic Tradition: Realized or Potential Eschatology?' in Adelbert Denaux (ed.), *John and the Synoptics* (BETL, 101; Leuven, Belgium: Leuven University Press, 1992), pp. 473–80.
Carson, D. A., *The Gospel According To John* (PNTC; Grand Rapids: Eerdmans, 1991).
—'1–3 John', in G. K. Beale and D. A. Carson (eds), *Commentary on the New Testament Use of the Old Testament* (Grand Rapids: Baker, 2007), pp. 1063-67.
Carson, D. A., and H. G. M. Williamson (eds), *It is Written: Scripture Citing Scripture: Essays in Honor of Barnabas Lindars* (Cambridge: Cambridge University Press, 1988).
Casey, Maurice, *Son of Man: The Interpretation and Influence of Daniel 7* (London: SPCK, 1979).
—'Idiom and Translation: Some Aspects of the Son of Man Problem', *NTS* 41 (1995), pp. 164–82.
—'Aramaic Idiom and the Son of Man Problem: A response to Owen and Shepherd', *JSNT* 25 (2002), pp. 3–32.
Charles, Robert H., *A Critical and Exegetical Commentary on the Book of Daniel* (Oxford: Clarendon, 1929).
Charles, Robert H. (ed.), *The Apocrypha and Pseudepigrapha of the Old Testament in English* (2 vols; Oxford: Clarendon, 1913).
Charlesworth, James H., *John and the Dead Sea Scrolls* (New York: Crossroad, 1990).
Charlesworth, James H. (ed.), *The Old Testament Pseudepigrapha* (Vol. 1; New York: Doubleday, 1983).
—*The Old Testament Pseudepigrapha* (Vol. 2; New York: Doubleday, 1985).
—*Rule of the Community and Related Documents* (The Dead Sea Scrolls: Hebrew, Aramaic, and Greek Texts with English Translations; Vol. 1; Tübingen: Mohr (Siebeck), 1994).
Chazon, Esther G., and Michael Stone (eds), *Pseudepigraphic Perspectives: The Apocrypha and Pseudepigrapha in Light of the Dead Sea Scrolls* (Leiden: Brill, 1999).
Childs, Brevard S., *Isaiah* (OTL; Louisville: Westminster John Knox, 2001).
Chilton, Bruce D., 'John 12.34 and Targum Isaiah 52.13', *NovT* 22 (1980), pp. 176–78.
Churgin, P., 'Targum and LXX', *AJSL* 50 (1933–1934), pp. 41–65.
Clark-Soles, Jaime, *Scripture Cannot be Broken: The Social Function of the Use of Scripture in the Fourth Gospel* (Leiden: Brill, 2003).
Clements, R. E., *Prophecy and Covenant* (London: SCM, 1965).
—*Isaiah 1–39* (NCB; Grand Rapids: Eerdmans, 1987).
—*Jeremiah* (Interpretation; Atlanta: John Knox, 1988).
Clifford, Richard J., 'History and Myth in Daniel 10–12', *BASOR* 220 (1975), pp. 23–26.
Coetzee, J. C., 'The Holy Spirit in 1 John', *Neot* 13 (1979), pp. 43–67.
Coggins, R. J., and M. A. Knibb, *The First and Second Books of Esdras* (CBC; Cambridge: Cambridge University Press, 1979).
Collins, Adela Yarbro, *Mark* (Hermeneia; Minneapolis: Fortress, 2007).
Collins, John J., 'The Date and Provenance of the Testament of Moses', in George W. E. Nickelsburg (ed.), *Studies in the Testament of Moses* (Cambridge, MA: SBL, 1973), pp. 15–32.
—'Son of Man and the Saints of the Most High in the Book of Daniel', *JBL* 93 (1974), pp. 50–66.
—'Apocalyptic Literature', in Robert A. Kraft and George W. E. Nickelsburg (eds), *Early Judaism and Its Modern Interpreters* (Philadephlia: Fortress, 1986), pp. 345–70.
—'The Son of Man in First-Century Judaism', *NTS* 38 (1992), pp. 448–66.
—*Daniel: A Commentary on the Book of Daniel* (Hermeneia; Minneapolis: Fortress, 1993).
—'Teacher and Messiah? The One Who Will Teach Righteousness at the End of Days', in Eugene Urlich and James VanderKam (eds), *The Community of the Renewed Covenant: The Notre Dame Symposium on the Dead Sea Scrolls* (Notre Dame, Ind.: University of Notre Dame Press, 1994), pp. 193–210.

—*The Scepter and the Star: The Messiahs of the Dead Sea Scrolls and Other Ancient Literature* (New York: Doubleday, 1995).

—*The Apocalyptic Vision of the Book of Daniel* (HSM, 16; Missoula, Mont.: Scholars, 1997).

—*Apocalypticism in the Dead Sea Scrolls* (LDSS; New York: Routledge, 1997).

—'The Expectation of the End in the Dead Sea Scrolls', in Craig A. Evans and Peter W. Flint (eds), *Eschatology, Messianism, and the Dead Sea Scrolls* (Grand Rapids: Eerdmans, 1997), pp. 74–90.

Collins, John J., and Peter W. Flint (eds), *The Book of Daniel: Composition and Reception* (2 vols; Leiden: Brill, 2001).

Cothenet, E., 'Temoinege de l' Esrit et interpretation de l' ecriture dans la corpus johanique', in H. Cazelles (ed.), *La vie de la parole: De l'Ancien au Nouveau Testament, Mélanges P. Grelot* (Paris: Desclée de Brouwer, 1987), pp. 367–77.

Craigie, Peter C., Page H. Kelley and Joel F. Drinkard, Jr., *Jeremiah 1–25* (WBC, 26; Dallas: Word, 1991).

Crenshaw, James L., *Joel: A New Translation with Introduction and Commentary* (AB, 24C; New York: Doubleday, 1995).

Cross, B. F. M., *The Ancient Library of Qumran* (London: Duckworth, 1958).

Culpepper, R. Alan, *Anatomy of the Forth Gospel: A Study in Literary Design* (Philadelphia: Fortress, 1983).

—'The AMHN AMHN Sayings in the Gospel of John', in Robert B. Sloan and Mikeal C. Parsons (eds), *Perspectives on John: Method and Interpretation in the Fourth Gospel* (NABPRSS, 11; New York: Mellen, 1993), pp. 57–102.

Curtis, Edward M ., 'The First Person Plural in 1 John 2.18-27', *EvJ* 10 (1992), pp. 27–36.

Dahl, Nils Alstrup, '"Do Not Wonder!": John 5.28-29 and Johannine Eschatology Once More', in Robert T. Fortna and Beverly R. Gaventa (eds), *The Conversation continues: Studies in Paul and John: In Honor of J. Louis Martyn* (Nashville: Abingdon, 1990), pp. 322–36.

Dahms, J. V., 'Isaiah 55.11 and the Gospel of John', *EvQ* 53 (1981), pp. 78–88.

Davidson, Richard M., *Flame of Yahweh: Sexuality in the Old Testament* (Peabody, Mass.: Hendrickson, 2007).

Davies, Philip R., *1QM, the War Scroll from Qumran: Its Structure and History* (Rome: Biblical Institute Press, 1977).

de la Potterie, Ignace, 'L'exaltation du Fils de l'homme (Jn 12.31-36)', *Greg* 49 (1968), pp. 460–78.

—'Anointing of the Christian by Faith', in Ignace de la Potterie and Stanislaus Lyonnet (eds), *The Christian Lives by the Spirit* (New York: Alba House, 1971), pp. 99–109.

—'"Sin is Iniquity" (1 Jn 3.4)', in Ignace de la Potterie and Stanislaus Lyonnet (eds), *The Christian Lives by the Spirit* (New York: Alba House, 1971), pp. 36–55.

—*La vérité dans Saint Jean: Tome 2* (AnBib, 74; Rome: Editrice Pontifico Istituto Biblico, 1999).

Denaux, Adelbert (ed.), *John and the Synoptics* (BETL, 101; Leuven, Belgium: Leuven University Press, 1992).

Dennis, John A., *Jesus' Death and the Gathering of True Israel* (Tübingen: Mohr (Siebeck), 2006).

DeVries, Simon J., *Yesterday, Today and Tomorrow* (Grand Rapids: Eerdmans, 1975).

Dillard, Raymond, 'Joel', in Thomas Edward McComiskey (ed.), *The Minor Prophets: An Exegetical and Expository Commentary* (Vol. 1; Grand Rapids: Baker, 1992), pp. 239-314.

Dodd, C. H., *The Johannine Epistles* (MNTC; London: Hodder and Stoughton, 1946).

—*According to the Scriptures* (London: Nisset, 1953).

—*The Interpretation of the Fourth Gospel* (Cambridge: Cambridge University Press, 1958).

—*Historical Tradition in the Fourth Gospel* (Cambridge: Cambridge University Press, 1963).

—'A Hidden Parable in the Fourth Gospel', in C. H. Dodd (ed.), *More New Testament Studies* (Manchester, England: Manchester University Press, 1968), pp. 30–40.

Doyle, Brian, *The Apocalypse of Isaiah Metaphorically Speaking: A Study of the Use, Function and Significance of Metaphors in Isaiah 24–27* (BETL, 151; Leuven, Belgium: Leuven University Press, 2000).

Draper, Jonathan A., 'Holy Seed and the Return of the Diaspora in John 12.24', *Neot* 34 (2000), pp. 347–59.

du Rand, J. A., 'Studies in the Johannine Letters: A discourse Analysis of 1 John', *Neot* 13 (1981), pp. 1–42.

Dunn, James D. G., '"Son of God" as "Son of man" in the Dead Sea Scrolls: A Response to John Collins on 4Q246', in Stanley E. Porter and Craig A. Evans (eds), *Scrolls and the scriptures: Qumran Fifty Years After* (Sheffield: Sheffield University Press, 1997), pp. 198–210.

Eichrodt, Walther, *Theology of the Old Testament* (Vol. 1; London: SCM Press, 1961).

Elledge, C. D., *Life After Death in Early Judaism* (WUNT, 208; Tübingen: Mohr (Siebeck), 2006).

Elliger, K., *Das Buch der zwölf kleinen Propheten, 2* (ATD, 25; Göttingen, 1964).

Ellis, E. Earle, *Paul's Use of the Old Testament* (Edinburgh: Oliver and Boyd, 1957).

—*The Old Testament in Early Christianity: Canon and Interpretation in Light of Modern Research* (Grand Rapids: Baker, 1992).

Ensor, Peter W., *Jesus and His Works: The Johannine Sayings in Historical Perspective* (WUNT, 85; Tübingen: Mohr (Siebeck), 1996).

—'The Authenticity of John 12.24', *EvQ* 74 (2002), pp. 99–107.

Ernst, Josef, *Die eschatologischen Gegenspieler in den Schriften des Neuen Testaments* (BU, 3; Regensburg, Germany: Passavia Passau, 1967).

Evans, Craig A., 'On the Quotation Formulas in the Fourth Gospel', *BZ* 26 (1982), pp. 79–83.

—'Jesus and the Dead Sea Scrolls', in Peter W. Flint and James C. VanderKam (eds), *The Dead Sea Scrolls After Fifty Years: A Comprehensive Assessment* (Vol. 2; Leiden: Brill, 1999), pp. 585–88.

—'Daniel in the New Testament: Visions of God's Kingdom', in John J. Collins and Peter W. Flint (eds), *The Book of Daniel: Composition and Reception* (Vol. 2; Leiden: Brill, 2001), pp. 490–527.

—*Mark 8.27–16.20* (WBC, 34B; Dallas: Word, 2002).

—*Ancient Texts for New Testament Studies: A Guide to the Background Literature* (Peabody, Mass.: Hendrickson, 2005).

Evans, Craig A., and James A. Sanders (eds), *Early Christian Interpretation of the Scriptures of Israel: Investigations and Proposals* (JSNTSup, 148; Sheffield: Sheffield Academic Press, 1997).

Evans, Craig A,. and W.R. Stegner (eds), *The Gospels and the Scriptures of Israel* (JSNTSup, 104; Sheffield: Sheffield Academic Press, 1994).

Eynikel, Erik, and Katrin Hauspie, 'The Use of καιρός and χρόνος in the Septuagint', *ETL* 73 (1997), pp. 369–85.

Fascher, E., 'Johannes 16.32', *ZNW* 39 (1940), pp. 171–230.

Ferch, Arthur J., *The Son of Man in Daniel Seven* (Berrien Springs, MI: Andrews University Press, 1983).

Ferraro, Giuseppe, *L' "ORA" Di Cristo Nel Quarto Vangelo* (Rome: Herder, 1974).

Fishbane, M., *Biblical Interpretation in Ancient Israel* (New York: Oxford University Press, 1985).

Fisk, Bruce N., *Do You Remember? Scripture, Story and Exegesis in the Rewritten Bible of Pseudo-Philo* (JSPSup, 37; Sheffield: Sheffield Academic Press, 2001).

Fitzmyer, Joseph A., 'The Use of Explicit Old Testament Quotations in Qumran Literature and the New Testament', *NTS* 7 (1960–1961), pp. 297–333.

Flint, Peter W., 'The Daniel Tradition at Qumran', in Craig A. Evans and Peter W. Flint (eds), *Eschatology, Messianism, and the Dead Sea Scrolls* (Grand Rapids: Eerdmans, 1997), pp. 41–60.

Floyd, Michael H., *Minor Prophets: Part 2* (FOTL, 22; Grand Rapids: Eerdmans, 2000).

Fortna, R.T., *The Gospel of Signs: A Reconstruction of the Narrative Source Underlying the Fourth Gospel* (Cambridge: Cambridge University Press, 1970).

Fortna, R. T., and B. R. Gaventa (eds), *The Conversation Continues: Studies in Paul and John: In Honor of J. Louis Martyn* (Nashville: Abingdon, 1990).

France, R. T., *The Gospel of Matthew* (NICNT; Grand Rapids: Eerdmans, 2007).

Franke, A. H., *Das alte Testament bei Johannes: Ein Beitrag zur Erklärung und Beurteilung der johaneischen Schriften (Göttingen: Vandenhoeck and Ruprecht, 1885).*

Freed, E. D., *Old Testament Quotations in the Gospel of John* (NovTSup, 11; Leiden: Brill, 1965).

Frey, Jörg, *Die johanneische Eschatologie I: Ihre Probleme im Spiegel der Forschung seit Reimarus* (WUNT, 96; Tübingen: Mohr [Siebeck], 1997).

—*Die johanneische Eschatologie II: Das johanneische Zeitverständis* (WUNT, 110; Tübingen: Mohr (Siebeck), 1998).

—*Die johanneische Eschatologie III: Die eschatologische Verkundigung in den johanneischen Texten* (WUNT, 117; Tübingen: Mohr [Siebeck], 2000).

Frey, Jörg, Jan G. van der Watt and Ruben Zimmermann, *Imagery in the Gospel of John: Terms, Forms, Themes, and Theology of Johannine Figurative Language* (WUNT, 200; Tübingen: Mohr (Siebeck), 2006).

Fröhlich, Ida, *'Time and Times and Half a Time': Historical Consciousness in the Jewish Literature of the Persian and Hellenistic Eras* (JSPSup, 19; Sheffield: Sheffield Academic Press, 1996).

Frost, S. B., 'Eschatology and Myth', *VT* 2 (1952), pp. 70–80.

—*Old Testament Apocalyptic* (London: Epworth Press, 1952).

Garrett, Duane A., *Hosea, Joel* (NAC, 19A; Nashville: Broadman & Holman Publishers, 1997).

Gese, Hartmut, 'Das medische Reich im Geschichtsbild des Danielbuches—eine hermeneutische Frage', in Jutta Hausmann and Hans-Jürgen Zobel (eds), *Alttestamentlicher Glaube und biblische Theologie: Festschrift für Horst Dietrich Preuss zum 65. Geburtstag* (Stuttgart, Germany: Kohlhammer, 1992), pp. 298–308.

Gieschen, Charles A., 'The Different Functions of a Similar Melchizedek Tradition in 2 Enoch and the Epistle to the Hebrews', in Craig A. Evans and James A. Sanders (eds), *Early Christian Interpretation of the Scriptures of Israel* (JSNTSup, 148; Sheffield: Sheffield Academic Press, 1997), pp. 364–79.

Gladd, Benjamin L., *Revealing the Mysterion: The Use of Mystery in Daniel and Second Temple Judaism with Its Bearing on First Corinthians* (Berlin: Walter de Gruyter, 2008).

Glasson, T. Francis, 'Exodus Typology in the Fourth Gospel', *JBL* 81 (1962), pp. 329–42.

—*Moses in the Fourth Gospel* (London: SCM, 1963).

Goldingay, John E., *Daniel* (WBC, 30; Dallas: Word, 1998).

—'Kayyom Hazzeh "On This Very Day"; Kayyom "On The Very Day"; Ka'et "At The Very Time"', *VT* 43 (2001), pp. 112–15.

Gooding, D. W., 'The Literary Structure of Daniel and Its Implications', *TynBul* 32 (1981), pp. 43–79.

Goppelt, Leonhard, *Typos: The Typological Interpretation of the Old Testament in the New* (Grand Rapids: Eerdmans, 1982).

Gowan, Donald E., *Eschatology in the Old Testament* (Edinburgh: T&T Clark, 2000).

Greenberg, Moshe, *Ezekiel 1–20: A New Translation with Introduction and Commentary* (AB, 22; New York: Doubleday, 1983).

—*Ezekiel 21–37: A New Translation with Introduction and Commentary* (AB, 22A; New York: Doubleday, 1997).

Greenfield, J. C., and M. E. Stone, 'The Enochic Pentateuch and the Date of the Similitudes', *HTR* 70 (1977), pp. 51–65.

Griffith, Terry, 'A Non-Polemical Reading of 1 John: Sin, Christology and the Limits of Johannine Christianity', *TynBul* 49 (1998), pp. 253–76.

—*Keep Yourselves from the Idols: A New Look at 1 John* (JSNTSup, 233; London: Sheffield Academic Press, 2002).

Gry, L., *Les Dires Prophetiques D'Esdras (4. ESDRAS)* (Paris: Librairie Orientaliste Paul Geuthner, 1938).

Guilding, Aileen, *Fourth Gospel and Jewish Worship* (Oxford: Clarendon Press, 1960).

Gurney, R. J. M., *God in Control* (Worthing, England: H. E. Walter, 1980).

Haenchen, Ernst, *John 1: A Commentary on the Gospel of John, Chapters 1–6* (Hermeneia; Philadelphia: Fortress Press, 1984).

—*John 2: A Commentary on the Gospel of John, Chapters 7–27* (Hermeneia; Philadelphia: Fortress, 1984).

Hamid-Khani, Saeed, *Revelation and Concealment of Christ: A Theological Inquiry into the Elusive Language of the Fourth Gospel* (WUNT, 120; Tübingen: Mohr (Siebeck), 2000).

Hamilton, Victor P., *The Book of Genesis: Chapters 18–50* (NICOT; Grand Rapids: Eerdmans, 1995).

Hammer, Raymond, *The Book of Daniel* (CBC; Cambridge: Cambridge University Press, 1976).

Hansford, Keir L., 'The Underlying Poetic Structure of 1 John', *JOTT* 5 (1992), pp. 126–74.

Hanson, Anthony Tyrrell, *The Prophetic Gospel: A Study of John and the Old Testament* (Edinburgh: T&T Clark, 1991).

Hanson, P. D., *The Dawn of Apocalyptic: The Historical and Sociological Roots of Jewish Apocalyptic Eschatology* (Philadelphia: Fortress Press, 1979).

Hare, Douglas R. A., *The Son of Man Tradition* (Minneapolis: Augsburg Fortress, 1990).

Harnisch, W., *Verhängnis und Verheißung der Geschichte: Untersuchungen zum Zeit- und Geschichtsverständnis im 4. Buch Esra und in der syr. Baruchapokalypse* (FRLANT, 97; Göttingen: Vandenhoeck & Ruprecht, 1969).

Hartingsveld, L. van, *Die Eschatologie des Johannesevangeliums* (Assen, Netherlands: van Gorcum, 1962).

Hartman, Lars, *Prophecy Interpreted: The Formation of Some Jewish Apocalyptic Texts and of the Eschatological Discourse Mark 13 Par* (CBNTS, 1; Lund, Sweden: Gleerup, 1966).

Hartman, Louis F., and Alexander A. Di Lella, *The Book of Daniel* (AB, 23; Garden City, N.Y.: Doubleday & Company, 1978).

Hasel, Gerhard F., 'Resurrection in the Theology of Old Testament Apocalyptic', *ZAW* 92 (1980), pp. 267–84.

Hays, R. B., *Echoes of Scripture in the Letters of Paul* (New Haven: Yale University Press, 1989).

Helyer, Larry R., *Exploring Jewish Literature of the Second Temple Judaism* (Downers Grove: InterVarsity Press, 2002).

Hengel, M., *Judaism and Hellenism: Studies in Their Encounter in Palestine During the Early Hellenistic Period* (2 vols; London: SCM, 1974).

—'The Old Testament in the Fourth Gospel', *HBT* 12 (1990), pp. 19–41.

Hillers, Delbert R., *Micah* (Hermeneia; Philadelphia: Fortress Press, 1984).

Hodges, Zane C., 'Those Who Have Done Good — John 5.28-29', *BSac* 136 (1979), pp. 158–66.

Hoffman, Yair, 'Eschatology in the Book of Jeremiah', in Henning Graf Reventlow (ed.), *Eschatology in the Bible and in Jewish and Christian Tradition* (JSOTSup, 243; Sheffield: Sheffield Academic Press, 1997), pp. 75–97.

Holladay, William L., *Jeremiah 1: A Commentary on the Book of the Prophet Jeremiah, Chapters 1–25* (Hermeneia; Minneapolis: Fortress Press, 1986).

—*Jeremiah 2: A Commentary on the Book of the Prophet Jeremiah, Chapters 26–52* (Hermeneia; Minneapolis: Fortress, 1989).

Hollander, John, *The Figure of Echo: A Mode of Allusion in Milton and After* (Berkeley: University of California Press, 1981).

Horbury, William, 'Messianism in the Old Testament Apocrypha and Pseudepigrapha', in John Day (ed.), *King and Messiah in Israel and the Ancient Near East: Proceedings of the Oxford Old Testament Seminar* (JSOTSup, 270; Sheffield: Sheffield Academic Press, 1998), pp. 422–27.

Hoskins, Paul M., *Jesus as the Fulfillment of the Temple in the Gospel of John* (Eugene: Wipf and Stock, 2006).

Hoskyns, E. C., *The Fourth Gospel* (London: Faber & Faber, 1947).

Houtman, Cees, 'An der Swelle zum Eschaton: Prophetische Eschatologie im Deuteronomium', in F. Postma, K. Spronk, and E. Talstra (eds), *The New Things: Eschatology in Old Testament Prophecy, Festschrift for Henk Leene* (ACEBT, SS3; Maastricht: Shaker, 2002), pp. 119–28.

Howard, Wilbert F., 'Father and the Son: An Exposition of John 5.19-29', *Int* 4 (1950), pp. 3–11.

Hubbard, David A., *Joel and Amos* (TOTC; Downers Grove: InterVarsity, 1989).

Huey, F. B. Jr., *Jeremiah Lamentations* (NAC, 16; Nashville: Broadman & Holman Publishers, 1993).

Huie-Jolly, M. R., *The Son Enthroned in Conflict: A Socio-Rhetorical Interpretation of John 5.17-23* (Dunedin: University of Otago, 1994).

—'Threats Answered by Enthronement: Death/Resurrection and the Divine Warrior Myth in John 5.17-29, Psalm 2 and Daniel 7', in Craig A. Evans and James A. Sanders (eds), *Early Christian interpretation of the scriptures of Israel* (Sheffield: Sheffield Academic Press, 1997), pp. 191–217.

Hunter, A. M., *The Gospel According to John* (CBC; Cambridge: Cambridge University Press, 1965).

Irshai, Oded, 'Dating the Eschaton: Jewish and Christian Apocalyptic Calculations in Late Antiquity', in Albert I. Baumgarten (ed.), *Apocalyptic Time* (Leiden: Brill, 2000), pp. 113–53.

Isaac, E., '1 (Ethiopic Apocalypse of) Enoch', in James H. Charlesworth (ed.), *The Old Testament Pseudepigrapha: Vol. 1* (New York: Doubleday, 1983), pp. 5–89.

Jackson, David R., *Enochic Judaism: Three Defining Paradigm Exemplars* (London: T&T Clark, 2004).

Jacobson, Howard, *A Commentary on Pseudo-Philo's Liber Antiquitatum Biblicarum* (2 vols; Leiden: Brill, 1996).

Jeansonne, Sharon Pace, *The Old Greek Translation of Daniel 7–12* (CBQMS, 19; Washington: The Catholic Biblical Association of America, 1988).

Jellicoe, Sidney, *The Septuagint and Modern Study* (Winona Lake: Eisenbrauns, 1993).

Jeppesen, Knud., Kristen Nielsen, and Bent Rosendal (eds), *In the Last Days: On Jewish and Christian Apocalyptic and its Period* (Aarhus: Aarhus University Press, 1994).

Jeske, Richard L., 'John 12.20-36', *Int* 43 (1989), pp. 292–95.

Jobes, Karen H., and Moises Silva, *Invitation to the Septuagint* (Grand Rapids: Baker, 2000).

Johnson, Dan G., *From Chaos to Restoration: An Integrative Reading of Isaiah 24–27* (JSOTSup, 61; Sheffield: Sheffield Academic Press, 1988).

Jones, D. R., *Haggai, Zechariah, and Malachi* (TBC; London: SCM, 1962).

Jones, Larry Paul, *The Symbol of Water in the Gospel of John* (Sheffield: Sheffield Academic Press, 1997).

Jones, Peter Rhea, 'Structural Analysis of 1 John', *RevExp* 67 (1970), pp. 433–44.

Karlberg, Mark W., 'Israel and the Eschaton', *WTJ* 52 (1990), pp. 117–30.

Kaufman, Y., *Toldot Haemunah Hyisraelil* (Jerusalem: Mosad-Bialik-Devir, 1960).

Keener, Craig S., *The Gospel of John: A Commentary* (2 Vols; Peabody: Hendrickson Publishers, 2003).

Kelber, Werner H., 'Hour of the Son of Man and the Temptation of the Disciples (Mark 14.32-42)', in Werner H. Kelber and John R. Donahue (eds), *The Passion in Mark: Studies on Mark 14–16* (Philadelphia: Fortress, 1976), pp. 39–60.

Keown, Gerald L., Pamela J. Scalise, and Thomas G. Smothers, *Jeremiah 26–52* (WBC, 27; Dallas: Word, 1995).

Kerr, Alan R., *The Temple of Jesus' Body: The Temple Theme in the Gospel of John* (Sheffield: Sheffield Academic Press, 2002).

Keulers, J., 'Die eschatologische Lehre des vierten Esrabuches', *BibS(F)* 20.2–3 (1922), pp. 1–204.

Kim, Seyoon, *'The "Son of Man"' as the Son of God* (WUNT, 30; Tübingen: Mohr (Siebeck), 1983).

Kittel, G., 'אִזְדְּקֵף = ὑψωθῆναι = gekreuzigt werden', *ZNW* 35 (1936), pp. 282–85.

Kittel, Gerhard, and Gerhard Friedrich (eds), *Theological Dictionary of the New Testament* (Geoffrey W. Bromiley [trans.]; 10 vols; Grand Rapids: Eerdmans, 1964–1976).

Klauck, Hans-Josef, 'Antichrist und das johanneische Schisma: zu 1 Joh 2.18-19', in Karl Kertelge (ed.), *Christus bezeugen* (Leipzig: St. Benno, 1989), pp. 237–48.

—'Zur rhetorischen Analyse der Johannesbriefe', *ZNW* 81 (1990), pp. 205–24.

—*Der erste Johannesbrief* (EKKNT, 23/1; Zurich: Benziger Verlag, 1991).

Klein, Günther, 'Das wahre Licht schent shon', *ZTK* 68 (1971), pp. 261–326.

Klijn, A. F. J., '2 (Syriac Apocalypse of) Baruch', in James H. Charlesworth (ed.), *The Old Testament Pseudepigrapha: Vol. 1* (New York: Doubleday, 1983), pp. 615–52.

Knibb, Michael A., *The Ethiopic Book of Enoch* (Oxford: Oxford University Press, 1978).

Knöppler, Thomas, *Die theologia cruces des Johannesevangeliums: Das Veraständnis des Todes Jesu im Rahmen der johanneischen Inkarnation – und Erhöhungschristologie* (Düsseldorf: Neukirchener Verlag, 1994).

Koch, K., 'Die Herkunft der proto-Theodotion-Übersetyung des Danielbuches', *VT* 23 (1973), pp. 262–65.

Koehler, Ludwig, and Walter Baumgartner, *The Hebrew and Aramaic Lexicon of the Old Testament* (5 vols; Leiden: Brill, 1994–2001).

Kosmala, Peter, 'At the End of the Days', *ASTI* 2 (1963), pp. 27–37.

Köstenberger, Andreas J., *John* (BECNT; Grand Rapids: Baker Academic, 2004).

—'John', in G. K. Beale and D. A. Carson (eds), *Commentary on the New Testament Use of the Old Testament* (Grand Rapids: Baker, 2007), pp. 415–512.

Kovacs, Judith L., '"Now Shall the Ruler of This World Be Driven Out": Jesus' Death as Cosmic Battle in John 12.20-36', *JBL* 114 (1995), pp. 227–47.

Kristeva, Julia, *Desire in Language: A Semiotic Approach to Literature and Art* (New York: Columbia University Press, 1980).

—*Revolution in Poetic Language* (New York: Columbia University Press, 1984).

Krötke, Wolf, 'Das menschliche Eschaton: zur anthropologischen Dimension der Eschatologie', in Konrad Stock (ed.), *Zukunft der Erlösung* (Gütersloh: Chr Kaiser, 1994), pp. 132–46.

Kruse, Colin G., *The Letters of John* (PNTC; Grand Rapids: Eerdmans, 2000).

—'Sin and Perfection in 1 John', *ABR* 51 (2003), pp. 60–70.

Kvanvig, Helge S., *Roots of Apocalyptic: The Mesopotamian Background of the Enoch Figure and of the Son of Man* (Neukirchen-Vluyn: Neukirchener, 1988).

Kyle, Richard, *The Last Days are Here Again: A History of the End Times* (Grand Rapids: Baker, 1998).

Kysar, Robert, *John* (ACNT; Minneapolis: Augsburg, 1986).

Lane, William L., *The Gospel of Mark* (NICNT; Grand Rapids: Eerdmans, 1974).

Leaney, A. R. C., *The Rule of Qumran and Its Meaning: Introduction, Translation, and Commentary* (Philadelphia: Westminster Press, 1966).

Leon-Dufour, X., 'Trois chiasmes johanniques', *NTS* 7 (1960–1961), pp. 249–55.

Lieu, Judith, '"Authority to Become Children of God": A Study of 1 John', *NovT* 23 (1981), pp. 210–28.

—'What Was from the Beginning: Scripture and Tradition in the Johannine Epistles', *NTS* 39 (1993), pp. 458–77.

Lightfoot, R. H., *The Gospel Message of St. Mark* (Oxford: Clarendon, 1958).

Lincoln, Andrew T., *The Gospel According to Saint John* (BNTC; New York: Continuum, 2005).

Lindars, Barnabas, *New Testament Apologetic: The Doctrinal Significance of the Old Testament Quotations* (London: SCM Press, 1961).

—*The Gospel of John* (NCB; Grand Rapids: Eerdmans, 1982).

—*Jesus Son of Man: A Fresh Examination of the Son of Man Sayings in the Gospels* (London: SPCK, 1983).

Lindblom, Johannes, 'Gibt es eine Eschatologie bei den alttestamentlichen Propheten?' *ST* 6 (1953), pp. 79–114.

Link, Christian, 'Points of Departure for a Christian Eschatology', in Henning Graf Reventlow (ed.), *Eschatology in the Bible and in Jewish and Christian Tradition* (JSOTSup, 243; Sheffield: Sheffield Academic Press, 1997), pp. 98–110.

Lipinski, E., 'b'hryt hymym dans les texts preexiliques', *VT* 20 (1970), pp. 445–50.

Longenecker, Bruce W., *2 Esdras* (Sheffield: Sheffield Academic Press, 1995).

Lucas, Ernest, *Daniel* (AOTC; Downers Grove: InterVarsity, 2002).

Lundbom, Jack R., *Jeremiah 1–20* (AB, 21A; New York: Doubleday, 1999).

—*Jeremiah 21–36* (AB, 21B; New York: Doubleday, 2004).

Mackay, Ian D., *John's Relationship with Mark: An Analysis of John 6 in Light of Mark 6–8* (Tübingen: Mohr [Siebeck], 2004).

Malina, Bruce J., *The Gospel of John in Sociolinguistic Perspective: Protocol of the Forty-Eighth Colloquy* (Berkeley: Graduate Theological Union and the University of California, 1985).

Malina, Bruce J., and Richard L. Rohrbaugh, *Social-Science Commentary on the Gospel of John* (Minneapolis: Fortress, 1998).

Manning, Gary T., Jr., *Echoes of a Prophet: The Use of Ezekiel in the Gospel of John and in Literature of the Second Temple Period* (JSNTSup, 270; New York: T&T Clark International, 2004).

March, W., 'The Study of Two Prophetic Compositions in Isaiah 24.1–27.1' (unpublished dissertation; Union Theological Seminary, 1966).

Marcos, Natalio Fernandez, *The Septuagint in Context: Introduction to the Greek Versions of the Bible* (Leiden: Brill, 2000).

Marshall, I. Howard, *The Epistles of John* (NICNT; Grand Rapids: Eerdmans, 1978).

—'Slippery Words: 1. Eschatology', *The Expository Times* 89 (1978), pp. 264–69.

—*1 and 2 Thessalonians* (NCB; Grand Rapids: Eerdmans, 1983).

Martin-Achard, Robert, *From Death to Life: A Study of the Development of the Doctrine of the Resurrection in the Old Testament* (Edinburgh: Oliver & Boyd, 1960).

Martinez, Florentino Garcia, *Qumran and Apocalyptic: Studies on the Aramaic Texts from Qumran* (Leiden: Brill, 1992).

Martinez, Florentino Garcia, and Eibert J. C. Tigchelaar, *The Dead Sea Scrolls: Study Edition* (vol. 1; Grand Rapids: Eerdmans, 1997).

Martyn, J. Louis, *History and Theology in the Fourth Gospel* (Louisville: John Knox, 2003).

Mason, Rex, *The Books of Haggai, Zechariah, and Malachi* (CBC; Cambridge: Cambridge University Press, 1977).

Mays, James Luther, *Micah: A Commentary* (OTL; Philadelphia: Westminster, 1976).

McAlpine, Thomas H., *Sleep, Divine and Human in the Old Testament* (JSOTSup, 38; Sheffield: JSOT, 1987).

McKane, William, *Jeremiah Vol 2* (ICC; Edinburgh: T&T Clark, 1996).

McLay, R. Timothy, *The OG and The Versions of Daniel* (SBLSCS, 43; Atlanta: Scholars, 1996).

—*The Use of the Septuagint in New Testament Research* (Grand Rapids: Eerdmans, 2003).

McNamara, M., 'The Ascension and the Exaltation of Christ in the Fourth Gospel', *Scr* 19 (1967), pp. 66–69.

McNeil, Brian, 'Quotation at John 12.34', *NovT* 19 (1977), pp. 22–33.

McWhirter, Jocelyn, *The Bridegroom Messiah and the People of God* (Cambridge: Cambridge University Press, 2006).

McWilliams, Warren, 'Interpretations of the Antichrist', *BI* (1990), pp. 50–53.

Meadowcroft, T. J., *Aramaic Daniel and Greek Daniel: A Literary Comparison* (JSOTSup, 198; Sheffield: Sheffield Academic Press, 1995).

Meeks, Wayne A., 'The Man from Heaven in Johannine Sectarianism', *JBL* 91 (1972), pp. 44–72.

—*The Prophet-King: Moses Traditions and the Johannine Christology* (NovTSup, 12; Leiden: Brill, 1975).

—'Equal to God', in Robert T. Fortna and Beverly R. Gaventa (eds), *The Conversation Continues: Studies in Paul and John* (Nashville: Abingdon, 1990), pp. 309–21.

Menken, M. J. J., *Old Testament Quotations in the Fourth Gospel: Studies in Textual Form* (CBET, 18; Kampen: Kok, 1996).

Metso, Sarianna, 'The Use of Old Testament Quotations in the Qumran Community Rule', in Frederick H. Cryer and Thomas L. Thompson (eds), *Qumran between the Old and New Testaments* (JSOTSup, 290; Sheffield: Sheffield Academic Press, 1998), pp. 217–31.

Metzger, B. M., 'The Fourth Book of Ezra', in James H. Charlesworth (ed.), *The Old Testament Pseudepigrapha: Vol. 1* (New York: Doubleday, 1983), pp. 517–59.

Milik, J. T., *The Books of Enoch: Aramaic Fragments of Qumran Cave 4* (Oxford: Clarendon Press, 1976).

Miller, Stephen R., *Daniel* (NAC, 18; Nashville: Broadman & Holman, 1994).

Mills, Donald W., 'The Holy Spirit in 1 John', *DBSJ* 4 (1999), pp. 33–50.

Miner, Earl, 'Allusion', in Alex Preminger and T. V. F. Brogan (eds), *The New Princeton Encyclopedia of Poetry and Poetics* (Princeton: Princeton University Press, 1993), pp. 38–39.

Moloney, Francis J., *The Johannine Son of Man* (Rome: LAS, 1978).

—*The Gospel of John* (SP, 4; Collegeville: The Liturgical Press, 1998).

—*The Gospel of John: Text and Context* (BIS, 72; Leiden: Brill Academic Publishers, 2005).

Montgomery, James A., *A Critical and Exegetical Commentary on the Book of Daniel* (ICC; Edinburgh: T&T Clark, 1950).

Moo, Douglas J., *The Old Testament in the Gospel Passion Narratives* (Sheffield: Almont Press, 1983).

Morgan, R., 'Fulfillment in the Fourth Gospel: The Old Testament Foundations', *Int* 11 (1957), pp. 155–65.

Morkholm, O., *Antiochus IV of Syria* (Copenhagen: Gyldendalske Boghandel, 1966).

Morris, Leon, *The Gospel According to John* (Grand Rapids: Eerdmans, 1995).

Motyer, J. Alec., *The Prophecy of Isaiah: An Introduction and Commentary* (Downers Grove: InterVarsity Press, 1993).

Mounce, Robert H., *The Book of Revelation* (NICNT; Grand Rapids: Eerdmans, 1998).

Mowinckel, Sigmund, *He That Cometh: The Messiah Concept in the Old Testament and Later Judaism* (Grand Rapids: Eerdmans, 2005).

Moyise, Steve, *The Old Testament in the Book of Revelation* (JSNTSup, 115; Sheffield: Sheffield Academic Press, 1995).

—'Intertextuality and the Study of the Old Testament in the New Testament', in Steve Moyise (ed.), *The Old Testament in the New Testament: Essays in Honor of J. L. North* (JSNTSup, 189; Sheffield: Sheffield Academic Press, 2000), pp. 14–41.

Mulder, M. J. (ed.), *Mikra: Text, Translation, Reading, and Interpretation of the Hebrew Bible in Ancient Judaism and Early Christianity* (Minneapolis: Fortress, 1990).

Munch, Peter Andreas, *The Expression Bajjôm Hāhū': is it an eschatological terminus technicus?* (Oslo: I Kommisjon Hos Jacob Dybwad, 1936).

Murphy, Frederick J., *The Structure and Meaning of Second Baruch* (SBLDS, 78; Atlanta: Scholars, 1985).

—*Pseudo-Philo: Rewriting the Bible* (Oxford: Oxford University Press, 1993).

Myers, J. M., *1 and 2 Esdras* (AB, 42; Garden City: Doubleday, 1974).

Neusner, J., and W. S. Green (eds), *Writing with Scripture: The Authority and Uses of the Hebrew Bible in the Torah of Formative Judaism* (Minneapolis: Fortress, 1989).

Neyrey, Jerome H., S. J., *The Gospel of John* (NCBC; Cambridge: Cambridge University Press, 2007).

Ng, Wai Yee, 'Johannine Eschatology as Demonstrated in First John' (unpublished thesis; Westminster Theological Seminary, 1988).

—*Water Symbolism in John: An Eschatological Interpretation* (StudBL, 15; New York: P. Lang, 2001).

Nichols, Stephen J., 'Prophecy Makes Strange Bedfellows: On the History of Identifying the Antichrist', *JETS* 44 (2001), pp. 75–85.

Nickelsburg, George W. E., *Resurrection, Immortality, and Eternal Life in Intertestamental Judaism* (HTS, 26; Cambridge: Harvard University Press, 1972).

—*Jewish Literature between the Bible and the Mishnah* (Minneapolis: Fortress, 2005).

Nickelsburg, George W. E., and James C. VanderKam, *1 Enoch: A New Translation* (Minneapolis: Fortress, 2004).

Niederwimmer, Kurt, 'Zur Eschatologie im Corpus Johanneum', *NovT* 39 (1997), pp. 105–16.

Nir, Rivka, *The Destruction of Jerusalem and the Idea of Redemption in the Syriac Apocalypse of Baruch* (Atlanta: SBL, 2003).

Obermann, Andreas, *Die christologische Erfüllung der Schrift im Johannesevangelium: Eine Untersuchung zur johanneischen Hermeneutik anhand der Schriftzitate* (WUNT, 83; Tübingen: Mohr [Siebeck], 1996).

O'Day, Gail R., *Revelation in the Fourth Gospel: Narrative Mode and Theological Claim* (Philadelphia: Fortress, 1986).

—'"I Have Overcome the World" (John 16.33): Narrative Time in John 13–17', *Semeia* 53 (1991), pp. 153–66.

Odeberg, Hugo, *3 Enoch or The Hebrew Book of Enoch* (New York, KTAV, 1973).

—*The Fourth Gospel* (Amsterdam: Grüner, 1974).

Odendaal, Dirk H., *The Eschatological Expectation of Isaiah 40–66 with Special Reference to Israel and the Nations* (Philadelphia: Presbyterian and Reformed, 1970).

Olsson, Birger, *Structure and Meaning in the Fourth Gospel: A Text-Linguistic Analysis of John 2.1-11 and 4.1-42* (Lund, Sweden: CWK Gleerup, 1974).

Osborne, Grant R., *Revelation* (BECNT; Grand Rapids: Baker, 2002).

Oswalt, John N., *The Book of Isaiah: Chapters 1–39* (NICNT; Grand Rapids: Eerdmans, 1986).

Painter, John, 'The "Opponents" in 1 John', *NTS* 32 (1986), pp. 48–71.

—'The Enigmatic Johannine Son of Man', in F. Van Segbroeck, et al. (eds), *The Four Gospels: Festschrift Frans Neirynck* (3 vols; Leuven: Leuven University Press, 1992), pp. 1869–87.

Pamment, Margaret, 'The Son of Man in the Fourth Gospel', *JTS* 36 (1985), pp. 56–66.

Pancaro, S., *The Law in the Fourth Gospel: The Torah and The Gospel, Moses and Jesus, Judaism and Christianity According to John* (NovTSup, 42; Leiden: Brill, 1975).

Parry, Donald W., 'Garden of Eden: Prototype Sanctuary', in Donald W. Parry (ed.), *Temples of the Ancient World: Ritual and Symbolism* (Salt Lake City: Deseret, 1994), pp. 126–51.

Paul, Shalom M., *Amos* (Hermeneia; Minneapolis: Fortress, 1991).

Peckham, Brian, 'History and Time', in R. Chazan, W. W. Hallo, and L. H. Schiffman (eds), *Ki Baruch Hu: Ancient Near Eastern, Biblical, and Judaic Studies in Honor of Baruch A. Levine* (Winona Lake: Eisenbrauns, 1999), pp. 295–314.

Perkins, Pheme, 'Koinōnia in 1 John 1.3-7: The Social Context of Division in the Johannine Letters', *CBQ* 45 (1983), pp. 631–41.

Petersen, David L., *Zechariah 9–14 and Malachi: A Commentary* (OTL; Louisville: John Knox, 1995).

Pines, S., 'Eschatology and the Concept of Time in the Slavonic Book of Enoch', in R. J. Zwi Werblowsky and C. Jouco Bleeker (eds), *Types of Redemption* (Leiden: Brill, 1970), pp. 72–87.

Pitre, Brant, *Jesus, the Tribulation, and the End of the Exile* (Tübingen: Mohr [Siebeck], 2005).

Pöhlmann, Wolfgang, 'Bestimmte Zukunft: Die Einheit von "Eschaton" und "Eschata" in neutestamentlicher Sicht', in Jostein Adna, Scott J. Hafemann, and Otfried Hofius (eds), *Evangelium, Schriftauslegung, Kirche: Festschrift für Peter Stuhlmacher zum 65. Geburtstag* (Göttingen: Vandenhoeck & Ruprecht, 1997), pp. 337–46.

Porteous, Norman W., *Daniel: A Commentary* (OTL; Philadelphia: Westminster, 1965).

Porter, Stanley E., 'The Use of the Old Testament in the New Testament: A Brief Comment on

Method and Terminology', in Craig A. Evans and James A. Sanders (eds), *Early Christian Interpretation of the Scriptures of Israel: Investigations and Proposals* (JSNTSup, 148; Sheffield: Sheffield Academic Press, 1997), pp. 79–96.

Postma F., K. Spronk, and E. Talstra (eds), *The New Things: Eschatology in Old Testament Prophecy, Festschrift for Henk Leene* (ACEBT, SS3; Maastricht: Shaker, 2002).

Puech, Emile, 'Messianism, Resurrection, and Eschatology at Qumran and in the New Testament', in Eugene Urlich and James VanderKam (eds), *The Community of the Renewed Covenant: The Notre Dame Symposium on the Dead Sea Scrolls* (Notre Dame: University of Notre Dame Press, 1994), pp. 235–56.

Reim, Günter, *Studien zum alttestamentlichen Hintergrund des Johannesevangeliums* (SNTSMS, 22; Cambridge: Cambridge University Press, 1974).

Reventlow, Henning Graf, 'The Eschatologization of the Prophetic Books: A Comparative Study', in Henning Graf Reventlow (ed.), *Eschatology in the Bible and in Jewish and Christian Tradition* (JSOTSup, 243; Sheffield: Sheffield Academic Press, 1997), pp. 169–88.

Reventlow, Henning Graf (ed.), *Eschatology in the Bible and in Jewish and Christian Tradition* (JSOTSup, 243; Sheffield: Sheffield Academic Press, 1997).

Ridderbos, Herman, *The Gospel of John: A Theological Commentary* (Grand Rapids: Eerdmans, 1997).

Romanowsky, John W., '"When the Son of Man Is Lifted Up": The Redemptive Power of the Crucifixion in the Gospel of John', *Hor* 32 (2005), pp. 100–16.

Sacchi, P., *Apocrifi dell'Antico Testamento* (Turin: Union Tipogratico—Editrice Torinese, 1989).

Saebø, Magne, *Sacharja 9–14: Undersuchungen von Text und Form* (WMANT, 34; Neukirchen-Vluyn: Neukirchener Verlag, 1969).

—'Eschaton und Eschatologia im Alten Testament—in traditionsgeschichtlicher Sicht', in Jutta Hausmann and Hans-Jürgen Zobel (eds), *Alttestamentlicher Glaube und biblische Theologie: Festschrift für Hosrt Dietrich Peuss zum 65. Geburtstag* (Stuttgart: Kohlhammer, 1992), pp. 321–30.

—'Old Testament Apocalyptic in its Relation to Prophecy and Wisdom: The View of Gerhard von Rad Reconsidered', in Knud Jeppesen, Kristen Nielsen, and Bent Rosendal (eds), *In the Last Days: On Jewish and Christian Apocalyptic and its Period* (Aarhus: Aarhus University Press, 1994), pp. 78–91.

Salvoni, Fausto, 'Nevertheless, My Hour Has Not Yet Come (John 2.4)', *ResQ* 7 (1963), pp. 236–41.

Santo, Charles de, 'A Theological Key to the Gospel of John', *EvQ* 34 (1962), pp. 83–90.

Sayler, Gwendolyn B., *Have the Promises Failed? A Literary Analysis of 2 Baruch* (SBLDS, 72; Chico: Scholars, 1984).

Schnackenburg, Rudolf, *The Gospel According to St. John* (3 Vols; New York: Crossroad, 1987).

—*The Johannine Epistles: A Commentary* (New York: Crossroad, 1992).

Schneiders, Sandra M., 'The raising of the new temple: John 20.19-23 and Johannine ecclesiology', *NTS* 52 (2006), pp. 337–55.

Schottroff, Luise, 'Heil als innerweltliche Entweltlichung: der gnostische Hintergrund der johanneischen Vorstellung vom Zeitpunkt der Erlösung', *NovT* 11 (1969), pp. 294–317.

Schuchard, B. G., *Scripture within Scripture: The Interrelationship of Form and Function in the Explicit Old Testament Citations in the Gospel of John* (SBLDS, 133; Atlanta: Scholars, 1992).

Schunack, Gerd, *Die Briefe des Johannes* (ZBKNT, 17; Zürich: Theologischer Verlag, 1982).

Schwarz, Günther, 'In der Welt habt ihr Angst? (Jn 16.33)', *BN* 63 (1992), pp. 49–51.

Scott, James M., 'Geographic Aspects of Noachic Materials in the Scrolls at Qumran', in Stanley E. Porter and Craig A. Evans (eds), *The Scrolls and the Scriptures: Qumran Fifty Years After* (JSPSup, 26; Sheffield: Sheffield Academic Press, 1997), pp. 368–81.

Shaw, Charles S., *The Speeches of Micah: A Rhetorical-Historical Analysis* (JSOTSup, 145; Sheffield: Sheffield Academic Press, 1993).

Sheldon, Martin E., 'The Eschatological Son of Man in Jewish and Christian Literature', *EvJ* 17 (1999), pp. 60–75.

Simon, U. E., 'Eternal Life in the Fourth Gospel', in F. L. Cross (ed.), *Studies in the Fourth Gospel* (London: Mowbray, 1957), pp. 97–110.

Slater, Thomas B., 'One Like a Son of Man in First-Century CE Judaism', *NTS* 41 (1995), pp. 183–98.

Smalley, Stephen S., *The Revelation to John: A Commentary on the Greek Text of the Apocalypse* (Downers Grove: InterVarsity, 2005).

—*1,2,3 John* (WBC, 51; Nashville: Thomas Nelson, 2007).

Smit, Sibinga J., 'A Study in 1 John', in *Studies in John* (NovTSup, 24; Leiden: Brill, 1970), pp. 194–208.

Smith, Moody D., *John Among the Gospels: The Relationship in Twentieth Century Research* (Columbia: University of South Carolina Press, 2001).

Smith, Ralph L., *Micah-Malachi* (WBC, 32; Dallas: Word, 1984).

Snaith, N. H., 'Time in the Old Testament', in F. F. Bruce (ed.), *Promise and Fulfillment* (Edinburgh: T&T Clark, 1963), pp. 175–86.

Soderlund, Sven, *The Greek Text of Jeremiah: A Revised Hypothesis* (JSOTSup, 47; Sheffield: Sheffield Academic Press, 1985).

Stanley, Christopher D., 'The Rhetoric of Quotations: An Essay on Method', in Craig A. Evans and James A. Sanders (eds), *Early Christian Interpretation of the Scriptures of Israel: Investigations and Proposals* (JSNTSup, 148; Sheffield: Sheffield Academic Press, 1997), pp. 44–58.

Stibbe, Mark W. G., *John* (Sheffield: Sheffield Academic Press, 1993).

Stone, Michael E., 'Coherence and Inconsistency in the Apocalypses: The Case of "The End" in 4 Ezra', *JBL* 102 (1983), pp. 229–43.

—*Jewish Writings of the Second Temple Period* (Philadelphia: Fortress, 1984).

—*Features of the Eschatology of IV Ezra* (HSS; Atlanta: Scholars, 1989).

—*Fourth Ezra* (Hermeneia; Minneapolis: Fortress, 1990).

—*Selected Studies in Pseudepigrapha and Apocrypha* (Leiden: Brill, 1991).

Stordalen, Terje, *Echoes of Eden: Genesis 2–3 and Symbolism of the Eden Garden in Biblical Hebrew Literature* (CBET, 25; Leuven: Peeters, 2000).

Strecker, George, 'Der Antichrist: zum religionsgeschichtlichen Hintergrund von 1 Joh 2.18-22; 4.3 und 2 Joh 7', in Tjitze Baarda, *et al.* (eds), *Text and Testimony: Essays on New Testament and Apocryphal Literature* (Kampen: Kok, 1988), pp. 247–54.

—*The Johannine Letters: A Commentary on 1, 2, and 3 John* (Minneapolis: Fortress, 1996).

Stuckenbruck, Loren T., '"One like a Son of Man as the Ancient of Days" in the Old Greek Recension of Daniel 7.13: Scribal Error or Theological Translation?' *ZNW* 86 (1995), pp. 268–76.

Sweeney, Marvin, A. *Isaiah 1–39: With an Introduction to Prophetic Literature* (FOTL, 16; Grand Rapids: Eerdmans, 1996).

—*Zephaniah* (Hermeneia; Philadelphia: Fortress, 2003).

Talbert, C. H., *Reading John: A Literary and Theological Commentary on the Fourth Gospel and the Johannine Epistles* (New York: Crossroads, 1992).

Thomas, John Christopher, 'The Literary Structure of 1 John', *NovT* 40 (1998), pp. 369–81.

Thompson, Alden L., *Responsibility and Evil in the Theodicy of IV Ezra* (SBLDS, 29; Missoula: Scholars, 1977).

Thompson, J. A., *The Book of Jeremiah* (NICNT; Grand Rapids: Eerdmans, 1980).

Thomson, J. G. S., 'The Shepherd-Ruler Concept in the Old Testament and Its Application in the New Testament', *SJT* 8 (1955), pp. 406–18.

Thyen, Hartwig, *Studien zum Corpus Iohanneum* (WUNT, 214; Tübingen: Mohr (Siebeck), 2007).

Tollefson, Kenneth D., 'Certainty within the Fellowship: Dialectical Discourse in 1 John', *BTB* 29 (1999), pp. 79–89.

Torrey, Charles Cutler., '"When I Am Lifted Up from the Earth", John 12.32', *JBL* 51 (1932), pp. 320–22.

Tov, Emanuel, *The Septuagint Translation of Jeremiah and Baruch: A Discussion of an Early Revision of the LXX of Jeremiah 29–52 and Baruch 1.1–3.8* (HSM, 8; Missoula: Scholars, 1976).

—'Die griechischen Bibelübersetyungen', *ANRW* 2,20 (1986), pp. 121–89.

Tromp, Johannes, *The Assumption of Moses: A Critical Edition with Commentary* (Leiden: Brill, 1992).

Tsuchido, Kiyoshi, 'Tradition and Redaction in John 12.1-43', *NTS* 30 (1984), pp. 609–19.

Tuckett, Christopher M., 'The Son of Man and Daniel 7: Q and Jesus', in Andreas Lindemann (ed.), *The Sayings Source Q and the Historical Jesus* (Louvain: Leuven University Press, 2001), pp. 371–94.

Um, Stephen T., *The Theme of Temple Christology in John's Gospel* (New York: T&T Clark, 2006).

Unterman, Jeremiah, *From Repentance to Redemption: Jeremiah's Thought in Transition* (JSOTSup, 54; Sheffield: Sheffield Academic Press, 1987).

van der Kooij, Arie, '"Coming" Things and "Last" Things: Isaianic Terminology as Understood in the Wisdom of Ben Sira and in the Septuagint of Isaiah', in F. Postma, K. Spronk, and E. Talstra (eds), *The New Things Eschatology in Old Testament Prophecy: Festschrift for Henk Leene* (Maastricht: Shaker, 2002), pp. 135–40.

van der Merwe, D. G., '"Ωρα, A Possible Theological Setting for Understanding Johannine Eschatology', *APB* 13 (2002), pp. 255–87.

van der Ploeg, J. P. M., 'Eschatology in the Old Testament', *OTS* 17 (1972), pp. 89–99.

van der Watt, J. G., 'A New Look at John 5.25-9 in the Light of the Use of the Term "Eternal Life" in the Gospel According to John', *Neot* 19 (1985), pp. 71–86.

—'The Use of 'ΑΙΩΝΙΟΣ in the Concept ΖΩΗ 'ΑΙΩΝΙΟΣ in John's Gospel', *NovT* 31 (1989), pp. 217–28.

van Unnik, Willem Cornelis, 'The Quotation from the Old Testament in John 12.34', *NovT* 3 (1959), pp. 174–79.

VanderKam, James C., *Enoch and the Growth of an Apocalyptic Tradition* (Washington: The Catholic Biblical Association of America, 1984).

—'Righteous One, Messiah, Chosen One, and Son of Man in 1 Enoch 37–71', in James H. Charlesworth (ed.), *The Messiah: Developments in Earliest Judaism and Christianity* (Minneapolis: Fortress, 1992), pp. 169–91.

—'Apocalyptic Tradition in the Dead Sea Scrolls and the Religion of Qumran', in John J. Collins and Robert A Kugler (eds), *Religion in the Dead Sea Scrolls* (Grand Rapids: Eerdmans, 2000), pp. 113–34.

—*An Introduction to Early Judaism* (Grand Rapids: Eerdmans, 2001).

VanGemeren, Willem A., 'The Spirit of Restoration', *WTJ* 50 (1988), pp. 81–102.

Vanhoye, A., 'La composition de Jn 5.19-20', in André de Halleux (ed.), *Melanges B. Rigaux* (Gembloux: Duculot, 1970), pp. 259–74.

Vlaardingerbroek, Johannes, *Zephaniah* (HCOT; Leuven: Peeters, 1999).

von Rad, Gerhard, 'The Origin of the Concept of the Day of Yahweh', *JSS* 4 (1959), pp. 97–108.

von Wahlde, Urban C., 'The Stereotyped Structure and the Puzzling Pronouns of 1 John 2.28–3.10', *CBQ* 64 (2002), pp. 319–38.

Vos, Geerhardus, *The Eschatology of the Old Testament* (Phillipsburg: P&R Publishing, 2001).

Waltke, Bruce, 'Micah', in Thomas Edward McComiskey (ed.), *The Minor Prophets: An Exegetical and Expository Commentary* (vol. 2; Grand Rapids: Baker, 1993), pp. 591-764.

Wanamaker, Charles, *The Epistles to the Thessalonians* (NIGTC; Grand Rapids: Eerdmans, 1990).

Ward, Ronald A., 'Theological Pattern of the Johannine Epistles', *SwJT* 13 (1970), pp. 23–39.

Watson, Duane F., '1 John 2.12-14 as Distributio, Conduplicatio, and Expolitio: A Rhetorical Understanding', *JSNT* 35 (1989), pp. 97–110.

—'Amplification Techniques in 1 John: The Interaction of Rhetorical Style and Invention', *JSNT* 51 (1993), pp. 99–123.

Watts, J. D. W., *Isaiah 1–33* (WBC, 24; Dallas: Word, 1998).

Weinfield, M., 'Jeremiah and the Spiritual Metamorphosis of Israel', *ZAW* 88 (1976), pp. 17–56.

Wenham, Gordon J., 'Sanctuary Symbolism in the Garden of Eden Story', in Richard S. Hess and David Toshio Tsumura (eds), *'I Studied Inscriptions from Before the Flood': Ancient New Eastern, Literary, and Linguistic Approaches to Genesis 1–11* (Winona Lake: Eisenbrauns, 1994), pp. 399–404.

Wernberg-Moller, P., *The Manual of Discipline: Translated and Annotated with an Introduction* (Leiden: Brill, 1957).

Westermann, Claus, *Isaiah 40–66* (OTL; Philadelphia: Westminster, 1977).

—*Genesis 37–50: A Continental Commentary* (Minneapolis: Augsburg, 1986).

Whitacre, R. A., *Johannine Polemic: The Role of Tradition and Authority* (SBLDS, 67; Chico: Scholars, 1982).

Whitters, Mark F., *The Epistle of Second Baruch: A Study in Form and Message* (JSPSup, 42; Sheffield: Sheffield Academic Press, 2003).

Wilch, John R., *Time and Event: An Exegetical Study of the Use of 'ēth in the Old Testament in Comparison to Other Temporal Expressions in Classification of the Concept of Time* (Leiden: Brill, 1969).

Wildberger, Hans, *Isaiah 1–12: A Continental Commentary* (Minneapolis: Fortress, 1991).

—*Isaiah 13–27: A Continental Commentary* (Minneapolis: Fortress, 1997).

Willett, Tom W., *Eschatology in the Theodicies of 2 Baruch and 4 Ezra* (JSPSup, 4; Sheffield: Sheffield Academic Press, 1989).

Witherington III, Ben, *John's Wisdom: A Commentary on the Fourth Gospel* (Louisville: Westminster John Knox, 1995).

Wolff, Hans Walter, *Joel and Amos* (Hermeneia; Philadelphia: Fortress, 1977).

Wrege, H. T., 'Jesusgeschichte und Jüngergeschick nach Joh 12.20-23 und Hebr 5.7-10', in Joachim Jeremias, Eduard Lohse, *et al.* (eds), *Der Ruf Jesu und die Antwort der Gemeinde* (Göttingen: Vandenhoeck & Ruprecht, 1970), pp. 259–88.

Wright, J. Edward, 'The Social Setting of the Syriac Apocalypse of Baruch', *JSP* 16 (1997), pp. 81–96.

Wright, N. T., *The Resurrection of the Son of God* (Minneapolis: Fortress, 2003).

Yadin, Yigael, *The Scroll of the War of the Sons of Light Against the Sons of Darkness* (Oxford: Oxford University Press, 1962).

Yarid, John R, Jr., 'Reflections of the Upper Room Discourse in 1 John', *BSac* 160 (2003), pp. 65–76.

Yates, Roy, 'The Antichrist', *EvQ* 46 (1974), pp. 42–50.

Young, Edward J., *The Prophecy of Daniel: A Commentary* (Grand Rapids: Eerdmans, 1957).

Young, F. W., 'A Study of the Relation of Isaiah to the Fourth Gospel', *ZNW* 46 (1955), pp. 215–33.

Zimmermann, Ruben, *Christologie der Bilder im Johannesevangelium: Die Christopoetik des vierten Evangeliums unter besonderer Berücksichtigung von Joh 10* (WUNT, 171; Tübingen: Mohr (Siebeck), 2004).

INDEX OF REFERENCES